# Essentials of Mortgage Loan Origination

I0047541

**First Edition**

Donna Welschmeyer
Ellen Barski
Stephen Mettling
Ryan Mettling

**Performance Programs Company**
6810 190th Street East
Bradenton, Florida 34211
www.performanceprogramscompany.com

Material in this book is not intended to represent legal advice and should not be so construed.
Readers should consult legal counsel for advice regarding points of law.

© 2026 by Performance Programs Company
6810 190th Street East, Bradenton, FL 34211
info@performanceprogramscompany.com
www.performanceprogramscompany.com

All rights reserved.  No part of this book may be reproduced in any form by any means without the express written consent of the publisher.

ISBN 978-1965482315

# Table Of Contents

# PREFACE

**About the text**

*Essentials of Mortgage Loan Origination (EMLO)* contains the essential national content required for aspiring mortgage loan originators preparing to meet the standards of the 20-hour SAFE Act NMLS prelicense course. This textbook is tailored to the needs of pre-license students entering the mortgage industry as licensed professionals.

This text is designed to:
- Make it easy for students to learn and retain the material
- Prepare students for practical, real-world applications in mortgage origination
- Emphasize both practical skills and required theoretical knowledge

EMLO is streamlined, direct, and to the point. It includes multiple learning reinforcements and a student-centered organization both within and across chapters. Its examples, explanations, and exercises are grounded in the authors' many years of experience in real estate and mortgage education.

Whether you are new to the industry or transitioning from a related field, EMLO is built to guide you through the foundational knowledge and practices needed to pass your NMLS licensing exam and begin your career as a mortgage loan originator.

**Inside the cover**

Each chapter begins with an overview of the main section heads and learning objectives covered in the chapter. As each of these heads is expanded, the subheads are displayed in the margin. Key terms are printed in bold type the first time they are used and defined. The chapters conclude with a study aid called the "Snapshot Review," which compresses the main points of the chapter into one or two pages.

**About the authors**

Donna Welschmeyer is an active real estate investor and a licensed real estate agent. A Colorado native, Donna's career in adult education has spanned over 35 years. With 13 years of active involvement in real estate and six years of real estate education development, Donna's knowledge and expertise convey a unique perspective that allows her to interpret and clarify the complexities of real estate for students and clients alike.

Ellen Barski has enjoyed a career as a writer, editor, and content developer for close to 30 years, the last eight of which have been in real estate-related education. She has written and developed pre-license, post-license, test prep, and continuing education courses in multiple states.

Stephen Mettling has been a real estate educator and custom training program developer specializing in real estate over the past forty years. During that time, he has written or co-developed over 100 books, professional training programs and texts covering all aspects of residential, commercial, and corporate real estate for national trade organizations and real estate companies. Additionally, Steve has directed numerous statewide real estate schools and served as vice president of Dearborn Financial Services where he headed up the country's largest real estate, securities and insurance license training network.

Ryan Mettling, partner and publisher of Performance Programs, is an experienced online curriculum designer, author, and course developer.

## About the Contributing Editor

Dee Kumar is an award-winning real estate and NMLS-approved instructor with more than 30 years of experience in mortgage and real estate education. He has trained tens of thousands of mortgage loan originators and real estate professionals nationwide.

Dee contributes extensive expertise in federal mortgage regulations—including RESPA, TILA, ECOA, HMDA, Dodd-Frank, and CFPB requirements—helping ensure this publication aligns with NMLS functional specifications and federal compliance standards.

For additional mortgage education resources, visit:
YouTube: https://www.youtube.com/@DeeKumarOnline

# Rules of Conduct for NMLS Approved Pre-Licensure (PE) and Continuing Education (CE) Courses
Updated March 20, 2024

The Secure and Fair Enforcement for Mortgage Licensing Act (SAFE ACT) requires that state-licensed MLO's complete pre-licensing (PE) and continuing education (CE) courses as a condition to be licensed. The SAFE Act also requires that all education completed as a condition for state licensure be NMLS approved. Since 2009 NMLS has established course design, approval, and delivery standards which NMLS approved course providers are required to meet. To further ensure students meet the education requirements of the SAFE Act, NMLS has established Rules of Conduct (ROC). The ROC, which have been approved by the NMLS Mortgage Testing & Education Board, and the NMLS Policy Committee, both of which are comprised of state regulators, are intended to stress that NMLS approved education be delivered and completed with integrity.

## Rules of Conduct

NMLS approved course providers are not authorized by NMLS to grant exceptions to these rules and that I alone am responsible for my conduct under these rules. I also understand these rules are in addition to whatever applicable rules the course provider may have set.

Additionally, I understand that the course provider or others may report any alleged violations to NMLS. NMLS may conduct an investigation into alleged violations and may report alleged violations to the state(s) in which I am seeking licensure or maintain licenses, or to other states.

As an individual completing PE or CE I attest the course format I am being credit banked for has been entirely completed by myself alone and have met required below:

### Classroom (live)
- Completed sign-in by providing my signature prior to the start of the course
    - Provided government issued ID at time of sign-in of the course to verify identity
- Engaged with other students and instructor(s)
- Returned from breaks and lunches on time as required
- Participated and was engaged throughout the entire course
- Properly completed the entire seat-time the SAFE Act required for the approved NMLS course in order to receive an end-of-course completion certificate

### Classroom Equivalent (webinar)
- Provided at the time of entering the webinar platform:
    - Government issued ID
    - Knowledge-Based Authentication
- Returned from breaks and lunches on time as required

- Properly completed the entire seat-time the SAFE Act required for the approved NMLS course in order to receive an end-of-course completion certificate by the following means:
  - Provided adequate camera access to ensure visibility for the entire duration of the course by enabling the proctor to ensure I was visible from the shoulders up
- Understand that if I fail to maintain camera presence for a period of greater than 10 minutes I will be removed from the class and not receive credit
- Engaged and completed all course quizzes and case studies
- Engaged and completed all polls
- Understand at various times during the CEQ/webinar course, I will be required to authenticate my identity and engagement.
- Engaged with other students and facilitators/instructor(s)

**Online Instructor-Led (online with instructor)**
- Provided at the time of entering the Learning Management System (LMS):
  - Personal identification requirements set forth by the provider
- Have not and will not divulge my login ID or password or login credentials to another individual for any online course
- Used my own personal login information to complete the NMLS approved online course
- Properly completed the entire seat-time the SAFE Act required for the approved NMLS course in order to receive an end-of-course completion certificate by the following means:
- Engaged and completed all course quizzes and case studies
- Engaged with other students and facilitators/instructor(s)

**Online Self-Study (online without instructor)**
- Provided at the time of entering the Learning Management System (LMS):
  - Personal identification requirements set forth by the provider
  - Used and authenticated my own personal login for BioSig to enter and complete the NMLS approved online course
- Have not and will not divulge my login ID or password or login credentials to another individual for any online course
- Understand at various times during the online course, I will be required to authenticate my identity through a biometric system.
- Properly completed the entire seat-time the SAFE Act required for the approved NMLS course in order to receive an end-of-course completion certificate by the following means:
- Engaged with all the course content and completed all course quizzes and case studies

ROC for NMLS Approved PE and CE Courses V4. Updated 03/20/2024.

Additionally, I

1. Attest that I am the person who I say I am and that all my course registration information is accurate.

2. Acknowledge that I am required to show a current government issued form of identification prior to class entry and that the name on the identification matches the name as it appears on this course registration.

3. Understand that the SAFE Act and state laws require me to spend a specific amount of time in specific subject areas. Accordingly, I will not attempt to circumvent the requirements of any NMLS approved course. I will not use or attempt to use any artificial intelligence and/or large language model chatbots and/or other assistance to complete any NMLS approved course.

4. Will not give or attempt to give assistance to any other person who is registered to take an NMLS approved pre-licensure or continuing education course.

5. Understand that the course provider has the right to dismiss anyone from class that creates a disturbance or interferes with the administration of the course or other students' learning, including, but not limited to cell phone/smart watch usage.

6. Acknowledge that any outside activities are prohibited while attending class and grounds for immediate removal from class.

7. Will not engage in any conduct that would be contrary to good character or reputation or engage in any behavior that would cause the public to believe that I would not operate in the mortgage loan business lawfully, honestly or fairly.

8. Will not engage in any conduct that is dishonest, fraudulent, or would adversely impact the integrity of the course(s) I am completing or the conditions for which I am seeking licensure or renewal of licensure.

9. Understand and acknowledge my responsibility to report any violations or misconduct involving any of the above ROC to the (MTEB).

10. Understand the CSBS Privacy Notice is applicable to these Rules of Conduct. The CSBS Privacy Notice can be found here: https://www.csbs.org/privacy-policy

ROC for NMLS Approved PE and CE Courses V4. Updated 03/20/2024.

Chapter 1: Federal Mortgage-Related Laws  9

By signing below, I understand the Rules of Conduct listed above, and that any violations to these rules will be subject to an investigation by the state(s) in which I am seeking licensure in or maintaining licenses in. The results of any investigation may subject me to disciplinary actions by the state(s) or the State Regulatory Registry (SRR), including but not limited to:

- Revocation, suspension, or denial of license
- Disqualification from receiving class credit
- Retraction of class credit
- Fines
- Additional education

Print Name:_____          Course Number(s): _____

Signature: _____          Date (mm/dd/yyyy):_____
Email: _____              NMLS ID# _____

# *1* Federal Mortgage-Related Laws

Introduction
Regulatory authority
Real Estate Settlement Procedures Act (RESPA) (12 U.S.C. §2601 et seq.)
Equal Credit Opportunity Act (ECOA) (15 U.S.C. §1691 et seq.) & Regulation B (12 CFR §1002)
Truth in Lending Act (TILA) & Regulation Z
TILA-RESPA Integrated Disclosure Rule (TRID)
Other federal laws and guidelines

## Learning Objectives

- Describe the purpose and major provisions of RESPA.
- Describe the purpose and major provisions of the ECOA.
- Describe the purpose and major provisions of TILA.
- List and briefly describe the purpose and major provisions of additional federal laws and guidelines that govern the financial industry.

**INTRODUCTION**

Numerous federal laws and regulations govern individuals and entities involved in the mortgage lending industry. These regulations impact mortgage lending institutions, individual lenders, mortgage brokers, and third-party service providers. Most of these laws and regulations aim to protect consumers from unscrupulous lending practices.

In presenting the laws that impact the mortgage industry, this textbook will frequently reference both federal laws and related regulations. It is important to understand how those laws and regulations interact. At the federal level, the legislature creates laws that govern actions. Administrative agencies promulgate detailed regulations (rules) to implement and enforce laws. For example, **Regulation B** implements the **Equal Credit Opportunity Act** or **ECOA** (15 U.S.C. §1691 et seq.) (12 CFR §1002), and **Regulation X** implements the **Real Estate Settlement and Procedures Act** or **RESPA** (12 CFR §1024). You may hear the acts referred to as the implementing regulations.

We will begin with a discussion of agencies that regulate the financial industry and then discuss various laws and regulations that protect consumers in the mortgage market.

## REGULATORY AUTHORITY

**Consumer Financial Protection Bureau**
**Department of Housing and Urban Development**
**Federal Housing Finance Agency**
**Office of the Comptroller of the Currency**
**Federal Deposit Insurance Corporation**

### Consumer Financial
Protection Bureau

Essentials. The Consumer Financial Protection Bureau (CFPB) (12 U.S.C. §5481 et seq.) exerts major influence over the mortgage market. Created by the Dodd-Frank Wall Street Reform and Consumer Protection Act (Dodd-Frank Act) (H.R. 4173/P.L. 111-203) in 2010, the CFPB is charged with protecting consumers in the financial sector by regulating lenders and loan originators. The CFPB is a federal agency, but it operates independently. Under this act, the CFPB ensures transparency in mortgage lending and watches for discriminatory lending practices.

**UDAAP.** It also protects consumers from *unfair, deceptive, or abusive financing acts or practices* (UDAAP), which are defined as practices that harm consumers financially and that they cannot reasonably avoid. These practices do not benefit consumers or enhance market competition as a tradeoff for the potential harm.

A few examples of **UDAAP** related to the real estate industry might be a loan servicer that refuses to release a lien after a consumer pays off a mortgage loan, a lender that misrepresents loan terms to a borrower, or sales practices that focus on monthly payments in an attempt to hide the true cost of a loan. A later chapter in this text addresses UDAAP in greater detail.

Among the responsibilities of the CFPB is the enforcement of various consumer financial protection laws, rules, orders, standards, and prohibitions, including some or all provisions of the many acts, including the Consumer Financial Protection Act (12 U.S.C. §5481 et seq.), the Equal Credit Opportunity Act, the Gramm-Leach-Bliley Act (15 U.S.C. §6801 et seq.), the Truth in Lending Act, and the SAFE Act (12 U.S.C. §5101 et seq.).

**CFPB jurisdiction.** As part of its oversight role, the CFPB also has jurisdiction over numerous financial entities and actions:

- ▸ U.S. banks
- ▸ credit unions
- ▸ securities firms
- ▸ mortgage-servicing firms
- ▸ payday lenders
- ▸ foreclosure relief services

- ▸ debt collectors
- ▸ private (for-profit) colleges
- ▸ automobile financing
- ▸ student loan servicing
- ▸ international money transfer
- ▸ consumer reporting, including services such as TransUnion, Equifax, and Experian

The CFPB ensures that financial entities comply with federal consumer financial laws and provides a platform consumers can use to file complaints about issues they encounter with financial products.

The CFPB is also charged with enforcing laws and regulations, primarily by investigating companies, conducting examinations, and taking legal action for violations of consumer financial laws. The agency collects and publishes consumer financial product and service data, including mortgage data, and works in conjunction with other federal and state agencies to ensure a cohesive regulatory environment.

The CFPB strives to educate consumers about their rights related to financial products and offers consumer resources such as guides, calculators, and other tools to help consumers better understand mortgage terms, choose the best options, and avoid unfair practices. For more information about CFPB consumer resources, see https://www.consumerfinance.gov/consumer-tools/.

## Check Your Understanding

Which of these statements about the Consumer Financial Protection Bureau is true?

- A. The CFPB, originally called the Consumer Bureau of Financial Oversight, was established in 2010 by the Equal Credit Opportunity Act.
- B. The CFPB established the Dodd-Frank Act in 2010 in response to the 2008 financial and housing crisis.
- C. The Dodd-Frank Act established the CFPB in 2012 in response to the financial crisis brought about by the events of 9/11.
- D. The Dodd-Frank Act established the CFPB in 2010 in response to the 2008 financial and housing crisis.

If you selected "D," you are correct. The Dodd-Frank Wall Street Reform and Consumer Protection Act established the Consumer Financial Protection Bureau in 2010. This was an attempt to protect consumers as well as the general economy by regulating lenders and loan originators.

**Department of Housing and Urban Development (HUD)**

**HUD.** The **Department of Housing and Urban Development (HUD)** was established in 1965 as a cabinet-level federal agency to address housing issues, especially in the context of urban renewal and development. The agency oversees federal housing programs, including numerous aspects of the housing market and mortgage lending. It focuses on fair practices and affordable housing. HUD's goals include increasing both homeownership and access to affordable housing, ridding the housing industry of discriminatory practices, and supporting community development.

**FHA.** The **Federal Housing Administration (FHA)**, a Department of Housing and Urban Development (HUD) division, was established in 1934 to stimulate the housing market following the Great Depression. Today's FHA primarily serves to insure mortgages made by approved lenders. This "insurance" protects lenders against losses resulting from borrower loan defaults. It enables more consumers, especially first-time homebuyers and those with lower incomes or credit scores, to access mortgage financing. Many of these buyers do not qualify for conventional loans. FHA lenders may accept lower down payments and less favorable credit scores than conventional lenders, though borrowers may be required to purchase mortgage insurance.

HUD sets residential underwriting standards and ensures compliance with federal housing laws. It plays a strong role in holding the mortgage industry accountable for loan products and services provided to those who are buying or trying to keep their home. HUD monitors FHA-approved lenders and gathers mortgage data. FHA uses this data to evaluate loan performance and identify lenders that fail to comply with FHA standards to **originate**, **underwrite**, and **service** mortgages. HUD also sets Minimum Property Standards (MPS) for single-family homes, multi-family housing, and healthcare facilities constructed under HUD housing programs. In addition, homes purchased through HUD loan programs, including FHA, must meet certain minimum building standards.

HUD enforces the **Fair Housing Act** (42 U.S.C. §3601 et seq.) (42 USC 3601), which prohibits discrimination in housing and mortgage lending by investigating discrimination complaints, conducting compliance reviews, and taking action against individuals and organizations that violate Fair Housing regulations.

The agency administers programs for housing rehabilitation and supports low-income individuals with housing by providing rental assistance. It approves and funds Section 8 housing vouchers to assist with rental payments and provides federal aid to local public housing authorities to manage community-based public housing projects. HUD also provides grants to support housing and services for the homeless and assists in rebuilding communities affected by natural disasters.

## Check Your Understanding

Which of these statements most accurately summarizes HUD's role in the mortgage lending industry?

    A.  HUD's primary role is to oversee FHA financing of homes.
    B.  HUD's primary focus is strengthening the housing market and meeting the need for quality housing.
    C.  HUD focuses primarily on housing in rural and agricultural areas.
    D.  HUD oversees private housing developments to ensure affordability.

If you selected "B," you are correct! HUD's primary role is to oversee federal housing programs, ensure decent and affordable housing, and promote community development.

## Federal Housing Finance Agency

The **Federal Housing Finance Agency (FHFA)** was established by the **Housing and Economic Recovery Act of 2008 (HERA)** (P.L. 110-289). FHFA is an independent federal government agency (that regulates and supervises **Fannie Mae** and **Freddie Mac**, the two **government-sponsored enterprises (GSEs)** that purchase mortgages from lenders. This text includes additional information on these GSEs in a later section.

The FHFA also governs the **Federal Home Loan Bank System (FHLBanks or FHLB)**, ensuring they are financially sound, well-capitalized, and able to raise funds. The **Office of Finance (OF)**, which is part of the **Federal Home Loan Bank System**, also falls under the Agency's purview and acts as the fiscal agent for the FHL Bank System.

Most local lending institutions finance at least a portion of their lending through low-cost loans provided by regional Federal Home Loan Banks. The private sector, not taxpayer dollars, provides the capital for each FHLBank. This system of banks plays an important role in the residential mortgage market by providing a continuous flow of funds to lenders.

FHLBanks raise funds by issuing debt securities or consolidated obligations through the "system" of FHLBs. The OF issues and manages all issued debt securities on behalf of the FHLB System. The federal government does not insure these securities and obligations. FHLBanks use the funds they generate to provide advances to member banks. For additional information on the Federal Home Loan Bank System, review this document published by the Federal Deposit Insurance Corporation: https://www.fdic.gov/resources/bankers/affordable-mortgage-lending-center/guide/part-3-docs/federal-home-loan-bank-system.pdf.

**Check Your Understanding**

What role does the Federal Home Loan Bank System play in mortgage financing?

    A. It provides direct-to-consumer loans for borrowers who do not meet the criteria for other mortgage loans.
    B. It oversees the Federal Housing Finance Agency to ensure GSEs perform as required.
    C. It provides government-backed financing to Federal Home Loan banks.
    D. It uses private capital to provide funds to Federal Home Loan banks.

If you selected "D," you are correct! The Federal Home Loan Bank System, governed by the Federal Housing Finance Agency, raises private capital to fund loans to Federal Home Loan banks, which in turn provide funding to other member banks for consumer loans.

## Office of the Comptroller of the Currency

The **Office of the Comptroller of the Currency (OCC)** is charged with ensuring that national banks and federal savings and loan associations function safely, provide fair access to financial services, treat customers fairly, and abide by all pertinent laws and regulations. Like the FHFA, the OCC is an independent branch of the U.S. Department of the Treasury. It charters and oversees national banks and federal savings associations. The OCC has enforcement authority over OCC-governed banks if they violate laws and regulations or engage in unsafe practices. This Agency also has the authority to ensure banks do not discriminate against customers or consumers.

The OCC impacts the mortgage industry through its oversight of national banks that participate in mortgage lending. It sets underwriting standards, including minimum credit score requirements, debt-to-income ratios, and appraisal standards. The entity monitors mortgage performance metrics, identifying potential credit, interest rate, and concentration risk, and encourages banks to implement strong risk management strategies. *Concentration risk* refers to the level of risk in a lender's portfolio that occurs from focusing on a single sector or country rather than diversifying.

The OCC publishes quarterly information about first-lien mortgages held by national banks. This information includes delinquency rate data, foreclosure activity, and loan modification, all of which provide insights into the health of the mortgage market.

The OCC oversees compliance with the **Home Mortgage Disclosure Act (HMDA)** and other mortgage regulations, helping to ensure fair lending practices and protect against discrimination. Finally, the OCC monitors trends in the mortgage market, helping to identify risks and guide banks on effectively managing those risks.

## Check Your Understanding

Which one of the following statements best describes the primary function of the OCC in the mortgage lending industry?

A. The OCC governs foreclosure processes to ensure that consumers receive fair treatment.
B. The OCC oversees national banks to ensure they operate within the law and adhere to safe, non-discriminatory practices.
C. The OCC oversees state banks that may or may not be subject to the same regulations as national banks.
D. The OCC is the regulatory authority in charge of mortgage brokers and governs related compensation and disclosures.

If you selected "B," you are correct. The Office of the Comptroller of the Currency regulates and governs national banks and federal savings and loan associations to ensure they remain solvent and implement safe practices.

**Federal Deposit Insurance Corporation**

The **Federal Deposit Insurance Corporation (FDIC)**, created in 1933, is yet another independent agency of the U.S. government. Its primary mission is to protect consumer deposits and generate confidence in the country's financial system. This agency insures up to $250,000 per depositor per insured bank for each account ownership category. Ownership categories include single accounts, joint accounts, IRAs, trust accounts, employee benefit plan accounts, business accounts, and government accounts. According to the FDIC, account "categories" do not encompass account types such as checking or savings. These two types of accounts are functionally equivalent under FDIC regulations.

The FDIC does not insure credit unions, but credit unions carry equivalent federal insurance.

**FDIC insurance example 1:** A consumer has three individual checking accounts at her bank. The accounts have a $75,000 balance, a $50,000 balance, and a $150,000 balance, respectively. Because these accounts are all at one bank, owned by one depositor, and fall into a single ownership category, the FDIC insures only a total of $250,000, leaving $25,000 uninsured.

**FDIC insurance example 2:** A couple has three accounts at a single bank. Each has an individual checking account, and they have a joint account. The FDIC insures each of these accounts for up to $250,000 because two separate people own the individual accounts, and the joint account is in a separate ownership category.

**FDIC insurance example 3:** A consumer has an individual account at two separate banks. The FDIC insures each account for up to $250,000 because they are at separate banks.

The FDIC plays a role in supervising financial institutions to ensure they safely house consumer deposits; thus, its role in the mortgage industry is to ensure the stability of banks that originate mortgages. This means that if a bank fails, the FDIC can step in, not only to protect depositors but also to manage loan servicing processes for existing mortgages.

In addition, the FDIC regulates lending practices, including mortgage lending, to ensure lenders employ responsible underwriting practices and comply with consumer protection laws. The FDIC monitors the financial health of banks, scrutinizing their mortgage lending practices to identify risks and ensure compliance with mortgage regulations. The FDIC's authority and actions allow it to influence the overall quality of the mortgage market.

### Check Your Understanding

Select the statement below that most accurately reflects FDIC insurance of consumer bank accounts.

A. A depositor has an individual checking account and a savings account at the same bank. Each of these accounts is insured for up to $250,000.

B. A depositor has an individual checking account and a joint account with his sister. Each of these accounts is insured for up to $250,000.

C. A depositor has an individual checking account at one bank and an individual savings account at another. The FDIC insures these accounts up to a total of $250,000.

D. A depositor has an individual savings account at a credit union and a checking account at another bank. The FDIC insures both of these accounts for up to $250,000.

If you selected "B," you are correct! An individual checking account and a joint account are separate ownership categories, so each would be insured for the full amount.

# REAL ESTATE SETTLEMENT PROCEDURES ACT

**Overview of RESPA**

**History.** The **Real Estate Settlement Procedures Act (RESPA)** was passed in 1974 and enacted on June 20, 1975. The law exists as Title 12, Chapter 27 of the United States Code: 12 U.S. C. §§ 2601-2617.

Congress originally charged the Department of Housing and Urban Development with administering RESPA. HUD promulgated Regulation X (12 CFR §1024) to implement the law in 1975. Regulation X details the rules for RESPA compliance.

In 1990, the **National Affordable Housing Act (NAHA)** amended RESPA to include disclosure requirements for lenders that transferred, sold, or assigned mortgage servicing to a new entity. NAHA also requires lenders to disclose escrow account information to borrowers at inception and annually after that, making it clear to borrowers the charges they must pay and the charges the servicer pays out of the escrow account.

**Affiliated business arrangements.** Another short amendment in 1992 extended RESPA's authority to cover subordinate lien loans (second and subsequent property loan liens). In 1996, the **Economic Growth and Regulatory Paperwork Reduction Act** further amended RESPA to better define **affiliated business arrangements**. A HUD-issued RESPA Reform Rule in 2008 made substantial changes to existing regulations. These changes included standardizing the **Good Faith Estimate** form and a revised **HUD-1 Settlement Statement**. This rule also permitted lenders to provide RESPA disclosures electronically.

In 2010, the Dodd-Frank Act granted RESPA rule-making authority and enforcement to the CFPB. We will address the Dodd-Frank Act in more detail later in this chapter.

Multiple Regulation X changes in 2013 and 2014 incorporated some Dodd-Frank Act provisions and adjustments to force-placed insurance (insurance purchased by the lender when a homeowners policy lacks adequate coverage or lapses), mortgage servicing rules, and escrow account requirements. These changes are often referred to as the "2013-2014 Amendments."

**Mortgage servicing rules**

**Mortgage servicers**. Mortgage lenders must disclose to borrowers the possibility of their mortgage loans being transferred to a **mortgage servicer**. A mortgage servicer is a third-party company to which lenders transfer loans for continued management. Servicers may assume any one or more of several tasks:

- ▸ collecting and processing payments
- ▸ tracking loan balances, including principal and interest paid
- ▸ generating tax forms, such as the year-end 1098 form
- ▸ managing escrow accounts
- ▸ processing mortgage insurance cancellation requests
- ▸ managing loss mitigation programs
- ▸ initiating foreclosure proceedings when warranted

In some instances, mortgage servicers charged excessive fees related to foreclosures or loan modifications, initiated foreclosure proceedings without proper notice to homeowners, and failed to participate in loss mitigation processes with borrowers. Changes to Regulations X (RESPA) and Z (aka the Truth in Lending Act, or TILA) attempted to alleviate these concerns.

**TILA-RESPA Integrated Disclosure Rule**. In December 2013, the CFPB published final Dodd-Frank Act rules, some of which created and implemented the **TILA-RESPA Integrated Disclosure Rule**, or **TRID**. Regulation Z (12 CFR §1026) became the "home" for the new integrated forms —the **Loan Estimate (LE)** and the **Closing Disclosure (CD)**, which took the place of the Good Faith Estimate and HUD-1 Settlement Statement—as well as details regarding timing and disclosure requirements for most closed-end consumer mortgage loans.

**Purpose of RESPA**

RESPA's primary purpose is **consumer protection**. The law and its implementing regulation mandate numerous safeguards for residential mortgage borrowers and govern the loan process from application to settlement. As it is currently written, RESPA has two primary purposes.

First, RESPA facilitates an efficient method for consumers to shop for settlement services by requiring lenders to disclose financing costs to borrowers before they become contractually obligated for a loan. The required disclosure information, prepared on a standardized Loan Estimate form, allows consumers to make informed decisions about financing alternatives and housing affordability.

Second, RESPA prohibits illegal and unethical business practices, including kickbacks, illegal referral fees, and undisclosed compensation that increase the cost of borrowing.

**Mortgage bankers vs. mortgage brokers.** Most mortgage lenders, including mortgage brokers, are subject to RESPA requirements. What is the difference between these types of mortgage professionals?

**Mortgage bankers** and **loan officers** both originate and fund loans for the lending institutions where they are employed. These lenders work directly with consumers and manage the loan process from application through funding. The institution may keep the loans it funds in its portfolio and continue to service those loans, or it may sell the loans to another lender or to the secondary market and continue to service them for a fee. Another alternative is to sell the servicing rights to its loans for a service release premium (SRP) fee. While most lending institutions offer a variety of loan products, available loans and loan terms are somewhat restricted based on the institution's policies.

**Portfolio lending.** Portfolio lending is the lender's practice of keeping and servicing loans it funds instead of selling them. Some lenders sell some of their loans and keep others. Loans that lenders keep in their portfolios may be nonconforming, which means those borrowers do not meet the standard credit score, debt-to-income ratio, down payment, or loan amount criteria that conforming loans require. A conforming loan meets the criteria that allow the lender to sell it to the secondary market. Depending on the loan, portfolio loans may or may not be subject to RESPA. Mortgage loans insured by the federal government or made with funds from a federally regulated lender are likely subject to RESPA terms. Non-consumer loans (business, commercial, or agricultural), temporary loans, or loans for properties with 25 or more acres are likely not subject to RESPA.

Portfolio lenders may be able to offer more favorable terms than those available for loans they will sell, or they may charge higher interest rates or other fees because of the additional risk involved. Because these loans are more flexible than traditional mortgage loans, borrowers with nontraditional incomes, such as self-employed buyers or those with less-than-stellar credit histories, may qualify for a mortgage loan through portfolio lending when they do not qualify for other loans.

**Mortgage brokers** do not fund or service loans and are not "lenders" themselves. They are employed by a mortgage brokerage firm rather than a financial institution. They act as intermediaries between borrowers and lenders by shopping multiple lending institutions for the best terms for the borrower, and they are subject to RESPA disclosures and restrictions just as typical mortgage lenders are.

Mortgage brokers advise consumers on available loan programs, help with the application process, provide required disclosures, process the loan, and submit it to the lender. Brokers also help borrowers respond to follow-up requests from lenders or underwriters, and they often attend the closing to ensure the loan closing process goes smoothly. Consumers work directly with the mortgage broker, not the lender, throughout the process. Many consumers who work with a mortgage broker have little to no contact with the lender until the loan is funded and loan servicing begins. Mortgage brokers typically can offer a wider array of loan products than traditional lending institutions because they partner with multiple lenders.

## Applicable loan types

RESPA's jurisdiction applies to **federally related mortgage loans**. Two factors determine if a mortgage loan is federally related.

**Must be a residential loan**. A RESPA-regulated loan must be a first lien on a one- to four-unit residential property securing the loan. Why is this important? These properties are considered "residential" (non-commercial). Residential properties with more than four units are considered commercial and are thus subject to different requirements. Residential property includes permanently placed manufactured homes, condominiums, and cooperatives that the borrower will use as a principal residence.

**Must have a specified purpose**. The second requirement for a loan to be a federally-regulated loan is that the loan fall into at least one of the following categories:

- ▸ The loan is made by a lending institution for which the federal government insures consumer deposits.
- ▸ The loan is made or insured by a federal government agency (e.g., Federal Housing Authority – FHA; Veterans Administration – VA; United States Department of Agriculture – USDA).
- ▸ The loan is made in connection with a housing or urban development program that the federal government administers.
- ▸ The lender intends to sell the loan to the secondary market
- ▸ The loan is the subject of a home equity conversion or reverse mortgage issued by a lender that must comply with RESPA regulations.

**Specific RESPA-regulated loans**. In general, most residential mortgage transactions are governed by RESPA, including the following types of loans:

- ▸ conventional loans
- ▸ government-insured or guaranteed loans (FHA, VA, USDA)
- ▸ purchase loans
- ▸ reverse mortgages
- ▸ lender-approved loan assumptions
- ▸ refinancing loans

- ▸ property improvement loans
- ▸ home equity lines of credit (**HELOC**)
- ▸ installment sales contracts (land contracts) if the seller funding the loan is funded by another RESPA-governed loan on the property

In short, any loan that is guaranteed by a federal government entity or that will be sold to the secondary mortgage market is subject to RESPA.

**RESPA transaction exemptions.** RESPA regulations do NOT apply to the following transaction types:

- ▸ cash purchases
- ▸ seller financing (except as noted previously)
- ▸ business or commercial loans
- ▸ assumptions that do not require lender approval
- ▸ loan conversions, e.g., converting from an adjustable-rate to a fixed-rate mortgage
- ▸ temporary construction loans (unless the loan automatically converts to permanent financing)
- ▸ bridge loans
- ▸ vacant or unimproved property loans unless a dwelling unit will be added to the property within two years
- ▸ lender loan sales to the secondary market

These transactions are not subject to RESPA, but they are subject to other federal regulations, such as the Truth in Lending Act.

### Check Your Understanding

Which of these situations is subject to RESPA regulations?

A. An investor pays cash for a single-family residential home that he will use as a rental.
B. A lender sells a package of mortgages to the secondary market.
C. A corporation expands housing offerings by purchasing a 35-unit apartment complex.
D. An Army veteran uses VA benefits to purchase a new residence.

If you selected "D," you are correct. Cash purchases, lender sales to the secondary market, and commercial transactions are exempt from RESPA regulations.

**Prohibitions, limitations, exemptions**

**Referral fees.** One of RESPA's primary consumer protections is achieved by prohibiting real estate settlement service providers from receiving or giving any "thing of value" (e.g., **kickback**, fee split, or unearned fee) for referrals in a mortgage transaction without performing an actual service (12 CFR §1024.14 (12 CFR §1024.14) and 15).

RESPA makes it illegal to give or receive any kind of payment or reward (fees or kickbacks), aka thing of value, for referring settlement services associated with federally related mortgage loans. These rules ensure that there are no financial incentives or arrangements for referring settlement services in mortgage transactions.

**Fee splitting.** RESPA also prohibits individuals from giving or accepting any part of a fee for settlement services in a federally related mortgage loan transaction unless the fee corresponds to actual services performed. All fees must be earned. This rule aims to prevent people from charging fees without actually providing a service.

**Thing of value.** The definition of a **thing of value** is far-reaching. Following are just a few of the items considered things of value:

- money, including salaries, commissions, and fees
- physical items
- discounts
- duplicate payment of charges
- stock, dividends, or partnership profit distributions
- franchise royalties
- credits representing monies to be paid at a later date
- increased equity in a parent or subsidiary entity
- special or free rates for services, sales, or rentals
- tips for and payments of another person's expenses
- reduction in credit against an existing obligation

### Case Study – Kallai vs. Jatola Homes, LLC

In 2022, a federal district court judge in the court case *Kallai vs. Jatola Homes, LLC*, emphasized RESPA's definition of a "thing of value" to be "any payment, advance, funds, loan, service, or other consideration," as well as "credits representing monies that may be paid *at a future date*" or "the opportunity to participate in a money-making program."

The judge noted that *payment* or *compensation* does not refer only to financial compensation. This definition closed a loophole that some providers took advantage of, wherein they promised to provide compensation (financial or otherwise) at a later date. For more information, visit https://www.foley.com/insights/publications/2022/01/federal-court-allow-unusual-respa-section-8-claim/.

**Case Study – Realty Connect USA Long Island, Inc.**

In August 2023, the Bureau issued an order against Realty Connect USA Long Island, Inc., a real estate brokerage firm in Suffolk County, New York, for accepting things of value in exchange for referring mortgage loans to Freedom Mortgage Corporation. The realty firm accepted various things of value, including subscription services, event tickets, and monthly marketing services agreement payments. These actions violated RESPA and Regulation X, the implementing regulation.

The Bureau ordered Realty Connect to cease the illegal activity and pay a $200,000 civil penalty.

In the same case, the Bureau also took separate action against Freedom Mortgage Corporation for the lender's part in providing things of value in violation of RESPA. The lender was ordered to cease the illegal activity and pay a civil penalty of $1.75 million. For more details, visit https://www.consumerfinance.gov/enforcement/actions/realty-connect-usa-long-island-inc/.

## Check Your Understanding

Which of these is NOT acceptable under RESPA provisions?

    A. A title insurance company gives hockey tickets to a real estate broker who frequently recommends the company to clients.
    B. A lender calculates a borrower's annual escrow payment to be $1,500 and requires the borrower to fund the account at closing with $250.
    C. A lender permits a borrower to opt out of escrow requirements but charges the borrower a one-time $300 fee for the opt-out.
    D. Because the HOA increased its assessment, a borrower's escrow account is short; the lender requires the borrower to increase the escrow payment.

If you chose "A," you are correct! RESPA prohibits the exchange of anything of value between settlement service providers.

**Additional RESPA Protections**

**Cannot mark-up fees**. RESPA also prohibits service providers (primarily lenders) from marking up charges from other settlement service providers. For example, a lender paying $45 for a consumer's credit report can charge the consumer only that amount.

**Cannot require a given provider**. An additional RESPA protection prohibits service providers such as lenders or real estate agents from requiring buyers to use a particular settlement company as a condition of sale. This prohibition is of particular significance for service providers that have affiliated business arrangements with other providers, but it applies to ALL other service providers. For example, a lender may not require borrowers to use a specific title company, whether that company is fully or partially owned by the lender or is completely separate. However, the lender may provide suggestions to the borrower.

Many large builders and developers offer financial incentives to buyers who use a builder's preferred lender. Do these incentives constitute a RESPA violation? No. These sellers can offer different terms, etc., to buyers who use the seller's preferred lender; they may not, however, *require* buyers to use that lender.

**Cannot require a given title insurer**. In addition, sellers cannot require that buyers use a specific title insurance company unless the seller agrees to pay the title insurance premium and any other title-related charges.

**Cannot charge a fee for doc prep**. RESPA prohibits lenders or loan servicers from charging a fee to prepare loan documents, including the Loan Estimate (LE), Closing Disclosure (CD), the annual escrow statement, or other required disclosures.

## RESPA enforcement and penalties

Many agencies are involved in enforcing RESPA, including the Comptroller of the Currency, the Board of Governors of the Federal Reserve System, the Board of Directors for the Federal Deposit Insurance Corporation, the Federal Trade Commission, and the Consumer Financial Protection Bureau.

Violators are subject to civil liability for actual and punitive damages. It is important to note that actions that violate RESPA provisions often also violate other federal laws. Penalties for a violation can be severe and include criminal and civil financial penalties, injunctive action, and even imprisonment in severe cases.

## RESPA–regulated settlement services

Settlement service providers are one of the primary targets of RESPA and Regulation X. What are settlement services? Regulation X defines this term as *any service provided in connection with a prospective or actual settlement.*

What mortgage-related settlement services and providers does RESPA govern?

- loan origination of a federally related mortgage loan, including the loan application, loan document preparation, loan processing, credit reporting, underwriting, and funding
- mortgage brokerage services and processes
- escrow account management

> ▸ title services, searches, abstracts, title commitments, title insurance policies
> ▸ appraisers and appraisals
> ▸ mortgage, hazard, flood, and casualty insurance
> ▸ settlement document preparation, notarization, and recordation

The law does not govern post-settlement service providers (providers not actively involved in a transaction before settlement), such as contractors engaged for maintenance or repair activities after closing.

**Escrow regulation**

RESPA (12 CFR §1024.17) regulates how lenders manage escrow accounts. Most residential lenders require borrowers to fund an escrow account from which the lender pays the borrower's annual property taxes and hazard insurance premiums. Some loans/lenders permit the borrower to opt out of escrow payments, and some charge borrowers an upfront fee to exercise this option.

Borrowers whose mortgages include mortgage insurance will usually be required to fund an escrow account. All government-insured or guaranteed loans (VA, FHA, USDA) require escrow accounts. Higher-priced loans require a funded escrow account for at least the first five years of the loan term.

**Funding limitations.** To protect borrowers from excessive escrow funding requirements, RESPA permits lenders to require escrow deposits of only 1/12 of the annual estimated property tax, insurance, and other impounds, plus a cushion (that cannot exceed 1/6 of the total amount to be paid out of the escrow account annually).
To illustrate, suppose a lender anticipates the total annual payment from an escrow account to be $1,200. The borrower's monthly escrow payment cannot exceed $100 (1/12 of $1,200), and the escrow cushion cannot exceed $200 (1/6 of $1,200).

At closing, borrowers subject to an escrow account may have to fund the account with an amount equal to twice the ongoing monthly escrow payment. Using the example in the previous paragraph of a $1,200 annual escrow payment, lenders may require that borrowers fund an escrow account with $200 at closing. Note that this equates to the previously mentioned 1/6 escrow "cushion" permitted by law.

If the escrow account is overfunded by $50 or more, the lender must return funds to the borrower. If the account is underfunded based on tax and insurance estimates for the upcoming year, the lender may increase the borrower's escrow payment.

In some rare instances, lenders must collect escrow funds for items billed for a period longer than a year. For instance, some flood insurance premiums are billable every three years. In this situation, the lender may collect 1/36 of the anticipated payment each month.

**Escrow reporting requirements.** Lenders must provide borrowers with an initial escrow statement either at closing or within 45 days of closing. The statement must itemize the estimated expenditures the account is intended to cover.

After initial escrow account funding, lenders must perform an annual escrow analysis to determine if the account holds more or less funds than necessary. The lender must then provide the borrower with an annual escrow statement detailing all expenditures and deposits made during the year. The report must note any overage or shortage in the account, along with information about refunds due or additional escrow payments required.

**Loan application requirements**

In addition to regulating settlement services and escrow accounts, RESPA imposes certain application requirements on mortgage loan originators (MLOs).

**Loan application required information.** One of the RESPA application requirements is that the lender issue a Loan Estimate to the borrower within a statutory amount of time after a borrower submits a loan application. Six pieces of information are required to constitute "submission" of a loan application that triggers RESPA disclosure requirements:

- name
- income
- Social Security or other identifying number
- property address
- estimated property value
- mortgage loan amount requested

Are lenders that issue borrower pre-approvals required to provide Loan Estimates? Generally, they are not, because a property address is required to trigger loan disclosures under RESPA.

Of course, lenders require a considerable amount of information on a loan application in addition to these six items, but this information does not trigger the requirement to issue a Loan Estimate.

**RESPA foreclosure protections**

RESPA also includes consumer foreclosure protections. To better understand these protections, let us first review some mortgage-related terminology and processes.

**Mortgage loans and documents.** Mortgage loans are traditionally secured by the property they fund. The mortgaged property serves as loan **collateral,** assuring lenders they have an asset permitting them to recoup their losses if the borrower defaults.

How does this process unfold? When obtaining a mortgage, borrowers sign a **promissory note**, which is the borrower's promise to repay the loan. The note establishes the borrower's payment terms.

Borrowers also sign a **security instrument** (either a **mortgag**e or trust deed) that establishes the consequences for nonpayment of the note. By signing the security instrument, the borrower **hypothecates** the purchased property, meaning the property is pledged as collateral for the loan. The security instrument type determines the lender's allowable actions if the borrower defaults.

Security instruments typically include an **acceleration clause**, which permits a lender to "accelerate" a loan's due date to the present date if the borrower defaults.

What triggers the acceleration clause? Any form of loan default can set this clause in motion. Failure to make prescribed mortgage payments is the most common cause of default. However, other borrower actions may result in loan default, such as failing to maintain property insurance or pay taxes, filing for bankruptcy, and/or transferring the property without lender approval.

Most mortgages also include a **due-on-sale clause** (aka **alienation clause**). This clause comes into play if a borrower transfers property ownership without paying off the loan or receiving the lender's permission. For instance, a borrower who transfers ownership to a trust or business, even though the trust or business is in the borrower's name, may activate the due-on-sale clause, which in turn triggers a mortgage acceleration.

**Foreclosure process**   While some borrowers who default due to unpaid mortgage payments can catch up on their payments and avoid lender foreclosure actions, many cannot. When this occurs, the lender can initiate a loan foreclosure process. The foreclosure process is complex and can be lengthy, depending on the lender, the property, the real estate market in general, and the type of foreclosure process required.

**Lien theory and title theory.** Another concept related to mortgage loan security foreclosures is lien theory versus title theory. Some states follow one or the other, while others incorporate a blend of the two theories. The underlying premise of each of these theories impacts how lenders can approach the foreclosure process.

In **lien theory** states, the verbiage in the security instrument used creates a lien against the collateral property. The borrower must repay the associated loan to remove the lien, and lenders generally must use a judicial foreclosure process, which involves filing a lawsuit to obtain permission to foreclose.

In **title theory** states, the security instrument gives legal title to the lender and equitable title to the borrower, which means the borrower has all legal rights to the property except the actual title. When the borrower repays the loan, full legal title is then vested in the borrower's name. Because title is essentially in the lender's name, a non-judicial foreclosure process may be used if necessary.

These states typically use **trust deeds** (a **deed of trust**) as the security instrument. A trust deed involves three parties: the lender, the borrower, and a trustee. Using a trust deed transfers financial interest in the title to a disinterested third party (the **trustee**).

> ▸ The trustee holds legal title to the property, subject to the terms outlined in the trust deed. Each state determines who may serve as a trustee.
> ▸ The lender is the **beneficiary** and retains the note and the deed of trust.
> ▸ The borrower is the **trustor** and has equitable title that allows possession of the property.

**Non-judicial foreclosure process.** Two categories of non-judicial foreclosure proceedings exist. The first and most common requires public notice and document recording. Lenders must make required public notice and publications and record all necessary documents to initiate and complete the foreclosure. The trustee becomes responsible for foreclosing on the property under a power of sale clause in the trust deed.

The second, much less common process is **strict foreclosure**, which requires no public notice or document recording requirement. As of this writing, only two states permit strict foreclosures: Connecticut and Vermont.

The following content addresses the more common non-judicial foreclosure process. State laws vary, but here are the general steps in a non-judicial foreclosure process:

1. The lender notifies the borrower of the default and the potential for foreclosure sale. Depending on the state, the lender may provide these notices together or separately.

2. The borrower has a specified number of days to bring the loan current (aka redeem the loan). If the borrower cannot do so, the lender can authorize the trustee to schedule a property sale.

3. The trustee provides all required notices to the borrower and the public regarding the sale date and location.

4. On the auction date, the lender can place a credit bid on the property. A **credit bid** means that the lender is not offering cash. Instead, they offer credit against the mortgage loan. The highest bidder takes the property.

**Mortgages as security instruments.** Lenders typically use a mortgage as the security instrument in states that employ lien theory.

A mortgage involves just two parties: the lender and the borrower. When lenders use a mortgage as the security instrument for a loan, the borrower (mortgagor) conveys interest in the property to the lender in the form of a **voluntary lien**. The borrower holds legal title to the property. If a borrower defaults on the loan, the lender generally must use a **judicial foreclosure** process. However, if the loan documents include a power of sale clause, lenders may use a **non-judicial foreclosure** process.

**Judicial foreclosure processes.** To initiate a judicial foreclosure process, the lender must file a lawsuit against the borrower. This lawsuit is a petition to the court for permission to initiate foreclosure proceedings. If the court determines the lender has a rightful foreclosure claim, the lender can begin foreclosure.

Again, the steps involved in a judicial foreclosure process differ from one state to another; however, in general, the following actions will occur:

1. The lender uses the acceleration clause in the security instrument to call the loan due and sends a pre-foreclosure notice to the borrower. This notice informs the borrower that the lender will start the foreclosure process if the borrower does not bring the loan into compliance.

2. The lender files a foreclosure lawsuit, asking the court for authorization to proceed with the foreclosure sale.

3. In most states, the lender must notify the public of the sale date and location by placing ads in a newspaper in the county where the property is located. These ads must run for a specified period of time.

4. The property will be sold to the highest bidder. The lender may place a credit bid on the property to ensure it sells for enough to cover the debt and other fees. Often, the lender wins the bid, and the property becomes real estate owned (REO).

The borrower must voluntarily vacate the property by the stated date or be evicted.

If sale proceeds are sufficient to satisfy the loan and pay off other liens, expenses, and foreclosure costs, the lender must refund any surplus to the borrower.

## Check Your Understanding

A borrower signs a mortgage when purchasing a new residence. The borrower subsequently defaults on the loan, and the lender initiates foreclosure proceedings. Which one of the following statements is correct?

A. The lender must use a judicial foreclosure process because the security instrument is a mortgage.
B. The lender must use a non-judicial foreclosure process because the security instrument is a mortgage.
C. The lender may use either a judicial or non-judicial foreclosure process, depending on whether the mortgage includes a power of sale clause.
D. Depending on whether the borrower signed a trust deed, the lender may use a judicial or non-judicial foreclosure process.

If you selected "C," you are correct! When lenders use a mortgage as the security instrument (as in a strict lien theory state), they must use a judicial foreclosure process unless the mortgage includes a power of sale clause.

**Borrower foreclosure protections.** No matter what foreclosure process they use, lenders must carefully follow all federal and state regulations.

Many consumer protections under RESPA are the direct result of unscrupulous actions by lenders in loan and foreclosure processes.

Regulation X mandates that lenders work with borrowers to resolve delinquencies before initiating the foreclosure process. Called **loss mitigation**, this process requires the borrower to apply to request assistance to prevent foreclosure and requires lender approval. Several options exist:

> ▶ forbearance (a temporary pause in mortgage payments)
> ▶ deferral or partial claim (permission to add missed payments to the end of the mortgage loan)
> ▶ repayment plan (an adjusted payment schedule that adds back payments to monthly payments until the loan is caught up)\
> ▶ loan modification (original loan terms change to roll past-due payments into the loan, bringing the loan current)
> ▶ reinstatement (repaying past-due payments immediately after completing forbearance)

Transactions in the pre-foreclosure stage may not proceed after borrowers submit a loss mitigation application unless one of the following occurs:

> 1) the lender denies the application,
> 2) the borrower rejects loss mitigation options the lender presents, or
> 3) the borrower fails to perform the terms of a loss mitigation agreement.

Federal regulations require lenders to notify borrowers of missed payments and prohibit lenders from sending a default notice to borrowers unless the borrower meets one of the following criteria:

▸ The mortgage payment delinquency is 120 days or more.
▸ The borrower has triggered the due-on-sale clause.
▸ Another creditor has initiated a foreclosure action against the same property.

Some states give borrowers a redemption period, sometimes called an **equitable right of redemption**, which is an opportunity to redeem the loan and prevent foreclosure by paying all funds owed to the lender. Some states also provide a **statutory right of redemption**, which allows borrowers to redeem the foreclosure for a certain period after the foreclosure sale.

## Check Your Understanding

Regulation X requires lenders to cooperate with borrowers who are in danger of foreclosure by discussing loss mitigation options. Which one of the following statements regarding loss mitigation is FALSE?

A. The lender must invite eligible borrowers to complete a loss mitigation application.
B. Borrowers must complete a loss mitigation application to begin the process.
C. Lenders must wait at least 120 days after receiving a loss mitigation application before initiating a foreclosure process.
D. Lenders must receive court approval to deny a loss mitigation application.

If you selected "B," you are correct! Borrowers must apply to enter into a loss mitigation process with a lender. The lender may deny the application based on certain criteria, or the borrower may reject solutions offered by the lender.

**Foreclosure alternatives.** Borrowers who face foreclosure have options that may better suit their needs. To avoid foreclosure action and having the foreclosure appear on their credit history, borrowers may negotiate with the lender to provide a **deed in lieu of foreclosure**. If the lender approves the request, this action conveys the property to the lender. The lender adds the property to its "real estate owned" portfolio and then sells it.

Another option buyers may use is a **short sale**. Borrowers who owe more on a property than its market value may attempt to negotiate a short sale agreement with their lender. If approved, the borrowers can sell the property for less than they owe, with all proceeds going to the lender.

**Deficiency judgments.** When a foreclosure sale, a deed in lieu of foreclosure, or a short sale occurs, lenders may be able to pursue a **deficiency judgment** against borrowers for any difference between the sale proceeds and the loan balance. Some states prohibit deficiency judgments, and some mortgage agreements spell out whether or not a deficiency judgment is an option.

## RESPA disclosure requirements

In addition to certain disclosures required when borrowers apply for a mortgage loan and prepare to close on a property, RESPA requires lenders to provide certain other disclosures to consumers.

**Affiliated business arrangement disclosure.** Lenders must supply borrowers with an **Affiliated business arrangement disclosure** if the lender refers a borrower to a third-party service provider with which the lender has an ownership or other beneficial interest. For example, if a lender has an ownership interest in a title insurance firm and refers borrowers to that firm, the lender must disclose the affiliation to the borrower when making the referral. The lender may generally NOT require the borrower to use the referred service provider.

However, if the lender chooses a provider (such as an attorney, credit reporting agency, or appraiser) to represent the *lender's* interests in a transaction, the lender can require the borrower to use the named provider. For instance, borrowers do not select the appraiser for a transaction, but must compensate the lender for the appraisal.

**Mortgage Servicing Disclosure Statement.** Within three days of receiving a borrower's mortgage loan application, lenders must issue a **Mortgage Servicing Disclosure Statement** to notify borrowers of the possibility that the lender will transfer loan servicing tasks to a third party.
Within this same period, lenders must provide mortgage loan applicants with a special information booklet titled, "Your Home Loan Toolkit: A Step-by-Step Guide." The CFPB provides this guide, which contains information about real estate **settlement services** and documents.

**Servicing Transfer Statement.** Another RESPA-required disclosure is the **Servicing Transfer Statement**. Lenders typically provide this disclosure after closing when they intend to transfer servicing rights to another entity. The lender must provide this disclosure at least 15 days before the effective date of the transfer.

See also the section entitled **TILA-RESPA Integrated Disclosure rules**.

## EQUAL CREDIT OPPORTUNITY ACT (ECOA) AND REGULATION B

**Purpose of ECOA**
**Protected classes**
**Discrimination types**
**Loan denial criteria**
**Regulation B and ECOA implementation**
**Action notices to borrowers**
**Acceptable income**
**Creditworthiness**
**Enforcement**

**Purpose of ECOA**    The Equal Credit Opportunity Act (ECOA) of 1974 is one of the primary consumer protection laws prohibiting discrimination in lending practices. Congress passed this law when lenders often discriminated against women who applied for credit, but soon amended the law to include a number of protected classes.

The ECOA is implemented through Regulation B and administered by the Consumer Financial Protection Bureau. This act prohibits discrimination in providing credit, including taking, evaluating, and approving or denying loan applications. It governs both residential and business loan applicants and protects both applicants and any co-signors. The act prohibits lenders from discouraging consumers from applying for loans. It ensures that all consumers have an equal chance to obtain credit and requires lenders to base approval or denial on creditworthiness.

The ECOA originally prohibited discrimination based only on sex or marital status. The law eventually led to a requirement that credit bureaus create and maintain separate credit files for married spouses. In 1976, the law added the remaining classes that the ECOA protects today.

The act prohibits typical lenders from funding **stated loans**, which do not require income verification. Instead, the lender allows borrowers to simply state their income. These loans are also called no-doc mortgages or no-income verification mortgages.

**Protected classes**    The Equal Opportunity Act protects borrowers against discrimination based on the following categories, some of which are the same as the Fair Housing Act:

> ▶ race
> ▶ religion
> ▶ nationality
> ▶ ethnicity
> ▶ sex

- marital status
- age (applicant must have the capacity to enter into a contract)
- income source (legal sources of income)

It also protects consumers against backlash based on their having exercised rights under the **Consumer Credit Protection Act (CCPA)** (15 U.S.C. §1601 et seq.).

The ECOA prohibits discrimination in any part of the lending process and is not limited to mortgage lending. Any organization that offers credit is subject to the provisions of this act.

## Discrimination types

ECOA addresses three types of discrimination: **overt discrimination, disparate treatment, and indirect discrimination**.

**Overt discrimination.** Overt discrimination means explicit or blatant prejudicial behavior. While blatant discrimination still exists, it is less common than it once was.

**Disparate treatment.** Intentionally treating individuals differently based on any protected characteristic is called **disparate treatment**.

**Disparate impact.** An often-unintentional form of discrimination, **disparate impact,** also called **indirect discrimination**, occurs when a particular action or policy, while not discriminatory on its face, negatively impacts members of a protected class disproportionately. <u>Regardless of the intentionality of the action or policy, disparate treatment is illegal</u>.

For example, consider a suburb that creates zoning regulations prohibiting the construction of affordable housing. By itself, the regulation doesn't appear to discriminate against any particular class. However, in areas where people of color, for instance, are more likely to be in lower-income households, the zoning regulation described disproportionately keeps these individuals from living in this suburb. Zoning regulations of this kind are referred to as **exclusionary zoning** and are examples of disparate impact.

## Loan denial criteria

What criteria can a lender use to deny a loan?

- insufficient income
- poor credit history or score or lack of credit history
- high debt-to-income ratio
- inadequate collateral to secure a loan (property has insufficient value)
- unstable employment or lack of employment history
- immigration status, but only as it relates to repayment ability

**Regulation B and ECOA implementation**

Regulation B, which implements the Equal Credit Opportunity Act, provides additional guidelines, prohibitions, and requirements beyond the ECOA itself. This regulation prohibits lenders from requiring information unrelated to the applicant's creditworthiness and places certain requirements on lenders when they deny an application.

In determining the information lenders can legally require applicants to provide, it is important to note that they may request information that appears to be discriminatory but is actually legal for limited use, such as age, marital status, income source, and citizenship.

**Permissible forms of ECOA-required information**

**Applicant's age.** Lenders may consider an applicant's age to determine if the applicant is old enough to legally enter into a contract (usually age 18) or when the applicant's age relates to other creditworthiness factors (such as impending retirement and subsequently reduced income). Lenders may consider age in a valid credit scoring system. Such systems may not *disfavor* elderly applicants, defined by the ECOA as age 62 or older, but may *favor* such applicants.

**Spouses and children.** The ECOA prohibits lenders from inquiring about an applicant's marital status. In addition, lenders may not ask about a spouse (regarding income, for example) except under the following circumstances:

▶ The spouse is part of a joint credit application and will use the account or be liable for repayment.
▶ The applicant and spouse agree that the spouse's income can be considered in making any credit decisions.
▶ The property purchased serves as collateral for the loan and is in a state that grants property rights to spouses, e.g., states that recognize community property laws or dower/curtesy rights.

Lenders may not ask applicants about plans to have children, but they can ask about dependent expenses.

**Additional income sources.** Applicants are NOT required to report alimony, child support, or separate maintenance to a lender unless they wish to use those funds as a basis for repayment. Lenders may ask, however, if an applicant is required to make such payments.

**Legal residence and citizenship.** Lenders may inquire about the applicant's permanent residence and immigration status, but only to determine creditworthiness.

Under the ECOA, which one of these criteria may a lender use to deny a loan application?

    A. The applicant has a low debt-to-income ratio.
    B. The applicant's source of employment is stable but part-time.
    C. The applicant is not a U.S. citizen.
    D. The applicant is retiring in six months and will see a significant income reduction.

If you selected "D," you are correct! Lenders may deny a loan application if the applicant's impending retirement income is insufficient to support the mortgage payment.

**Action notices to borrowers**

**Notice of Action Taken**. Regulation B requires lenders to provide loan applicants with a **Notice of Action Taken** within 30 days of 1) receiving a consumer's completed application or an incomplete application, or 2) taking adverse action on an existing account.

**Adverse actions** regarding credit decisions include denying the loan, offering terms other than those initially offered or requested, or changing the terms of existing credit accounts. Lenders must disclose certain information to borrowers in writing upon taking an adverse credit action:

    ▸ the creditor's name and address, and a description of the action taken
    ▸ the specific reason(s) for denial, such as employment history or credit score, or a statement informing the applicant of the right to request a reason for denial within 60 days
    ▸ the name of the federal agency charged with enforcing compliance with the act
    ▸ negative credit report details, if applicable
    ▸ notification of the right to receive a copy of the lender's property appraisal, if applicable, to prove the unfavorable value of the collateral property
    ▸ specific reasons for less favorable loan terms than originally discussed

Lenders can provide these disclosures verbally but must confirm them in writing within 30 days of the applicant's request for the information.

The CFPB provides samples of forms lenders can use for notification in either English or Spanish at
https://www.consumerfinance.gov/compliance/compliance-resources/other-applicable-requirements/equal-credit-opportunity-act/model-credit-application-and-sample-notification-forms/

Several variations of the form are available for use depending on the reason(s) for application denial. The following two images are examples of CFPB forms a lender would use when providing action notices.

**Sample Form C-3: Notice of Action Taken and Statement of Reasons**
**(Credit Score Disclosure)**

---

[Number of recent inquiries on consumer report, as a key factor]

[If you have any questions regarding your credit score, you should contact [entity that provided the credit score] at:

Address: _____

[Toll free] Telephone number: ___ ]


You should know that the Federal Equal Credit Opportunity Act prohibits creditors, such as ourselves, from discriminating against credit applicants on the basis of their race, color, religion, national origin, sex, marital status, age (provided the applicant has the capacity to enter into a binding contract), because they receive income from a public assistance program, or because they may have exercised their rights under the Consumer Credit Protection Act. If you believe there has been discrimination in handling your application you should contact the [name and address of the appropriate Federal enforcement agency listed in appendix A].


Sincerely,

---

**Sample Form C-4: Notice of Action Taken and Statement of Reasons – Counteroffer Disclosure**

Date

Dear Applicant: Thank you for your application for _____. We are unable to offer you credit on the terms that you requested for the following reason(s):

_____

We can, however, offer you credit on the following terms:_____

_____

If this offer is acceptable to you, please notify us within [amount of time] at the following address:_____

_____

Our credit decision on your application was based in whole or in part on information obtained in a report from [name, address and [toll-free] telephone number of the consumer reporting agency]. You have a right under the Fair Credit Reporting Act to know the information contained in your credit file at the consumer reporting agency. The reporting agency played no part in our decision and is unable to supply specific reasons why we have denied credit to you. You also have a right to a free copy of your report from the reporting agency, if you request it no later than 60 days after you receive this notice. In addition, if you find that any information contained in the report you receive is inaccurate or incomplete, you have the right to dispute the matter with the reporting agency.

[We also obtained your credit score from the consumer reporting agency and used it in making our credit decision. Your credit score is a number that reflects the information in your consumer report. Your credit score can change, depending on how the information in your consumer report changes.

Your credit score:_____

Date: _____

Scores range from a low _____ to a high of _____.

Key factors that adversely affected your credit score:

_____

_____

# Check Your Understanding

An "action notice" relative to a loan application is a notice provided to consumers about the documents and information they must submit in order to complete their application.

    A. True

    B. False

If you selected "B," you are correct! An action notice is required when lenders have denied a borrower's loan application or agree to offer the loan but under different terms than the borrower originally requested.

**Acceptable income**

**Cannot discriminate based on income**. Lenders may not discriminate based on any legal source of income. They must consider all consistent/permanent income from public assistance, part-time employment, Social Security, pensions, or annuities. In short, lenders may consider only whether the applicant's income is adequate and stable enough to support the loan. If applicants provide information about income from alimony, child support, or separate maintenance payments, lenders may ask for proof of the reliability of this income, but must consider it valid.

**Cannot discriminate based on applicant's sex or marital status**. Lenders may not discount income because of an applicant's sex or marital status and must accept someone other than a spouse as a co-signer if the applicant chooses this option.

**Creditworthiness**

While the ECOA requires lenders to evaluate an applicant's creditworthiness when reviewing loan applications, this act does not specify or provide credit analysis guidelines. Lenders may use standard credit scoring, lending ratios, and judgment when evaluating loan applications. They may NOT consider family status and must consider all legal forms of income, as discussed in the previous paragraphs.

**Applicants not required to answer questions regarding race or gender.** In keeping with federal financing mandates, credit applications focus on the applicant's creditworthiness. Applications can include questions regarding race, gender, and ethnicity for statistical purposes, but applicants are not required to answer those questions. Lenders can note that the applicant "did not wish to furnish" such information if they do so in good faith.

If a lender receives an incomplete application, the lender must provide the previously discussed Action Notice to notify the applicant. The notification may include a deadline by which the applicant must respond. If the applicant does not respond, the lender may close the application.

**Lenders must verify information.** Lenders are responsible for verifying application information, typically through the underwriting process, to ensure that borrowers are qualified and meet "ability to repay" criteria.

**Enforcement**

Per the CFPB, "The CFPB safeguards household financial stability by ensuring that consumer financial markets are fair, transparent, and competitive." Consumers can research enforcement actions on the CFPB website at https://www.consumerfinance.gov/enforcement/.

The CFPB may investigate allegations against lenders before initiating legal action under federal consumer financial law. It does so by issuing **civil investigative demands (CIDs)**, which may require recipients to provide documents, emails, and reports, answer questions, and provide oral testimony.

Creditors who violate the ECOA may be subject to civil penalties, including actual and punitive damages as awarded by a United States district court. In many cases, the defendant is ordered to compensate victims. If a defendant cannot provide the ordered compensation, the CFPB can compensate victims through the **Civil Penalty Fund** established by the Dodd-Frank Act.

How serious is the Bureau about enforcement?

In 2023 alone, the CFPB filed 29 enforcement actions and resolved six other cases from lawsuits that had been filed previously. These actions resulted in more than $3 billion in compensation to victims and nearly $500 million in civil financial penalties. (https://www.consumerfinance.gov/enforcement/enforcement-by-the-numbers/)

In 2025, the CFPB filed a lawsuit against Vanderbilt Mortgage and Finance, accusing the firm of violating the Truth in Lending Act by originating loans without addressing the consumer's ability to repay the loan. (https://www.consumerfinance.gov/enforcement/actions/vanderbilt-mortgage-finance-inc/)

The CFPB occasionally issues warning letters to inform recipients that certain activities could potentially breach consumer financial laws. These letters do not allege wrongdoing. Instead, they prompt recipients to review their practices and confirm compliance with federal regulations.

# TRUTH IN LENDING ACT (TILA) AND REGULATION Z

**Purpose**
**TILA-covered loans**
**Definitions**
**Regulation Z disclosures**
**Notice of Right to Rescind**
**Seller contributions**
**HOEPA**
**Higher-priced mortgage loans**
**MLO compensation**
**TILA-regulated advertising**

**Purpose**

The **Truth in Lending Act (TILA)** (15 U.S.C. §1601 et seq.) preceded the ECOA by six years, and, like the ECOA and RESPA, it has a broad impact on the mortgage lending industry. Enacted in 1968 and administered by the Consumer Financial Protection Bureau, TILA is a federal law designed to better inform consumers about the cost of consumer credit.

Regulation Z implements TILA, which is part of Title 1 of the Consumer Protection Act. It was intended to increase consumer knowledge about loan applications and terms, allowing consumers to make more knowledgeable decisions about borrowing. Legislation in 2008, 2009, and 2010 amended TILA to address significant disclosure and lending concerns.

Regulation Z promotes clear, understandable loan information, including costs and terms, before consumers commit to them. The law also promotes the informed use of consumer credit by requiring lenders to disclose loan terms and the cost to borrow money. It also standardizes how lenders calculate and disclose required loan information, such as interest rates, amount financed, total payments, and the payment schedule.

**TILA-covered loans**

TILA governs loans that incur interest charges or are supported by a written agreement requiring at least four installment payments. Thus, residential mortgage loans, home equity loans, home equity lines of credit, credit cards, personal loans, auto loans, retail installment sales, and short-term loans such as payday loans all fall under TILA requirements.

Commercial and business loans are exempt from TILA requirements, including loans extended to buy, refinance, or rehabilitate non-owner-occupied properties. However, the residency requirement is minimal. For the purposes of this law, a property becomes owner-occupied if the owner lives in it for more than 14 days.

**Definitions**

To fully understand TILA's requirements, you must understand certain related vocabulary.

**APR**. The **APR**, or **annual percentage rate**, is not the same as the interest rate on a loan. Rather, it refers to the total cost of the loan to the borrower, stated as a percentage. The APR will nearly always be higher than a loan's stated interest rate. Because the loan costs that make up the APR are standard, consumers can compare the APR across various loans instead of trying to compare individual interest rates, fees, and other loan costs.

**Finance charge.** Related to APR, **a finance charge** is any fee a borrower pays, either directly or indirectly, to obtain credit; i.e., it is the cost of credit stated as a dollar amount. Finance charges (and, therefore, the APR) include interest, loan origination or discount points, loan fees, assumption fees, and finder's fees. By definition, finance charges include any lender-required charge the consumer pays directly or indirectly.

Finance charges do NOT include seller's points, title examination fees, title insurance, appraisals, inspections, surveys, preparation fees, credit reporting fees, or escrow account funds.

**Dwelling**. For TILA purposes, a **dwelling** is any residential structure of one to four units.

**Residential mortgage loan**. A **residential mortgage loan** is a loan secured by the property itself as collateral and is used to purchase or refinance a residential property.

## Regulation Z Disclosures

**Disclose prior to consummation**. Regulation Z requires written disclosures from lenders when they offer credit to consumers. Disclosures must be made before a loan is consummated and in a form the consumer can keep and refer to when needed. The loan agreement can include the disclosures, but all disclosures must be easily identifiable and separated from other loan details.

**Consumer Handbook on ARMs**. Lenders cannot charge the consumer any fees until they provide the required disclosures. Additional disclosure requirements, which will be addressed later in this section, focus on advertising.

Specifically, Regulation Z requires lenders to provide TILA-RESPA integrated disclosures, a booklet entitled, "*Consumer Handbook on Adjustable Rate Mortgages*" (**CHARM**) for adjustable rate mortgages, and a booklet entitled "*When Your Home is on the Line*" for home equity installment loans and lines of credit. In addition, lenders must disclose to borrowers any impending rate adjustments in adjustable-rate mortgages, including any related change in payment amounts, as well as information about the initial rate period length and permitted adjustments.

**Lender records retention requirements.** In general, lenders must retain evidence of compliance with most disclosure requirements for at least **two years**. However, the Loan Estimate and related documents, loan originator compensation documents, and minimum qualification standards require a three-year retention period. The Closing Disclosure and related documents must be retained for five years.

## Check Your Understanding

A consumer applies for a loan to fund the purchase of an investment property. Under which of these circumstances is the loan subject to TILA regulations?

  A. The property consists of 12 individual residential units.
  B. The property consists of a 5,000-square-foot warehouse space plus offices.
  C. The property is a residential duplex.
  D. The loan includes three installment payments over the next three years.

If you selected "C," you are correct! TILA does not apply to commercial properties or properties with more than four residential units. It applies to loans with four or more installment payments.

**Notice of Right to Rescind**

TILA protects some borrowers from "buyer's remorse" by providing a right to cancel a loan transaction within a specified period, usually three business days, without incurring penalties, fees, or other obligations. This right extends only to refinancing and home equity loans.

**Statement of Right to Rescind**. Lenders must provide borrowers with a TILA-mandated disclosure and two copies of a notice that explains the buyer's right to rescind. This notice includes a **Statement of Right to Rescind**, instructions for exercising the rescission right, and an explanation of what happens if the borrower exercises this right.

Based on the three-business-day rule, the rescission period starts the day after all lending conditions are met: The loan has closed, the rescission notice is delivered, and the buyer has received all TILA disclosures.

**Seller contributions**

Many residential mortgage transactions include some form of seller contributions (aka contract concessions), and TILA restricts how borrowers may use seller-contributed funds. Buyers may use these funds for closing costs, prepaid expenses, or loan discount points. They may NOT apply the funds to the down payment.

The loan type and, for primary residence loans, the down payment amount govern seller contribution limits. The following table details these limits.

**Seller Contribution Limits**

| Loan Type | Down Payment | Seller Contribution Maximum |
|---|---|---|
| Conventional, primary resident | <10% | 3% |
| Conventional, primary resident | 10 – 25% | 6% |
| Conventional, primary resident | >25% | 9% |
| Conventional, investment | n/a | 2% |
| FHA and USDA | n/a | 6% |
| VA | n/a | 4% of sales price + reasonable/customary loan costs |

**HOEPA**

**HOEPA essentials.** The **Home Ownership and Equity Protection Act (HOEPA)** (15 U.S.C. §1639), was a 1994 amendment to TILA. The Dodd-Frank Act puts the CFPB in charge of HOEPA and broadened HOEPA's relevance by including purchase-money mortgages and open-ended lines of credit, such as home equity lines of credit. It applies to "high-cost" mortgages on a principal residence. This act does not apply to construction loans or reverse mortgages.

To understand the definition of a high-cost mortgage, it's important to understand the definition of the Average Prime Rate Offer (**APOR**). The APOR is a benchmark rate based on the average interest rates, fees, and other mortgage terms lenders offer to highly qualified buyers. Lenders calculate it as of the loan lock-in date.

Based on this definition, a **high-cost mortgage** exceeds an annually inflation-adjusted percentage (depending on the loan amount) of at least one of the following criteria:

> ▸ a first or second mortgage APR exceeds the Average Prime Rate Offer (APOR)
> ▸ total closing costs, fees, and points exceed a specified percentage of the total loan amount
> ▸ total closing costs, fees, and points exceed the specified percentage of the loan amount or a stated "adjusted points and fees dollar trigger," whichever is less

For example, in 2024, if the first mortgage APR exceeded the APOR by 2.25 percentage points for a loan greater than or equal to $130,461, it was classified as a high-cost mortgage.

To protect consumers from pressure tactics, lenders that grant HOEPPA-governed loans must thoroughly review a borrower's finances, including debt, credit history, assets, and income. Lenders must provide certain disclosures to affected borrowers at least three business days before completing the mortgage transaction. These disclosures are in addition to any other disclosures required by law. Lenders must disclose the following information to consumers:

- APR
- regular payment amount (including any balloon payment)
- loan amount (when the amount borrowed includes credit insurance premiums such as mortgage insurance premium [MIP] or private mortgage insurance [PMI])
- maximum monthly payment (for variable-rate loans)
- total amount borrowed relative to the face amount of the original note (for refinancing)

**Higher- priced mortgage loans**

**HPMLs and jumbos.** A definition within Regulation Z, born of the **Housing and Economic Recovery Act** of 2008, denotes a **higher-priced mortgage loan (HPML)** as one for which the APR exceeds the average prime rate offer by 1.5% for a first-lien mortgage, 2.5% for a first-lien **jumbo loan**, or 3.5% for a subordinate-lien (aka second-lien) mortgage loan. Loans for $32,400 or less were exempt effective June 1, 2024. This threshold is adjusted annually based on the Consumer Price Index for Urban Wage Earners and Clerical Workers (CPI-W). Note that the HPML is not the same as a high-cost mortgage.

A jumbo loan is a mortgage loan in an amount that is more than the conforming loan limits set by the Federal Housing Finance Agency.

**Borrower protections**. Loans classified as higher-priced mortgages require lenders to provide added borrower protections. Lenders must use more than the loan collateral to approve the loan. Instead, they must verify a buyer's ability to repay the loan. The Dodd-Frank Act requires that creditors carefully evaluate a borrower's ability to repay a mortgage loan based on verified and documented information such as income, other assets, and current obligations in place when funding the loan. The required information must indicate that the consumer has a reasonable ability to repay the loan according to its terms, as well as all related taxes, insurance, and assessments.

Lenders may have to obtain a full appraisal of the property and provide a second free appraisal for "flipped" homes (homes acquired by the seller less than 180 days before the sale). Typically, these loans require that borrowers maintain an escrow account for at least five years.

**Mortgage Loan Originator (MLO) compensation**

The Dodd-Frank Act amended the Truth in Lending Act in an effort to provide additional consumer protections in the lending industry. The implementation framework of Regulation Z included provisions related to mortgage loan originator (MLO) compensation. Remember that a mortgage loan originator does not fund loans but instead acts as a liaison between borrowers and mortgage lenders.

**MLO defined**. The Dodd-Frank Act defines a mortgage loan originator as anyone who performs the following acts for compensation:

- takes residential mortgage loan applications
- helps consumers obtain or apply to obtain a residential mortgage loan
- offers or negotiates residential mortgage loan terms (or individuals who represent or advertise that they perform such services)

**Licenses not required for admins**. Those who perform clerical tasks related to mortgage loan origination are not included in the previous definition, nor are manufactured home retailer employees who do not advise consumers about loan terms. Also excluded from the definition are persons, estates, or trusts that finance the sale of five or fewer properties in a 12-month period, as long as the financing is fully amortizing, the borrower has the ability to repay, and the loan is either fixed or adjustable after five years. Other conditions apply as well.

**Compensation not based on loan terms**. MLOs cannot receive compensation based on loan terms or conditions. Additionally, mortgage broker compensation to employees who originate loans must abide by this restriction. MLOs may not be compensated by more than one person or entity.

**Prohibited compensation**. MLO may not base compensation on any of the following:

- interest rate or other loan terms and conditions
- mortgage loan yield spread premium (additional compensation paid to a mortgage broker for higher-interest loans)
- steering borrowers to loans with higher interest rates, prepayment penalties, or less favorable terms
- steering borrowers to affiliated businesses
- proxy for a term of a transaction, e.g., steering consumers to a portfolio loan to receive a higher MLO commission

Compensation may consist of any of the following:

- a flat fee identified at the beginning of the transaction
- a salary or an hourly rate
- a fixed percentage of the loan amount
- bonuses, profit-sharing, retirement plans
- a percentage based on the number of closed loan transactions
- payment for tasks not specifically related to loan origination

**TILA-regulated advertising**

**Terms that trigger disclosures**. Under the Truth in Lending Act, lenders must provide certain disclosures in advertising depending on the advertisement's content. General wording, such as "flexible payment terms," does not place additional requirements on advertisers. However, if an advertisement incorporates certain terms, it must comply with Regulation Z provisions, including APR disclosure.

Certain terms in mortgage advertisements, regardless of the advertising medium, trigger additional disclosure requirements. These terms, called "**trigger**" or "**triggering**" terms, include the following:

- percentage or amount of down payment
- number of payments or period of repayment
- amount of any payment
- amount of any finance charge

Advertisements for traditional mortgages (closed-end credit) that mention triggering terms must include additional information as shown in the table below.

| Triggering Terms | Required Disclosures |
|---|---|
| Down payment amount | • Down payment amount or percentage |
| Number of payments or repayment period | • Repayment terms (over the entire loan term and including any balloon payment) |
| Finance charge amount | • Annual percentage rate (with a note stating the APR may increase after closing, if applicable) |
| Payment amount | |

**Trigger term examples.** If a lender advertises an interest rate and that rate may change over the life of the loan, the advertisement must state the effective length of each interest rate, as well as the APR for each rate. If the interest rate is variable based on an index and margin, the lender must use a reasonably current index and margin. The advertisement must also state the APR.

If a lender advertises a specific payment amount for a covered mortgage loan, the advertisement must disclose the amount of each payment over the life of the loan, including any balloon payments. The advertisement must also state the period of time during which any payment will apply, and if a first lien on the dwelling will secure the advertised loan, it must note if the payments will be higher after adding escrow payments for taxes and insurance.

In addition, lenders may not advertise a low annual percentage rate that they do not intend to offer. Lenders may advertise terms that are available for a limited time or in the future if the advertisement is made in good faith.

**Check Your Understanding**

A lender placed an advertisement on her Facebook page with the following information:

- 5/1 Adjustable-Rate Mortgage (ARM)
- 5/1 ARM with a fixed interest rate for the first five years, after which the rate adjusts annually during the remaining term of the mortgage
- interest rate of 4.625%

Which of these pieces of information is NOT required in this ad?

- A. down payment amount
- B. annual percentage rate (APR)
- C. minimum credit score
- D. repayment terms

If you selected "C," you are correct! An advertisement that mentions the interest rate must also include the down payment amount or percentage, the repayment terms, and the APR.

---

## TILA-RESPA INTEGRATED DISCLOSURE RULE (TRID) ·

**Purpose**
**Covered loans**
**Loan Estimate (LE)**
**Change of circumstances**
**TILA – RESPA Special information booklet**
**Closing Disclosure (CD)**

---

**Purpose of TRID**     The **TILA-RESPA Integrated Disclosure** (**TRID**) rules, sometimes referred to as "Know Before You Owe," streamline and simplify the mortgage application process for lenders and borrowers. Before TRID, lenders provided an initial truth-in-lending (TIL) disclosure and a good faith estimate (GFE) when a borrower applied for a mortgage loan. Closing documents included a settlement statement (the HUD-1) and a final truth-in-lending disclosure. TRID combines the initial TIL and good faith estimate into a single disclosure and the HUD-1 and final TIL into a second document that is presented before closing.

Born of a desire to harmonize RESPA and TILA disclosures and regulations, TRID standardizes lender disclosures, thereby helping borrowers make better-informed decisions when choosing a lender or loan product. The rule also provides clarified guidelines for lenders regarding required disclosures and disclosure timing. TRID replaced the Good Faith Estimate (GFE) with the Loan Estimate (LE) and the HUD-1 Settlement Statement with the Closing Disclosure

(CD) for most closed-end mortgage transactions that use the subject property as loan collateral.

**Covered loans**

Lenders follow TRID rules for residential mortgage loans, including fixed-rate and adjustable loans, as well as FHA, VA, and USDA loans. It does not impact reverse mortgages, home equity lines of credit (HELOCs), loans secured by a residence not attached to real property (e.g., a mobile home), or loans made by an entity that funds five or fewer mortgages annually. Lenders that take applications for these loans may continue to use the two **TIL disclosures,** the GFE, the HUD-1, or all three.

Lenders for commercial and residential cash transactions may still use the HUD-1 Settlement Statement, and reverse mortgage lenders may use the GFE.

**Loan Estimate**

The **Loan Estimate (LE)** informs borrowers of the key features, costs, and risks of a mortgage loan before they commit to the loan. It provides a standardized form to borrowers, making it easier for them to compare loans across different lenders.

Lenders must deliver the LE to the borrower or place it in the mail within three business days after they receive a borrower's loan application.

Previously, you read that six key pieces of information trigger legal "receipt" of an application, which in turn requires lenders to prepare and deliver a Loan Estimate. Note that if an applicant provides this information online but fails to complete the remainder of the application, the lender is not obligated to deliver an LE. "Submission" does not include situations where the lender has the information from a previous application unless the borrower indicates the lender should use it.

Note that borrowers who submit all triggering information to obtain a pre-qualification or pre-approval letter are still entitled to receive the Loan Estimate. However, in most cases, the borrower will not have the property address and thus will not have submitted the required six pieces of information to trigger the LE.

Delivery of the LE must also occur at least seven days before **loan consummation**, which is the date the borrower signs the loan documents and becomes contractually obligated to repay the loan. This is NOT the same as the closing or settlement process in which the seller conveys the property to the buyer, though it typically occurs simultaneously.

Preparation of the LE is typically a joint venture between the lender and the settlement agent. Why? The settlement agent identifies costs unrelated to the loan that must be included on the LE, such as the settlement services fee, title insurance premiums, document recording fees, and other expenses paid at closing.

## Check Your Understanding

A couple has submitted the information necessary to obtain a loan pre-approval. Which one of these factors eliminates the lender's requirement to provide a Loan Estimate?

    A. The applicants have an existing home financed through this lender.
    B. The lender makes an upfront disclosure stating that it does not issue an LE until the buyers are under contract on a property.
    C. The applicants are just beginning the mortgage process and do not yet have a specific property in mind.
    D. The applicants are purchasing the property as an investment.

If you selected "C," you are correct! Applicants must submit all six triggering pieces of information to receive an LE. Without a property address, the lender will not issue an LE.

**Loan Estimate examples.** The following illustrations depict completed sections of a Loan Estimate for a conventional 30-year mortgage. Carefully review the description and sample of each section.

This sample is available from the CFPB website. You will find examples of the completed form for other loan types and terms at this same site: https://www.consumerfinance.gov/compliance/compliance-resources/mortgage-resources/tila-respa-integrated-disclosures/forms-samples/#loan-estimate-sample.

### Loan Estimate Section 1: Basic Information

The first section of the LE identifies the issuing lender, the date issued, the applicant's name and address, the subject property, and the sale price. Also included are the loan term and purpose, the product (fixed or adjustable), the loan type (Conventional, FHA, VA, or other), and the loan ID number. Finally, this section indicates whether a rate lock is in place and, if so, when it expires.

---

4321 Random Boulevard · Somecity, ST 12340               *Save this Loan Estimate to compare with your Closing Disclosure.*

## Loan Estimate

| | | | |
|---|---|---|---|
| | | **LOAN TERM** | 30 years |
| | | **PURPOSE** | Purchase |
| **DATE ISSUED** | 2/15/2013 | **PRODUCT** | Fixed Rate |
| **APPLICANTS** | Michael Jones and Mary Stone | **LOAN TYPE** | ☒ Conventional ☐ FHA ☐ VA ☐_____ |
| | 123 Anywhere Street | **LOAN ID #** | 123456789 |
| | Anytown, ST 12345 | **RATE LOCK** | ☐ NO ☒ YES, until 4/16/2013 at 5:00 p.m. EDT |
| **PROPERTY** | 456 Somewhere Avenue | | *Before closing, your interest rate, points, and lender credits can* |
| | Anytown, ST 12345 | | *change unless you lock the interest rate. All other estimated* |
| **SALE PRICE** | $180,000 | | *closing costs expire on* **3/4/2013** *at 5:00 p.m. EDT* |

## Loan Estimate Section 2: Loan Terms

The second section of the LE addresses the loan terms, including the loan amount, interest rate, and monthly principal and interest payment. It indicates whether the loan includes a prepayment penalty or balloon payment. It includes information about whether each identified item can increase after closing, which is particularly important with adjustable-rate mortgages.

| Loan Terms | | Can this amount increase after closing? |
|---|---|---|
| Loan Amount | $162,000 | NO |
| Interest Rate | 3.875% | NO |
| Monthly Principal & Interest<br>See Projected Payments below for your Estimated Total Monthly Payment | $761.78 | NO |
| | | Does the loan have these features? |
| Prepayment Penalty | | YES • As high as $3,240 if you pay off the loan during the first 2 years |
| Balloon Payment | | NO |

## Loan Estimate Section 3: Projected Payments

The third section of the Loan Estimate provides the consumer with information regarding the principal, interest, mortgage insurance, and estimated escrow payment amounts. In this example, the total payment amount decreases in years 8-30 because the mortgage insurance premium drops off in year eight. The section also identifies the estimated property taxes, insurance, and assessments, noting that these amounts can change over time and indicating whether the amounts will be held in escrow.

| Payment Calculation | Years 1-7 | Years 8-30 |
|---|---|---|
| Principal & Interest | $761.78 | $761.78 |
| Mortgage Insurance | + 82 | + — |
| Estimated Escrow<br>Amount can increase over time | + 206 | + 206 |
| Estimated Total Monthly Payment | $1,050 | $968 |

| Estimated Taxes, Insurance & Assessments<br>Amount can increase over time | $206<br>a month | This estimate includes<br>[X] Property Taxes<br>[X] Homeowner's Insurance<br>[ ] Other:<br>See Section G on page 2 for escrowed property costs. You must pay for other property costs separately. | In escrow?<br>YES<br>YES |

## Loan Estimate Section 4: Costs at Closing

The next section of the Loan Estimate provides an estimate of the closing costs the borrower will pay, as well as the estimated cash to close that will be needed. This section refers the borrower to the following section for additional details.

| Costs at Closing | | |
|---|---|---|
| **Estimated Closing Costs** | $8,054 | Includes $5,672 in Loan Costs + $2,382 in Other Costs - $0 in Lender Credits. *See page 2 for details.* |
| **Estimated Cash to Close** | $16,054 | Includes Closing Costs. *See Calculating Cash to Close on page 2 for details.* |

## Loan Estimate Section 5: Closing Cost Details

The next section of the Loan Estimate provides details about closing cost calculations, including origination, application, and underwriting fees; taxes and other governmental fees; services the consumer can and cannot shop for; and prepaid items such as homeowners insurance, mortgage insurance premiums, interest, and property taxes. Also included in this section is a calculation of the initial escrow payment required and other closing costs, including the owner's title policy premium.

Notice that Item J in this section corresponds with the estimated closing costs identified in the previous section. The Estimated Cash to Close at the bottom right of this section matches the amount specified in the previous section.

### Closing Cost Details

**Loan Costs**

| A. Origination Charges | $1,802 |
|---|---|
| .25 % of Loan Amount (Points) | $405 |
| Application Fee | $300 |
| Underwriting Fee | $1,097 |

| B. Services You Cannot Shop For | $672 |
|---|---|
| Appraisal Fee | $405 |
| Credit Report Fee | $30 |
| Flood Determination Fee | $20 |
| Flood Monitoring Fee | $32 |
| Tax Monitoring Fee | $75 |
| Tax Status Research Fee | $110 |

| C. Services You Can Shop For | $3,198 |
|---|---|
| Pest Inspection Fee | $135 |
| Survey Fee | $65 |
| Title – Insurance Binder | $700 |
| Title – Lender's Title Policy | $535 |
| Title – Settlement Agent Fee | $502 |
| Title – Title Search | $1,261 |

| D. TOTAL LOAN COSTS (A + B + C) | $5,672 |
|---|---|

**Other Costs**

| E. Taxes and Other Government Fees | $85 |
|---|---|
| Recording Fees and Other Taxes | $85 |
| Transfer Taxes | |

| F. Prepaids | $867 |
|---|---|
| Homeowner's Insurance Premium ( 6 months) | $605 |
| Mortgage Insurance Premium ( months) | |
| Prepaid Interest ( $17.44 per day for 15 days @ 3.875%) | $262 |
| Property Taxes ( months) | |

| G. Initial Escrow Payment at Closing | $413 |
|---|---|
| Homeowner's Insurance $100.83 per month for 2 mo. | $202 |
| Mortgage Insurance per month for mo. | |
| Property Taxes $105.30 per month for 2 mo. | $211 |

| H. Other | $1,017 |
|---|---|
| Title – Owner's Title Policy (optional) | $1,017 |

| I. TOTAL OTHER COSTS (E + F + G + H) | $2,382 |
|---|---|

| J. TOTAL CLOSING COSTS | $8,054 |
|---|---|
| D + I | $8,054 |
| Lender Credits | |

**Calculating Cash to Close**

| Total Closing Costs (J) | $8,054 |
|---|---|
| Closing Costs Financed (Paid from your Loan Amount) | $0 |
| Down Payment/Funds from Borrower | $18,000 |
| Deposit | - $10,000 |
| Funds for Borrower | $0 |
| Seller Credits | $0 |
| Adjustments and Other Credits | $0 |
| Estimated Cash to Close | $16,054 |

Lenders may not charge the borrower any fees or accept a credit or debit card from the borrower to pay for any fees except the exact fee required to run a credit report until the borrower receives the required disclosures and indicates an intent to move forward with the loan process.

The stated cost of all settlement services the lender provides on the LE must remain effective for at least ten business days after delivery. Any expiration date on these charges is noted in the rate lock area of the LE (see the example in Loan Estimate Section 1, above). This does not include the interest rate or any other related terms.

Borrower *receipt* of disclosures is determined based on how the lender delivers the disclosures. If the borrower has indicated an intent to move forward, the lender may begin to charge other fees as follows:

> ▶ the day of delivery, if the lender hand-delivers the LE
> ▶ the day after a return receipt verifying delivery to the borrower is returned to the lender if the documents are delivered
> ▶ the day after a signed document verifying borrower receipt is faxed to the lender if the original documents are faxed
> ▶ three business days after the documents are mailed

## Change of circumstances

Federal regulations require lenders to provide a new Loan Estimate if the estimated charges to the borrower increase due to certain circumstances:

> ▶ an extraordinary event outside the parties' control results in increased settlement costs
> ▶ the appraisal comes in lower than anticipated
> ▶ the consumer requests changes, such as a larger loan amount, a smaller down payment, or a different loan product
> ▶ altered circumstances impact the borrower's eligibility, e.g., changes to employment, credit score, or lending ratios or a low appraisal
> ▶ an action such as locking in a loan rate causes points or lender credits to change
> ▶ the borrower does not notify the lender of the intent to proceed with the loan within ten business days after the LE is delivered

Lenders may revise only those charges impacted by changed circumstances. They must send the revised LE no more than three business days after receiving any new, relevant information and at least four business days before consummating the loan. For purposes of the revised LE, the four-business-day rule counts any day but Sunday or a federal holiday.

Lenders may not issue a revised LE after delivering the Closing Disclosure, and consumers may request that lenders describe the details that resulted in a revised LE.

In addition, lenders are charged with providing a good-faith Loan Estimate, meaning that borrowers can assume they are receiving an accurate estimate of their costs. Federal regulations define *good faith* and require that the Loan Estimate and Closing Disclosure calculations be within certain tolerance levels to meet the good faith requirement.

In general, if the final closing costs on the CD are greater than those on the LE by a certain tolerance limit, it is assumed that the lender did NOT issue the LE in good faith. If the CD closing costs are less than those on the LE, the lender is assumed to have prepared the LE in good faith.

**Tolerance limits .** TILA regulates **tolerance limits**. Relative to these limits, charges to the borrower fall into one of three categories when comparing the LE to the CD:

> ▸ charges that may change without regard to a tolerance limit
> ▸ charges subject to a 10% cumulative tolerance limit
> ▸ charges that may not change by any amount

**No tolerance limit.** Certain charges can change without regard to a tolerance limit. Those charges include prepaid interest, property insurance premiums, and escrow, impound, or reserve account funding amounts. Additionally, increased charges are permitted if borrowers shop for required services and use a provider not listed by the lender. Finally, any charges paid to third-party service providers for services the creditor does not require are not subject to a limitation. However, the CFPB notes that lenders may only charge customers more than they estimated if the original estimate (or lack thereof) was based on the "best information reasonably available" to them when they provided the disclosure.

**10% cumulative tolerance limit.** Some changes are limited to a 10% cumulative tolerance. For example, if one charge goes up and another goes down, keeping the total changes in this category under 10%, the charges are acceptable. These charges include recording fees and charges from third parties not affiliated with or recommended by the lender that the borrower shops and pays for directly.

**Zero-tolerance changes.** The final category prohibits any change from the LE to the CD unless changed circumstances, as previously discussed, occur. These charges include fees the borrower pays to the creditor, a mortgage broker, or an affiliate of either one. Also included are transfer taxes as well as charges paid to an unaffiliated third party if the lender did not allow the borrower to shop for the service.

If the consumer's costs at closing exceed any of the tolerances noted above, the lender must refund the excess to the consumer within 60 calendar days after loan consummation. For charges subject to zero tolerance, the lender must refund any amount charged beyond the amount noted on the Loan Estimate. For charges subject to a 10% cumulative tolerance, the lender must refund only the amount in excess of the total 10% tolerance.

**Mortgage brokers and initial disclosures.** If a borrower works through a mortgage broker, either the lender or the mortgage broker may provide the initial disclosures. However, disclosures made by a mortgage broker must include the lender's name.

## TILA-RESPA Special Information Booklet

As discussed previously, the lender (or mortgage broker) must present the borrower with a special information booklet when providing the LE. If a loan involves multiple borrowers, delivery to one borrower is sufficient.

**Settlement Costs Booklet**. The Special Information Booklet, also called the "*settlement costs booklet,*" helps familiarize borrowers with the homebuying and mortgage process. It addresses the steps in the home buying process, the mortgage process, associated fees, and disclosures.

No special information booklet is required if a lender denies a credit application before the three-day delivery requirement or for the following loan types:

- ▸ refinances
- ▸ closed-end loans when the lender takes a subordinate lien
- ▸ reverse mortgages
- ▸ other federally related mortgage loans, the purpose of which is NOT to buy a one- to four-unit residential property

## Closing disclosure

The **Closing Disclosure (CD)** is the "other half" of the TILA-RESPA disclosure requirement. Lenders must provide this disclosure to consumers at least three business days before closing.

**Responsibility for the Closing Disclosure.** Like the LE, the CD details both loan-related and other expenses related to closing on the purchase, enabling the lender and settlement agent to partner to prepare the CD. Alternatively, the lender can authorize the settlement agent to prepare and deliver the CD. However, the lender is ultimately responsible for ensuring that the CD is prepared and delivered as required by the CFPB.

The settlement agent shares responsibility for the accuracy of the CD. The agent may deliver a copy of the borrower's disclosure to the seller if the CD includes the seller's charges and costs. However, the settlement agent often prepares a separate CD for the seller that outlines only the seller's information, thereby maintaining confidentiality for both parties.

**Closing Disclosure receipt.** The borrower has "received" the CD on the date the lender provides it in person, three business days after mailing it or sending it electronically, or according to proof of delivery the lender may obtain.

Borrowers should use the time between receiving the CD and the closing date to compare the CD to the LE and ensure that the details have not changed significantly. The Closing Disclosure should detail actual loan terms and costs. However, it is important to remember that the costs can vary somewhat from the LE, depending on the amount and type of change.

**Closing Disclosure revision prior to loan consummation.** Usually, the first CD issued before closing is a true and accurate representation of the loan terms and the buyer's costs. However, in some circumstances, preparers may need to estimate costs that are not yet known. In this situation, the lender must provide an accurate CD to the borrower at or before loan consummation.

Three revision categories exist: 1) changes before loan consummation that require a revised CD, 2) changes before loan consummation that do not require a revised CD, and 3) changes that occur after consummation.

Certain loan changes force a new three-day waiting period and require the lender to provide a new CD:

  ▸ changes in loan terms that result in a new APR calculation
  ▸ changes in the loan product, e.g., from an FHA to a conventional loan
  ▸ addition of a prepayment penalty

Like the LE, the APR on the CD is subject to certain tolerance limits that determine whether a new CD and waiting period are required. Generally, for **regular transactions** (most fixed-rate loans), an APR change of more than .125% triggers a new CD and waiting period. For **irregular transactions,** which generally means an **adjustable-rate mortgage (ARM)**, an APR change of .250% is the trigger.

Note that a fixed-rate mortgage with an interest-only feature for a certain time or a graduated-payment feature may be considered irregular and thus subject to the .250% tolerance limit. Similarly, an ARM with an initial rate equal to the fully indexed rate may be considered regular and thus subject to the lower tolerance limit of .125%.

No new waiting period is required if a previous CD overstated the APR but was accurate under Regulation Z. An overstated APR that was inaccurate under Regulation Z triggers a new waiting period.

**Closing Disclosure revision after consummation.** If, no more than 30 days after loan consummation, a CD is found to have been in error, the lender must issue a corrected CD. The timing of the corrected CD depends on the circumstances.

If the previous CD contained a clerical error, the lender must issue the corrected CD within 30 calendar days of discovering the error. If the error results in a lender tolerance cure, the lender must issue a corrected disclosure and refund within 60 days. If the new CD corrects a non-numerical clerical error, the lender must issue it within 60 days. Sellers may also receive corrected CDs for the same types of errors.

**The 3/7/3 Rule.** To summarize the required timelines for mortgage loan disclosures (the LE and CD) and to help you remember them, consider the 3/7/3 Rule for disclosure timing. You likely remember the timing schedule: Lenders have **three days** to **send the initial LE**. A mandatory **seven-day waiting period is required before the loan can close** after LE receipt. A revision to the LE triggers a new **three-day waiting period.**

This rule was part of a 2008 amendment to TILA called the **Mortgage Disclosure Improvement Act (MDIA).** This act includes specific verbiage outlining the waiting periods required for delivering mortgage disclosure documents.

## Sample Closing Disclosure

The following pages illustrate a completed sample Closing Disclosure for the conventional 30-year mortgage previously addressed in the sample Loan Estimate. You can find this sample, as well as other iterations of the CD, on the CFPB website: https://www.consumerfinance.gov/compliance/compliance-resources/mortgage-resources/tila-respa-integrated-disclosures/forms-samples/#closing-disclosure-blank

The CD includes all final loan costs and terms. A statement at the top encourages borrowers to compare the CD with the LE they previously received. Compare the following sample Closing Disclosure with the Loan Estimate presented previously to detect similarities and differences.

# Closing Disclosure

This form is a statement of final loan terms and closing costs. Compare this document with your Loan Estimate.

## Closing Information

| | |
|---|---|
| Date Issued | 4/15/2013 |
| Closing Date | 4/15/2013 |
| Disbursement Date | 4/15/2013 |
| Settlement Agent | Epsilon Title Co. |
| File # | 12-3456 |
| Property | 456 Somewhere Ave |
| | Anytown, ST 12345 |
| Sale Price | $180,000 |

## Transaction Information

| | |
|---|---|
| Borrower | Michael Jones and Mary Stone |
| | 123 Anywhere Street |
| | Anytown, ST 12345 |
| Seller | Steve Cole and Amy Doe |
| | 321 Somewhere Drive |
| | Anytown, ST 12345 |
| Lender | Ficus Bank |

## Loan Information

| | |
|---|---|
| Loan Term | 30 years |
| Purpose | Purchase |
| Product | Fixed Rate |
| Loan Type | ☒ Conventional ☐FHA |
| | ☐VA ☐_____ |
| Loan ID # | 123456789 |
| MIC # | 000654321 |

## Loan Terms

| | | Can this amount increase after closing? |
|---|---|---|
| Loan Amount | $162,000 | NO |
| Interest Rate | 3.875% | NO |
| Monthly Principal & Interest *See Projected Payments below for your Estimated Total Monthly Payment* | $761.78 | NO |
| | | Does the loan have these features? |
| Prepayment Penalty | | YES • As high as $3,240 if you pay off the loan during the first 2 years |
| Balloon Payment | | NO |

## Projected Payments

| Payment Calculation | Years 1-7 | | Years 8-30 | |
|---|---|---|---|---|
| Principal & Interest | | $761.78 | | $761.78 |
| Mortgage Insurance | + | 82.35 | + | — |
| Estimated Escrow *Amount can increase over time* | + | 206.13 | + | 206.13 |
| **Estimated Total Monthly Payment** | | **$1,050.26** | | **$967.91** |

| Estimated Taxes, Insurance & Assessments *Amount can increase over time* *See page 4 for details* | $356.13 a month | This estimate includes | In escrow? |
|---|---|---|---|
| | | ☒ Property Taxes | YES |
| | | ☒ Homeowner's Insurance | YES |
| | | ☒ Other: Homeowner's Association Dues | NO |
| | | See Escrow Account on page 4 for details. You must pay for other property costs separately. | |

## Costs at Closing

| | | |
|---|---|---|
| Closing Costs | $9,712.10 | Includes $4,694.05 in Loan Costs + $5,018.05 in Other Costs – $0 in Lender Credits. See page 2 for details. |
| Cash to Close | $14,147.26 | Includes Closing Costs. See Calculating Cash to Close on page 3 for details. |

## Closing Cost Details

| Loan Costs | | Borrower-Paid | | Seller-Paid | | Paid by Others |
|---|---|---|---|---|---|---|
| | | At Closing | Before Closing | At Closing | Before Closing | |
| **A. Origination Charges** | | **$1,802.00** | | | | |
| C1  0.25 % of Loan Amount (Points) | | $405.00 | | | | |
| C2  Application Fee | | $300.00 | | | | |
| C3  Underwriting Fee | | $1,097.00 | | | | |
| C4 | | | | | | |
| C5 | | | | | | |
| C6 | | | | | | |
| C7 | | | | | | |
| C8 | | | | | | |
| **B. Services Borrower Did Not Shop For** | | **$236.55** | | | | |
| C1  Appraisal Fee | to John Smith Appraisers Inc. | | | | | $405.00 |
| C2  Credit Report Fee | to Information Inc. | | $29.80 | | | |
| C3  Flood Determination Fee | to Info Co | $20.00 | | | | |
| C4  Flood Monitoring Fee | to Info Co | $31.75 | | | | |
| C5  Tax Monitoring Fee | to Info Co | $75.00 | | | | |
| C6  Tax Status Research Fee | to Info Co | $80.00 | | | | |
| C7 | | | | | | |
| C8 | | | | | | |
| C9 | | | | | | |
| 10 | | | | | | |
| **C. Services Borrower Did Shop For** | | **$2,655.50** | | | | |
| C1  Pest Inspection Fee | to Pests Co. | $120.50 | | | | |
| C2  Survey Fee | to Surveys Co. | $85.00 | | | | |
| C3  Title – Insurance Binder | to Epsilon Title Co | $650.00 | | | | |
| C4  Title – Lender's Title Insurance | to Epsilon Title Co | $500.00 | | | | |
| C5  Title – Settlement Agent Fee | to Epsilon Title Co | $500.00 | | | | |
| C6  Title – Title Search | to Epsilon Title Co | $800.00 | | | | |
| C7 | | | | | | |
| C8 | | | | | | |
| **D. TOTAL LOAN COSTS (Borrower-Paid)** | | **$4,694.05** | | | | |
| Loan Costs Subtotals (A + B + C) | | $4,664.25 | $29.80 | | | |

| Other Costs | | Borrower-Paid | | Seller-Paid | | Paid by Others |
|---|---|---|---|---|---|---|
| **E. Taxes and Other Government Fees** | | **$85.00** | | | | |
| C1  Recording Fees | Deed: $40.00    Mortgage: $45.00 | $85.00 | | | | |
| C2  Transfer Tax | to Any State | | | $950.00 | | |
| **F. Prepaids** | | **$2,120.80** | | | | |
| C1  Homeowner's Insurance Premium ( 12 mo ) to Insurance Co | | $1,209.96 | | | | |
| C2  Mortgage Insurance Premium (    mo.) | | | | | | |
| C3  Prepaid Interest ( $17.44 per day from 4/15/13 to 5/1/13 ) | | $279.04 | | | | |
| C4  Property Taxes  ( 6 mo ) to Any County USA | | $631.80 | | | | |
| C5 | | | | | | |
| **G. Initial Escrow Payment at Closing** | | **$412.25** | | | | |
| C1  Homeowner's Insurance $100.83  per month for 2 mo. | | $201.66 | | | | |
| C2  Mortgage Insurance       per month for   mo. | | | | | | |
| C3  Property Taxes       $105.30  per month for 2 mo. | | $210.60 | | | | |
| C4 | | | | | | |
| C5 | | | | | | |
| C6 | | | | | | |
| C7 | | | | | | |
| C8  Aggregate Adjustment | | - 0.01 | | | | |
| **H. Other** | | **$2,400.00** | | | | |
| C1  HOA Capital Contribution | to HOA Acre Inc | $500.00 | | | | |
| C2  HOA Processing Fee | to HOA Acre Inc | $150.00 | | | | |
| C3  Home Inspection Fee | to Engineers Inc. | $750.00 | | $750.00 | | |
| C4  Home Warranty Fee | to XYZ Warranty Inc. | | | $450.00 | | |
| C5  Real Estate Commission | to Alpha Real Estate Broker | | | $5,700.00 | | |
| C6  Real Estate Commission | to Omega Real Estate Broker | | | $5,700.00 | | |
| C7  Title – Owner's Title Insurance (optional)    to Epsilon Title Co | | $1,000.00 | | | | |
| C8 | | | | | | |
| **I. TOTAL OTHER COSTS (Borrower-Paid)** | | **$5,018.05** | | | | |
| Other Costs Subtotals (E + F + G + H) | | $5,018.05 | | | | |

| | | Borrower-Paid | | Seller-Paid | | Paid by Others |
|---|---|---|---|---|---|---|
| **J. TOTAL CLOSING COSTS (Borrower-Paid)** | | **$9,712.10** | | | | |
| Closing Costs Subtotals (D + I) | | $9,682.30 | $29.80 | $12,800.00 | $750.00 | $405.00 |
| Lender Credits | | | | | | |

## Calculating Cash to Close

Use this table to see what has changed from your Loan Estimate.

| | Loan Estimate | Final | Did this change? |
|---|---|---|---|
| Total Closing Costs (J) | $8,054.00 | $9,712.10 | YES • See Total Loan Costs (D) and Total Other Costs (I) |
| Closing Costs Paid Before Closing | $0 | – $29.80 | YES • You paid these Closing Costs before closing |
| Closing Costs Financed (Paid from your Loan Amount) | $0 | $0 | NO |
| Down Payment/Funds from Borrower | $18,000.00 | $18,000.00 | NO |
| Deposit | – $10,000.00 | – $10,000.00 | NO |
| Funds for Borrower | $0 | $0 | NO |
| Seller Credits | $0 | – $2,500.00 | YES • See Seller Credits in Section L |
| Adjustments and Other Credits | $0 | – $1,035.04 | YES • See details in Sections K and L |
| **Cash to Close** | **$16,054.00** | **$14,147.26** | |

## Summaries of Transactions

Use this table to see a summary of your transaction.

### BORROWER'S TRANSACTION

| K. Due from Borrower at Closing | $189,762.30 |
|---|---|
| 01 Sale Price of Property | $180,000.00 |
| 02 Sale Price of Any Personal Property Included in Sale | |
| 03 Closing Costs Paid at Closing (J) | $9,682.30 |
| 04 | |
| **Adjustments** | |
| 05 | |
| 06 | |
| 07 | |
| **Adjustments for Items Paid by Seller in Advance** | |
| 08 City/Town Taxes to | |
| 09 County Taxes to | |
| 10 Assessments to | |
| 11 HOA Dues 4/15/13 to 4/30/13 | $80.00 |
| 12 | |
| 13 | |
| 14 | |
| 15 | |

| L. Paid Already by or on Behalf of Borrower at Closing | $175,615.04 |
|---|---|
| 01 Deposit | $10,000.00 |
| 02 Loan Amount | $162,000.00 |
| 03 Existing Loan(s) Assumed or Taken Subject to | |
| 04 | |
| 05 Seller Credit | $2,500.00 |
| **Other Credits** | |
| 06 Rebate from Epsilon Title Co. | $750.00 |
| 07 | |
| **Adjustments** | |
| 08 | |
| 09 | |
| 10 | |
| 11 | |
| **Adjustments for Items Unpaid by Seller** | |
| 12 City/Town Taxes 1/1/13 to 4/14/13 | $365.04 |
| 13 County Taxes to | |
| 14 Assessments to | |
| 15 | |
| 16 | |
| 17 | |

### SELLER'S TRANSACTION

| M. Due to Seller at Closing | $180,080.00 |
|---|---|
| 01 Sale Price of Property | $180,000.00 |
| 02 Sale Price of Any Personal Property Included in Sale | |
| 03 | |
| 04 | |
| 05 | |
| 06 | |
| 07 | |
| 08 | |
| **Adjustments for Items Paid by Seller in Advance** | |
| 09 City/Town Taxes to | |
| 10 County Taxes to | |
| 11 Assessments to | |
| 12 HOA Dues 4/15/13 to 4/30/13 | $80.00 |
| 13 | |
| 14 | |
| 15 | |
| 16 | |

| N. Due from Seller at Closing | $115,665.04 |
|---|---|
| 01 Excess Deposit | |
| 02 Closing Costs Paid at Closing (J) | $12,800.00 |
| 03 Existing Loan(s) Assumed or Taken Subject to | |
| 04 Payoff of First Mortgage Loan | $100,000.00 |
| 05 Payoff of Second Mortgage Loan | |
| 06 | |
| 07 | |
| 08 Seller Credit | $2,500.00 |
| 09 | |
| 10 | |
| 11 | |
| 12 | |
| 13 | |
| **Adjustments for Items Unpaid by Seller** | |
| 14 City/Town Taxes 1/1/13 to 4/14/13 | $365.04 |
| 15 County Taxes to | |
| 16 Assessments to | |
| 17 | |
| 18 | |
| 19 | |

### CALCULATION (Borrower)

| | |
|---|---|
| Total Due from Borrower at Closing (K) | $189,762.30 |
| Total Paid Already by or on Behalf of Borrower at Closing (L) | – $175,615.04 |
| **Cash to Close [X] From [ ] To Borrower** | **$14,147.26** |

### CALCULATION (Seller)

| | |
|---|---|
| Total Due to Seller at Closing (M) | $180,080.00 |
| Total Due from Seller at Closing (N) | – $115,665.04 |
| **Cash [ ] From [X] To Seller** | **$64,414.96** |

## Additional Information About This Loan

**Loan Disclosures**

### Assumption
If you sell or transfer this property to another person, your lender
- ☐ will allow, under certain conditions, this person to assume this loan on the original terms.
- ☒ will not allow assumption of this loan on the original terms.

### Demand Feature
Your loan
- ☐ has a demand feature, which permits your lender to require early repayment of the loan. You should review your note for details.
- ☒ does not have a demand feature.

### Late Payment
If your payment is more than 15 days late, your lender will charge a late fee of 5% of the monthly principal and interest payment.

### Negative Amortization (Increase in Loan Amount)
Under your loan terms, you
- ☐ are scheduled to make monthly payments that do not pay all of the interest due that month. As a result, your loan amount will increase (negatively amortize), and your loan amount will likely become larger than your original loan amount. Increases in your loan amount lower the equity you have in this property.
- ☐ may have monthly payments that do not pay all of the interest due that month. If you do, your loan amount will increase (negatively amortize), and, as a result, your loan amount may become larger than your original loan amount. Increases in your loan amount lower the equity you have in this property.
- ☒ do not have a negative amortization feature.

### Partial Payments
Your lender
- ☒ may accept payments that are less than the full amount due (partial payments) and apply them to your loan.
- ☐ may hold them in a separate account until you pay the rest of the payment, and then apply the full payment to your loan.
- ☐ does not accept any partial payments.

If this loan is sold, your new lender may have a different policy.

### Security Interest
You are granting a security interest in
456 Somewhere Ave., Anytown, ST 12345

You may lose this property if you do not make your payments or satisfy other obligations for this loan.

### Escrow Account
**For now,** your loan
- ☒ will have an escrow account (also called an "impound" or "trust" account) to pay the property costs listed below. Without an escrow account, you would pay them directly, possibly in one or two large payments a year. Your lender may be liable for penalties and interest for failing to make a payment.

| Escrow | | |
|---|---|---|
| Escrowed Property Costs over Year 1 | $2,473.56 | Estimated total amount over year 1 for your escrowed property costs: *Homeowner's Insurance Property Taxes* |
| Non-Escrowed Property Costs over Year 1 | $1,800.00 | Estimated total amount over year 1 for your non-escrowed property costs: *Homeowner's Association Dues* You may have other property costs. |
| Initial Escrow Payment | $412.25 | A cushion for the escrow account you pay at closing. See Section G on page 2 |
| Monthly Escrow Payment | $206.13 | The amount included in your total monthly payment |

- ☐ will not have an escrow account because ☐ you declined it ☐ your lender does not offer one. You must directly pay your property costs, such as taxes and homeowner's insurance. Contact your lender to ask if your loan can have an escrow account.

| No Escrow | |
|---|---|
| Estimated Property Costs over Year 1 | Estimated total amount over year 1. You must pay these costs directly, possibly in one or two large payments a year. |
| Escrow Waiver Fee | |

**In the future,**
Your property costs may change and, as a result, your escrow payment may change. You may be able to cancel your escrow account, but if you do, you must pay your property costs directly. If you fail to pay your property taxes, your state or local government may (1) impose fines and penalties or (2) place a tax lien on this property. If you fail to pay any of your property costs, your lender may (1) add the amounts to your loan balance, (2) add an escrow account to your loan, or (3) require you to pay for property insurance that the lender buys on your behalf, which likely would cost more and provide fewer benefits than what you could buy on your own.

## Loan Calculations

**Total of Payments.** Total you will have paid after you make all payments of principal, interest, mortgage insurance, and loan costs, as scheduled.     $285,803.36

**Finance Charge.** The dollar amount the loan will cost you.     $118,830.27

**Amount Financed.** The loan amount available after paying your upfront finance charge.     $162,000.00

**Annual Percentage Rate (APR).** Your costs over the loan term expressed as a rate. This is not your interest rate.     4.174%

**Total Interest Percentage (TIP).** The total amount of interest that you will pay over the loan term as a percentage of your loan amount.     69.46%

**Questions?** If you have questions about the loan terms or costs on this form, use the contact information below. To get more information or make a complaint, contact the Consumer Financial Protection Bureau at
**www.consumerfinance.gov/mortgage-closing**

## Other Disclosures

**Appraisal**
If the property was appraised for your loan, your lender is required to give you a copy at no additional cost at least 3 days before closing. If you have not yet received it, please contact your lender at the information listed below.

**Contract Details**
See your note and security instrument for information about
- what happens if you fail to make your payments,
- what is a default on the loan,
- situations in which your lender can require early repayment of the loan, and
- the rules for making payments before they are due.

**Liability after Foreclosure**
If your lender forecloses on this property and the foreclosure does not cover the amount of unpaid balance on this loan

☒ state law may protect you from liability for the unpaid balance. If you refinance or take on any additional debt on this property, you may lose this protection and have to pay any debt remaining even after foreclosure. You may want to consult a lawyer for more information.

☐ state law does not protect you from liability for the unpaid balance.

**Refinance**
Refinancing this loan will depend on your future financial situation, the property value, and market conditions. You may not be able to refinance this loan.

**Tax Deductions**
If you borrow more than this property is worth, the interest on the loan amount above this property's fair market value is not deductible from your federal income taxes. You should consult a tax advisor for more information.

## Contact Information

| | Lender | Mortgage Broker | Real Estate Broker (B) | Real Estate Broker (S) | Settlement Agent |
|---|---|---|---|---|---|
| **Name** | Ficus Bank | | Omega Real Estate Broker Inc. | Alpha Real Estate Broker Co. | Epsilon Title Co. |
| **Address** | 4321 Random Blvd. Somecity, ST 12340 | | 789 Local Lane Sometown, ST 12345 | 987 Suburb Ct. Someplace, ST 12340 | 123 Commerce Pl. Somecity, ST 12344 |
| **NMLS ID** | | | | | |
| **ST License ID** | | | 2765416 | 261456 | 261616 |
| **Contact** | Joe Smith | | Samuel Green | Joseph Cain | Sarah Arnold |
| **Contact NMLS ID** | 12345 | | | | |
| **Contact ST License ID** | | | P16415 | P51461 | PT1234 |
| **Email** | joesmith@ficusbank.com | | sam@omegare.biz | joe@alphare.biz | sarah@epsilontitle.com |
| **Phone** | 123-456-7890 | | 123-555-1717 | 321-555-7171 | 987-555-4321 |

## Confirm Receipt

By signing, you are only confirming that you have received this form. You do not have to accept this loan because you have signed or received this form.

_____     _____     _____     _____
Applicant Signature          Date          Co-Applicant Signature          Date

## Check Your Understanding

What is the relationship between the LE and the CD?

    A. The CD provides additional details about the information presented in the LE.

    B. The LE is a lender-issued document that details only loan and closing costs. The CD is a closing agent-issued document that details only closing costs.

    C. The LE is the initial disclosure issued to loan applicants. The CD is the final disclosure issued and must closely match the LE.

    D. The CD is issued to provide initial estimates of loan and closing costs. The LE is issued to provide final numbers to the borrower.

If you selected "C," you are correct! Lenders issue the LE to loan applicants. Numbers on the LE must closely match those of the later-issued CD.

**Borrower's Right of Recission**.  Borrowers may cancel a refinance or home equity loan within three days after closing. This right of rescission does NOT apply to home purchase mortgage loans.

---

## OTHER FEDERAL LAWS AND GUIDELINES

**Home Mortgage Disclosure Act**
**Fair Credit Reporting Act**
**Privacy Protection; Do Not Call Registry**
**Bank Secrecy Act/Anti-Money Laundering**
**USA Patriot Act/Freedom Act**
**Dodd-Frank Act**
**Qualified Mortgages**
**Gramm-Leach-Bliley Act**
**Mortgage Act & Practices (MAP)**
**Electronic Signatures (E-sign Act)**
**Homeowner's Protection Act**

---

## Home Mortgage Disclosure Act

In addition to the major mortgage lending legislation previously discussed, many additional federal laws impact the industry. These laws focus on consumer protections and federal government oversight designed to prevent money laundering and terrorism. The first such law to review is the Home Mortgage Disclosure Act.

**Primary purpose of the HMDA**.  The primary goal of the Home Mortgage Disclosure Act (HMDA) (12 U.S.C. §2801 et seq.), adopted in 1975, is to ensure fair and equitable access to housing finance and to combat discriminatory lending practices such as redlining (arbitrarily denying mortgage applications based on geographical area instead of an applicant's financial qualifications). Regulation C (12 CFR §1003) is the implementing rule, and the Consumer Financial Protection Bureau is responsible for enforcing the Act.

**Reporting to the CFPB**. Unlike many other federal mortgage-related laws, the HMDA focuses on lender-to-regulator action instead of lender-to-consumer action. This act requires lenders to collect, report, and publicly disclose housing-related lending activities. This data is related to home acquisition loans, home improvement loans, and refinances to create greater transparency and protect residential mortgage borrowers.

Lenders must report the following data annually:

▸ applicant race, gender, ethnicity, and gross annual income
▸ application date and loan type, purpose, and amount
▸ collateral type and location
▸ loan status (approved, denied, withdrawn, or incomplete and closed)

In their reports, lenders must identify the reason(s) for denying a loan application. It is important to note that while lenders must report demographic data received, they may not require applicants to provide such information.

What is the purpose of this data collection? The CFPB uses this data to identify patterns of discriminatory practices by lenders, allowing the Bureau to take action against entities that engage in discrimination and unfair treatment. The following two cases illustrate the use of mortgage data collected and the federal government's view on the serious nature of lending bias and discrimination by both public and private lenders.

### Case Study: CFPB vs. Bank of America

In November 2023, the CFPB issued an order against Bank of America for violating the HMDA and Regulation C, the HMDA's implementing regulation, as well as the Consumer Financial Protection Act of 2010. The Bureau found that for at least four years (from 2016 to late 2020), many of the bank's loan officers were not asking applicants for the required race, ethnicity, and sex disclosure information. Instead, these banks falsely reported that the applicants chose not to provide the information.

The CFPB ordered Bank of America to pay a $12 million penalty, citing the lender for filing false mortgage lending information. The bank must take the steps necessary to prevent the illegal data collection processes it previously engaged in. The Bureau also noted that the bank knew as early as 2013 that mortgage loan officers were not collecting the required data but failed to take appropriate steps to stop the practice.

(https://www.consumerfinance.gov/enforcement/actions/bank-of-america-na-hmda-data-2023/)

**Case Study: CFPB vs. Trident Mortgage**

In a first-of-its-kind settlement, the CFPB and Department of Justice took action against a nonbank mortgage lender, Trident Mortgage Company. In 2022, Trident was accused of redlining majority-minority neighborhoods in Philadelphia by actively discouraging people in these neighborhoods from applying for mortgage loans or refinancing. Data indicates that Trident loan applications were overwhelmingly from non-minority neighborhoods, and of the applications accepted from minority neighborhoods (12% of total applications accepted), more than half were from white applicants.

Trident employees, including loan officers and their assistants, distributed emails with "racial slurs and racist content," pejorative language related to property locations and appraisals, and verbiage targeting residents of majority-minority neighborhoods.

Of Trident's 53 Philadelphia offices, 51 were located in majority white neighborhoods, while the remaining two were in neighborhoods split equally between white and minority residents. Marketing campaigns and advertisements pictured almost exclusively white employees and models; advertisements were targeted at majority white neighborhoods.

On September 14, 2022, the court entered a consent order requiring Trident to perform the following activities:

- invest $18.4 million to fund a Loan Subsidy Program to increase credit extended in Philadelphia's minority neighborhoods
- invest $750,000 to develop organizations to provide financial, homeownership, or foreclosure prevention services in minority neighborhoods
- invest $875,000 in advertising and outreach in minority neighborhoods
- invest $375,000 for consumer financial education
- pay a $4 million civil penalty to the CFPB
- retain an independent credit-needs-assessment consultant to create a report on the credit needs of Philadelphia metropolitan minority neighborhoods
- agree to biannual staff training from a third-party trainer on topics related to bias and discrimination

https://www.consumerfinance.gov/about-us/newsroom/cfpb-doj-order-trident-mortgage-company-to-pay-more-than-22-million-for-deliberate-discrimination-against-minority-families/

**Fair Credit
Reporting Act
(FCRA)**

**FCRA and FACTA essentials**. The **Fair Credit Reporting Act (FCRA)** (15 U.S.C. §1681 et seq.) is Title VI of the Consumer Credit Protection Act. It aims to ensure accuracy, fairness, and privacy in collecting, sharing, and using consumer credit information to make lending decisions, including granting mortgage loans, employment, insurance underwriting, court orders, and other legitimate business reasons.

Regulation V (12 CFR §1022) implements the Act. The **Fair and Accurate Credit Transactions Act (FACTA)** amended the FCRA in 2003 largely to enhance consumer identity theft protections.

**Consumer Identity theft protections**. FCRA and FACTA permit lenders to request credit information only if loan applicants have authorized the request. These Acts also require that credit bureaus provide one free credit report to consumers annually (upon request).

Similar to ECOA requirements, the FCRA requires lenders to notify applicants in writing when taking an adverse action based wholly or in part on information obtained from credit reports. The notice must include the reporting credit bureau's name, address, and toll-free phone number. Note that adverse credit information can remain on a consumer's credit reports for only seven years; Chapter 7 bankruptcy information may remain on credit reports for no more than ten years from the filing date.

**Freezing credit reports**. These laws also allow consumers to place a credit freeze on their credit reports, making reports inaccessible to all lenders unless the consumer lifts the freeze. Consumers can place three types of fraud alerts on their credit files:

- ▶ one-call (initial) for individuals who believe they may be victims of fraud or identity theft; this alert lasts for one year, and consumers can renew it
- ▶ extended for victims of identity theft who have a police report or **Federal Trade Commission (FTC)** Identity Theft Report; this alert lasts for seven years
- ▶ active duty for military personnel on active duty; this alert lasts for one year, but consumers can renew it

Lenders must clear fraud alerts before extending credit.

According to Nolo (https://www.nolo.com/legal-encyclopedia/most-common-violations-the-fcra.html) there are seven common FCRA violations:

- ▶ furnishing and reporting outdated consumer information
- ▶ furnishing and reporting inaccurate consumer information
- ▶ mixing one consumer's file with another's

- ▸ failing to follow debt dispute procedures
- ▸ violating privacy
- ▸ requesting credit information for an impermissible purpose
- ▸ withholding required notices

**FTC red flags rule.** Under FACTA, lenders must follow "**red flag rules**" to prevent and detect identity theft. Numerous red flags exist:

- ▸ discrepancies in account or credit report information
- ▸ alerts, notifications, and credit bureau warnings
- ▸ unusual account activity
- ▸ suspicious documents or personally identifying information
- ▸ fraud alerts on a consumer report
- ▸ attempt to use suspicious account application documents

Red flag rules govern accounts used primarily for personal, family, or household purposes that involve multiple payments or transactions, e.g., credit card accounts, mortgage loans, vehicle loans, checking or savings accounts, or utility accounts. Also impacted are other accounts that pose a reasonably foreseeable risk of identity theft, such as small business, sole proprietorship, or single-transaction accounts.

Creditor programs must detail appropriate actions to address red flags.

## Privacy Protection/ Do Not Call Registry

While not specific to the mortgage industry, the **National Do Not Call Registry** impacts MLOs by restricting telemarketing and protects consumers by prohibiting telemarketing deception and abuse. The Federal Communications Commission established the Do Not Call Registry in 2003. In that same year, Congress passed the **Do Not Call Implementation Act**, permitting the Federal Trade Commission to enforce the Do Not Call Registry. Though somewhat embattled in the early years, the Registry survived numerous legal challenges.

**Do Not Call requirements**. A few states have their own versions of do-not-call laws, while most rely on federal legislation. State laws may cover more types of communications, require telemarketers to register separately with the state, require callers to update their no-call lists more often, or comply with additional privacy safeguards. Some, such as California, even require telemarketers to give consumers more rights to opt out of marketing communications.

Under today's regulations, telemarketing businesses must access the national registry every 31 days; these businesses then have 31 days from the date a cell phone or landline number is registered to stop calling that number. Mortgage professionals must check the registry before initiating calls unless they have an established business relationship with the consumer. Regulations prohibit telemarketers from using an automated dialer to call cell phones.

**Do Not Call exempted parties**. Certain organizations and circumstances are exempt from Do Not Call restrictions:

- businesses with which a consumer has a relationship (up to 18 months after the business relationship ends)
- political organizations
- charitable or non-profit organizations (calling on their own behalf)
- survey takers
- businesses to which a consumer submitted an application or inquiry (up to three months after the last contact)
- bill collectors (may only call during reasonable hours

Under do-not-call regulations, telemarketers must identify themselves and the purpose of their call. They must describe the nature of the goods or services they are marketing and note that no purchase or payment is required to participate in an offered promotion.

**Do Not Call prohibitions**. The legislation prohibits telemarketers from the following:

- using threats, profanity, or intimidation tactics
- making false or misleading statements
- calling before 8:00 a.m. or after 9:00 p.m. (local time)
- requiring advance payment of any kind to obtain a loan or loan extension
- charging for goods or services without a consumer's knowledge or permission
- failing to transmit a phone number identifiable by Caller ID
- calling consumers listed on a state or national do-not-call list

**Records retention**. Telemarketers must retain certain records for at least 24 months:

- advertising and marketing materials
- customer information (name, address, purchases, cost)
- current and former employee information (name, address, phone)
- authorizations or consent agreements that consumers signed

Penalties. The FTC categorizes violations of do-not-call laws as "unfair and deceptive trade practices." Penalties can be up to $53,088 for each violation, and each day the practice continues is considered a separate violation.

**Case Study: Do-Not-Call violation**

The FTC charged EduTrek, LLC, a telemarketing operation, with making millions of illegal, unsolicited calls about educational programs to consumers who had provided contact information on websites that offered assistance with job searches, public benefits, and other programs unrelated to EduTrek's business activities.

In September 2023, an Illinois judge found the defendants guilty of calling consumers listed on the Do Not Call Registry. The charges eventually led to a $28.7 million fine. EduTrek was also permanently banned from performing any telemarketing activities. For additional details, see https://www.ftc.gov/legal-library/browse/cases-proceedings/152-3126-edutrek-llc.

**Check Your Understanding**

Which one of the following laws was primarily written to collect and analyze data to ensure non-discriminatory lending?

    A. Home Mortgage Disclosure Act
    B. Fair Credit Reporting Act
    C. FTC Red Flags Rule
    **D.** Do Not Call

If you selected "A," you are correct. The HMDA requires lenders to maintain and report information regarding loan applications and funding.

## Bank Secrecy Act/ Anti-Money Laundering

The **Currency and Foreign Transactions Reporting Act of 1970**, along with its amendments and other statutes relating to financial crimes such as money laundering, have come to be referred to as the **Bank Secrecy Act** (31 U.S.C. §5311 et seq.) **of 1970**. These regulations were established to detect, report, and prevent money laundering and other financial crimes. This legislation requires financial institutions to keep detailed records of cash purchases of negotiable instruments, file reports such as the **Currency Transaction Report (CTR)** for "suspicious" transactions exceeding $10,000 daily, and report any suspicious activity that might signal illegal behaviors.

With the passage of the Patriot Act in 2001, the BSA was amended to require that financial institutions perform due diligence for financial transactions, including *Know Your Customer* processes to verify clients' identity (in tandem with the USA Patriot Act (P.L. 107-56)) and assess potential risks of illegal intentions.

**Suspicious Activity Reports**. Banks must file a **Suspicious Activity Report (SAR)** with the Financial Crimes Enforcement Network if they suspect suspicious activity that might indicate money laundering, fraud, terrorist funding, tax evasion, or other criminal activities. SARs alert authorities about activity that may need to be investigated, such as

- unusual transaction patterns
- sudden, unexplained deposits
- transactions not relevant to the stated business type or typical volume
- an unusually complex series of transactions with multiple accounts, parties, and banks
- unusual mixed deposits in a business account
- transactions attempting to avoid reporting and recordkeeping requirements

Institutions must submit SARs within 30 days after the institution detects the suspicious activity. They may not alert the individuals being investigated and must retain all documentation for at least five years.

**Activity triggering a SAR -- Example.** An account holder with a number of investment properties has had a business checking account with a local bank for six years. Since opening the account, the account holder has made six deposits under $2,000 each at the beginning of each month and pays expenses throughout the month. In the past three months, the account holder has made the typical deposits as well as multiple large deposits ($6,000+) and then immediately transferred those additional funds to an account at another financial institution.

Because this activity is far different from the previous account activity, it may trigger the institution to file a SAR.

**USA Patriot Act/
USA FREEDOM Act
(P.L. 114-23)**

The **Uniting and Strengthening America by Providing Appropriate Tools Required to Intercept and Obstruct Terrorism Act**, more concisely known as the **USA Patriot Act** or just the Patriot Act, was enacted in 2001 in response to the terrorist attacks of September 11, 2001.

**Purpose of the Patriot Act.** The Act's stated purpose was to enhance national security and prevent future terrorist activities. The act significantly expanded the search and surveillance authority of federal law enforcement and intelligence agencies related to suspected terrorists by relaxing requirements for search warrants. The act also made it easier to detain and deport immigrants suspected of terrorism-related acts and <u>included significant measures to prevent and prosecute international **money laundering and terrorism financing**</u>.

Under this Act, the Secretary of the Treasury gained additional authority to combat money laundering.

**The Freedom Act of 2015.** In 2015, in response to continued concerns regarding government overreach, the **Uniting and Strengthening America by Fulfilling Rights and Ensuring Effective Discipline Over Monitoring (USA**

**FREEDOM Act**) replaced the USA Patriot Act, curtailing the government's authority to collect data. This move was precipitated largely by Edward Snowden's exposure of the government's vast collection of phone and internet records. The USA Freedom Act permits the federal government to gather or access such data only after obtaining permission from the U.S. Foreign Intelligence Surveillance Court.

**Dodd-Frank Act**

The Dodd-Frank Act (Dodd-Frank Wall Street Reform and Protection Act) was enacted in 2010 in response to the 2008 financial crisis. Then President Barack Obama hailed this act as a "sweeping overhaul of the United States financial regulatory system." The act implemented the most comprehensive changes to financial regulation since the Great Depression, eliminating some agencies, creating new ones, and reassigning jobs to other agencies.

**Dodd Frank essentials**. Dodd-Frank targets mortgage financing systems, including banks, insurance companies, investment banking firms, mortgage lenders, and credit rating agencies, all believed to have played a part in the housing market crash of 2007-2008. Mortgage bankers/brokers and loan officers fall under the Dodd-Frank Act and the CFPB governing umbrella.

One of the key components of the Dodd-Frank Act was to **establish the CFPB**, thereby consolidating financial oversight duties previously distributed among several agencies. The CFPB is responsible for protecting consumers in the financial sector, overseeing financial products and services, and ensuring that banks, lenders, and other financial institutions treat consumers fairly.

The act created the **Financial Stability Oversight Council (FSOC)**. It charged the Council with identifying risks to the nation's financial stability, promoting market discipline, and responding to emerging threats to U.S. financial system stability.

**The Volcker Rule**. Dodd-Frank also instituted the **Volcker Rule**. This rule **prevents banks from taking on too much risk** by restricting them from making certain kinds of speculative investments that do not benefit customers.

Another provision of the act provides incentives and protections for whistleblowers who report securities law violations to the Securities and Exchange Commission (SEC). Additional provisions introduced new mortgage lending standards and processes to avoid the risky lending practices that contributed to the housing bubble and crash of 2008. These provisions include ability-to-repay requirements, standards for qualified mortgages, and new disclosure requirements (as outlined in the RESPA section, covered previously).

**Minimum underwriting requirements and exemptions.** Establishing **Ability-to-repay (ATR)** requirements under Dodd Frank involved setting minimum underwriting requirements for residential mortgages. These requirements do NOT impact home equity lines of credit, HELOCs, time-share plans, reverse mortgages, temporary or bridge loans with terms of a year or less, the construction phase of less than a year for construction-to-permanent loans, consumer credit transactions secured by vacant land, or loan modifications. In addition, lenders who refinance homeowners from a risky loan to a standard loan may be exempt from ATR requirements.

**Qualified Mortgages**

Related to the ability-to-repay requirements, a **qualified mortgage** is a loan with certain less risky features that make it more likely that consumers can afford it. A qualified mortgage

- ▶ may not have an interest-only period,
- ▶ cannot allow negative amortization;
- ▶ cannot contain a, balloon payment;
- ▶ cannot have a term in excess of 30 years.

Equally important, the APR on a qualified mortgage may not exceed a specified threshold (depending on the loan type). In addition, excess upfront points and fees are prohibited. Finally, for a loan to be a qualified mortgage, the lender must consider and verify the borrower's current monthly income and assets (excluding the value of the property to be purchased) as well as monthly debt. Lenders must also consider the borrower's debt-to-income ratio or residual income.

**No MLO compensation based on loan terms**. Dodd-Frank imposes rules for MLO compensation, eliminating incentives for MLOs to steer borrowers into higher-cost or riskier loans. These rules prohibit compensation based on loan terms.

**Limited prepayment penalties**. Another Dodd-Frank protection limits prepayment penalties on affected loans. Such penalties may not last more than three years on a residential mortgage and cannot exceed 2% of the loan's outstanding balance if the borrower pays the loan off in the first two years or 1% if the borrower pays the loan off in the third year. This act prohibits prepayment penalties on adjustable-rate mortgages (ARMs), high-cost mortgage loans, and higher-priced mortgage loans.

**Oversight of larger banks**. The Act increased regulatory oversight and standards for large banks and financial institutions, requiring higher capital reserve balances, enhanced risk management standards, and more rigorous supervision.

Dodd-Frank requires large financial companies to develop plans to address financial distress and establishes a process for liquidating financial companies that pose a significant risk to the financial stability of the U.S.

**Gramm-Leach-Bliley Act**

Also known as the Financial Services Modernization Act of 1999, the Gramm-Leach-Bliley Act (GLB) (15 U.S.C. §6801 et seq.) charged the FTC with implementing regulations to carry out the act's privacy provisions. The act comprises three primary components: The Financial Privacy Rule, the Safeguards Rule, and Pretexting Protection, all designed to protect consumers' nonpublic personal information (NPI).

**The Privacy Rule**. The Privacy Rule requires companies that offer financial products or services such as loans, financial or investment advice, or insurance to provide a privacy notice explaining their information-sharing practices to their customers and consumers. Firms that do not share customer NPI still must provide this notice when the transaction begins and annually thereafter. Mortgage lenders and firms that service mortgage loans are subject to GLB provisions.

Under the Privacy Rule, a consumer is an individual who obtains or has obtained a financial product or service from a financial institution. It does not apply to commercial clients, including sole proprietorships. Customers are a subcategory of consumers. These individuals have a continuing relationship with the financial institution, such as a credit card account, automobile lease, mortgage loan, or investment adviser. The rule classifies individuals who use an institution's peripheral services regularly (such as an ATM at a bank where they do not have an account) as consumers, not customers.

In the mortgage industry, a special rule defines customer relationships when more than one financial institution is involved in a mortgage transaction. For example, a mortgage loan originator who sells the loan but retains the servicing rights still has a customer relationship with the individual. If the lender transfers the servicing rights but keeps an ownership interest in the loan, the borrower is a consumer of the bank and a customer of the loan servicer. Any other institutions with an ownership interest in the loan (but not servicing rights) have a consumer relationship with the individual.

The privacy notice provides the following details:

> ‣ personally identifiable information the firm collects
> ‣ where the firm shares this information
> ‣ how the information is used
> ‣ how the information is protected
> ‣ the consumer's opt-out options

The opt-out option must allow clients to refuse permission for the institution to share their information with affiliated parties. The Fair Credit Reporting Act requires this opt-out, but the GLB requires the notification.

**The Safeguards Rule.** The Safeguards Rule requires that financial institutions assess their NPI-related security measures and develop, implement, and maintain comprehensive information security programs to protect consumer information.

## Mortgage Acts and Practices: Advertising (Regulation N)

**Regulation N** (12 CFR §1014).  Also known as the **Mortgage Acts and Practices Advertising Rule**, Regulation N is a rule the CFPB and FTC established after the 2008 financial crisis. It governs mortgage advertising through any medium, from print to broadcast to online. The **rule prohibits lenders from making deceptive claims** related to any loan product regarding mortgage terms, including misrepresentations of:

- the type, amount, or existence of fees related to a mortgage product
- the mortgage type
- the mortgage terms, payments, amounts, insurance, or taxes
- the nature of the interest rate (variable or fixed), payment amounts, or term lengths
- the percentage of the monthly payment that will be used to pay down interest, the loan amount, or the total amount due
- refinancing or loan modification potential
- prepayment penalties
- default potential and actions that constitute default
- the consumer's right to live in the property being purchased
- the type and availability of mortgage-related expert advice or counseling

**Advertising clarity required**.  The rule requires that advertisers use clear, concise, and specific wording in advertisements related to the APR, repayment terms, and down payment amounts. In addition, advertisements related to any type of credit must include terms easily available to the public.

## Electronic Signatures (E-SIGN Act)

The **Electronic Signatures in Global and National Commerce Act (E-Sign Act)** (15 U.S.C. §7001 et seq.) of 2000 validates the general use of electronic records and signatures for interstate or foreign commerce transactions. It allows the use of electronic records to satisfy any law, rule, or regulation that requires documents to be in writing and gives electronic signatures the same legal standing as traditional handwritten signatures. It is important to note that under some circumstances, consumers must consent to using electronic records. For instance, consumers must consent electronically to the use of electronic TRID notices. Lenders who use e-signatures must validate that signers are who they say they are and that documents are delivered to the intended recipients. Thus, when multiple parties intend to e-sign documents, the lender typically sends a separate email to each party's email address with instructions for signing electronically, usually through a secure third-party signature system.

The act requires electronic records to reflect any agreements correctly and be properly stored and easily retrievable for all parties involved in the transaction.

Related to the mortgage industry, this act impacts Regulation B, which implements the Equal Credit Opportunity Act; Regulation E, which implements the Electronic Fund Transfer Act; and Regulation M, which implements the Truth in Lending Act.

Electronic signatures are invalid for some documents, including wills, divorce or adoption documents, <u>loan acceleration or foreclosure documents</u>, evictions, and certain court documents.

Most states have a version of the E-SIGN Act, but the federal act permits electronic documents and signatures in interstate commerce.

Fannie Mae accepts eSignatures and eNotarizations on most loan documents.

## Homeowners Protection Act

The **Homeowners Protection Act** (12 U.S.C. §4901 et seq.), also known as the **PMI Cancellation Act**, provides financial relief to borrowers whose loans require **private mortgage insurance (PMI)**.

**Requires release from PMI requirement**. Borrowers who obtain conventional mortgage loans with less than a 20% down payment are generally required to purchase private mortgage insurance. This insurance aims to protect lenders from borrowers who default on mortgage loans and force foreclosure actions. This act is intended to ensure that borrowers do not pay for mortgage insurance longer than necessary.

The act, which became law in 1999, includes the following key provisions:

- It **requires automatic termination of PMI** on a loan when the borrower's mortgage balance is first scheduled to reach 78% of the home's original value, as long as the borrower is current on payments.
- It permits borrower-requested PMI termination when the mortgage balance reaches or is first scheduled to reach 80% of the home's original value.

Appreciation of real property values in recent years permitted some homeowners to terminate PMI earlier than anticipated.

**Must disclose PMI details**. The act also requires lenders to disclose PMI details, including cost, cancellation policies, and the borrower's rights to borrowers when consummating the loan. Lenders must also provide an annual notice to borrowers detailing their rights to cancel and the cancellation requirements.

**Does not apply to FHA loans**. Note that these provisions do NOT impact the **MIP (Mortgage Insurance Premium)** on FHA loans. FHA borrowers who received their loans before June of 2013 may be able to terminate their MIP after five years if they made at least a 10% down payment. FHA borrowers who received their loans after June of 2013 may be able to remove MIP after 11 years if their down payment was at least 10%. No matter when borrowers obtain their loans, they must pay MIP for the life of the loan if they made a down payment of less than 10%. Borrowers who refinance into a conventional loan and make at least a 20% down payment will eliminate PMI.

The following table summarizes the mortgage-related laws herein presented and the implementing regulations, where applicable.

# Federal Mortgage-Related Law:
## Legislation Summary

| Law/Rule | Implementing Regulation | Purpose |
|---|---|---|
| Real Estate Settlement Procedures Act (RESPA) | Regulation X | Provides numerous protections for residential mortgage borrowers, governs the mortgage loan process, prohibits kickbacks and referral fees to/from settlement service providers, and requires certain disclosures. |
| Equal Credit Opportunity Act (ECOA) | Regulation B | Prohibits discrimination in providing credit from the application process through and beyond loan funding. |
| Truth in Lending Act (TILA) | Regulation Z | Allows consumers to make better-informed decisions about consumer loans, including mortgage loans, by requiring standardized loan calculations and disclosures. |
| TILA/RESPA (TRID) | | Streamlines and simplifies the mortgage process for consumers and lenders. Requires timely disclosure of mortgage loan costs and implements the standardized Loan Estimate and Closing Disclosure forms. |
| Home Mortgage Disclosure Act (HMDA) | Regulation C | Protects consumers against discrimination by requiring lenders to report certain data to the federal government annually. |
| Fair Credit Reporting Act (FCRA) | Regulation V | Amended by the Fair and Accurate Credit Transaction Act (FACTA), FCRA is intended to protect consumers' private financial information. |
| FTC Red Flags Rule | | Required by FACTA, the rule identifies red flags lenders must be aware of when working with individuals' private financial information. |
| Privacy Protection/Do Not Call | | Protects consumers by prohibiting unwanted phone calls, as well as telemarketing deception and abuse |
| Bank Secrecy Act/Anti-Money Laundering | | Prevents financial crimes by requiring financial institutions to be aware of and report banking activities that may signal illegal activities |
| USA Patriot Act/USA FREEDOM ACT | | The Patriot Act enhanced the federal government's search and surveillance authority in the wake of the World Trade Center attack. The FREEDOM Act curtailed some of the authority the Patriot Act granted |
| Dodd-Frank Act | | Protects consumers and the economy by regulating mortgage financing systems and consolidating financial oversight duties under the CFPB |
| Graham-Leach-Bliley Act | Regulation P | Requires financial service and product providers to implement plans for protecting consumer information and advising consumers of those plans |
| Mortgage Acts and Practices Advertising Rule | Regulation N | Protects consumers by prohibiting deceptive mortgage loan advertising |
| E-SIGN Act | | Gives electronic documents and signatures the same legal standing as traditional handwritten documents and signatures |
| Homeowners Protection Act | | Protects consumers by regulating Private Mortgage Insurance and stipulating when consumers can remove PMI from loans |

| | |
|---|---|
| **Regulatory authority** | • **Consumer Financial Protection Bureau (CFPB):** Regulates lenders protects consumers from unscrupulous lending practices.<br><br>• **Department of Housing and Urban Development (HUD):** Provides rental assistance, insures mortgages, sets underwriting standards, and administers the Fair Housing Act.<br><br>• **Federal Housing Finance Agency (FHFA):** Regulates and supervises Fannie Mae and Freddie Mac; governs the Federal Home Loan Bank System.<br><br>• **Office of the Comptroller of the Currency (OCC):** Charters national banks and federal savings and loan associations; monitors them to avoid risk and prevent discrimination.<br><br>• **Federal Deposit Insurance Corporation (FDIC):** Insures consumer bank accounts up to $250,000 per depositor per insured bank for each account ownership category. |
| **Real Estate Settlement Procedures Act** | • Mandates disclosures to loan applicants, including the Loan Estimate (LE) and Closing Disclosure (CD).<br><br>• Prohibits kickbacks and illegal referral fees between service providers.<br><br>• Regulates settlement service costs and prohibits professionals from requiring loan applicants to use a specific title insurance company or other provider.<br><br>• Impacts lenders and mortgage brokers who offer federally related mortgage loans.<br><br>• Limits the amount of escrow funds lenders can require.<br><br>• Provides foreclosure protections to borrowers. |
| **Equal Credit Opportunity Act** | • Governs residential and business loans, requiring that all consumers have an equal chance to obtain credit.<br><br>• Prohibits discrimination in the lending process based on any one of eight protected classes.<br><br>• Governs the information lenders can require of loan applicants and criteria they can use to deny a loan. |
| **Truth in Lending Act; Regulation Z** | • Requires lenders to provide certain disclosures to loan applicants.<br><br>• Mandates that mortgage advertisers include specific information in advertisements if other certain trigger terms are included.<br><br>• HOEPA, a 1994 TILA amendment, defines a "high-cost mortgage" as one secured by the borrower's primary residence on which the APR and lender fees exceed certain thresholds. Lenders must carefully evaluate borrowers' ability to repay. |

- Regulation Z, the implementing regulation for TILA, defines a higher-priced mortgage as a loan secured by a primary residence with an APR that exceeds a certain threshold. Lenders may not use only loan collateral to approve a higher-priced mortgage, but must evaluate the borrower's ability to repay.
- MLOs cannot receive compensation based on loan terms or conditions and may not be compensated by more than one person or entity.

**TILA-RESPA Integrated Disclosure rules (TRID)**

- Also called "Know Before you Owe," requires an (LE) upon application receipt and a (CD) before closing on most mortgage loans. Strict timelines apply.
- LE is only triggered if an application is considered "received," which requires applicant to submit name, income, identifying number, property address, estimated property value, and mortgage amount requested.
- Amounts on the LE must be within specific range (tolerance limit) of the amount on the CD, or additional disclosure is required.
- The "3/7/3 rule" summarizes timelines for delivery of the LE and CD. Lenders have three days from application receipt to deliver the LE. Seven days must elapse before closing, and the CD must be delivered three days before closing.
- Borrowers have a three-day right of rescission after loan closing for refinance or home equity loans.

**Other federal laws and guidelines**

- The **Home Mortgage Disclosure Act (HMDA)** combats discrimination by requiring lenders to collect, report, and publicly disclose mortgage lending data.
- The **Fair Credit Reporting Act (FCRA)** focuses on accuracy, fairness, and privacy in the lending process.
- The **Federal Trade Commission (FTC)** Red Flag Rule requires lenders to identify red flags in the lending process to prevent and detect identity theft.
- Privacy protection and Do Not Call rules protect consumers from unsolicited telemarketing calls. Legislation governs telemarketer contact with consumers.
- The **Bank Secrecy Act (BSA)** was designed to prevent money laundering by requiring lenders to monitor cash purchases of negotiable instruments and report suspicious activity. The Patriot Act amended the BSA to implement processes to verify client identity and assess the risk of illegal intentions.
- The **Patriot Act** expanded the government's search and surveillance authority to prevent terrorism. The **USA Freedom Act** curtailed some of the authority granted by the Patriot Act and requires court permission to gather or access data.
- Banks must file a **Suspicious Activity Report** (SAR) if they suspect activity that might signal money laundering, terrorist funding, tax evasion, or other illegal activities.
- The **Dodd-Frank Act** governs finance entities involved in mortgage lending. It established the CFPB and the Financial Stability Oversight Council (FSOC).
- Dodd-Frank prevents qualified mortgages from having an interest-only period, negative amortization, balloon payments, or terms longer than 30 years. It establishes other consumer protections as well.

- The Gramm-Leach-Bliley Act (15 U.S.C. §6801 et seq.) focuses on consumer privacy and places restrictions and requirements on financial service providers to address privacy concerns.

- The **Mortgage Acts and Practices Rule (MAP)**: Advertising (Regulation N) protects consumers from misleading and deceptive advertising.

- The **Electronic Signatures Act (E-Sign Act)** validates the use of electronic records and signatures for certain processes.

- The **Homeowners Protection Act** protects consumers by requiring lenders to terminate private mortgage insurance when borrower's mortgage loans reach certain thresholds.

# Chapter 1 Quiz: Federal Mortgage-Related Laws

1. Which of these statements most accurately describes the relationship between the Dodd-Frank Act (P.L. 111-203) Act and the Consumer Financial Protection Bureau?

   a. The Dodd-Frank Act created the Consumer Financial Protection Bureau in response to the housing and financial crisis of 2007-2008.
   b. HUD implemented the Dodd-Frank Act by creating the Consumer Financial Protection Bureau.
   c. The Consumer Financial Protection Bureau implements the Dodd-Frank Act.
   d. The Dodd-Frank Act was part of the legislation that established both HUD and the Consumer Financial Protection Bureau in 1965.

2. Which of the following agencies enforces the Fair Housing Act (42 U.S.C. §3601 et seq.)?

   a. CFPB
   b. HUD
   c. FHFA
   d. OCC

3. What is HUD's primary focus?

   a. Implementing RESPA (12 U.S.C. §2601 et seq.) provisions
   b. Protecting homebuyers from unscrupulous developers
   c. Developing housing in rural areas
   d. Fostering homeownership and affordable housing

4. Which of the following is NOT a function of the Federal Housing Finance Agency (FHFA)?

   a. Regulate and supervise Fannie Mae and Freddie Mac
   b. Govern the Federal Home Loan Bank System
   c. Purchase mortgage loans from independent lenders
   d. Issue debt securities to provide funding for member banks

5. Which agency monitors mortgage market trends to identify risks to banks?

   a. CFPB
   b. HUD
   c. FHFA
   d. OCC

6. A couple has three bank accounts at banks insured by the FDIC. In which of the following situations would all three accounts be insured for the FDIC maximum of $250,000?

   a. Each person has an individual checking account, and they have a joint checking account—all at the same bank.
   b. The couple has three joint checking accounts; two are at one bank, and one is at a separate bank.
   c. The couple has one joint checking account, one joint savings account, and one joint business account—all at the same bank.
   d. The couple has a joint checking account and a joint savings account at one bank, and one individual has an individual checking account at a separate bank.

7. Which one of the following disclosures is NOT required by RESPA?

   a. Servicing Transfer Statement
   b. Affiliated business arrangement disclosure
   c. Mortgage Servicing Disclosure Statement
   d. Seller's financial condition statement

8. Under RESPA disclosure requirements, what exempts lenders from having to issue a Loan Estimate (LE) to a loan applicant who requests preapproval?

   a. The applicant waives the right to receive the LE.
   b. The applicant has not supplied an address for the property to be purchased.
   c. The lender agrees to close within 30 days from the date of application.
   d. The applicant has an existing mortgage loan with the lender.

9. Lenders who retain and service all or part of the loans they fund instead of selling them are called _____.

   a. Secondary lenders
   b. Loan servicers
   c. Portfolio lenders
   d. Mortgage brokers

10. Carlton works with mortgage loan applicants. He does not fund or service mortgage loans but instead acts as an intermediary between borrowers and lenders, assisting borrowers in finding the most suitable mortgage loan from a wide range of lenders. Carlton must be a

    a. mortgage broker
    b. portfolio lender
    c. mortgage banker
    d. loan officer

11. Which of the following transactions is exempt from RESPA provisions?

    a. A first-time homebuyer is financing a purchase with a conventional mortgage
    b. A homeowner is applying for a HELOC to upgrade a home
    c. An investor is paying cash for a property to fix up and resell
    d. An investor is applying for a real estate loan to purchase a four-unit residential property

12. Select the entity that is not considered a third-party settlement services provider under RESPA provisions.

    a. Lenders
    b. Movers
    c. Appraisers
    d. Surveyors

13. Select the escrow calculation that meets RESPA funding limitation requirements.

    a. The borrower's estimated annual escrow amount for taxes and insurance is $3,217. The lender calculates the borrower's monthly escrow payment to be $268.08.
    b. The borrower's estimated annual escrow amount for taxes and insurance is $2,506. The lender calculates an initial funding amount at closing to be $417.67.
    c. The borrower's estimated annual property tax bill is $1,875, insurance is $1,295, and a three-year flood insurance policy is $2,160. The lender calculates the borrower's monthly escrow payment to be $444.17.
    d. The borrower's estimated annual escrow amount for taxes and insurance is $4,197. The lender calculates the initial funding amount at closing to be $699.50.

14. Which of the following scenarios describes an illegal action related to settlement service providers?

    a. A lender refers a borrower to the lender's affiliated title insurance and closing firm after making the required disclosures.
    b. A lender offers a substantial discount to buyers who choose to use its preferred title company.
    c. A developer offers financial incentives to buyers who use the builder's preferred lender.
    d. A closing firm provides event tickets worth $500 to a real estate agent who routinely refers clients to the firm.

15. Under which circumstances can a seller require a buyer to use a specific title insurance company?

    a. The seller is paying for the title insurance and all related services.
    b. The seller is also the housing developer.
    c. The seller is offering seller financing to the buyer.
    d. The seller disclosed his affiliated business relationship with the title insurance company.

16. Which of the following might cause a lender to invoke the due-on-sale clause in a mortgage?

    a. The borrower failed to make the required mortgage payments for three consecutive months.
    b. The borrower goes under contract on the sale of the property, with the mortgage to be paid off at closing.
    c. The borrower refinanced the original mortgage loan.
    d. The borrower conveyed title to the property into the borrower's trust.

17. Which of the following accurately describes protected classes under the Equal Credit Opportunity Act and the Fair Housing Act (42 U.S.C. §3601 et seq.)?

    a. Both laws prohibit discrimination based on race, religion, age, and sex.
    b. Both laws prohibit discrimination based on race, religion, nationality, and sex.
    c. Neither law prohibits discrimination based on age or marital status.
    d. Both laws prohibit discrimination based on source of income.

18. Select the situation that most accurately depicts disparate impact.

    a. After accepting a mortgage application from a Hispanic couple, the lender refused to consider the application because the couple's real estate agent was difficult to work with.
    b. A mortgage lender funds loans to white applicants more often than to Asian applicants, even though the Asian applicants were often more qualified financially.
    c. A lender established a policy not to offer loans for single-family residences for less than $150,000.
    d. A lender refused to fund a mortgage loan to a qualified buyer due to the neighborhood in which the buyer's property was located.

19. Which of the following is a reason a lender can use to deny a loan?

    a. Insufficient income
    b. Part-time employment
    c. Low debt-to-income ratio
    d. High credit score

20. In which situation can a lender NOT inquire about an applicant's marital status?

    a. Steve is applying for a mortgage loan based on only his income. The property will be titled in his name. He is married, and he and his spouse live in a state that recognizes spousal rights.
    b. Margaret is applying for a mortgage loan based on only her income. The property will be titled in her name, though her spouse will reside with her.
    c. A married couple plans to use both their incomes to qualify for a mortgage loan, even though the property will be titled in just one of their names.
    d. A married couple makes a joint application for a mortgage loan, and both parties will be responsible for repaying the loan.

21. Which of these questions can a lender ask loan applicants, assuming the applicant has provided proof of sufficient income for the loan requested?

    a. Do you plan to have children?
    b. Do you receive alimony or child support?
    c. What is your immigration status?
    d. Do you have a second job?

22. Select the factor that would NOT be considered an adverse credit action requiring the lender to provide a Notice of Action Taken.

    a. Loan approval
    b. Loan denial
    c. Incomplete loan application
    d. Offering terms other than those requested

23. Which of the following statements regarding income sources is most accurate?

    a. Lenders may consider whether an applicant's income is from public assistance.
    b. Lenders may not discriminate based on any legal source of income.
    c. Lenders may not consider alimony or child support as sources of income.
    d. Lenders must include spousal income if the applicant is married.

24. The primary purpose of TRID is to

    a. require lenders to make appropriate disclosures to consumers regarding the cost of a loan
    b. require borrowers to submit truthful, accurate loan documentation
    c. provide lenders with guidance regarding high-cost loans
    d. provide information to the federal government regarding mortgage loans funded

25. The Loan Estimate

    a. must be provided to borrowers within three days after submission of an application
    b. must exactly match the calculations on the Closing Disclosure
    c. must be provided at least ten days before loan consummation
    d. includes information about loan costs, closing costs, and the down payment submitted

26. Which of the following statements regarding the Loan Estimate is correct?

    a. Lenders can issue a new Loan Estimate after the CD is issued.
    b. Lenders must issue the Loan Estimate at least three days before the loan closes.
    c. Lenders must issue a new LE if the borrower's work hours, and thus wages, were reduced.
    d. Mortgage brokers are not authorized to issue Loan Estimates; only the lender may do so.

27. A family has received clearance to close on their mortgage loan. Which one of the following situations is most likely to cause a delay in closing due to an unpermitted increase from the Loan Estimate to the Closing Disclosure?

    a. The lender origination charge increased by $250.
    b. The title insurance premium increased by 2%, and the price for the title search increased by 3%.
    c. The amount due for prepaid property taxes increased by $550.
    d. The initial escrow funding calculation increased by $350.

28. Two days before closing, a borrower receives an unexpected work bonus that permits a larger down payment. The borrower wants to switch from an FHA loan to a conventional loan. What is the impact on closing and the Closing Disclosure?

    a. There is no impact. Closing can proceed as planned.
    b. The lender must provide a new CD, and a new three-day waiting period is required.
    c. The closing can go on as planned if the lender can make the necessary changes in time.
    d. The borrower must start the loan application process over again.

29. The Home Mortgage Disclosure Act is designed primarily to

    a. protect borrowers by requiring lenders to make certain disclosures to them
    b. protect lenders by requiring appraisers and home inspectors to comply with industry standards in their work
    c. prevent discriminatory lending by requiring lenders to gather and report certain lending information
    d. protect lenders by allowing them to sell qualifying loans to investors

30. Which of the following laws addresses credit reporting accuracy?

    a. RESPA
    b. HMDA (12 U.S.C. §2801 et seq.)
    c. TRID
    d. FCRA

31. Do-Not-Call laws prohibit telemarketers from

    a. contacting a consumer for more than 12 months after the business relationship ended
    b. calling consumers before 9:00 a.m. or after 8:00 p.m. local time
    c. failing to provide a telephone number via Caller ID
    d. retaining call records for more than 12 months

32. When is a bank required to file a Suspicious Activity Report?

    a. When an account holder makes sudden, unexplained deposits
    b. Any time an account holder deposits $10,000 or more
    c. Quarterly, with data on all account holders
    d. When an account holder adds a co-signor to the account

33. The _____ directed the Federal Trade Commission to implement regulations protecting consumers' personal financial information. It requires financial services companies to explain how they share consumer information.

    a. Mortgage Acts and Practices—Advertising
    b. Dodd-Frank Act
    c. Truth in Lending Act
    d. Gramm-Leach-Bliley Act (15 U.S.C. §6801 et seq.) Act

34. The Mortgage Acts and Practices Advertising Rule (Regulation N) prohibits misleading marketing or advertising

    a.  related to the number of mortgage loans a broker has funded
    b.  related to a lender's average number of days to close
    c.  regarding the lender's qualifications, staffing, and funding processes
    d.  regarding the loan terms of any of the lender's loan products

35. In the mortgage industry, the E-SIGN Act

    a.  requires handwritten (wet) signatures on loan documents
    b.  requires conversion of electronically signed documents to paper for storage
    c.  allows electronic documents to take the place of printed documents
    d.  identifies a specific platform lenders must use for electronic signatures and documents

36. Under the Homeowners Protection Act,

    a.  borrowers can request PMI termination when the mortgage balance reaches 80% of the home's original value based on payments made or appreciation
    b.  lenders must automatically terminate PMI or MIP when the borrower's mortgage balance reaches 78% of the home's original value
    c.  borrowers can request PMI termination when the mortgage balance first reaches 80% of the home's original value based solely on payments made
    d.  lenders must automatically terminate MIP when the borrower's mortgage balance reaches 80% of the home's original value

# 2 General Mortgage Knowledge

The mortgage market and mortgage loan programs
Mortgage loan products
Terms used in the mortgage industry

## Learning Objectives

- Describe the differences between qualified mortgages (QMs) and non-qualified mortgages (non-QMs), including their key features and regulatory standards.
- Distinguish between conventional/conforming loans and conventional/non-conforming loans based on underwriting guidelines and loan limits.
- Identify the characteristics and eligibility requirements of major government-backed mortgage programs, including FHA, VA, and USDA loans.
- Explain the functions of the primary and secondary mortgage markets and their roles in mortgage lending and liquidity.
- Summarize the features, benefits, and risks associated with common mortgage loan products, including fixed-rate, ARM, interest-only, and balloon loans.
- Describe the purpose and structure of specialty loan products such as reverse mortgages, construction loans, and purchase money second mortgages.
- Identify commonly used mortgage terms and concepts.

---

## THE MORTGAGE MARKET AND MORTGAGE LOAN PROGRAMS

Mortgage market overview
Mortgage loans
General mortgage loan categories
Conventional / conforming loans
Qualified mortgages (QMs)
Non-qualified mortgages (non-QMs)
Conventional / non-conforming loans
FHA loans
VA loans
USDA loans
Office of Public and Indian Housing loans
Interested party contributions
Late fees
Mortgage-backed securities

---

## Mortgage market overview

The mortgage market is divided into two primary components: the primary mortgage market and the secondary mortgage market, each serving distinct functions essential to the overall system.

**Primary mortgage market.** In the **primary mortgage market**, loans are originated as borrowers work directly with lenders to secure new mortgages. This market is where the initial transaction occurs, as borrowers receive funds to finance their properties, and lenders issue loans that are secured by the property itself. The primary market is critical because it enables individuals and businesses to access the financing necessary to purchase real estate.

**Secondary mortgage market.** The **secondary mortgage market** plays a vital role by buying and selling existing mortgages, which are bundled into mortgage-backed securities (MBS). In this market, there is no direct interaction with borrowers; instead, loans are traded between financial entities.

The secondary market exists to provide liquidity to lenders in the primary market, enabling them to continue issuing new loans. This market also helps reduce the risk associated with interest rates for lenders by allowing them to diversify their portfolios across various loan products and investor categories. Additionally, the secondary market establishes industry-wide standards for credit requirements, loan types, and documentation, which brings uniformity and reliability to the lending process.

Key players in the secondary mortgage market include government-sponsored enterprises (GSEs) and federal agencies, specifically the Federal National Mortgage Association (Fannie Mae), the Federal Home Loan Mortgage Corporation (Freddie Mac), the Government National Mortgage Association (Ginnie Mae), and the Federal Home Loan Bank System, along with a range of private investors. These institutions facilitate the buying, pooling, and selling of mortgage loans, ensuring that funds continue to circulate through the mortgage market and sustain lending activity.

**Federal National Mortgage Association (FNMA) (Fannie Mae).** The **Federal National Mortgage Association (Fannie Mae)** was created by Congress in 1938 during the Great Depression with the purpose of buying loans from primary market lenders to provide local banks with federal funds for financing home mortgages. This initiative aimed to stabilize the housing market and support economic recovery. In 1968 Fannie Mae was rechartered and became a privately held, for-profit organization and in 1972 it began purchasing conventional loans.

The largest investor in residential mortgages, Fannie Mae is classified as a government-sponsored enterprise (GSE), a financial services corporation established by Congress to improve the flow of credit, particularly within the housing sector. Although privately held, Fannie Mae is supported by the federal government, which bolsters its credibility and ensures its continued operations in times of financial strain.

**Mortgage pools**. Fannie Mae purchases mortgages from primary market lenders, such as commercial banks, savings and loans, and mortgage companies, and then pools these purchased loans into mortgage-backed securities (MBS), or mortgage bonds. Through a process known as **securitization**, Fannie Mae sells these MBS to investors. A core aspect of its service is guaranteeing that investors receive timely principal and interest payments on the MBS, even in cases where the original borrower defaults on the loan. This guarantee makes MBS investments more appealing and reliable for a broad range of investors, including individuals, pension funds, state governments, investment management funds, and foreign government entities.

**Create FNMA underwriting standards**. As a major player in the mortgage market, Fannie Mae sets underwriting standards for the mortgages it is willing to purchase. These standards impact industry-wide underwriting practices, influencing the types of loans that lenders create and the criteria used to assess borrower eligibility. Additionally, Fannie Mae sets annual loan limits on the mortgages it will buy, adjusting these limits each year based on market conditions and housing prices.

**Lender approval process**. Fannie Mae also implements a formal lender approval process to establish annual contracts with lending institutions. This approval process ensures that lenders meet specific requirements in areas such as capital, profitability, experience, underwriting standards, licensing, technology, insurance, and legal compliance. By maintaining stringent criteria, Fannie Mae promotes responsible lending practices and helps ensure the quality of loans within the housing market.

**Federal Home Loan Mortgage Corporation (Freddie Mac)**. The **Federal Home Loan Mortgage Corporation (Freddie Mac)** was established in 1970 by Congress as a government-sponsored enterprise (GSE) to enhance the liquidity and stability of the U.S. mortgage market. Like Fannie Mae, Freddie Mac plays a crucial role in the secondary mortgage market by purchasing loans from primary market lenders, such as commercial banks, credit unions, and mortgage lenders. By buying these loans, Freddie Mac provides lenders with the capital needed to issue new mortgages, thereby helping to support homeownership across the country.

**Securitize mortgage pools for sale to investors**. Freddie Mac pools the purchased mortgages into mortgage-backed securities (MBS) and sells these securities to investors, transferring the risk of the loan from the lender to investors. Freddie Mac guarantees that investors will receive their principal and interest payments on time, even if the borrower defaults on the mortgage. This assurance attracts a range of investors, including individuals, institutional funds, pension funds, and government entities, as it reduces investment risk. Freddie Mac also sets underwriting standards that influence the broader mortgage market, ensuring that loans meet specific quality criteria. These standards impact loan origination practices, creating industry consistency in evaluating borrower creditworthiness.

In addition, Freddie Mac has an approval process for lenders that wish to sell loans to them, assessing factors such as capital adequacy, profitability, experience, and compliance with underwriting guidelines. This structured approach fosters a strong and sustainable mortgage lending environment, which benefits both lenders and borrowers.

**NOTE**: Fannie Mae and Freddie Mac will *only* buy conforming loans.

**Government National Mortgage Association (Ginnie Mae).** The **Government National Mortgage Association (Ginnie Mae)**, established in 1968, functions differently from its GSE counterparts (Fannie Mae and Freddie Mac) as it operates directly under the U.S. Department of Housing and Urban Development (HUD) instead of being privately held. Ginnie Mae's primary role is to **guarantee mortgage-backed securities** that include loans insured or guaranteed by federal agencies, such as the Federal Housing Administration (FHA), the Department of Veterans Affairs (VA), and the U.S. Department of Agriculture (USDA). Unlike Fannie Mae and Freddie Mac, Ginnie Mae does not buy or sell mortgages. Instead, it backs the securities created from federally insured loans, providing an additional layer of security to investors.

**Guaranteed mortgage pools**. By guaranteeing MBS, Ginnie Mae ensures that investors receive principal and interest payments even if borrowers default on their loans. This guarantee is critical for attracting a broader range of investors, including foreign governments and institutional funds, as it reduces the perceived risk associated with investing in mortgages for low- to moderate-income, rural, or veteran borrowers. The assurance provided by Ginnie Mae allows lenders to continue offering loans under federal programs, knowing that these loans can be bundled and sold as secure investments in the secondary market. Ginnie Mae's role supports affordable housing initiatives by maintaining a steady flow of funds to housing programs, thereby promoting homeownership opportunities for underserved populations.

**Federal Home Loan Bank System (FHLB).** The **Federal Home Loan Bank System (FHLB)** was created in 1932, during the Great Depression, to provide stable and low-cost funding to financial institutions for home mortgage and economic development loans. The system was established to strengthen local lending and stimulate economic growth by enabling financial institutions to continue issuing loans in their communities, even in challenging economic times. By supporting lending at the local level, the FHLB system helps to maintain access to affordable housing and fosters economic development across the country.

**FHLB structure**. The FHLB system is made up of 11 regional Federal Home Loan Banks, serving more than 8,000 financial institution members nationwide. Membership in the FHLB is voluntary and includes a diverse range of financial institutions such as banks, credit unions, insurance companies, and community development financial institutions. Each of the 11 regional banks operates as a privately capitalized, cooperatively owned corporation, where member institutions act as both owners and customers. This cooperative governance model allows the FHLB system to focus on the specific needs of its members while providing stability to the financial system.

**Housing finance stabilization**. The FHLB channels resources into housing finance and community development projects within their geographic regions, ensuring that funds are available for projects that benefit their local economies. This regional structure also allows the FHLB system to offer targeted support to smaller financial institutions, which may have fewer options for funding compared to larger, national banks. In this way, the FHLB system promotes both diversity and stability within the financial sector, helping to create a resilient and robust framework for housing finance and community development across the United States.

**Private investors**

In addition to government entities, **private investors** play a significant role in the mortgage market by investing in mortgage-backed securities (MBS) and other mortgage-related financial products. These investors include individuals, corporations, financial institutions, hedge funds, insurance companies, and various other non-governmental entities. Private investors provide essential capital to the mortgage market by purchasing securities backed by pools of mortgages, thereby supporting the flow of funds into the housing sector.

Private investors' mortgage-related investments come in several forms, including mortgage-backed securities (MBS), collateralized mortgage obligations (CMOs), and real estate mortgage investment conduits (REMICs). These products allow investors to access the mortgage market and earn returns based on the performance of the underlying loans.

# MONEY FLOW IN THE MORTGAGE MARKET

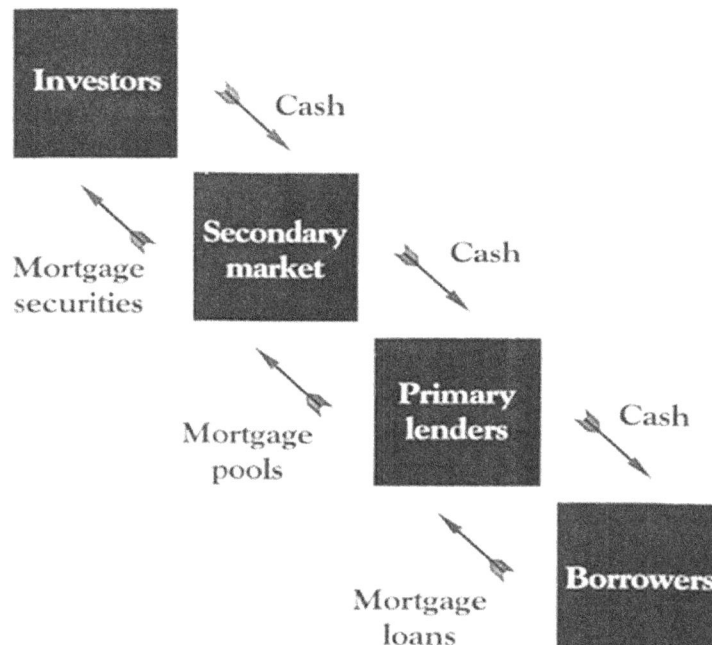

**Investors**

Cash

Mortgage securities

**Secondary market**

Cash

Mortgage pools

**Primary lenders**

Cash

Mortgage loans

**Borrowers**

## Check Your Understanding

The primary function of the secondary mortgage market is to:

A.  provide liquidity to lenders in the primary market, enabling them to continue issuing new loans.
B.  insure loans to reduce lenders' risks associated with mortgage loans.
C.  enable borrowers to work directly with lenders to secure new mortgages.
D.  securitize mortgage-backed securities.

The correct answer is A! The secondary market exists to provide liquidity to lenders in the primary market, enabling them to continue issuing new loans.

**Mortgage loans**

A mortgage loan is a type of loan secured by real property and documented through an agreement that establishes both the existence of the loan and an encumbrance on the property itself. An **encumbrance** is a legal claim, right, or restriction on a property that can affect that property's transfer (sale or other conveyance) or reduce its value. With a loan to buy real property, the encumbrance takes the form of a mortgage, which acts as collateral to secure the loan.

In the context of "a loan secured by real property," *secured by* means that the loan is backed by an asset—in this case, real property (like a house or land)—that serves as **collateral**. When a loan is secured by an asset, the lender has the legal right to claim or take possession of that asset if the borrower defaults or fails to make required loan payments.

For example, with a mortgage loan secured by real property, if the borrower does not fulfill the payment obligations, the lender has the right to foreclose on the property, selling it to recoup the remaining loan balance. This security reduces the lender's risk, because the lender has a tangible asset to fall back on if the borrower does not repay the loan.

The terms (specifics) of mortgage loans can vary widely, with differences in loan amount, maturity period, interest rate, repayment method, and other features. These factors shape the overall structure and cost of the loan.

In general, the term **mortgage** is often used interchangeably with **mortgage loan** to describe the financing arrangement.

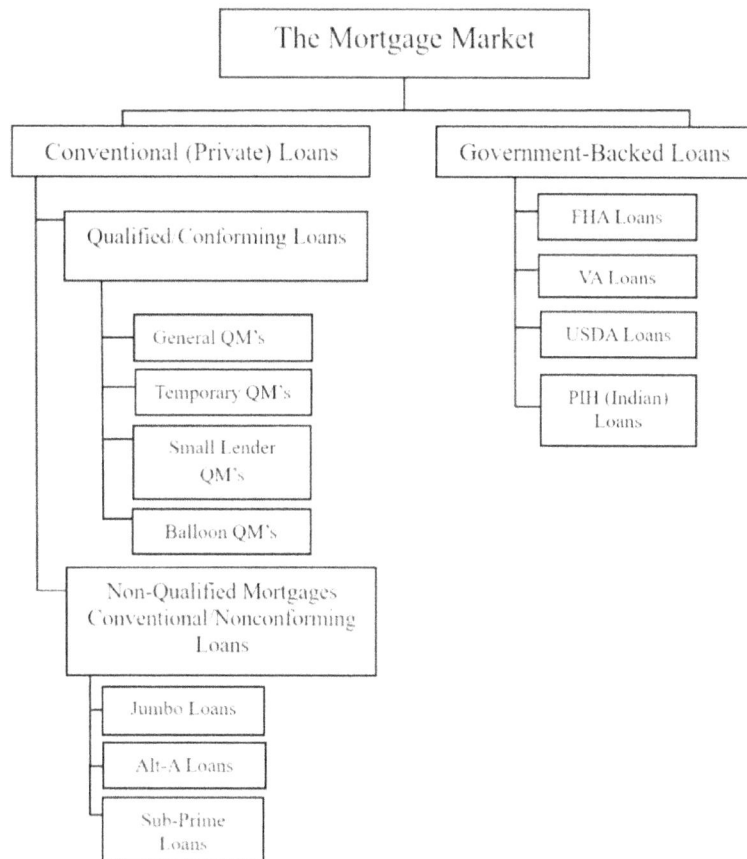

```
                         ┌─────────────────────────┐
                         │   The Mortgage Market    │
                         └─────────────────────────┘
              ┌────────────────────────┴────────────────────────┐
    ┌──────────────────────────────┐            ┌──────────────────────────┐
    │ Conventional (Private) Loans  │            │  Government-Backed Loans   │
    └──────────────────────────────┘            └──────────────────────────┘
              │                                                │  ┌──────────────┐
    ┌──────────────────────────────┐                          ├──│  FHA Loans    │
    │  Qualified/Conforming Loans   │                          │  └──────────────┘
    └──────────────────────────────┘                          │  ┌──────────────┐
              │   ┌──────────────┐                             ├──│  VA Loans     │
              ├───│  General QM's │                            │  └──────────────┘
              │   └──────────────┘                             │  ┌──────────────┐
              │   ┌──────────────┐                             ├──│  USDA Loans   │
              ├───│ Temporary QM's│                            │  └──────────────┘
              │   └──────────────┘                             │  ┌──────────────┐
              │   ┌──────────────┐                             └──│ PIH (Indian)  │
              ├───│  Small Lender │                                │    Loans     │
              │   │      QM's     │                                └──────────────┘
              │   └──────────────┘
              │   ┌──────────────┐
              └───│  Balloon QM's │
                  └──────────────┘
    ┌──────────────────────────────┐
    │  Non-Qualified Mortgages      │
    │ Conventional/Nonconforming    │
    │           Loans               │
    └──────────────────────────────┘
              │   ┌──────────────┐
              ├───│  Jumbo Loans  │
              │   └──────────────┘
              │   ┌──────────────┐
              ├───│  Alt-A Loans  │
              │   └──────────────┘
              │   ┌──────────────┐
              └───│  Sub-Prime    │
                  │    Loans      │
                  └──────────────┘
```

**General mortgage
Loan categories**

In categorizing loan types, the primary types are **conventional loans** and **government-backed loans**.

A **conventional loan** is a type of mortgage funded by private lenders. These mortgages are typically subject to the lender's own requirements as well as the mortgage industry's general guidelines.

A **government-backed loan** is insured or guaranteed by a government agency, such as the Federal Housing Administration (**FHA**), Department of Veterans Affairs (**VA**), or the U.S. Department of Agriculture (**USDA**).

Conventional loans are classified into two categories:

- **conventional conforming loans**: loans that meet the standards set by Fannie Mae and Freddie Mac, including limits on loan size, borrower creditworthiness, and property type
- **conventional non-conforming loans**: loans that do not meet these standards, such as jumbo loans (which exceed conforming loan limits) or loans for borrowers with unique financial situations

### Check Your Understanding

Which loan is best defined as a type of mortgage that is funded by private lenders?

A. conforming
B. conventional
C. government insured
D. fixed rate

If you answered B, you are correct! A conventional loan is a type of mortgage that is funded by private lenders.

**Conventional /
conforming loans**

**Not insured or guaranteed**. Conventional / conforming loans represent a significant category within the mortgage market, offering borrowers access to loans that are not insured or guaranteed by the federal government. Again, a **conventional loan** is simply a mortgage that falls outside government-backed programs like FHA, VA, or USDA loans.

**Conforming loans**

Conventional loans can either be conforming or non-conforming. A **conforming loan** is any loan that meets the standards set by Fannie Mae and Freddie Mac. These guidelines are intended to promote stability and reduce risk, making these loans appealing to investors in the secondary mortgage market. A **non-conforming loan** does not adhere to these guidelines.

**Loan limits**. To qualify as a conforming loan, certain key standards and requirements must be met, which Fannie Mae and Freddie Mac periodically update. One fundamental criterion is the **conforming loan limit**: as of 2025, the baseline limit for single-unit properties is $806,500 in most areas, though in high-cost areas, it can reach up to $1,209,750. These limits are adjusted annually in response to changes in U.S. home prices.

**Higher credit scores**. Additionally, **credit score requirements** for conforming loans generally start at 620, with higher scores offering borrowers better interest rates and loan terms. A **minimum down payment** of 3% is typically expected, though borrowers who put down less than 20% are required to pay for private mortgage insurance (PMI) until they reach 20% equity in the property.

**Specific income requirements**. Conforming loans also specify limits on the **debt-to-income (DTI) ratio**—the portion of a borrower's monthly income that goes toward debt payments. For most conforming loans, a DTI ratio of 45% or lower is required.

**Minimum LTVs**. Another important measure is the **loan-to-value (LTV) ratio**, which compares the loan amount to the property's appraised value. Higher LTV ratios indicate greater risk, so conforming loans typically impose maximum LTV limits, which vary depending on the loan program and borrower qualifications, but a general good rule of thumb is a maximum of 97%. Borrowers must also provide thorough documentation of their financial standing, including proof of income, employment, assets, and debts—typically in the form of W-2 statements, tax returns, bank statements, and credit reports. Furthermore, a property appraisal is required to ensure the property value meets or exceeds the loan amount, safeguarding the lender's interest in case of default. Only specific property types are eligible for conforming loans, including primary residences, second homes, and investment properties, each with its own standards.

**Must qualify through underwriting systems**. Fannie Mae and Freddie Mac require that conforming loans go through automated underwriting systems, like Fannie Mae's **Desktop Underwriter (DU)** or Freddie Mac's **Loan Product Advisor (LPA)**, which assess borrower eligibility based on standardized guidelines. Additional borrower requirements may address issues such as a history of bankruptcy or foreclosure, as well as special considerations for self-employed individuals.

**Risk-based fee standards**. To address variations in borrower risk, Fannie Mae and Freddie Mac apply **Loan-Level Price Adjustments (LLPAs)**, which are fees charged to lenders based on specific loan characteristics. These risk-based fees, which lenders often pass along to borrowers, are determined by factors such as credit scores, LTV ratios, property type, loan purpose (e.g., purchase, refinance), and loan features like interest-only payments or terms longer than 30 years. LLPAs help Fannie Mae and Freddie Mac manage the risks associated with buying and guaranteeing mortgages, offsetting potential losses from defaults. These adjustments can significantly affect the loan's cost, especially for borrowers with lower credit scores or high LTV loans, and can be paid up front at closing, added to the loan's interest rate, or handled with a combination of both. Fannie Mae and Freddie Mac publish LLPA matrices that lenders use to determine applicable fees, but LLPAs do not apply to government-backed loans.

**HomeReady**. To make homeownership more accessible, Fannie Mae and Freddie Mac offer **low down payment programs** like **HomeReady** and **HomePossible**. These programs allow for down payments as low as 3%, translating to a 97% LTV. Designed for first-time and low- to moderate-income buyers, they permit the use of non-traditional income sources and flexible closing cost options. Typically, borrowers' income cannot exceed 80% of the area's median income.

Through these structured guidelines and offerings, conventional / conforming loans provide a balanced approach to risk management and accessibility, benefiting both borrowers and investors in the mortgage market.

### Check Your Understanding

Which of the following is a general criterion for a conforming loan?

    A. Maximum LTV of 99%
    B. Minimum down payment of 8%
    C. Minimum credit score of 700
    D. DTI ratio of 45% or lower

Did you choose D? For most conforming loans, a DTI ratio of 45% or lower is indeed required.

## Qualified mortgages (QMs)

**QMs defined.** A qualified mortgage (QM) is a type of mortgage that meets specific standards set by the Consumer Financial Protection Bureau (CFPB) to **ensure lenders issue loans that borrowers can realistically repay**. Introduced as part of the Dodd-Frank Act in 2014, qualified mortgages are designed to promote responsible lending and borrowing practices, thereby contributing to financial stability within the mortgage market. The concept of qualified mortgages was one component of the broader financial reforms enacted under the Dodd-Frank Act in 2010, intended to reduce the risks that contributed to the 2008 financial crisis.

**Limited points and fees.** To be classified as a qualified mortgage, a loan must meet several key features and requirements. First, limits are placed on the lender's total "points and fees" which may not exceed the following thresholds based on 2025 Federal Register annual adjustments: For loan amounts of $129,859 or more, points and fees cannot exceed 3 percent of the total loan amount. For loan amounts between $77,916 and $129,858, points and fees cannot exceed $3,896. For loan amounts between $48,947 and $77,915, points and fees cannot exceed 8 percent of the total loan amount. For loan amounts less than $48,947, points and fees cannot exceed the greater of 8 percent of the total loan amount or $3,896. These thresholds are adjusted annually by the CFPB to account for inflation.

**No risky loan features**. Additionally, qualified mortgages are prohibited from including **risky loan features** that increase financial vulnerability. For example, QMs cannot include **negative amortization** (where the loan principal grows over time), interest-only payments, balloon payments, or loan terms longer than 30 years. QMs must also involve a **reasonable and good-faith determination of the borrower's ability to repay**, which includes verifying the borrower's income, assets, debt obligations, and credit history. Furthermore, QMs generally enforce a **debt-to-income (DTI) cap** of 43%, meaning that the borrowers' total monthly debt obligations, including the mortgage, should not exceed 43% of their monthly pre-tax income.

**QMs protect against predatory lending**. Qualified mortgages serve a dual protective function. For consumers, they guard against predatory lending practices and reduce the risk of acquiring loans that they cannot afford to repay. For lenders, QMs provide legal protection, offering a "safe harbor" against borrower lawsuits related to the ability-to-repay requirement, as long as the lender has adhered to QM standards. As a result, qualified mortgages have become a standard in the mortgage industry, shaping how lenders assess borrower eligibility and set loan terms.

### QM classifications

Different categories of qualified mortgages exist to accommodate various lending circumstances:

- General QMs
- Temporary QMs
- Small lender QMs
- Balloon-payment QMs

**General QMs.** These mortgages adhere to all the basic QM requirements.

**Temporary QMs.** Introduced to provide a transition period when QM rules were first implemented under Dodd-Frank, temporary QMs allow lenders to continue issuing loans while adapting to new standards.

**Small lender QMs.** These mortgages are specifically designed for smaller lenders that might face challenges in meeting standard QM requirements. To qualify, lenders must have less than $2 billion in assets and originate fewer than 2,000 QMs annually. As a category, small lender QMs allow more flexibility in evaluating a borrower's DTI ratio.

**Balloon-payment QMs.** As the name suggests, these QMs allow loans with balloon payments at the end of the term—normally a feature excluded from QMs. However, this option is only available to small creditors operating in rural or underserved areas, helping to address the unique financing needs of these communities.

These distinctions within the qualified mortgage category offer flexibility within a structured framework, helping to balance the goals of consumer protection and accessibility to credit.

**Loan types exempted.** Certain types of loans, however, are **exempt from QM requirements**. These include open-ended credit plans, timeshare plans, reverse mortgages, bridge loans, short-duration construction-to-permanent loans, and consumer credit transactions secured by vacant land. These exemptions ensure that specific financing arrangements, often with unique repayment structures or temporary financing needs, remain accessible without needing to conform to QM standards.

## Non-qualified mortgages

**Do not follow Dodd Frank and CFPB underwriting requirements**. Non-qualified mortgages **(non-QMs)** are home loans that do not conform to the strict lending requirements set forth by the Dodd-Frank Act and the Consumer Financial Protection Bureau (CFPB), which were established to promote responsible lending practices and prevent scenarios like the 2008 subprime mortgage crisis. By sidestepping qualified mortgage (QM) standards, non-QMs offer an alternative for borrowers whose income or credit history do not meet the more stringent requirements of conventional mortgage programs.
**Higher DTIs.** Non-QM loans are particularly useful for individuals with debt-to-income ratios (DTIs) above 43% or those who need to use alternative documentation to verify income. These borrowers may be self-employed individuals who may rely on bank statements rather than W-2s or tax returns.

Unlike qualified mortgages, non-QMs may include higher-risk features such as:

- interest-only payment periods
- negative amortization
- balloon payments
- loan terms of more than 30 years

However, these terms often come at higher costs in the form of higher interest rates and upfront fees, making non-QMs more expensive over the life of the loan.

**Tighter default terms**. Borrowers of non-QMs receive less regulatory protection than those with qualified mortgages, as non-QMs lack the "safe harbor" provisions that protect lenders from liability as long as they follow QM standards. The application process for a non-QM is generally more lenient, often requiring less documentation than conventional loans. Despite this flexibility, the higher risk associated with non-QMs means they are offered by fewer lenders and come with a price premium, reflecting the added cost of taking on riskier loan features.

Non-qualified mortgages provide an essential option for borrowers who do not fit into traditional mortgage molds, offering a pathway to homeownership that might not otherwise be available.

Common non-QMs are **jumbo loans**, **Alt-A loans**, and **subprime loans**.

## Conventional / non-conforming loans

**Conventional / non-conforming loans** fall under the category of private mortgages, meaning they are not backed by any governmental agency and generally offer flexible terms. Unlike conforming loans, which adhere to the guidelines of Fannie Mae and Freddie Mac, **non-conforming loans** do not follow these government-sponsored standards.

These loans are often used for high-value properties, providing higher loan amounts beyond the FHFA limits. They can also work for buyers who need more flexible borrower requirements, such as having lower credit scores. However, they often command higher down payments and interest rates, as well as potentially more stringent lending criteria, depending on the lender.

### Jumbo loans

**Costs and underwriting**. Jumbo loans are a prominent type of non-conforming loan used to finance properties with values exceeding the conforming loan limits, such as homes in high-cost real estate markets. For instance, in 2024, the FHFA's baseline limit for single-family conforming loans was $766,550, though this limit is higher in pricier regions.

Jumbo loans come with more stringent qualification standards, often requiring excellent credit scores (typically 700 or higher) and larger down payments, generally 20% or more. Borrowers must also meet rigorous DTI requirements that demonstrate borrowers' ability to manage debt alongside a larger mortgage payment.

While interest rates on jumbo loans can be competitive, they may be slightly higher than those for conforming loans due to lenders' increased risk with larger loan amounts. Lenders also generally require more rigorous income verification, detailed property appraisals, and extensive documentation, as they have the freedom to set their criteria without government backing.

### Alt-A loans

Alt-A loans (Alternative A-paper loans) are suitable for borrowers with unique financial situations that may not meet the strict documentation or credit requirements of a conforming loan. Individuals with diverse financial backgrounds, such as those with non-traditional income sources, lower credit scores, higher DTIs, or less conventional documentation, may be a good fit for an

Alt-A loan. Borrowers often use Alt-A loans as a short- to medium-term financing solution, with plans to refinance into a standard mortgage later.

Due to their elevated risk for lenders, Alt-A loans typically have higher interest rates and closing costs. Further, they are not typically bought or sold in the secondary mortgage market. Even though Alt-A loans are considered riskier than prime (A-paper) loans, they are generally viewed as less risky than subprime loans.

**Subprime loans**

Subprime loans are designed for borrowers with poor credit scores or other financial challenges, making them higher-risk loans for lenders. Characteristics of a subprime borrowers often include:

- credit score below 660
- history of late payments
- foreclosure or bankruptcy
- DTI of 50% or more

To offset the increased risk, subprime loans have higher interest rates than traditional loans. Over the years, regulatory changes have been introduced to protect subprime borrowers, ensuring that they do not take on more debt than they can reasonably afford.

**"Guidance on Non-Traditional Mortgage Product Risk"**

The *Guidance on Non-Traditional Mortgage Product Risk* was established in 2006 as a set of guidelines for lenders offering non-conforming loans. It focuses on risks associated with non-traditional mortgage products and encourages responsible underwriting standards. These include urging lenders to carefully assess a borrower's ability to repay the loan, especially in scenarios where loan payments may increase due to features like interest-only payments, negative amortization, balloon payments, and payment-option ARMs.

Additionally, lenders are encouraged to provide borrowers with clear, comprehensive information on the potential risks associated with non-traditional mortgage products and to disclose potential future payment increases at the time of loan selection and throughout the loan term. To ensure adherence, the guidance recommends that lenders conduct regular reviews and audits to maintain compliance with relevant regulations and prioritize sound underwriting practices in all non-traditional mortgage transactions.

## Check Your Understanding

Which conventional / non-conforming loan product is designed for borrowers with poor credit scores or other financial challenges?

   A. Jumbo loan
   B. Subprime loan
   C. FHA loan
   D. Alt-A loan

If you selected B, subprime loans, you are right! These loans are designed for borrowers with poor credit scores or other financial challenges, making them higher-risk loans for lenders.

## Government-backed Loans

Loans backed by the government are **non-conventional loans**. They include **FHA loans, VA loans, and USDA loans**. Government-backed mortgage programs offer structured support for specific borrower groups, which makes homeownership more accessible and more affordable homeownership for buyers across different income levels and in geographic areas.

## FHA loans

**Federal Housing Administration (FHA) loan essentials**

**Insured, smaller down payments**. Federal Housing Administration (FHA) loans are a type of government-backed mortgage designed to protect lenders against borrower default through federal insurance. Primarily aimed at first-time homebuyers and lower-income individuals, FHA loans offer low down payments—typically as low as 3.5% of the purchase price—and more flexible credit requirements than conventional loans.

Refinancing options under FHA include streamline, cash-out, rate-and-term, and rehab loans, among others. Additionally, FHA loans come with anti-flipping provisions to prevent quick resale practices. For example, properties resold within 90 days are ineligible, and those resold between 91 and 180 days for more than 100% of the previous price require a second appraisal at the lender or seller's expense.

FHA loans are assumable, allowing future buyers to take over the loan under the original terms, subject to lender and HUD approval. Also, no prepayment penalties are permitted.

**FHA credit scores**. Borrowers with a credit score of 580 or above are eligible for the FHA minimum down payment of 3.5% of the purchase price. Borrowers with a credit score between 500 and 579 may still qualify for an FHA loan but are required to make a 10% down payment. FHA loans are generally not available to borrowers with credit scores below 500.

Beyond the FHA's minimum credit score requirements, lenders may impose higher standards, known as "overlays." Many lenders prefer borrowers to have a score of at least 620 or higher, especially if they want to access the 3.5% down payment option, even though FHA guidelines allow for lower scores. It is important for borrowers to compare different lenders to find one that best supports their credit situation.

**FHA loan limits and minimum property requirements**

FHA loans have limits, and those limits are determined by a percentage of the Federal Housing Finance Agency's conforming loan limits, with amounts varying by county based on local housing prices. In 2024, for example, the "floor" limit for most counties was $498,257 and the "ceiling" for high-cost areas was $1,149,285.

FHA loans also impose loan-to-value (LTV) limits.

> ‣ purchases: maximum LTV is 96.5%, with a minimum 3.5% down payment
> ‣ rate-and-term refinances: maximum LTV of 97.75%
> ‣ cash-out refinances: capped at 80%

**Acceptable physical condition**. To qualify for an FHA loan, properties must meet HUD's minimum property requirements (MPR), covering safety, security, and soundness standards. Homes with issues related to structural integrity or sanitation are ineligible, and appraisals must be conducted by FHA-approved appraisers. FHA loans finance various property types, including single-family homes, multi-family residences, and manufactured homes, with a requirement that borrowers must occupy the property within 60 days of closing and live there for at least a year.

**Mortgage insurance**

FHA loans require two forms of mortgage insurance: an **upfront mortgage insurance premium (UFMIP)**, and an **annual mortgage insurance premium (MIP)**, which is. These loans are offered by FHA-approved financial entities such as banks, credit unions, mortgage companies, and online lenders, making them widely accessible.

> **UFMIP**: a one-time fee typically set at 1.75% of the loan amount, which can be paid at closing or financed into the loan
> **MIP**: an annual premium that's divided into monthly payments added to the monthly mortgage payment; rate is based on loan amount and term; generally 0.45% to 1.05% of the loan balance annually; typically required for the entire loan term

## Underwriting requirements for FHA-approved lenders

To issue FHA loans, lenders must be approved by the Department of Housing and Urban Development (HUD), which oversees the FHA. Basic requirements include:

- ▸ complete an application with HUD, pay an application fee, and submit documentation for HUD review
- ▸ demonstrate sound financial health, including minimum net worth and liquidity requirements based on the type and volume of FHA loans issued
- ▸ implement and maintain a quality control program to ensure that loans meet FHA standards and that all employees are trained in FHA lending guidelines
- ▸ conduct regular audits and quality control reviews to ensure compliance
- ▸ follow FHA's underwriting criteria, which includes evaluating borrower credit, income, debt, and other factors according to FHA guidelines
- ▸ complete an annual recertification with HUD, updating financial and operational information and paying a renewal fee
- ▸ meet technology requirements for HUD's loan systems

All FHA-approved lenders must have a minimum net worth of $1 million. Lenders whose FHA mortgages exceed $25 million must also have an additional 1% of total volume that exceeds that $25 million in loans.

*Example*:

A lender that originates $30 million in FHA-guaranteed loans must have a net worth of the base amount of $1 million PLUS the additional amount of: ($30 million - $25 million) × 1% = $50,000. That's a total of $1,050,000 in net worth.

The FHA's maximum net worth for lenders is $2.5 million, with at least 20% of that in liquid assets

## FHA Case Numbers

The lender assigns an FHA case number through the FHA's system, **FHA Connection**, shortly after the borrower applies for an FHA loan. The case number is a unique identifier that functions as a tracking and reference tool for the FHA, lenders, and other parties involved in the loan process. Each case number is specific to a single property and borrower and remains associated with that loan until it either fails to close, is paid off, or is otherwise terminated.

**VA loans**

**U.S. Department of Veterans Affairs (VA)**

**VA targeted borrowers**. VA loans are specifically designed to assist veterans, active service members, and their families in financing owner-occupied homes. Loan options include purchase loans, Interest Rate Reduction Refinance Loans (IRRRLs), and cash-out refinance loans. The VA guarantees these loans, minimizing lender risk and allowing institutions like banks and mortgage companies to offer favorable terms.

**No down payment, no mortgage insurance, lower rates**. Eligible borrowers include veterans, active-duty service members, National Guard members, reservists, and certain surviving spouses, though eligibility depends on service type and duration. VA loans typically require no down payment and do not involve private mortgage insurance, regardless of the down payment size. They generally feature lower interest rates than conventional loans, with limited allowable closing costs and no prepayment penalties. VA loans are also assumable, provided the new borrower meets VA and lender criteria.

**Must have stable income, meet DTI standards**. VA loans have no government-set loan limits for borrowers with full entitlement, though county-based limits apply for those with partial entitlement. Borrowers are expected to have stable income and a **debt-to-income (DTI) ratio** of 41% or lower, alongside sufficient residual income after expenses, which varies based on family size and regional costs. The VA does not mandate a minimum credit score, but most lenders prefer scores around 620.

**Certificate of Eligibility (COE). A Certificate of Eligibility (COE)** is required to prove eligibility. The COE is a critical first step for obtaining a VA loan, as it confirms to lenders that the borrower meets the service requirements and is eligible for the program's benefits, which can include zero down payment, no private mortgage insurance (PMI), and competitive interest rates. The COE is available to:

> ‣ veterans who served during wartime or peacetime, meeting minimum active-duty service requirements
> ‣ active-duty service members who have served at least 90 continuous days
> ‣ National Guard and reserve members with six years of service or who meet specific active-duty requirements
> ‣ surviving spouses of service members who died in the line of duty or as a result of service-related injuries, in certain cases

The COE also indicates if the borrower is exempt from the VA funding fee, which is a one-time cost associated with most VA loans. Exemptions apply to veterans with service-connected disabilities, surviving spouses eligible for the loan benefit, and others who meet specific criteria.

**Minimum Property Requirements (MPRs).** VA loans must also meet **minimum property requirements (MPRs)**, covering safety, soundness, and sanitation, with appraisals conducted by VA-approved appraisers to determine value and compliance. MPR requirements protect both the borrower and the VA from potential issues with the property. They cover a range of property conditions and features to ensure that homes financed through the VA loan program provide a secure and stable living environment for veterans and service members.

**Funding fees.** Veterans and other permitted individuals who are using a VA loan pay a one-time, non-refundable funding fee to help offset the cost of the loan guarantee program and sustain it for future borrowers. It is typically financed into the loan, meaning it is added to the total loan balance rather than paid out of pocket. However, it can also be paid upfront at closing. Further, sellers may contribute up to 4% of the home's reasonable value to count toward closing costs, including the funding fee.

The VA funding fee for 2025 varies depending on several factors, including military status, whether the borrower has used a VA loan before, and the size of down payment.

**Current fee structure**. As a general guideline, VA fees are structured as follows:

- first-time VA loan users with no down payment or less than 5% down: 2.15%
- subsequent VA loan users with no down payment or less than 5% down: 3.3%
- 5% down payment: 1.5%
- 10% or more down payment: 1.25%
- interest rate reduction refinances: 0.50%
- cash-out refinance loans with any down payment amount:
  - first-time VA loan use: 2.15%
  - subsequent VA loan use: 3.3%

Some funding fee exemptions apply, including veterans who are living with service-related disabilities and surviving spouses of veterans who died in service or as a result of a service-connected disability.

Lenders are also permitted to charge a <u>loan origination fee of up to 1% of the loan amount</u>.

**Requirements for VA-approved lenders.** Like the FHA, the VA also has an approval process for lenders that is designed to ensure that lenders understand the unique aspects of VA loans and can meet the needs of veterans and service members. Requirements include:

▸ submit an application to the VA and pay a fee

▸ establish a quality control program to monitor VA loan processing, underwriting, and closing procedures

▸ conduct regular quality audits and have dedicated staff who understand VA-specific requirements, such as eligibility verification, appraisals, and loan guarantees

▸ ensure that loan officers, underwriters, and staff involved in VA loans are trained in VA program guidelines, such as eligibility criteria, minimum property requirements (MPRs), and funding fee regulations

▸ understand VA-specific processes, including obtaining the Certificate of Eligibility (COE) for borrowers and coordinating with VA appraisers for property evaluations

▸ have access to the VA's automated systems, such as WebLGY, which manages borrower eligibility, loan guarantees, and appraisals

▸ complete an annual recertification to demonstrate continued compliance with VA standards, including financial requirements and quality control practices

The VA may also conduct an inspection of the lender's offices and facilities to ensure compliance with program standards. It also ensures that lenders have adequate financial stability to fulfill their obligations to borrowers and the VA.

**US Dept. of Agriculture (USDA) loans**

**USDA overview.** USDA loans cater specifically to rural and smaller community borrowers, offering an affordable path to homeownership. USDA loans require no down payment and tend to offer lower insurance rates and interest rates. There are two primary types of USDA loans: USDA Guaranteed Loans and USDA Direct Loans.

**USDA-guaranteed loans.** USDA loans are provided by private lenders but come with a USDA guarantee, making them accessible to low- and moderate-income borrowers who might struggle to secure conventional financing. Generally, applicants need a minimum credit score of 640, though exceptions may be made based on other financial factors. These loans apply exclusively to owner-occupied, single-family homes. USDA Guaranteed Loans come with an upfront guarantee fee of 1% of the loan amount, which can be financed, and an annual fee of 0.35% spread over monthly payments. The maximum LTV is 100% if the upfront fee is paid in cash or 101% if financed. USDA Guaranteed Loans typically enforce a front-end DTI of 29% and a back-end DTI of 41%.

**USDA direct loans.** Direct loans are issued directly by the USDA for very low- and low-income applicants, with income thresholds that vary by region and fall within 50% to 80% of the area's median income. Direct Loans do not require a down payment and feature subsidized interest rates, potentially as low as 1%, depending on the borrower's income and subsidy qualifications. Borrowers may also qualify for a payment assistance subsidy to reduce mortgage payments temporarily, based on family income. USDA Direct Loans allow repayment terms of up to 33 years, and up to 38 years for those with very low incomes who cannot manage a shorter term.

**Requirements for USDA-approved lenders.** Lenders seeking to issue USDA loans must apply for approval from the USDA and demonstrate their ability to originate, underwrite, close, and service loans that meet USDA standards. Further, the USDA prefers lenders who have experience with government-insured loan programs (such as FHA or VA loans) since USDA loans have similar guidelines and borrower protections.

Other requirements include:

- submit an application with detailed information on financial stability, experience with government-backed loans, and operational capacity
- demonstrate consistent financial stability, with regular financial reporting to the USDA to maintain approved status
- maintain a minimum net worth, which varies depending on the lender's size and volume of USDA-guaranteed loans
- understand USDA-specific processes, such as verifying borrower eligibility, handling income calculations for rural borrowers, and ensuring property eligibility
- establish a quality control program to oversee USDA loan origination, underwriting, closing, and servicing processes
- follow USDA underwriting guidelines, which include evaluating a borrower's credit, income, debt, and property eligibility based on USDA standards
- conduct regular internal audits and ongoing training for staff on USDA guidelines, particularly for underwriting and compliance with eligibility requirements
- use the USDA's Guaranteed Underwriting System (GUS), an automated underwriting system to assess eligibility for both the borrower and the property, as USDA loans have strict location and income requirements
- meet USDA's servicing standards for proper loan record maintenance, delinquency management, default resolution, borrower assistance, and foreclosure avoidance measures

Lenders must complete an annual recertification with the USDA, updating their financial and operational information and verifying continued compliance with USDA guidelines.

## Office of Public and Indian Housing (PIH) loans

**Loans for Native Americans, Alaska Natives, and lower-income families**. The PIH, a branch of the U.S. Department of Housing and Urban Development (HUD), provides various programs, including mortgage loan assistance, aimed at improving housing access and support for Native American communities, Alaska Natives, and low-income families. Its purpose is to mitigate some of the unique challenges related to property ownership and housing in these communities, such as:

- opportunities for affordable homeownership in underserved areas
- economic stability through fostering homeownership
- address specific property and land issues, such as leasing arrangements on trust land

**PIH loan programs.** PIH oversees two primary mortgage programs: the Section 184 Indian Home Loan Guarantee Program and the Section 184A Native Hawaiian Housing Loan Guarantee Program. Both programs feature loan guarantees for lenders and very low down payment requirements. They are also meant for primary residences only, whether to purchase, build, or rehabilitate / renovate an existing home. Further, both programs are only eligible in certain areas, such as federally recognized Indian reservations, designated tribal service areas, within certain approved areas for Alaska Natives, or for properties located on Hawaiian Home Lands.

**Requirements for PIH-approved lenders.** Lenders must apply for HUD approval to participate in Section 184 and Section 184A loan programs. This application process includes submitting documentation that demonstrates the lender's financial stability, operational capacity, and compliance with HUD's requirements. Approval also helps to ensure that a lender understands and is committed to serving the unique needs of tribal and Native Hawaiian borrowers. Beyond that, PIH generally prefers lenders with experience in government-insured or government-guaranteed loan programs, such as FHA, VA, or USDA loans, to help ensure compliance with PIH-specific processes.

Other PIH-lender requirements include:

- demonstrate they are financially capable of originating, underwriting, and servicing PIH loans
- establish a quality control program to oversee PIH loan origination, underwriting, closing, and servicing
- adhere to HUD's specific underwriting guidelines for Section 184 and 184A loans, such as evaluating borrowers' credit, income, and debt, while considering the unique circumstances often found in Native American and Native Hawaiian communities
- conduct regular internal audits, staff training on HUD guidelines, and systems monitoring to ensure that all PIH loans meet program standards
- navigate legal and procedural requirements for properties on trust or restricted lands to ensure proper loan documentation and enforceability
- understand these unique land situations, as they affect title, lien placement, and foreclosure processes
- provide financial updates to HUD periodically to maintain approved status

Lenders must recertify with HUD annually to verify their continued compliance with financial, operational, and program standards, as well as their capability in continuing to support Native American and Native Hawaiian borrowers. The process includes submitting updated financials and quality control documentation.

## Check Your Understanding

Which government loan program is primarily aimed at first-time homebuyers?

    A.  VA
    B.  USDA
    C.  FHA
    D.  PIH

Option C is correct! Federal Housing Administration (FHA) loans are primarily aimed at first-time homebuyers as well as lower-income individuals.

**Interested party contributions**

**Interested party contributions (IPCs)** are funds or financial incentives provided by parties involved in a real estate transaction—other than the buyer—toward the buyer's closing costs or other transactional expenses. Typically, these contributions come from sellers (aka seller's concessions), real estate agents, builders, or developers who have a vested interest in facilitating the sale. IPCs can cover items such as:

- closing costs, e.g., lender fees or title insurance
- prepaid expenses, e.g., property taxes and homeowners insurance
- interest rate buydowns, which reduce the borrower's interest rate

Different loan types have specific limits on how much can be contributed through IPCs. For example, **conventional conforming loan contribution limits** vary based on the loan's down payment. For primary residences and second homes:

- less than 10% down payment: 3% IPC cap
- 10% to 25% down payment: 6% IPC cap
- 25% or more down payment: 9% IPC cap

For investment properties, IPCs are usually capped at 2%, regardless of the down payment size.

**IPCs for government loans (FHA, VA, USDA).** FHA, VA, and USDA loans have their own specific limits and guidelines regarding IPCs, with generally lower or different caps than conventional loans.

- FHA limits seller concessions to 6% of the purchase price or appraised value, whichever is lower, regardless of the down payment amount. Sellers may not contribute to the down payment. When a seller contributes more than 6%, the sale price is reduced to make up for the overage. The lender then reduces the loan amount by the sum that exceeds the limit.

▸ With VA loans, sellers are not permitted to pay more than 4% of the total home loan in seller's concessions, but this rule only applies to certain costs, such as the VA funding fee. The limit does not apply to:
  ○ typical loan discount points
  ○ the buyer's closing costs

▸ The maximum for seller concessions for USDA loans is 6% of the purchase price. Exemptions to this limit include:
  ○ closing costs or prepaid items the lender pays through premium pricing
  ○ upfront guarantee fee
  ○ real estate commissions the seller pays on the buyer's behalf
  ○ single close construction loans, a type of mortgage that finances new home construction and then converts to a traditional mortgage after the home is built

**Excessive IPCs.** Excessive IPCs involved in a transaction tend to raise lender concerns because the IPCs may mask the property's true market value, potentially increasing the loan's risk. They do not actually affect the property's value, but they can indirectly impact it by inflating sale prices to offset the cost of these contributions. As a result, most loan programs cap IPCs, and lenders may require appraisers to consider the effect of any IPCs on the property's sale price.

*Example:* A buyer is interested in purchasing a house priced at $300,000. The buyer only has $45,000 for a down payment, which would result in a loan-to-value (LTV) ratio of 85%. However, the buyer wants a lower LTV ratio to avoid paying for private mortgage insurance (PMI).

The seller, who is eager to move, offers a solution: He will contribute $18,000 (more than the 6% IPC cap for this transaction) toward the buyer's closing costs and expenses if the buyer agrees to a final sale price of $315,000, enabling the seller to recoup $15,000 of the contribution. The seller's total contribution lowers the LTV ratio to 80% and eliminates the need for PMI for the buyer. The slight increase in price will only slightly affect the buyer's monthly payment on a 30-year loan.

On the surface, this seems like a win-win situation. The buyer gets a lower LTV ratio and avoids PMI, while the seller is able to sell their house faster. However, there are potential risks involved.

1. The $15,000 price increase to allow the seller to recoup most of the IPC may mask the true value of a property by artificially inflating the property's value. In this case, the house may not be worth the full $315,000.

2. In addition, this IPC can lead to appraisal issues. Appraisers may question the true value of the property if the sale price is significantly higher than recent comparable sales. This could delay the closing process and potentially lead to the loan being denied.

3. If the buyer defaults on the loan, the lender may only be able to recover a portion of the loan amount if the property is sold for less than the appraised value. This increases the risk of loss for the lender.

**Late fees**

Late fees on mortgages are penalties that lenders charge when a borrower fails to make a monthly mortgage payment by the designated due date. These fees are designed to encourage timely payments and compensate lenders for the additional administrative work and potential risk associated with late payments. Lenders are required to disclose all fee structures, including late fees, in the mortgage loan agreement and during the closing process.

Most mortgage agreements provide a short grace period, typically between 10 and 15 days after the payment due date, during which borrowers can make their payment without incurring a late fee. If a borrower pays within the grace period, the payment is considered on time, and no penalty is assessed.

Late fees are usually calculated as a percentage of the missed payment amount rather than a flat fee. Fannie Mae and Freddie Mac late fees are typically up to 5% of the principal and interest payment on conventional loan payments that are 16 or more days late. So, for example, if the mortgage payment is $1,500 and the late fee is 5%, the borrower would incur a $75 late fee if they miss the payment deadline.

Government-backed loans have their own requirements. For FHA loans made on or after March 16, 2016, a late charge cannot be more than 4% of the missed payment's principal and interest. Older loans may be assessed a late charge based on overdue principal, interest, taxes, and insurance, if the loan's terms and applicable laws permit it.

The USDA typically assesses a 4% late fee on the principal and interest of the late payment, unless the state in which the property is located stipulates a different percentage rate. VA loan late fees are typically capped at 4% of the late payment amount, which <u>must</u> be 16 or more days past due.

State laws and federal regulations can set limits on late fees, so lenders must comply with local restrictions, which might cap the maximum allowable fee or dictate when it can be assessed.

## Check Your Understanding

For which loan type are late fees capped at 5%?

A. Conventional
B. FHA
C. USDA
D. VA

The correct answer is A! Fannie Mae and Freddie Mac late fees are typically up to 5% of the principal and interest payment on conventional loan payments that are 16 or more days late.

## Mortgage-backed securities

**Mortgage-backed securities (MBS)** are financial instruments created by pooling together a group of mortgage loans and selling shares of this pool to investors in the secondary mortgage market. When homeowners make their monthly mortgage payments, the cash flows (principal and interest) are collected and distributed to MBS investors based on the terms of the security. MBS are divided into two main types: agency MBS and non-agency MBS, each with distinct risk and return profiles.

**Agency MBS** are issued by government-sponsored enterprises (GSEs) like Fannie Mae, Freddie Mac, or by Ginnie Mae, which are government-insured. These securities typically consist of **conforming loans**, meaning they meet the underwriting standards set by the GSEs, such as specific credit, loan-to-value, and income requirements. Because agency MBS generally include conforming, lower-risk loans, they are considered relatively safe investments with lower yields, appealing to risk-averse investors.

**Non-agency MBS**, on the other hand, are issued by private financial institutions, such as investment banks and mortgage companies, rather than government-backed entities. These securities frequently include **non-conforming loans**, which do not meet the guidelines set by Fannie Mae, Freddie Mac, or Ginnie Mae. Non-conforming loans can encompass various types, such as jumbo loans, subprime mortgages, and Alt-A mortgages. As a result, non-agency MBS often present higher risks but offer the potential for higher yields, making them attractive to investors with a greater risk tolerance.

Further, MBS can vary in structure and risk, with common types including:

**Pass-through securities**. Investors receive a proportional share of all principal and interest payments from the mortgage pool.

**Collateralized Mortgage Obligations** (CMOs). Payments are divided into "tranches" with varying levels of risk and payment schedules, allowing investors to choose a level of risk that suits their preferences.

## MORTGAGE LOAN PRODUCTS

**Fixed-rate mortgages**
**Adjustable rate mortgages (ARM)**
**Purchase money mortgages**
**Interest-only loans**
**Balloon mortgages**
**Reverse mortgages**
**HELOCs & home equity loans**
**Construction loans**

## Fixed-rate mortgage

A **fixed-rate mortgage** is a type of home loan in which the interest rate remains constant throughout the entire loan term. The rate is not affected by market fluctuations. This stability means that the <u>monthly principal and interest payments stay the same from the first payment to the last</u>, making fixed-rate mortgages predictable and easier to budget for over time.

One key advantage of a fixed-rate mortgage is that it acts as a form of protection against rising interest rates. If market rates increase, borrowers with fixed-rate mortgages continue to pay their agreed-upon interest rate, ensuring their housing costs are unaffected by external economic changes. Fixed-rate loans are typically offered in terms of 15, 20, or 30 years. While shorter terms result in higher monthly payments, they reduce the total interest paid over the life of the loan. Conversely, longer terms offer lower monthly payments but accrue more interest overall.

Fixed-rate mortgages are well-suited for borrowers who plan to stay in their homes for a long time, as they benefit from the predictability and stability of fixed payments. However, if interest rates drop significantly after securing the loan, borrowers can take advantage of lower rates by **refinancing** to a new mortgage, potentially lowering their monthly payments or shortening the loan term while still benefiting from stable rates.

## Adjustable rate mortgage (ARM)

An **adjustable-rate mortgage (ARM)** is a type of home loan in which the interest rate can change periodically throughout the loan term, generally after an initial fixed-rate period of 3, 5, 7, or 10 years. ARMs are tied to a specific **index**, which is a benchmark interest rate that reflects broader market conditions, such as the Constant Maturity Treasury (CMT) rate. As the index fluctuates, the ARM's interest rate adjusts accordingly, making monthly payments variable over time.

**Interest rate caps.** To prevent drastic changes, ARMs have built-in caps that limit how much the interest rate can adjust, both at each adjustment period and over the life of the loan:

1. **Initial cap**. The initial cap limits the rate increase at the first adjustment following the fixed-rate period.

2. **Periodic cap** (or adjustment cap). The periodic cap sets the maximum allowable increase for each subsequent adjustment period (e.g., annually or semi-annually).

3. **Lifetime cap**. The lifetime cap limits the total rate increase over the entire loan term.

**Margins and the fully indexed rate**. A key component of an ARM is the **margin**, which is a set percentage added to the index to determine the new interest rate at each adjustment. The **fully indexed rate** is the sum of the index and margin and typically represents the rate charged after the initial period ends. The **introductory rate** is the interest rate at closing, which may remain fixed for the duration of the initial period.

**Teaser rates in ARMs.** In some cases, lenders offer a **teaser rate**—an initial discounted rate below the fully indexed rate to attract borrowers. This rate applies only for a short period, after which the ARM's rate adjusts according to the index and margin. Teaser rates are often attractive to borrowers who plan to sell or refinance before the rate adjustments.

**Housing costs can increase.** Because the interest rate on an ARM is subject to periodic adjustment, monthly payments can become unpredictable, which makes this loan type appealing for borrowers who anticipate their income will rise or who plan to sell or refinance before the adjustments begin. However, ARMs can be riskier than fixed-rate loans if interest rates increase significantly or if a borrower's plans change, which can lead to "payment shock"—a sharp increase in monthly payments due to rate adjustments.

Borrowers who choose an ARM may later decide to refinance if they want to switch to a fixed-rate mortgage, especially if interest rates rise. While ARMs can be beneficial for borrowers who expect lower rates or plan to move within a few years, they require careful consideration of future financial stability and the potential for rising costs over time.

## Check Your Understanding

With an ARM, the _____ limits the rate increase at the first adjustment following the fixed-rate period.

   A. periodic cap
   B. introductory rate
   C. initial cap
   D. margin

Did you select C? The initial cap limits the rate increase at the first adjustment following the fixed-rate period.

**Purchase money mortgages**

A **purchase money mortgage** is a second-priority loan taken out by the buyer or a third party to help finance a home purchase. This loan can be used to supplement the primary mortgage or it can be a stand-alone loan for the entire purchase price.

For example, a buyer might use a purchase money second mortgage in an 80-10-10 arrangement to avoid paying private mortgage insurance (PMI). In this scenario, the primary mortgage covers 80% of the home's value, the second mortgage covers an additional 10%, and the buyer provides a 10% down payment. By using the second mortgage to bridge the financing gap, the buyer can avoid PMI while putting down less than 20%.

However, the interest rate on a purchase money second mortgage can be higher than the first mortgage since it is inherently riskier for the lender. Terms for second mortgages can vary; some may be short-term loans with a balloon payment, while others may be amortized over a longer period. Borrowers are responsible for making separate payments on both the primary and second mortgages. In the event of a foreclosure, the first mortgagor has priority for repayment, making the second mortgage riskier from the lender's perspective.

Advantages of a purchase money mortgage include:

- **lower down payment without PMI**: Buyers can purchase a home with less than a 20% down payment and avoid PMI, a significant monthly expense.
- **potential tax benefits**: Interest paid on both the first and second mortgages may be tax-deductible, providing a potential financial advantage for eligible borrowers.

Risks include:

- **Increased debt load**: A second mortgage increases the total amount of debt, which can strain the borrower's finances.
- **Two mortgage payments**: Borrowers must manage payments on both the primary and second mortgage, potentially resulting in higher overall monthly costs.
- **Risk of negative equity**: If home values decline, the borrower may end up owing more than the property is worth, particularly with a high combined loan amount.

Because of the added risk, lenders typically require good credit and a stable income for borrowers seeking a purchase money second mortgage. These qualifications help offset the lender's risk and provide assurance that the borrower can manage the dual payments.

## Check Your Understanding

Purchase money second mortgages are

A. almost always short-term with a balloon payment at the end of the term.
B. equally as risky for lenders as a first mortgage.
C. rolled into the first mortgage for ease in payments.
D. helpful in avoiding paying private mortgage insurance (PMI).

The answer is D!  A purchase money second mortgage can help buyers avoid paying private mortgage insurance (PMI).

## Interest-only loans

An **interest-only loan** is a mortgage option where the borrower pays only the interest for a set period, typically the first 5-10 years of the loan. During this interest-only phase, the borrower's payments are lower because principal payments are deferred, meaning the loan balance remains the same without reduction. Once the interest-only period ends, however, the loan generally converts to a standard amortizing loan, requiring payments on both principal and interest, which leads to a significant increase in monthly payments. Interest-only loans can come with either fixed or adjustable interest rates.

> ▸ **fixed-rate interest-only loan**: The interest rate remains the same throughout the loan, providing consistent interest payments during the interest-only period.
> ▸ **adjustable-rate interest-only loan**: The interest rate may change after the interest-only period ends, making future payments variable and potentially riskier due to potential rate increases.

Borrowers often choose interest-only loans if they expect their income to increase significantly in the future, plan to sell the property before the interest-only period concludes, or intend to refinance to a different loan. These loans are also popular among investors who want lower initial payments to enhance cash flow.

The lower monthly payments during the interest-only period can free up cash for other uses, such as investing, doing home improvements, or managing irregular income. However, risks include:

> ▸ payment shock when monthly payments increase substantially as principal payments are added
> ▸ refinancing challenges if the borrower's income does not grow as expected, or if property values do not increase

In a stagnant or declining market, the borrower may end up with a property worth less than the loan balance, complicating refinancing or a sale.

Interest-only loans can be more challenging to qualify for due to their elevated risk and are subject to availability based on market conditions. Borrowers considering these loans should carefully assess their future income expectations and market forecasts, as well as develop a plan for managing the higher payments once the interest-only period concludes.

**Balloon mortgages**

A **balloon mortgage** is a short-term loan that features relatively low monthly payments for an initial period, typically 5 to 7 years, followed by a large final payment known as the "balloon" payment. This balloon payment covers the remaining principal balance, resulting in a substantial one-time amount due at the end of the loan term.

Balloon mortgages are structured to offer lower initial payments compared to a standard fixed-rate mortgage, as the **amortization schedule** is often set for a longer term than the actual loan period. For example, a 5-year balloon mortgage might have payments calculated as if the loan were amortized over 30 years, resulting in lower monthly payments. However, at the end of the 5-year term, the remaining balance comes due in a single, large balloon payment.

Interest rates on balloon mortgages can vary and are sometimes higher to offset the lender's increased risk of a shorter loan term. Balloon mortgages are an option for <u>borrowers who plan to refinance, sell the property, or pay off the loan with cash</u> by the time the balloon payment is due. This strategy is common for individuals who expect their financial situation to improve in the near future or who intend to move within the loan term.

A significant risk is the borrower's potential inability to pay the large balloon payment when it comes due. If the borrower is unable to refinance or sell the property, they may face financial difficulty, which could lead to foreclosure.

Due to these risks, balloon mortgages are less common than fixed-rate or adjustable-rate mortgages and are sometimes used in commercial real estate or for specific scenarios where borrowers have a well-defined plan to handle the balloon payment.

### Check Your Understanding

How are balloon mortgages structured so that they offer lower initial payments that fixed-rate mortgages do?

A. The amortization schedule is often set for a longer term than the actual loan period.
B. Interest rates are higher to offset the lender's increased risk of a shorter loan term.
C. Monthly payments during the term are interest only.
D. Borrowers make separate payments: interest only for 5-7 years, and then PITI for the remainder of the loan term.

If you choose A, then you are right! Balloon mortgages are structured to offer lower initial payments compared to a standard fixed-rate mortgage, as the amortization schedule is often set for a longer term than the actual loan period.

**Reverse mortgages**  A **reverse mortgage** is a specialized loan product designed for seniors age 62 and older, allowing them to convert a portion of their home's equity into cash without selling the property or taking on additional debt. Instead of making monthly payments to a lender, as with a traditional mortgage, the homeowner receives payments from the lender, effectively borrowing from the equity they have accumulated in their home.

**Reverse mortgage mechanics.** The amount available to borrow depends on factors such as the home's current market value, the borrower's age, and prevailing interest rates. Reverse mortgage payments can be structured in various ways: as a lump sum, a line of credit, or regular monthly installments, depending on the homeowners needs and preferences.

Interest and fees do apply to reverse mortgages, and they can be higher than those associated with other loan types. These costs, which include origination fees, insurance, and closing costs, are typically deferred until a specific trigger event occurs. Common triggers include the homeowner selling the home, moving out permanently, or passing away. At that point, the home is usually sold, and the proceeds are used to repay the loan's principal, accumulated interest, and fees.

One of the unique aspects of reverse mortgages is that <u>borrowers do not risk defaulting due to non-payment</u>, as no monthly mortgage payments are required. Instead, the homeowners equity in the property decreases over time as payments are made against it, which can reduce the amount of equity heirs might inherit. However, federally insured reverse mortgages are non-recourse loans, meaning that neither the borrower nor their heirs can owe more than the home's value, even if the loan balance exceeds it.

Due to the complex nature of reverse mortgages, <u>HUD-approved financial counseling is generally required</u>. This counseling helps ensure that borrowers understand the implications of reverse mortgages, including their effect on home equity and inheritance, and are fully informed about the costs and repayment terms.

Reverse mortgages offer a flexible financial option for seniors who need access to cash or who want to remain in their home without traditional monthly mortgage payments. However, they are best suited for those who fully understand these implications and have a long-term plan in place.

## Check Your Understanding

One unique aspect of reverse mortgages is that:

    A.  interest and fees do not apply.
    B.  only small monthly mortgage payments are required.
    C.  borrowers do not risk defaulting due to non-payment.
    D.  they are available to all borrowers regardless of credit scores.

One of the unique aspects of reverse mortgages is that borrowers do not risk defaulting due to non-payment, as no monthly mortgage payments are required. Option C is correct.

## HELOCs and home equity loans

**HELOCS.** A **home equity line of credit (HELOC)** is a revolving line of credit that allows homeowners to borrow against the equity in their home. Since it is secured by the property itself, a HELOC provides a flexible borrowing option for homeowners. Borrowers are approved for a maximum loan amount, but they can withdraw funds as needed, up to this limit, rather than taking out the entire amount at once. They also only pay interest on the funds they actually use. HELOC interest rates are usually variable, meaning they fluctuate based on market conditions, making monthly payments potentially unpredictable. HELOCs are often used for home improvements, debt consolidation, emergency expenses, or educational costs, offering homeowners a flexible financing solution.

HELOCs have two main phases:

    ▶  **draw period**: During this initial phase, the borrower can withdraw funds as needed, often only paying interest on the borrowed amount.

    ▶  **repayment period**: When the draw period ends, the borrower enters the repayment phase, during which they repay both principal and interest.

**Home equity loans.** In contrast to a HELOC, a **home equity loan** provides the borrower with a lump sum amount based on the equity in the home. The loan is structured like a traditional loan with a fixed interest rate and fixed monthly payments over a set term, typically 5-15 years. Since the interest rate and payment schedule are fixed, home equity loans offer predictability, making them ideal for borrowers who need a specific amount of money for a one-time expense, such as a major home renovation or consolidating debt.

A _____ is a revolving line of credit that allows homeowners to borrow against the equity in their home.

    A. home equity loan
    B. purchase money second mortgage
    C. HELOC
    D. reverse mortgage

Option C is the correct answer! A home equity line of credit (HELOC) is a revolving line of credit that allows homeowners to borrow against the equity in their home.

## Construction loans

A **construction loan** is a short-term loan designed to finance the building of a new home or significant property renovation. Typically, construction loans last about a year, covering the duration of the project, after which borrowers refinance into a traditional mortgage, often called a "construction-to-permanent" loan.

Construction loans come with higher risks than standard mortgages, so lenders require stringent underwriting standards. Lenders assess not only the borrower's credit, income, and debt-to-income ratio but also the feasibility of the construction project itself. This includes reviewing a detailed construction plan, budget, timeline, and builder or contractor qualifications and stability. An appraisal is often required to confirm that the loan amount aligns with the property's projected value upon completion. Some loans may also include interest reserves to cover interest payments during construction and contingency funds for unexpected expenses.

Funds are disbursed in stages, known as "draws," to the builder as construction reaches specified milestones. Each draw requires inspection and approval to ensure that construction is proceeding as planned. Borrowers typically make interest-only payments during the construction phase, based only on the disbursed funds, not the full loan amount.

Due to the higher risk, construction loans generally carry higher interest rates and may require a substantial down payment, often 20-25%. Once construction is complete, the loan is converted to a traditional mortgage, securing long-term financing for the newly built property.

## Check Your Understanding

Construction loans differ substantially from other mortgage loans. Which of the following is NOT an attribute of construction loans?

    A. Funds are disbursed in draws to the builder as construction reaches specified milestones.
    B. Lenders assess the feasibility of the construction project itself in addition to assessing the borrower's criteria.
    C. Borrowers typically make interest-only payments during the construction phase, based only on the disbursed funds.
    D. Borrowers take out a second mortgage once the home is built while they pay off the construction loan.

Option D is correct! With construction loans, borrowers do not take out a second mortgage once the home is built while they pay off the construction loan. A construction loan is a short-term loan designed to finance the building of a new home or significant property renovation. Typically, construction loans last about a year, covering the duration of the project, after which borrowers refinance into a traditional mortgage, often called a "construction-to-permanent" loan.

## The Mortgage Market

- **Conventional (Private) Loans**
  - Qualified/Conforming Loans
    - General QM's
    - Temporary QM's
    - Small Lender QM's
    - Balloon QM's
  - Non-Qualified Mortgages Conventional/Nonconforming Loans
    - Jumbo Loans
    - Alt-A Loans
    - Sub-Prime Loans
- **Government-Backed Loans**
  - FHA Loans
  - VA Loans
  - USDA Loans
  - PIH (Indian) Loans

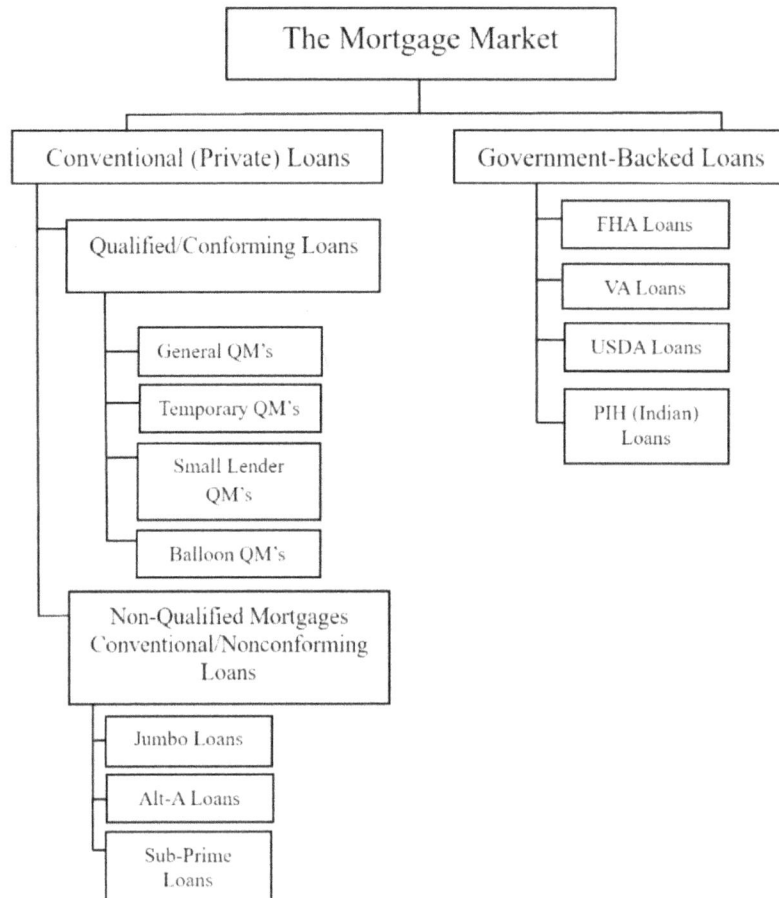

## TERMS USED IN THE MORTGAGE INDUSTRY

**acceleration clause**: a loan provision allowing the lender to demand full repayment if the borrower defaults or violates loan terms

**accrued interest**: interest on a loan or mortgage that accumulates over time but has not yet been paid; for mortgages, it is interest that has accrued each month between payments

**adjustable-rate mortgage (ARM)**: type of home loan with an interest rate that can change periodically over the life of the loan, typically after an initial fixed-rate period; rate adjusts based on an index plus a fixed margin

**amortization schedule**: a table detailing each periodic payment on a loan over time, showing how much goes toward principal and how much goes toward interest

**annual percentage rate (APR)**: broad measure of a loan's total cost; represents annual cost of funds over loan term; includes interest rate, broker fees, finance charges, discount points, and some closing costs, etc.; expressed as a percentage

**assumable loans**: mortgage loans that can be transferred from seller to buyer, who takes over mortgage payments, often benefiting from existing interest rates that may be lower than current market rates

**balloon payment**: a large payment due at the end of a balloon loan, covering the remaining principal balance: this type of loan typically has lower monthly payments with the balance due at maturity

**buydown**: financing option that allows a borrower to pay a lower interest rate and reduced mortgage payments by paying discount points up front; can be temporary or permanent

**2-1 buydown**: financing technique that reduces mortgage interest rate in a stepped fashion during loan's initial years, then reverts to standard rate for remaining term; e.g., 2% reduction in first year and 1% in second year ; buydown fee can be paid by borrower, home seller, or builder as incentive to purchase

**cash-out refinance**: a refinance option that allows the borrower to take out additional cash by refinancing for more than they owe and pocketing the difference

**Closing Disclosure (CD)**: a comprehensive form provided to borrowers at least three business days before closing; includes final loan terms, monthly payment details, fees, and closing costs, allowing borrowers to review all costs associated with the loan and compare them with the initial Loan Estimate

**commercial bank**: financial institution that provides services such as accepting deposits, providing business loans, offering basic investment products, and often offering mortgage loans

**conveyance**: act of transferring ownership of a property from one party to another; typically done through a legal document such as deed or title

**current index rate**: value of the chosen index at the time of an ARM adjustment; used to calculate new fully indexed rate in combination with the margin

**DTI ratio**: measures borrower's monthly debt load compared to gross monthly income; used to assess borrower's ability to manage monthly payments and repay debts

**debt consolidation**: combining multiple debts into a single loan with one monthly payment, often to lower monthly payments or interest rates

**deed of trust**: a legal document similar to a mortgage that involves a borrower, lender, and trustee; the trustee holds the title until the borrower repays the loan

**Desktop Underwriter (DU)**: Fannie Mae's automated underwriting system that analyzes a borrower's financial information to determine whether it meets Fannie Mae's lending guidelines

**discount point**: a fee equal to 1% of total loan amount, paid at closing to reduce interest rate

**discount rate**: the interest rate charged by the Federal Reserve to banks for borrowing funds; influences other interest rates, including mortgage rates

**down payment**: initial lump sum borrower pays upfront when purchasing a property, typically a percentage of total purchase price

**encumbrance**: a legal claim, right, or restriction on a property that can affect that property's transfer (sale or other conveyance) or reduce its value

**escrow**: funds lenders collect from borrowers and then hold to pay certain expenses related to homeownership, e.g., property taxes and homeowners' insurance

**escrow account**: third-party account that holds funds until transaction conditions are fulfilled; often holds buyer's earnest money or funds for property taxes and homeowners insurance

**escrow analysis**: a periodic review of escrow accounts by the lender to ensure enough funds are set aside for property taxes and insurance

**escrow payment**: a portion of a borrower's monthly mortgage payment placed into an escrow account to cover property taxes and insurance

**equity**: the difference between the current market value of the property and the outstanding mortgage balance; represents the homeowners ownership stake

**federal mortgage loan**: loans guaranteed or insured by the federal government; includes FHA loans, VA loans, and USDA loans

**FICO score**: a credit score developed by the Fair Isaac Corporation; commonly used by lenders to assess a borrower's credit risk

**finance charge**: total cost of borrowing, including interest, origination fee, discount points, mortgage insurance, lender charges, etc.; represents entire loan cost to borrower

**fixed-rate mortgage**: type of home loan where the interest rate remains constant throughout the life of the loan; borrower's monthly principal and interest payments do not change over time

**floating rate (adjustable rate)**: interest rate that changes over life of loan; typically tied to index like the prime rate

**fully indexed rate**: interest rate on an ARM after adjustments, calculated by adding the margin to the current index rate; the rate borrowers pay after initial fixed-rate period, subject to any caps

**housing ratio**: indicates the portion of income used to pay housing costs, including mortgage payments, insurance, property taxes, and homeowners association fees; aka front-end ratio

**index**: benchmark interest rate used in ARMs to reflect general market conditions; common indices include Constant Maturity Treasury (CMT), London Interbank Offered Rate (LIBOR), or Secured Overnight Financing Rate (SOFR)

**index rate**: specific interest rate value of the chosen index at a given time; serves as starting point for calculating adjustable interest rate on an ARM

**interest:** fee that lenders charge borrowers for the use of funds, typically expressed as a percentage of the loan amount; calculated over time and often paid in periodic installments

**interest rate cap**: a limit on the amount that an ARM's interest rate can increase at each adjustment period (periodic cap) or over the life of the loan (lifetime cap)

**Interested Party Contributions (IPCs):** funds or financial incentives provided to the buyer by other parties involved in a real estate transaction toward buyer's closing costs or other transactional expenses; typically paid by sellers but can also be paid by real estate agents, builders, or developers; limitations apply based on loan type

**lender credit**: funds lender provides to help cover borrower's closing costs, typically in exchange for higher interest rate; reduces amount of cash borrower needs at closing but typically results in higher costs over loan life

**lien**: legal claim or right against a property; often used as security for a debt in which property acts as collateral against amount owed; when debt is not paid, lien holder can seize property; common types include mortgage liens, tax liens, and mechanic's liens

Loan Estimate (LE): a standardized form that replaced the Good Faith Estimate (GFE) and the initial Truth in Lending (15 U.S.C. §1601 et seq.) Disclosure (TIL) for most residential loans; provided to borrowers within three business days of loan application, it details estimated loan costs, including the annual percentage rate (APR), interest rate, monthly payments, and closing costs, helping borrowers understand their financial commitment upfront

**loan modification**: a change made to the terms of an existing loan due to borrower hardship; may include lowering the interest rate, extending the loan term, or reducing the principal

**Loan Product Advisor (LPA)**: Freddie Mac's automated underwriting system that evaluates a borrower's financial profile to assess their eligibility for Freddie Mac's loan products

**loan subordination**: a lender agrees to position their loan claim below another lender's claim in terms of priority for debt repayment in event of default; most often relevant when refinancing a first mortgage and holder of second mortgage allows their loan to remain in secondary position

**LTV ratio**: compares loan amount to property's value; calculated by dividing loan amount by property's appraised value or purchase price, whichever is lower; used to assess lender's risk; higher LTV ratio is riskier

**margin**: fixed number of percentage points added to the index rate to determine the fully indexed interest rate on an ARM; set in the loan agreement and does not change over the life of the loan

**mortgage-backed securities (MBS)**: financial instruments created by pooling together a group of mortgage loans and selling shares of this pool to investors; two types exist: agency MBS and non-agency MBS

**mortgage banker:** an individual, firm, or corporation that originates, sells, and services mortgage loans; typically uses their own funds for financing or obtains them from a warehouse lender

**mortgage broker**: acts as an intermediary who brokers mortgage loans on behalf of individuals or businesses; does not fund loans but finds lenders for borrowers

**mortgage insurance premium (MIP)**: insurance required for FHA loans that protects the lender against borrower default; typically paid both as an upfront fee and an annual premium

**mortgage loan**: a type of loan that is secured by real property, documented through an agreement that establishes both the existence of the loan and an encumbrance on the property itself; aka **mortgage**

**negative amortization**: when monthly payments are not large enough to cover interest due on a loan; unpaid interest is added to principal balance, so total amount of debt increases over time

**origination fee**: a fee charged by the lender for processing a loan application, typically a percentage of the loan amount

**per diem interest**: interest that accumulates every day instead of monthly or another period; aka daily interest

**period interest:** interest that accumulates over a specific time period, often on a regular basis, such as monthly or annually; aka periodic interest

**permanent buydown:** allows borrower to secure a lower interest rate for entire life of the loan; aka fixed-rate buydown

**PITI:** the four components of a typical monthly mortgage payment: principal, interest, taxes, and insurance

**positive amortization**: loan balance decreases over time as payments are made; typical in standard loan repayment plans where monthly payments cover interest and portion of principal

**prepaid interest**: payment that borrowers pay at closing to cover interest that begins to accrue on the day after closing to the end of that same month

**prepaid items:** costs borrowers pay up front at closing to ensure certain expenses are covered in advance

**prepayment penalty**: a fee that some lenders charge if a borrower pays off the mortgage early, compensating the lender for the loss of interest payments

**primary market**: where borrowers and mortgage originators come together to negotiate terms and create a mortgage loan

**private mortgage insurance (PMI)**: a type of insurance that protects the lender if a borrower defaults on a conventional loan with a down payment of less than 20%; generally paid as a monthly premium; automatically removed once the LTV ratio reaches 78%; borrowers can request cancellation when their equity in the home reaches 20%

**promissory note**: a written promise to repay a loan, outlining terms such as interest rate, payment schedule, and penalties for default

**prorated items:** ongoing costs that are divided proportionately between buyer and seller at closing based on the length of time each party owns the property during the billing period

**Rate-lock agreement**: lender's promise to hold certain interest rate and specific number of points for a buyer for specified period while loan application processes; protects borrower from rate fluctuations during loan application process

**recasting**: the process of re-amortizing a mortgage after a large lump sum payment, which reduces the monthly payment while keeping the same loan term

**refinance:** process of replacing an existing mortgage with a new loan, typically to achieve better loan terms, such as a lower interest rate, reduced monthly payments, or a shorter loan term

**reserves:** liquid assets a borrower must show they have in reserve after closing, measured in the number of months of mortgage payments the funds could cover

**right of rescission**: under the Truth in Lending Act (TILA), this is the borrower's right to cancel a refinance or home equity loan within three business days of closing, without penalty; only applies to refinances of primary residences and not to new purchase loans

**secondary market**: where loans that originated in primary market are sold to investors; includes enterprises like Fannie Mae and Freddie Mac, which buy mortgages and package them into securities

**securitization**: the financial process of pooling various types of debt and transforming them into securities to be sold to investors

**servicing transfer**: occurs when a company handling and processing a loan (servicer) transfers this responsibility to another company; requires borrower notification and details, such as new servicer's name and contact details; does not affect borrower or other payment terms

**settlement**: conclusion of a real estate transaction; property's title transfers from seller to buyer, and all necessary payments and paperwork are completed

**subordinate loan**: type of loan ranked below primary loan in terms of claim on property assets in the event of default; subordinate loan creditors are paid after primary or senior debt holders; higher risk so typically a higher interest rate

**table funding**: mortgage broker originates and processes a loan but a third party (e.g., a wholesale lender) funds loan at closing table

**teaser rate**: an initial, temporarily low interest rate on an adjustable-rate mortgage (arm), which is lower than the rate will eventually adjust to

**temporary buydown:** reduces loan's interest rate for a specified period, e.g., three or fewer years

**third-party provider**: company that or individual who provides services to lenders or borrowers in the course of originating, processing, or closing a mortgage loan; includes appraisers, title companies, credit reporting agencies, and attorneys

**third-party provider**: company that or individual who provides services to lenders or borrowers in the course of originating, processing, or closing a mortgage loan; includes appraisers, title companies, credit reporting agencies, and attorneys

tolerance: limit on how much final closing costs can exceed estimates provided in Loan Estimate form; set by the Real Estate Settlement Procedures Act (RESPA (12 U.S.C. §2601 et seq.)); cost categories are zero tolerance, 10% cumulative tolerance, and no or unlimited tolerance, and each has specific rules on cost increases

**thrift**: financial institution that primarily accepts savings deposits and makes mortgage and other loans; aka savings and loan associations

**title insurance**: insurance that protects lenders and/or homeowners against losses due to disputes over property ownership or title defects

**underwriting**: the process a lender uses to assess the risk of lending money, examining factors like the borrower's credit, employment, income, debt obligations and net worth

**yield spread premium**: compensation a mortgage broker or loan officer receives for originating a loan with interest rate higher than lender's par rate, i.e., rate at which lender would not pay a rebate or charge a fee; profit a broker makes for selling a higher-than-par-rate loan

# Chapter 2: General Mortgage Knowledge
# Snapshot Review

**THE MORTGAGE MARKET AND MORTGAGE LOAN PROGRAMS**

**Mortgage market overview**

- primary market: where borrowers obtain loans from lenders.
- secondary market: where existing loans are sold to investors; major players include Fannie Mae, Freddie Mac, Ginnie Mae, FHLB, and private investors.
- **Fannie Mae and Freddie Mac:** GSEs that buy conforming loans and securitize them into MBS; set underwriting standards and loan limits; use automated underwriting (DU for Fannie; LPA for Freddie).
- **Ginnie Mae:** government agency that guarantees MBS with federally insured loans (FHA, VA, USDA); does not buy or sell loans directly.
- **Federal Home Loan Bank System (FHLB):** provides liquidity and support to more than 8,000 member institutions; focused on affordable housing and community development.
- private investors: purchase securities backed by mortgages

**Mortgage loans**

- loan secured by real property; mortgage creates an encumbrance

**General mortgage loan categories**

- conventional loans: Not backed by government; can be conforming or non-conforming.
- government loans: backed by FHA, VA, USDA.

**Conventional / conforming loans**

- meet Fannie/Freddie guidelines.
- not insured or guaranteed
- loan limit for 2025: $806,500 (higher in some areas).
- minimum credit score: 620; min down payment: 3%.
- PMI required less than 20% down.
- maximum DTI: ~45%; max LTV: ~97%.
- risk-based pricing via LLPAs.
- special low-down programs: HomeReady and HomePossible.

**Qualified mortgages (QMs)**

- meet CFPB standards: less risky features (e.g., negative amortization, balloons), max 30-year term, DTI cap of 43%.
- cap on fees (3% for most loans).

|  |  |
|---|---|
| | • offer lender legal protection ("safe harbor"). |
| | • categories: general, temporary, small lender, balloon-payment QMs. |
| | • exempt: reverse mortgages, bridge loans, timeshares, etc. |
| **Non-qualified mortgages (Non-QMs)** | • do not conform to Dodd-Frank or CFPB requirements |
| | • may have features like interest-only, balloon, longer terms. |
| | • higher costs and less regulatory protection. |
| | • often used by self-employed or high-DTI borrowers. |
| **Conventional / non-conforming loans** | • jumbo loans: exceed conforming loan limits; stricter criteria. |
| | • alt-A loans: for borrowers with non-traditional income or credit. |
| | • subprime loans: for high-risk borrowers (low credit scores, high DTI). |
| | • governed by 2006 "Guidance on Non-Traditional Mortgage Product Risk" |
| **Government-backed loans** | • non-conventional |
| | • provide structural support for borrowers |
| | • include FHA, VA, and USDA loans |
| **FHA loans** | • low down payments (3.5% with 580+ credit score). |
| | • UFMIP and annual MIP required. |
| | • strict appraisal and property standards. |
| | • loan limits vary by county. |
| | • assumable and no prepayment penalty. |
| **VA loans** | • no down payment or PMI. |
| | • eligibility via COE. |
| | • DTI up to 41%, residual income test. |
| | • one-time funding fee (waived for some). |
| | • assumable and favorable terms. |
| **USDA loans** | • for rural areas. |
| | • no down payment; income and location limits. |
| | • guaranteed loans: issued by lenders, backed by USDA |
| | • direct loans: issued by USDA; subsidized. |
| | • guarantee fees apply; must meet DTI caps. |
| | • PIH programs (Section 184/184A): |
| | • Native American and Native Hawaiian borrowers. |
| | • minimal down payment and loan guarantees. |
| | • only for primary residences in eligible areas. |

| | |
|---|---|
| **Interested party contributions (IPCs)** | • limits vary by loan type and down payment. |
| | • excessive IPCs can distort property value and create appraisal/lending issues. |
| | • sample limits by loan category: |
| |     ○ conventional: 3–9% based on down payment. |
| |     ○ FHA/USDA: capped at 6%. |
| |     ○ VA: capped at 4% for certain items. |
| **Late fees** | • typically assessed after 15-day grace period. |
| | • calculated as a percentage of principal and interest. |
| | • caps vary: conventional: up to 5%; FHA, VA, USDA: typically 4% |
| **Mortgage-backed securities (MBS)** | • created by pooling mortgage loans and selling shares to investors. |
| | • agency MBS: issued by GSEs, lower risk. |
| | • non-agency MBS: issued by private firms, higher risk/yield. |
| | • types include pass-through securities and CMOs. |

## MORTGAGE LOAN PRODUCTS

| | |
|---|---|
| **Fixed-rate mortgages** | • interest rate remains constant for the entire loan term. |
| | • monthly principal and interest payments are predictable and stable. |
| | • available in terms such as 15, 20, or 30 years. |
| | • ideal for long-term homeowners and stable budgets. |
| | • borrowers can refinance if market rates drop significantly. |
| **Adjustable-rate mortgages (ARM)** | • interest rate changes periodically after an initial fixed period (e.g., 3, 5, 7, 10 years). |
| | • Tied to an index + margin = fully indexed rate. |
| | • includes caps: initial, periodic, and lifetime. |
| | • may include teaser rates during the introductory period. |
| | • suitable for borrowers expecting income growth or short-term ownership. |
| | • risk of payment shock if rates rise significantly. |
| **Purchase money mortgages** | • commonly a second-priority junior loan taken back by seller to reduce the down payment on the underlying first loan. |
| | • common in 80-10-10 LTV structures to avoid PMI. |
| | • higher risk for lenders = higher interest rate than primary loan. |
| | • borrowers make two separate payments. |
| | • can increase debt burden and risk of negative equity (debt exceeds value). |

| | |
|---|---|
| **Interest-only loans** | • only interest is paid for an initial period (5–10 years). |
| | • loan balance does not decrease during this period. |
| | • lower initial payments; higher payments begin after the interest-only phase. |
| | • available with fixed or adjustable rates. |
| | • often chosen by investors or borrowers expecting higher future income. |
| | • risk: payment shock, refinance difficulty, negative equity in flat/down markets. |
| **Balloon mortgages** | • short-term loan (typically 5–7 years) with low monthly payments. |
| | • ends with a large lump-sum "balloon" payment. |
| | • payments often amortized over 30 years for lower monthly costs. |
| | • suitable for borrowers planning to sell, refinance, or pay off the loan before the balloon is due. |
| | • risk: inability to make the final payment may lead to default. |
| **Reverse mortgages** | • for homeowners aged 62+ to convert home equity into cash. |
| | • borrowers receive payments instead of making them. |
| | • no monthly mortgage payments required; loan repaid upon death, move, or sale. |
| | • federally insured reverse mortgages are non-recourse. |
| | • HUD-approved counseling required. |
| | • ideal for seniors wanting to stay in their home while accessing equity. |
| | • equity diminishes over time; can affect inheritance. |
| **HELOCS and home equity loans)** | • **HELOCS**: revolving credit line based on home equity; variable interest rates; pay interest only on funds used; two phases: draw period (interest-only) and repayment period (principal + interest); flexible and reusable for expenses like renovations or emergencies |
| | • **home equity loans**: lump sum loan based on home equity; fixed interest rate and fixed monthly payments; suitable for one-time expenses (e.g., large renovations, debt consolidation) |
| | • predictable payments over 5–15 years. |
| **Construction loans** | • short-term financing for building a new home or major renovation. |
| | • converts to permanent mortgage upon project completion. |
| | • higher interest rates; often interest-only during construction. |
| | • funds disbursed in draws as construction progresses. |
| | • requires detailed plans, appraisals, and strong borrower and contractor qualifications. |
| | • may include interest reserves and contingency funds. |

# Chapter 2 Quiz: General Mortgage Knowledge

1. Which of the following best describes an encumbrance in the context of a mortgage loan?

   a. A government grant used to subsidize closing costs
   b. A restriction or claim that may affect a property's value or transfer
   c. A type of private mortgage insurance
   d. An agreement between buyer and seller to add an easement to the deed

2. Which of the following would be classified as a non-conforming loan?

   a. A loan underwritten to Freddie Mac guidelines
   b. A USDA loan used for a rural property
   c. A jumbo loan that doesn't meet Fannie Mae standards
   d. A fixed-rate loan offered by a private bank

3. Jason just applied for a mortgage with his local credit union and was approved for a loan to purchase a home. Which part of the mortgage market is Jason participating in?

   a. Primary mortgage market
   b. Secondary mortgage market
   c. Government-backed securities market
   d. Mortgage insurance market

4. A mortgage company originates a conforming loan and sells it to Fannie Mae, which then bundles it with similar loans and sells it to investors as a mortgage-backed security. Why does this process appeal to investors?

   a. It guarantees investors a profit on every loan.
   b. It increases the number of loans investors can buy, since borrowers with lower credit scores can piggyback into packages with loans to borrowers with better credit.
   c. It ensures investors receive timely payments of principal and interest, even if the borrower defaults.
   d. It exempts investors from paying taxes on gains if any borrower defaults on a packaged loan.

5. An investor is looking for a relatively safe investment and prefers lower risk over high returns. Based on the characteristics of mortgage-backed securities (MBS) which of the following types of investment would best suit this investor?

   a. Subprime MBS
   b. Agency MBS
   c. Non-agency MBS
   d. Jumbo loan pool

6. Which of the following is a feature required for a loan to be classified as a qualified mortgage (QM)?

   a. The borrower's total debt-to-income (DTI) ratio must be 43% or less.
   b. The loan must include a balloon payment.
   c. The loan term must be exactly 30 years.
   d. The borrower must waive any right to sue.

7. A small rural lender approves a mortgage for a borrower in an underserved area. The lender meets the size and volume limits set for small creditors and follows all other qualified mortgage requirements. The loan has a large final payment due at the end of the term. What type of qualified mortgage does this describe?

   a. Temporary QM
   b. Small lender QM
   c. Balloon-payment QM
   d. General QM

8. A borrower applies for a loan of $900,000 to purchase a single-unit home in an area where the conforming loan limit is $806,500. Which of the following best describes this loan?

   a. It qualifies as a conforming loan because it is for a single-family home.
   b. It qualifies as a conventional, non-conforming loan due to the loan amount.
   c. It is a government-backed loan due to the high loan amount.
   d. It is automatically approved under Ginnie Mae's loan criteria.

9. Which of the following factors could trigger a Loan-Level Price Adjustment (LLPA)?

   a. The borrower uses the loan for home improvements.
   b. The borrower is approved for a VA-guaranteed mortgage.
   c. The property is located in a rural area with an average income lower than the national average.
   d. The borrower has a high LTV ratio and a low credit score.

10. Other than being paid upfront, what key characteristic distinguishes the Up Front MIP (UFMIP) from the MIP on an FHA loan?

    a. UFMIP has a higher rate, typically 1.75% of the loan amount.
    b. UFMIP is paid annually in addition to the regular mortgage payment.
    c. UFMIP is required only if the borrower puts down less than 10%.
    d. UFMIP varies based on property location and loan term.

11. Which of the following closing cost charges on a VA loan is limited by regulation and cannot exceed 1% of the loan amount?

    a. Title insurance
    b. VA funding fee
    c. Appraisal fee
    d. Loan origination fee

12. Which type of property is eligible for a USDA Guaranteed Loan?

    a. A single-family home the borrower uses as a vacation property when they want to get out of the city
    b. A two-unit investment property that includes designated farmland
    c. A primary residence for the borrower
    d. A commercial mixed-use building

13. Why do subprime loans usually have higher interest rates than traditional loans?

    a. They are only available to investors.
    b. They come with longer loan terms.
    c. They are backed by government guarantees.
    d. They carry higher risk for the lender.

14. A borrower has a remaining loan balance of $250,000 and an annual interest rate of 6%. What is the monthly interest amount based on this balance?

    a. $1,250
    b. $1,500
    c. $1,200
    d. $1,150

15. A borrower has a monthly principal payment of $850 and an interest payment of $450. Their annual property tax bill is $4,200, and their annual homeowner's insurance premium is $1,800. What is the borrower's total monthly PITI payment?

    a. $1,200
    b. $1,300
    c. $1,550
    d. $1,800

16. A borrower is putting down 15% on a primary residence using a conventional conforming loan. What is the maximum Interested Party Contribution (IPC) allowed?

    a. 2%
    b. 3%
    c. 6%
    d. 9%

17. A borrower chooses a 5/1 ARM with an initial teaser rate well below the fully indexed rate. What is one risk this borrower might face if they keep the loan long term and rates rise?

    a. The interest rate will convert to a high fixed rate automatically.
    b. They may experience payment shock when the teaser rate ends and adjustments begin.
    c. Their payment amounts will increase in equal increments over time.
    d. Their interest rate will stay locked at the teaser rate, and their loan term will automatically increase.

18. In an 80-10-10 financing structure for a purchase money second mortgage, what does the "80" represent?

    a. The borrower's total loan-to-value ratio
    b. The percentage of the home's value covered by the first mortgage
    c. The borrower's combined down payment and second mortgage
    d. The amount of equity required to avoid a second mortgage

19. What happens to the borrower's loan principal balance during the interest-only period of an interest-only loan?

    a. It gradually decreases as regular principal payments are made.
    b. It increases each month due to negative amortization.
    c. It remains the same because only interest is being paid.
    d. It is forgiven if the borrower meets eligibility requirements.

20. Which borrower would be best-suited for a balloon mortgage?

    a. Someone who expects to sell or refinance before the balloon payment is due
    b. Someone who wants to pay off their loan slowly over 30 years and avoid refinancing
    c. Someone who plans to keep the property long-term and is uncomfortable with large future payments
    d. Someone with a fixed income and limited savings for large future expenses

21. Elena, age 74, has built up substantial equity in her primary residence and wants to access some of that equity without selling or taking on monthly mortgage payments. She receives a lump sum through a reverse mortgage, which she plans to use to cover medical expenses. A few years later, she permanently moves into an assisted living facility. What happens next under the terms of her reverse mortgage?

    a. She must begin making monthly payments to cover the remaining loan balance.
    b. The loan becomes due, and the home will typically be sold to repay the loan.
    c. The lender forgives the debt as long as she used the funds for medical expenses.
    d. The reverse mortgage automatically converts into a standard fixed-rate loan.

22. Marcus has a HELOC with a 10-year draw period and a 20-year repayment period. During the draw period, he uses $20,000 of his $50,000 credit limit to renovate his kitchen. He's been making monthly interest payments for three years. What will change when Marcus enters the repayment period?

    a. He will no longer be able to access any of the unused credit.
    b. He will begin repaying both principal and interest on the full $50,000.
    c. His monthly payments will decrease because the credit limit resets.
    d. He will start receiving monthly disbursements from the lender.

23. What is the purpose of including contingency funds in a construction loan?

    a. To provide funds for future landscaping or furnishings
    b. To cover interest payments during the repayment period
    c. To prepare for unexpected expenses or cost overruns during construction
    d. To pay the borrower's income taxes during the build

24. How does the FHLB system support smaller financial institutions?

    a. By issuing reverse mortgages on their behalf
    b. By offering direct grants to individual borrowers
    c. By purchasing subprime loans from their portfolios
    d. By providing regional funding access that may not be available through national lenders

25. A borrower has proposed monthly housing expenses of $1,450 principal and interest, $250 property taxes, $50 homeowner's insurance, and $45 HOA dues. Their gross monthly income is $7,250. What is the borrower's housing DTI ratio?

    a. 24%
    b. 25%
    c. 26%
    d. 27%

26. Which of the following is true regarding occupancy requirements for FHA loans?

    a. Borrowers must begin renovations on the home within 30 days of closing.
    b. FHA loans are only available for rental investment properties.
    c. Borrowers must occupy the home within 60 days and live there for at least one year.
    d. The home must be used as a vacation residence for at least six months.

27. What is the primary purpose of VA loan minimum property requirements (MPRs)?

    a. To ensure the property will be the borrower's primary residence
    b. To confirm the property provides a safe and sanitary living environment
    c. To ensure the home meets local energy codes
    d. To reduce the interest rate on the loan

28. Compared to conforming loans, Alt-A loans typically come with:

    a. Lower interest rates and easier resale on the secondary market
    b. Higher risk for borrowers and fewer qualification requirements
    c. Lower fees but stricter documentation rules
    d. Higher interest rates and limited access to the secondary mortgage market

# *3* Mortgage Loan Origination Activities

**Application information and requirements**
**Qualification processing and underwriting**
**Closing**
**Financial calculations used in mortgage lending**

### Learning Objectives

- Describe the overall mortgage loan origination process.
- Identify the mandatory information needed and other requirements for the loan application.
- Explain the criteria and progression of loan qualification and underwriting.
- Summarize the borrower analysis steps in the mortgage loan origination process.
- Describe the role, value, and tasks of the settlement agent.
- Explain the fees and documents involved in closing a loan.
- Demonstrate financial calculations used in mortgage lending.

---

## APPLICATION INFORMATION AND REQUIREMENTS

**Loan origination process overview**
**Role of the MLO**
**Pre-qualification phase**
**Initial consultation**
**Borrower application**
**Application verification**
**Suitability of products and programs**
**Accuracy (tolerances)**
**MLO disclosure documents**

---

**Loan origination process overview**

**Pre-qualification**. The **loan origination process** itself encompasses a series of structured steps that begin well before a borrower receives final loan approval. The process typically starts with the **pre-qualification phase**, during which a prospective borrower submits preliminary financial information to a lender. Based on this information, the lender provides an estimate of the mortgage amount for which the borrower may qualify. It is important to note that this stage is generally **non-binding** and is intended solely to offer an initial assessment of the borrower's financial capability.

**Apply for the loan**. Following pre-qualification, the borrower proceeds to the **loan application** stage. At this point, the borrower completes a formal mortgage application, commonly referred to as the **Uniform Residential Loan Application or Form 1003**. This document requires comprehensive details regarding the borrower's employment history, income, assets, liabilities, and information pertaining to the subject property.

**Application processing**. Once the application is submitted, the **application processing** phase begins. The lender undertakes a detailed review to verify the information provided by the borrower. This includes confirming the borrower's employment and income, evaluating credit history, and arranging for an appraisal to determine the current market value of the property.

**Underwriting**. After processing, the file is transferred to **underwriting**. The underwriter is responsible for assessing the level of risk associated with granting the loan. This includes a thorough evaluation of the borrower's creditworthiness and the value of the property serving as collateral. The underwriter ensures that the loan application meets both regulatory guidelines and any specific criteria established by the lending institution.

**Credit decision**. Once underwriting is complete, a **credit decision** is rendered. The underwriter may approve the loan, suspend the decision pending additional information, or deny the application entirely. This decision is based on a holistic review of the borrower's ability to repay the loan and the adequacy of the property as security for the debt.

**Closing**. If the loan is approved, the process advances to **closing**. During this phase, all parties sign the legal documents required to finalize the mortgage agreement. These documents typically include the mortgage note, which outlines the terms and repayment schedule of the loan, and the mortgage or deed of trust, which secures the lender's interest in the property.

**Post-closing**. The final phase of the process is **post-closing**. After closing, the lender may either retain the loan in its own portfolio or sell it on the secondary mortgage market. The borrower begins making regular monthly mortgage payments in accordance with the loan terms. The lender, or its designated servicer, is responsible for managing the loan, which may include collecting payments and administering escrow accounts for taxes and insurance, when applicable.

## Role of the MLO

**MLO tasks**. At the center of the loan origination process is the **mortgage loan originator (MLO)**—a licensed professional who serves as the borrower's primary point of contact from the initial loan inquiry through to closing. The MLO evaluates financial readiness, explains available loan products, and gathers documentation to build a complete and compliant loan file. However, they are far from alone in this process.

Successful loan origination relies on the collaboration of several key professionals, including loan processors, underwriters, appraisers, title agents, and escrow officers. Each plays a specific role: ensuring the borrower qualifies, the property meets value requirements, the title is clear, and that all documents are accurate and legally binding.

## Pre-qualification Phase

**Gathering borrower's information**. The **loan origination process** typically begins with the **pre-qualification phase**, a preliminary but essential step that allows both the borrower and the lender to gauge financial readiness before diving into a formal loan application. During this stage, the prospective borrower provides basic financial information to the Mortgage Loan Originator (MLO), which may include details about income, employment, existing debts, assets, and estimated credit score. This information can often be submitted verbally, through an online form, or via a quick consultation, making the process relatively informal compared to later stages.

**Information evaluation**. Using the information provided, the MLO evaluates the borrower's financial profile and calculates an estimated loan amount for which the borrower may qualify. While this evaluation does not include a review of official documentation or a credit report, it does offer a useful ballpark figure. Based on standard debt-to-income (DTI) and loan-to-value (LTV) guidelines, the MLO can help the borrower understand potential price ranges for home shopping, estimate monthly mortgage payments, and discuss different loan programs that might be appropriate for their situation. The pre-qualification letter issued at this stage can serve as a basic demonstration of buying power, although it does not carry the same weight as a pre-approval letter.

**Evaluation is non-binding**. It is important to note that pre-qualification is non-binding and does not guarantee loan approval. No credit report is pulled, income documents are not verified, and underwriting has not yet begun. Because of this, pre-qualification should be viewed as an informational step—helpful for initial planning but not a substitute for the more rigorous pre-approval phase that typically follows. That said, it plays an important role in opening the lines of communication between the borrower and the MLO, setting expectations, and helping the borrower begin the home search with greater clarity and purpose.

**Pre-approval phase.** Following pre-qualification, borrowers ready to take the next step typically move into the **pre-approval phase**, a more formal and detailed financial evaluation. Unlike pre-qualification, which relies on self-reported information, pre-approval requires the borrower to submit **verifiable documentation**. This may include recent pay stubs, W-2 forms, tax returns, bank statements, and authorization for the lender to pull a full credit report. The Mortgage Loan Originator (MLO) reviews this information and works with the lender's processing team to assess the borrower's financial strength based on actual data.

**Compare borrower to modeled profiles**.  The goal of pre-approval is to determine whether the borrower meets the lender's guidelines for a specific loan amount and product. The lender calculates key financial ratios—such as the borrower's front-end and back-end debt-to-income (DTI) ratios—and examines the credit report for payment history, credit utilization, and public records. If the borrower meets the necessary criteria, the lender issues a pre-approval letter, which reflects a conditional commitment to lend up to a specified amount, subject to final underwriting and property approval. This letter holds considerably more weight in a competitive real estate market, as it shows sellers and agents that the buyer has been vetted and is financially capable of closing the deal.

**Pre-approval letters.**  Pre-approval not only strengthens a borrower's position when making an offer, but it also helps identify any issues early on—such as high DTI, limited credit history, or insufficient assets—that may require attention before moving forward. It's worth noting that pre-approval is also time-sensitive: most pre-approval letters are valid for 60 to 90 days, after which financial information may need to be updated. Still, for serious buyers, obtaining pre-approval is a crucial step that brings them much closer to loan commitment and ultimately, homeownership.

## Check Your Understanding

What is the main purpose of a pre-approval letter in the mortgage process?

    A.  It guarantees a specific interest rate.
    B.  It shows sellers the buyer's credit score.
    C.  It reflects a lender's conditional commitment to lend, based on verified data.
    D.  It is required before touring properties.

If you selected Option C, you are correct! A pre-approval letter shows the borrower has been vetted and conditionally approved, giving them a competitive edge in the market.

**Initial consultation**

**Establishing the groundwork for an actual application**.  Before a borrower fills out a formal application for loan approval, the initial consultation with a Mortgage Loan Originator (MLO) serves as a key relationship-building moment. Whether it takes place over the phone, in person, or via video conference, this early conversation allows the MLO to better understand the borrower's financial goals, concerns, and homeownership timeline. It is also the borrower's opportunity to ask questions, voice uncertainties, and begin evaluating whether they are ready to move forward with a mortgage—and whether the MLO and lending institution are the right fit.

During this consultation, the MLO will often ask broad questions about the borrower's income, employment stability, credit history, savings for a down payment, and any existing debts. They may also inquire about the type of property the borrower is interested in purchasing, potential price range, and whether the borrower has already spoken with a real estate licensee. Based on these answers, the MLO can suggest appropriate loan products, explain estimated monthly payments, and discuss the pros and cons of different financing options—conventional vs. FHA, fixed vs. adjustable, and so on.

Importantly, during this meeting, the MLO sets expectations for documentation, timelines, and the steps to come. They may walk the borrower through the difference between pre-qualification and pre-approval, outline what will be needed to complete a loan application, and provide a list of recommended next steps—such as gathering income documents or checking credit reports for errors. While no commitments are made at this stage, the initial consultation lays the groundwork for a productive borrower-lender relationship and helps ensure that when the time comes to formally apply, the borrower is informed, prepared, and confident.

**Interest rates.** While the initial consultation is not the time for **locking in a rate**, borrowers often ask about interest rates, and a well-informed MLO will be ready to discuss current market conditions and how rates might apply to the borrower's situation. The MLO may explain the difference between interest rates and annual percentage rates (APR), as well as the factors that influence a borrower's rate—such as credit score, loan type, down payment size, and loan term.

**Identifying the interest rate range**. At this point, the MLO can provide rate quotes based on generic or preliminary information, often showing a range of options (e.g., 30-year fixed, 15-year fixed, or ARM). However, these quotes are **non-binding** and typically labeled as subject to change until the borrower submits a full application and provides documentation for underwriting review. The MLO may also explain how discount points work if the borrower is interested in buying down the rate.

The purpose of this discussion is to set expectations and educate the borrower about how mortgage rates work—not to finalize terms. A savvy MLO uses this opportunity to help the borrower understand rate volatility, the importance of timing, and what steps must be taken to officially lock in a rate later in the process.

**Typical loan fees.** Typical fees associated with real estate loans are often introduced during the initial consultation so that borrowers are not caught off guard later in the process. While the exact amounts will vary based on the lender, loan type, and location, the MLO should provide a general breakdown to help borrowers understand the true cost of borrowing.

A categorized overview of common fees often includes:

▸ **lender fees (origination-related)**

The lender charges fees to process and underwrite the loan. These include:

- loan origination fee: often 0.5% to 1% of the loan amount
- application fee: may cover credit checks and admin costs
- processing fee: covers work done to gather and organize the file
- underwriting fee: charged for the risk assessment and final loan decision

▸ **third-party fees**

Third-party fees are paid to outside service providers involved in the transaction. These may include:

- appraisal fees: paid to the licensed appraiser
- credit report fees: cover the cost of pulling the borrower's credit
- flood certification fee: verifies whether the property is in a flood zone
- tax service fees: ensure property taxes are monitored and paid on time
- verification services: used to confirm employment, income, and assets

▸ **title-related fees**

These fees relate to verifying and insuring the property's title, including:

- title search and title insurance: protects against defects in ownership chain
- settlement or escrow fee: paid to the title or escrow company for managing the closing
- recording fees: charged by local government to record the deed and mortgage
- notary fees: if applicable, for official witnessing of document signing

**Prepaid items and escrows.** These are required upfront costs, not technically fees, but part of closing costs:

▸ **prepaid interest**: covers interest due between closing and the first mortgage payment
▸ **property taxes and homeowners insurance**: often collected in advance and deposited into escrow accounts

> ‣ **mortgage insurance premium**: if required (e.g., for FHA loans or low-down-payment conventional loans)

**Buydown discount points.** Borrowers can choose to pay additional discount points to "buy down" the interest rate. Here, the lender receives essentially prepaid interest up front. This effectively enables the lender to drop the face rate of interest on the loan since an increment of interest has already been paid.

Once the borrower submits a complete application, the lender is required to issue a **Loan Estimate (LE)** within three business days. The loan estimate gives the borrower a more precise breakdown of the costs.

### Check Your Understanding

What is the primary purpose of the initial consultation between a borrower and MLO?

  A. To build rapport and gather preliminary financial information
  B. To finalize the borrower's interest rate
  C. To collect the first mortgage payment
  D. To schedule the home appraisal

Option A is correct. The initial consultation helps the MLO understand the borrower's financial goals and timeline, setting the stage for a productive relationship.

**Borrower application**

One of the most important documents in the mortgage lending process is the **Uniform Residential Loan Application (URLA)**, also known as **the 1003**, which is Fannie Mae's designated form number. Freddie Mac refers to the same form as **Form 65**. Form 65 can be viewed here: - https://singlefamily.fanniemae.com/media/7896/display

**The URLA as the application standard.** The URLA is the industry standard for collecting borrower information during the mortgage application process. In 2021, the form underwent a significant redesign to improve functionality and compliance. Key enhancements included a streamlined format, updated terminology, improved accessibility, and better organization. The revised version also incorporated enhanced data collection features aligned with the Uniform Data Set (UDS), which standardizes mortgage application data collection across the lending industry to facilitate consistency and regulatory compliance.

The URLA is typically completed twice during the lending process—once at the initial application stage and again at closing to reflect final terms and conditions. The form itself is divided into several sections to capture comprehensive borrower and loan information.

Completing the application. Per the Equal Credit Opportunity (15 U.S.C. §1691 et seq.) Act (ECOA), a written loan application may be completed in various ways:

- ‣ face-to-face interview
- ‣ telephone interview
- ‣ fax or mail
- ‣ email or internet

**Borrower information**. The Borrower Information section includes details such as the applicant's name, alternate name (if applicable), Social Security number, date of birth, citizenship status, type of credit sought, marital status, dependents, contact information, and residential addresses. Additionally, it requires a thorough record of employment history and income sources, including any secondary employment and previous jobs if the current employment is less than two years in duration. Borrowers must also disclose their assets, liabilities, and any real estate they currently own. The form captures loan and property details, including the presence of other mortgages, rental income on the subject property, and any financial gifts or grants being used to assist with the transaction.

**Declarations**. Further sections of the application inquire about Declarations, which consist of specific questions relating to the borrower's financial background, including previous foreclosures, bankruptcies, judgments, and property occupancy plans. The borrower must also review and sign the **Acknowledgements and Agreements** section. Additional information may include military service status, demographic data required for government monitoring purposes, and Loan Originator Information, which the MLO completes.

The **Lender Loan Information** section of the URLA captures key details such as property and loan characteristics, title information (including how the estate will be held), and mortgage product specifics. It also outlines borrower qualification data, such as the minimum funds needed to complete the transaction. If more than one individual is applying for the mortgage, the **Additional Borrower** section is used, and it mirrors the data requirements for the primary borrower. There are also supplemental forms such as the **Unmarried Addendum**, which is required only when the borrower has selected "Unmarried" in Section 1, and the **Continuation Sheet**, which may be used when additional space is needed.

To formally accept an application, a lender must receive certain minimum information from the borrower. This includes:

- ‣ borrower's name, income, Social Security number
- ‣ property address
- ‣ estimated value of the property
- ‣ desired loan amount

Once this information is provided, the application is considered received, triggering specific disclosure and compliance obligations.

**MLO must manage borrower information**. As part of the origination process, the MLO may be involved in offering or negotiating loan terms with the borrower. This includes presenting a loan offer, which may be subject to verification of additional information or contingent on specific conditions. The MLO may also need to respond to borrower requests for alternative terms, such as a lower interest rate or a reduction in loan points. In such cases, a revised loan offer must be presented and documented appropriately.

Throughout the loan application process, the MLO bears the responsibility for managing all borrower-provided information. This includes ensuring that applications are complete, accurate, and accompanied by all required documentation. The MLO must also verify that all necessary disclosures are issued and review the application for inconsistencies or potential red flags. Accuracy in data collection and analysis is essential to maintaining regulatory compliance and ensuring loan quality.

**MLO must ascertain ability to repay loan**. While gathering borrower information, the MLO is permitted to ask questions that directly relate to the applicant's ability to repay the loan. These permissible questions include inquiries about income, credit history, assets, liabilities, and employment. Additionally, information related to ethnicity may be collected for government reporting purposes and to prevent discriminatory lending practices. Questions pertaining to an applicant's legal history, such as prior convictions or judgments, may also be appropriate when assessing loan eligibility.

**Using gift funds to obtain loan.** When borrowers intend to use financial gifts to cover part or all of their mortgage costs, **the MLO must confirm that gift funds are permissible, within accepted limits, and properly documented**. According to Fannie Mae guidelines, acceptable gift donors include individuals related to the borrower by blood, marriage, adoption, or legal guardianship. Other eligible donors include a domestic partner or their relative, a fiancé or fiancée, a former relative, or a godparent. Parties who are prohibited from providing gift funds include builders, developers, real estate agents involved in the transaction, and any individuals affiliated with these parties.

**Gift fund limits**. The acceptability of gift funds may vary depending on the loan type and the borrower's financial profile. For example:

> ▶ On conventional loans with a down payment of 20 percent or more, gift funds may be used to cover the entire cost of the loan transaction.

> ▶ For conventional loans with less than 20 percent down, there may be restrictions on how much of the cost can be covered by the gift, which will vary based on specific loan guidelines.

> ▶ For FHA and VA loans, if the borrower has a credit score of 620 or higher, gift funds may be used to cover all costs, regardless of the down payment amount. However, if the borrower's credit score is below 620, the borrower must contribute at least 3.5 percent of the down payment from their own funds.

To validate the use of gift funds, a signed gift letter from the donor is required. This letter must include the actual or maximum dollar amount of the gift, a statement confirming that no repayment is expected, the donor's name, address, and telephone number, and a clear explanation of the relationship to the borrower. In addition, the lender must verify both the availability of funds and the successful transfer of the gift to the borrower's account prior to closing.

**Incomplete applications.** The Equal Credit Opportunity Act (ECOA) requires that when an applicant submits an incomplete loan application, the mortgage loan originator (MLO) must take specific action. **The MLO must either issue a notice of incompleteness or send an Adverse Action Notice to the applicant**. The MLO may initially request the missing information verbally or in writing. However, if the applicant does not respond to a verbal request within a reasonable period of time, the MLO is then required to provide the request in writing to remain in compliance with ECOA requirements.

**Adverse Action Notice.** An Adverse Action Notice is a response back to the borrower where the response falls short of a loan approval. The Notice must contain:

- a statement of the action taken
- the name and address of the creditor taking action
- a specific notice of the consumer's rights
- CFPB's address as the ECOA's regulator
- a reason for the action being taken

### Check Your Understanding

Who of the following is an acceptable gift donor under Fannie Mae guidelines?

A. The borrower's real estate agent
B. A builder affiliated with the transaction
C. The seller of the home
D. A domestic partner

If you selected Option D, you are correct! Acceptable gift donors include people with close personal ties to the borrower, such as relatives, domestic partners, or godparents—not parties involved in the transaction like sellers or agents.

**Application Verification**

**A critical component of the loan origination process is the verification of borrower-supplied information**. To ensure the application's accuracy and to assess the borrower's financial stability and creditworthiness, lenders must confirm specific details through authorized third-party sources. This process involves obtaining verification documents using standardized forms, with the borrower's written consent.

An essential verification document is the **Verification of Deposit (VOD)**. This form is used to confirm both the availability and source of the funds that the borrower intends to use for the down payment, closing costs, or financial reserves.

The VOD typically includes details such as current account balances and recent account activity. Lenders generally prefer to see seasoned funds used for required funds, meaning that the money has been held in the account for at least 60 days. Seasoned funds helps demonstrate that the borrower has not recently acquired the funds through an undisclosed loan or other ineligible source.

This particular form can be viewed here:
https://singlefamily.fanniemae.com/media/13886/display

Another essential form in the verification process is the **Verification of Employment (VOE)**. This form is used to confirm the borrower's employment history, income level, and job stability. Lenders must be confident that the borrower has a reliable income source and a consistent work record. In order to validate income, lenders may request:

- ▶ pay stubs
- ▶ W-2 forms
- ▶ tax returns

As with the VOD, not all MLOs or lenders use the same VOE form, although the type of information requested is fairly consistent across the industry. Fannie Mae offers a standard VOE form (Form 1005) that many lenders use for written verifications. However, many lenders have their own in-house VOE forms that ask for the same core information but may be branded or slightly formatted for internal use. Some employes use third-party verification services, which respond to VOE requests electronically and securely.

Most lenders require that income be verifiable for the previous two years, and they frequently calculate a two-year average of income to determine qualification. To complete this process, MLOs typically reach out directly to the borrower's current employer—and if applicable, former employers—or they may utilize third-party services that specialize in employment verification.

Ten or so days before closing, lenders will often phone the employer to make sure the borrower is still employed.

### Check Your Understanding

Why do lenders prefer to see "seasoned" funds in a borrower's account?

- A. To ensure the borrower uses the same bank for the loan
- B. To confirm the borrower didn't recently acquire the money from an undisclosed loan
- C. To help the borrower earn more interest
- D. To meet credit score improvement requirements

Lenders prefer seasoned funds—typically held for at least 60 days—to verify that the borrower did not obtain the funds through ineligible or undisclosed means. Option B is correct!

**Suitability of products and programs**

**MLO must determine loan suitability**. Determining the suitability of loan products and programs is a fundamental responsibility of the mortgage loan originator (MLO). A key aspect of this responsibility involves developing a clear understanding of the borrower's financial goals, homeownership plans, and long-term objectives.

**Identify purpose of loan**. In order to recommend an appropriate loan product, the MLO must engage the borrower in a detailed conversation regarding the intended purpose of the loan—whether it is to purchase a home, refinance an existing mortgage, or access equity for other financial needs.

**Identify homeownership goals**. Beyond the immediate loan objective, **the MLO should explore the borrower's broader homeownership goals.** For example, it is important to determine whether the borrower plans to reside in the home long-term or anticipates selling or refinancing the property within a few years. This information directly informs the suitability of certain mortgage products, particularly those with variable interest rates or shorter-term features.

**Ascertain proper time horizon**. Timing considerations also play a significant role in product selection. Borrowers may be operating under time-sensitive circumstances, such as a job relocation, or they may have the flexibility to wait for optimal market conditions. Inquiries regarding future plans—such as retirement, anticipated refinancing, or intentions to pay off the mortgage early—can help ensure that the selected product aligns with the borrower's financial trajectory.

Life events, including marriage, divorce, or the need to relocate due to employment or family considerations, may further influence both the timeline and type of mortgage that is most appropriate. Similarly, planned property sales related to downsizing or other life changes should be considered during the selection process.

**Risk tolerance**. The MLO must assess the borrower's risk tolerance to determine which loan terms and features are most appropriate. This includes discussing the borrower's comfort level with potential fluctuations in interest rates, monthly payment amounts, and overall loan structure. Some borrowers may be attracted to the initial savings of an adjustable-rate mortgage (ARM) but may not fully understand the implications of future rate adjustments. The MLO has a duty to explain the risk-reward balance, ensuring the borrower is aware of the potential benefits and possible financial consequences associated with specific mortgage products.

By carefully aligning loan options with the borrower's financial circumstances, timeline, and risk profile, the MLO ensures that the selected mortgage product is both suitable and sustainable for the borrower's unique situation.

## Check Your Understanding

Why is it important for an MLO to ask about a borrower's future plans, such as anticipated refinancing or early payoff?

- A. To calculate the borrower's moving expenses
- B. To determine how soon the borrower can stop making payments
- C. To recommend a loan product that fits the borrower's timeline and financial goals
- D. To collect data for marketing purposes

The correct answer is Option C! Understanding future plans helps the MLO select a loan product that aligns with the borrower's long-term financial goals and expected timeline.

**Accuracy (tolerances)**

Maintaining accuracy in loan disclosures is a fundamental requirement in the mortgage lending process. To ensure transparency and protect borrowers from unexpected changes in loan terms and costs, the TILA-RESPA (12 U.S.C. §2601 et seq.) Integrated Disclosure (TRID) rule established three distinct tolerance thresholds. These thresholds govern how much certain charges disclosed in the Loan Estimate (LE) may vary by the time they appear in the final Closing Disclosure (CD).

**Zero tolerance factors**. The first category is **zero tolerance**, which applies to fees that must remain unchanged from the initial LE to the final CD. These fees include charges paid directly to the lender or mortgage loan originator, such as origination fees, as well as fees for services provided by affiliates of the lender or MLO. Additionally, transfer taxes fall under the zero tolerance rule. Any increase in these fees beyond what was originally disclosed is strictly prohibited.

**10% tolerance factors**. The second category is known as **10% cumulative tolerance**. Under this threshold, certain fees may collectively increase by no more than 10 percent from the LE to the CD. This category includes charges such as recording fees, fees paid to third-party service providers that are not affiliated with the lender, and charges for services selected by the borrower from the lender's list of preferred providers. While individual fees may fluctuate, the total of these charges must not exceed the ten percent limit.

**Unlimited tolerance**. The third category is referred to as **no or unlimited tolerance**, which applies to fees that may change without limitation between the LE and CD. These include fees for services the lender does not require, fees paid to third-party providers selected by the borrower who are not listed on the lender's preferred provider list, and charges for services where the borrower was permitted to shop and ultimately chose a provider outside of the lender's recommendations. Optional services, such as owner's title insurance, also fall into this category—provided that they are not mandated by the lender.

Understanding and adhering to these tolerance thresholds is essential for mortgage loan originators and lenders alike. Accurate and compliant disclosure practices not only build borrower trust but also ensure adherence to regulatory standards set forth under federal lending laws.

## MLO disclosure documents

Mortgage loan originators (MLOs) are required by federal law to provide a variety of disclosures to borrowers throughout the mortgage application process. The purpose of these disclosures is to promote transparency and ensure that borrowers are fully informed about the terms, costs, and potential risks associated with the mortgage loan. These requirements are primarily governed by the Truth in Lending (15 U.S.C. §1601 et seq.) Act (TILA) and the Real Estate Settlement Procedures Act (RESPA), as implemented by the TILA-RESPA Integrated Disclosure (TRID) rule.

**Loan Estimate.** One of the most significant disclosure documents is the **Loan Estimate (LE)**, a standardized form required under TILA. The LE outlines key loan terms, such as the interest rate, projected monthly payments, and whether those terms may change over time. It also provides an itemized estimate of closing costs, enabling borrowers to compare offers from multiple lenders. **The initial LE must be delivered within three business days of a completed loan application**. If specific circumstances change—such as an adjustment to the loan amount, interest rate, or other key terms—or if cumulative cost changes exceed tolerance limits, a revised LE may be issued. **Revised disclosures must be provided within three business days of the triggering event and received by the borrower no later than four business days before closing.** If the borrower does not indicate an intent to proceed within ten business days of receiving the initial LE, the estimate is considered expired.

**Mortgage Loan Servicing Disclosure.** Under RESPA, the **Mortgage Loan Servicing Disclosure** must also be provided within three business days of a completed application. This document informs the borrower whether the lender intends to retain the servicing of the loan or transfer it to another entity. There is no officially prescribed, government-mandated form like there is for the Loan Estimate or Closing Disclosure. However, the content of the Mortgage Servicing Disclosure Statement is strictly regulated under Regulation X (12 CFR § 1024.33). The lender or MLO must provide a written disclosure that includes:

> ▸ whether the lender intends to service the loan or transfer servicing
> ▸ a clear explanation of what mortgage loan servicing is
> ▸ a statement that if servicing is transferred, the borrower will be notified
> ▸ a summary of the borrower's rights under RESPA regarding loan servicing

Because the regulation requires specific disclosures, most lenders use a standardized in-house template that includes all required language to ensure compliance.

**Home Loan Toolkit.** For purchase transactions, borrowers must additionally receive the **CFPB's Home Loan Toolkit**, which is designed to guide them through the mortgage process. It contains valuable information about application steps, interest rates, mortgage terms, disclosure forms, and borrower rights. This toolkit must be delivered within three business days of application and applies only to purchase transactions.

**Prospective Settlement Service Providers List.** Another disclosure required under TILA is the list of **Prospective Settlement Service Providers**, which gives borrowers written options for services such as title insurance and settlement agents. Borrowers are not obligated to select a provider from the list and may choose any provider without penalty or discrimination. This list must also be provided within three business days of application.

**Affiliated Business Arrangement Disclosure.** If any of these prospective settlement service providers have financial or ownership affiliations with the lender or another party to the transaction, an **Affiliated Business Arrangement Disclosure (AfBA)** must be issued. This document discloses the nature of the relationship and includes estimated charges for the affiliated services. The borrower must be advised that they are not required to use any affiliated provider. The AfBA must be delivered at or before the time of loan application, and failure to provide this disclosure may result in significant penalties. Regulation X § 1024 Appendix D provides the standardized format and language that should be used to ensure compliance with RESPA regulations.

**ARM disclosures.** For borrowers considering adjustable-rate mortgages (ARMs), there are two key disclosures.

The first is the **Consumer Handbook on Adjustable-Rate Mortgages (CHARM Booklet)**, which is a federally required educational booklet designed to help consumers understand the risks and features of ARMs. It was originally created by the Federal Reserve Board and is now under the jurisdiction of the Consumer Financial Protection Bureau (CFPB).

The booklet provides general information about ARMs, such as:

- what an ARM is and how it differs from a fixed-rate loan
- how interest rates are determined (indexes, margins, rate caps)
- when and how payments can change
- risks of negative amortization (if applicable)
- how to evaluate if an ARM is right for you
- questions to ask lenders before choosing a loan
- comparison tips for shopping different ARM products

The second key disclosure related to ARMs is the **Adjustable-Rate Mortgage Disclosure**, which is specific to the loan product being offered. This disclosure is provided more than once.

The initial ARM disclosure content is regulated by 12 CFR § 1026.19(b) and must be in writing. It includes:

- an explanation of how the interest rate and payment can change
- index and margin used to determine rate adjustments
- frequency of adjustments (first adjustment and subsequent ones)
- interest rate and payment caps (periodic and lifetime limits)
- examples of how the borrower's payments may change over time
- negative amortization risk (if applicable)
- prepayment penalties or balloon payments (if applicable)
- statement of borrower rights regarding additional disclosures at each adjustment

Lenders must also provide ongoing ARM adjustment notices:

- **Initial Adjustment Notice**: Sent between 210 and 240 days before the first payment change
- **Ongoing Adjustment Notices**: Sent between 60 and 120 days before each subsequent change

These notices explain:

- the new interest rate
- the new payment amount
- the method used to calculate the adjustment
- contact information for questions or assistance

Both the CHARM booklet and ARM-specific disclosure **must be provided within three business days of receiving a completed ARM loan application**.

**Homeownership Counseling Disclosure.** TILA also requires that borrowers be notified of their right to seek homeownership counseling services through the **Homeownership Counseling Disclosure**. This document emphasizes the importance of consulting with qualified housing counselors, particularly for first-time homebuyers or those with complex financial needs.

**Closing Disclosure.** As the transaction nears completion, borrowers must receive a **Closing Disclosure (CD)**, which provides a detailed accounting of final loan terms and settlement costs. The CD allows borrowers to compare final figures with the initial LE and ensures accuracy before the loan is finalized. **The Closing Disclosure must be delivered at least three business days before the scheduled closing date.** If certain material changes occur after the CD is delivered—such as an increase in the annual percentage rate (APR) beyond regulatory thresholds, a switch in loan product, the addition of a prepayment penalty, a change in loan term, or increases in fees exceeding tolerance limits— then **a new three-day waiting period is required before closing may proceed**.

**The "3-7-3 Rule".** The **"3-7-3 Rule"** summarizes the timing requirements for initial disclosures under TILA and the Mortgage Disclosure Improvement Act

(MDIA) of 2008. According to this rule, lenders must provide required initial disclosures—such as the LE, Home Loan Toolkit, Homeownership Counseling Disclosure, CHARM booklet (if applicable), and ARM disclosure (if applicable)—within three business days of a completed loan application. **The loan may not close until at least seven business days have passed from the delivery of the initial disclosures. If any substantial change necessitates redisclosure, a new three-business-day waiting period must occur before closing.**

For TILA and TRID purposes, a business day includes all calendar days except Sundays and legal public holidays. Under RESPA, a business day is defined as any day on which the institution's offices are open and conducting regular business functions.

The method of disclosure delivery is also an essential consideration in determining when a borrower is deemed to have received required documents. If disclosures are sent via mail, they are presumed to be received on the third business day after mailing—commonly referred to as the **"mailbox rule."** If provided electronically, the borrower must first consent to electronic delivery, and the lender must ensure the format is accessible and retainable. Electronic disclosures are generally subject to the same three-day receipt rule unless the borrower provides a return receipt or other confirmation. Disclosures delivered via fax are considered received the day after successful transmission, while those delivered in person are considered received on the date of delivery.

## Check Your Understanding

The CHARM Booklet and ARM-specific disclosure must be delivered within three business days of receiving what?

- A.  A completed application for an ARM loan
- B.  The borrower's first mortgage payment
- C.  The loan approval letter
- D.  The Closing Disclosure

Option A is correct! Both disclosures must be delivered within three business days of a completed ARM loan application.

## QUALIFICATION PROCESSING AND UNDERWRITING

**Borrower analysis**
**Automated Underwriting Systems (AUS)**
**Appraisals**
**Title reports, binders, and title insurance**
**Insurance: hazard, homeowners, flood, mortgage**

**Borrower analysis**

**Borrower analysis** is a critical component of the mortgage loan origination process. Its purpose is to verify and validate the accuracy of information provided in the loan application and to assess the borrower's overall financial and creditworthiness. While the exact steps may vary by lender, the process generally includes reviewing the loan application for completeness and accuracy, preparing and delivering required initial disclosures, conducting a credit check, and submitting the completed file to underwriting for formal risk assessment.

**Evaluation of assets and liabilities.** A key element of borrower analysis is the evaluation of **assets**, which demonstrate the borrower's ability to meet financial obligations such as down payment, closing costs, and monthly payments, as well as the maintenance of escrow accounts, if applicable. Common asset types include funds in checking or savings accounts, money market accounts, certificates of deposit, retirement accounts, business accounts, stocks and bonds, proceeds from the sale of real estate or other assets, financial gifts, and down payment assistance programs.

Lenders typically categorize assets as either **liquid (current)**—those that can be readily converted to cash—or **fixed (non-current)**—those not easily converted. Moreover, the concept of seasoning is important; lenders often require that funds be in the borrower's account for at least 60 days to confirm legitimacy and rule out undisclosed borrowing. Verifying that the reported assets are both accurate and appropriately documented is a critical part of this analysis.

The borrower's **liabilities** are also carefully examined, as they directly affect the borrower's capacity to repay the mortgage loan. Common liabilities include existing mortgage obligations, installment loans such as auto, personal, or student loans, revolving credit accounts (e.g., credit cards), court-ordered payments such as alimony and child support, and any legal judgments or tax liens. **Contingent liabilities**, such as co-signed loans, are generally excluded from underwriting consideration if the lender can document that the primary borrower has made timely payments from their own funds over the past 12 months.

**Check Your Understanding**

Which of the following would typically be considered a liquid asset?

    A. Land owned in another state
    B. Funds in a savings account
    C. A rental property
    D. Income from a second job

If you selected Option B, that's correct! Liquid assets are those that can be easily converted to cash—such as checking or savings account funds.

**Income analysis.** Another central component of the loan application is **income analysis**. Lenders verify income documents such as recent pay stubs, W-2s, and tax returns to determine the stability and reliability of income streams. Most programs require that income be verifiable for at least two years, and when income varies—such as commissions or bonuses—a two-year average is often used.

Income with a defined expiration date, such as child support, long-term disability, or alimony, must be reasonably expected to continue for at least three years following the closing date.

Acceptable income sources, provided they are documented appropriately, include salaried and hourly employment, self-employment, rental income, retirement benefits, investment income, alimony, and non-taxable sources such as Social Security or permanent disability benefits.

Unemployment income may be accepted if it is part of a consistent seasonal work cycle and documented with two years of tax returns. However, unemployment benefits received due to layoff or termination cannot be used as qualifying income.

Some income, particularly non-taxable income, may be **grossed up** by multiplying it by 115% to 125%, depending on the lender's policy, to reflect its tax-free nature.

Self-employed borrowers must typically submit two years of federal income tax returns, including Form 1040 with Schedule C for sole proprietors, or relevant business tax returns for partnerships or corporations. If the borrower has experienced an employment gap, further explanation may be required. In cases where the gap is fewer than six months, current employment verification is usually sufficient. For gaps exceeding six months, the borrower may need to demonstrate at least six months of continuous full-time employment before qualifying.

## Check Your Understanding

What must be true for child support or alimony income to be counted in mortgage qualification?

    A. It must be received monthly for at least six months.
    B. It must be court-ordered.
    C. It must be expected to continue for at least three years after closing.
    D. It must be untaxed.

Option C is correct! For qualifying purposes, income with a defined expiration must be expected to continue at least three years post-closing.

**Credit requirements.** The **credit report** is a vital tool used in conjunction with other financial documents to evaluate the borrower's creditworthiness. Credit reports are obtained from one or more of the three national credit reporting agencies: Equifax, Experian, and TransUnion. These reports contain detailed records of the borrower's credit accounts, including payment histories, account balances, and any derogatory remarks.

**Credit scores**, such as the FICO Score or VantageScore, are calculated based on this data and typically range from 320 to 850. Higher scores reflect stronger creditworthiness and lower risk to the lender. Key factors influencing the score include on-time payments (35%), credit utilization (30%), account age (15%), credit mix (10%), and recent inquiries (10%). **Derogatory credit**, such as late payments, delinquencies, charge-offs, foreclosures, or bankruptcies, can significantly affect the borrower's ability to qualify.

**Undisclosed debt.** When a credit report reveals a substantial debt that the borrower failed to disclose on the mortgage application, the loan originator must follow up by requesting a written explanation for the omission. It is the originator's duty to investigate and ensure the borrower is not deliberately omitting financial obligations in an effort to appear more creditworthy or to qualify for the loan under false pretenses. Identifying and addressing such discrepancies is a critical part of responsible lending practices.

**Qualifying ratios.** Lenders rely on **qualifying ratios** to evaluate the borrower's ability to manage monthly mortgage obligations. These include the **Housing Ratio** (front-end ratio) and the **Debt-to-Income (DTI)** Ratio (back-end ratio).

The **Housing Ratio compares the borrower's gross monthly income to their total monthly housing expense**, which includes principal, interest, property taxes, homeowners insurance (PITI), and any applicable homeowners association fees. This ratio generally should not exceed **28% to 31% of gross monthly income**, depending on the loan program. However, this benchmark may be exceeded if the borrower presents compensating factors such as strong credit or substantial reserves. The formula for calculating the housing ratio is:

*Housing Ratio = PITI on Primary Residence ÷ Gross Monthly Income*

The DTI Ratio represents the percentage of gross monthly income that is allocated toward all monthly debt obligations, including PITI, installment debts, revolving debts, alimony, and child support. This ratio generally should not exceed **33% to 43%** of gross monthly income, although some lenders may allow higher ratios under certain circumstances. The DTI calculation excludes non-debt-related expenses such as utilities, groceries, education costs (excluding student loans), childcare (unless court-ordered), and insurance premiums. The formula for DTI is:

*DTI Ratio = Total Recurring Monthly Debt ÷ Gross Monthly Income*

**The LTV ratio.** Another essential financial measure is the **loan-to-value (LTV) ratio**, which compares the loan amount to either the appraised value or purchase price of the property—whichever is lower. This ratio helps assess whether the property's value adequately supports the requested loan. A higher LTV suggests a smaller down payment and therefore greater risk to the lender, while a lower LTV implies a larger down payment and less lender exposure.

LTV requirements vary by loan program. Government-backed loans such as FHA and VA loans typically allow for higher LTV ratios. For conventional loans, an LTV exceeding 80% usually requires the borrower to obtain private mortgage insurance (PMI). The formula used to calculate LTV is:

*LTV Ratio = Loan Amount ÷ Property Value*

To ensure responsible lending practices, federal law requires lenders to evaluate a borrower's ability to repay (ATR) the loan. These rules, established by the Consumer Financial Protection Bureau (CFPB) under the Dodd-Frank (12 U.S.C. §5301 et seq.) Wall Street Reform and Consumer Protection Act, mandate a comprehensive financial review. Lenders must document and verify key factors, including income, employment status, assets, housing costs, debt obligations, and credit history.

**Qualified mortgages.** If the loan qualifies as a **Qualified Mortgage (QM)**, the lender is presumed to be in compliance with ATR requirements. QM loans offer certain legal protections, such as the **Safe Harbor**, which applies when the borrower's DTI does not exceed 43% and other strict criteria are met. The **Rebuttable Presumption** applies to higher-DTI loans that meet QM standards but allow the borrower greater ability to challenge a lender's compliance. The ATR rules prohibit high-risk features such as balloon payments, negative amortization, no-documentation loans, and interest-only payments beyond the first five years. However, these rules do not apply to home equity lines of credit (HELOCs), reverse mortgages, timeshare loans, short-term bridge loans, or loans for business purposes.

**Refinance analyses.** When evaluating refinance transactions, lenders must ensure that the borrower will receive **a tangible net benefit** from the new loan. This may include:

- ▸ reducing interest rate or monthly payments
- ▸ shortening the loan term
- ▸ converting from an adjustable-rate to a fixed-rate mortgage
- ▸ eliminating private mortgage insurance
- ▸ consolidating debt

In some cases, borrowers may refinance to access home equity for other financial needs. Lenders must document and validate that such benefits exist. If a loan is refinanced repeatedly without a clear benefit to the borrower, this practice—known as **loan flipping** or **churning**—may constitute a form of loan fraud and can subject the lender to regulatory penalties.

## Check Your Understanding

Which of the following components has the greatest impact on a borrower's credit score?

- A. Length of credit history
- B. Credit mix
- C. On-time payment history
- D. Recent credit inquiries

Option C is correct! Payment history makes up 35% of a FICO credit score—the largest single factor influencing the score.

**Automatic Underwriting Systems (AUS)**

Modern mortgage lending relies heavily on **Automated Underwriting Systems (AUS)** to streamline the evaluation of borrower eligibility and loan risk. These systems analyze application data using standardized criteria to produce consistent and efficient underwriting recommendations. The two most widely used AUS platforms in the residential mortgage industry are Fannie Mae's **Desktop Underwriter (DU)** and Freddie Mac's **Loan Product Advisor (LPA)**.

**The Desktop Underwriter**. Desktop Underwriter (DU) is Fannie Mae's proprietary AUS. It is designed to assess a borrower's creditworthiness and determine whether the loan meets Fannie Mae's eligibility and underwriting requirements. DU integrates directly with the data provided on the Uniform Residential Loan Application (Form 1003), including the borrower's credit history, income, assets, and liabilities. By automating much of the underwriting process, DU reduces the need for manual file review and enables lenders to make lending decisions with greater consistency, accuracy, and efficiency. Based on the data submitted, DU generates a risk assessment and issues a recommendation. The system may indicate that the loan should be approved, referred for manual underwriting, or denied altogether.

**The Loan Product Advisor**. Freddie Mac's **Loan Product Advisor** (LPA) serves a similar purpose for lenders that sell loans to Freddie Mac. Like DU, LPA evaluates the borrower's application data against Freddie Mac's guidelines to determine eligibility. Both systems assist lenders by providing rapid, objective assessments of borrower risk and loan suitability.

It is important to note that while DU and LPA offer automated recommendations, *the final lending decision may also take into account lender-specific overlays, investor requirements, and other risk considerations beyond those evaluated by the AUS.* Furthermore, both systems are periodically updated to reflect changes in regulatory standards, market conditions, and underwriting practices, ensuring that their recommendations remain current and compliant with industry expectations.

## Appraisals

An appraisal is a critical component of the mortgage lending process, required to determine the fair market value of the property serving as collateral for the loan. Lenders rely on appraisals to ensure that the property's value justifies the loan amount. If the appraised value is lower than the purchase price, the lender may reduce the loan amount, requiring the borrower to cover the difference or renegotiate the contract. This protects the lender's investment by confirming that, in the event of borrower default, the property can be sold to recover the outstanding debt.

**Purpose and key concepts.** Appraisals are designed to establish the objective value of the subject property—the property being appraised—based on market data and standardized methodologies. One of the central components of this analysis is the use of comparable sales, or "comps," which are recently sold properties with similar characteristics in the same area. Appraisers make adjustments to account for differences in square footage, condition, amenities, or location to estimate the subject property's value more accurately.

**Primary appraisal methods.** Appraisers use one or more of the following three valuation approaches, depending on the property type and transaction context. These are the sales comparison approach, the cost approach, and the income approach.

### 1. Sales Comparison Approach

The most commonly used method for residential real estate, this approach involves analyzing the sale prices of comparable properties. The appraiser adjusts those prices to reflect any material differences between the comps and the subject property—such as the number of bedrooms, renovations, lot size, or garage space. The adjusted values are then reconciled to provide a final estimate of the subject property's market value.

### 2. Cost Approach

This method is typically used for new construction or unique properties with few comparable sales. The appraiser estimates the cost to rebuild the property using current labor and material costs, subtracts any depreciation—which may be physical, functional, or external—and then adds the value of the underlying land. The result is an estimate of the total property value.

### 3. Income Approach

Used primarily for income-generating properties such as apartment complexes or commercial real estate, this method bases the valuation on the property's **net operating income (NOI)** and a **capitalization rate (cap rate).**

Operating expenses, such as property taxes, maintenance, insurance, and management fees, are subtracted to calculate net operating income (NOI). The formula to calculate the NOI is:

*NOI = Estimated Potential Income - Operating Expenses*

The capitalization rate (cap rate), which reflects the investor's required rate of return, is then applied to the NOI using the formula:

*Value = NOI ÷ Cap Rate*

A higher NOI and lower cap rate typically result in a higher estimated value. This approach reflects the investment return a buyer might expect.

**Types of appraisals.** Depending on the nature of the transaction, lenders may order different types of appraisals:

  ▸ **full appraisal** (interior and exterior): the most thorough inspection, involving both interior and exterior observation.
  ▸ **exterior-only** (drive-by) appraisal: used in some refinance or low-risk scenarios; relies on limited in-person evaluation and public records.
  ▸ **desktop appraisal**: Conducted remotely using public records, MLS data, and third-party tools, without a physical site visit.

**Government Loan appraisal requirements.** FHA, VA, and USDA loans have additional appraisal requirements:

  ▸ **FHA**: Appraisals must confirm that the property meets Minimum Property Standards (MPS) related to safety and habitability.

  ▸ **VA**: Appraisals follow similar rules to ensure that properties are safe, structurally sound, and sanitary.

  ▸ **USDA**: Appraisals must confirm both the property's market value and its eligibility under USDA location and property guidelines.

**Appraisal reports and standard forms.** Most residential appraisals for conforming loans are documented using the **Uniform Residential Appraisal Report (URAR)**—Fannie Mae Form 1004 or Freddie Mac Form 70. This standardized form ensures that all essential components are addressed, including property condition, neighborhood characteristics, comparable sales, and reconciliation of value approaches.

**Appraisal rules, disclosure, and timing.** Under the **Equal Credit Opportunity Act (ECOA) Valuations Rule**, lenders are required to notify borrowers of their right to receive a copy of any appraisal or valuation developed in connection with their mortgage application. This disclosure must be delivered at the time of application or within three business days of receiving the application. Borrowers must submit a written request to receive a copy of the appraisal and may also waive this right, provided the waiver is made in writing. Regardless of whether a waiver is signed, lenders are required to deliver a copy of the appraisal or valuation no later than three business days prior to closing or upon completion—whichever occurs first.

**Appraisal regulatory framework: FIRREA and USPAP.** The Financial Institutions Reform, Recovery, and Enforcement Act of 1989 (FIRREA) was enacted in response to the savings and loan crisis and remains foundational to modern appraisal regulation. FIRREA mandates that appraisals used in federally related transactions—which include most mortgage loans involving federal oversight—must be conducted by state-licensed or certified appraisers and must comply with the **Uniform Standards of Professional Appraisal Practice (USPAP).**

FIRREA also established the Appraisal Subcommittee (ASC), which oversees the state appraisal licensing system and monitors compliance with federal requirements. Through the Appraisal Foundation, which includes the Appraiser Qualifications Board (AQB) and the Appraisal Standards Board (ASB), FIRREA enforces minimum competency standards and ethical guidelines for appraisers.

Some lower-risk transactions below a defined monetary threshold—currently $400,000 for residential real estate—may not require a full appraisal, but instead may qualify for an evaluation conducted by the lender.

All appraisals performed for federally related transactions must comply with the Uniform Standards of Professional Appraisal Practice **(USPAP).** Developed and maintained by the **Appraisal Standards Board (ASB)** of the **Appraisal Foundation**, USPAP sets forth the ethical obligations and performance standards required of professional appraisers in the United States.

USPAP covers a wide range of topics, including:

- ▶ competency requirements, ensuring that the appraiser is qualified to perform the assignment based on education, experience, and knowledge of the property type and market
- ▶ impartiality and objectivity, prohibiting appraisers from advocating for any party or allowing personal interests to affect the results
- ▶ scope of work disclosure, which requires the appraiser to explain the extent of research and analysis completed
- ▶ reporting standards, including clarity, transparency, and full documentation of valuation methods and conclusions

Appraisers must stay current with changes to USPAP. Revisions are issued regularly—typically every two years—to reflect evolving professional practices and regulatory needs. Lenders and mortgage professionals must ensure that appraisals they rely upon for underwriting meet these standards, as failure to comply with USPAP can result in regulatory violations, legal challenges, or the rejection of the appraisal.

**Appraiser independence requirements.** Federal regulations prohibit lenders from influencing or coercing appraisers in any way. Appraisers must be selected based on experience, training, and qualifications, not on their willingness to deliver a specific value. Appraisal Management Companies (AMCs) are often used to facilitate impartial ordering and oversight of appraisals. Lenders cannot base an appraiser's compensation on the appraised value, and any communication about potential errors in the report must be handled appropriately—without exerting pressure to change valuation conclusions.

**Appraisal reviews, reconsiderations, and second appraisals.** In some cases, especially with jumbo loans or loans with layered risk factors, the lender may require a second appraisal or conduct an appraisal review to verify accuracy. If a borrower or lender identifies a material error in the report—such as an overlooked comparable sale or factual inaccuracy—they may request a reconsideration of value, providing additional documentation for the appraiser's review. However, this request must not be used to pressure the appraiser to change their conclusion.

**Impact of appraisal outcomes.** If the appraised value comes in lower than the purchase price, the buyer may need to renegotiate with the seller, bring additional funds to closing, or cancel the transaction. If the value meets or exceeds the contract price, the transaction can proceed as planned. An appraisal that uncovers title defects, zoning issues, or condition problems may trigger required repairs or further underwriting scrutiny. In cases where repairs are required, the appraisal may be made "subject to" completion, and loan closing may be delayed until issues are resolved and verified.

**Appraisal updates and recertifications.** In some cases, lenders may require an **appraisal update** or **recertification of value**, particularly when the original appraisal report is several months old, or if the transaction has been delayed.

An appraisal update (also referred to as a **1004D** or **Appraisal Update and/or Completion Report**) is used to confirm that the original appraised value is still valid as of a new effective date. This is commonly needed when a loan has not closed within the typical appraisal validity window—often 120 days for FHA loans and 180 days for conventional loans.

A recertification of value is more specific. It is used to verify that conditions noted in the original appraisal have been satisfied, such as required repairs or the completion of new construction. It does not establish a new value, nor should it be confused with a reappraisal.

Appraisal updates and recertifications <u>must be performed by the same appraiser who completed the original report and must be consistent with USPAP requirements</u>. Lenders are responsible for determining whether the update is sufficient or if a new appraisal is required due to changes in market conditions, property condition, or the passage of time.

## Check Your Understanding

Under the ECOA Valuations Rule, when must the borrower receive a copy of their appraisal?

- A. Within three days of closing
- B. At least three business days before closing or upon completion, whichever is earlier
- C. At the time of the loan application
- D. Only upon request and payment of a fee

ECOA requires lenders to provide a copy of the appraisal to the borrower at least three business days before closing or upon completion—whichever comes first. Option B is correct!

**Title reports, binders, and title insurance**

**Marketable title.** Before a property can be legally transferred from seller to buyer, the seller must demonstrate the ability to convey **marketable title**—that is, ownership that is free from significant defects, encumbrances, or legal uncertainties that could limit the buyer's rights or result in future disputes. Marketable title does not mean perfect title, but it must be sufficiently clear that a reasonable buyer and lender would accept it without hesitation.

**Title search.** To confirm that marketable title exists, a title search is conducted. This search is a detailed review of public land records, typically performed by a title company, real estate attorney, or licensed title abstractor. The purpose of the title search is to identify and analyze any existing claims, liens, easements, encumbrances, restrictions, or ownership issues associated with the property. The search encompasses a review of recorded documents such as:

- ▶ deeds
- ▶ mortgages
- ▶ tax records
- ▶ court judgments
- ▶ probate filings
- ▶ divorce decrees
- ▶ easement agreements

**Chain of title.** A critical component of the title search process is establishing a clear and verifiable **chain of title**. The chain of title is <u>the sequential record of ownership transfers for a particular parcel of real estate, tracing all conveyances from the current owner back to the original source of title</u>. This sequence may span several decades and typically involves reviewing recorded deeds, wills, court records, and other legal instruments filed with the appropriate county or municipal recording office.

The purpose of verifying the chain of title is to ensure that:

> ▸ each prior transfer of ownership was legally valid and properly recorded.
> ▸ there are no gaps, breaks, or defects in ownership history.
> ▸ no unknown or unresolved claims, interests, or encumbrances have been passed down through previous owners.

Common issues discovered in a flawed chain of title may include:

> ▸ undisclosed, missing, or improperly recorded deeds
> ▸ undisclosed, unknown, or missing heirs with potential ownership claims
> ▸ unreleased prior mortgages or liens
> ▸ errors in public records
> ▸ improper legal descriptions
> ▸ unrecorded easements or encroachments
> ▸ forged or fraudulent documents
> ▸ name variations or identity errors
> ▸ pending lawsuits or bankruptcy proceedings
> ▸ gaps in chain of title
> ▸ restrictive covenants or deed restrictions

When these defects are discovered, they are referred to as **clouds on title**. These must be resolved—often through corrective deeds, affidavits, or legal action—before the property can be transferred with clear title. A clear and unbroken chain of title provides assurance that the seller has the legal right to convey ownership and that the buyer (and lender) will have uncontested rights to the property.

**Preliminary title report.** The **title abstractor or examiner** employed by the title company or attorney's office compiles the title search findings into a **preliminary title report**. Prepared shortly after the purchase agreement is executed, a preliminary title report—also known as a **title binder**—presents a snapshot of the title status at a specific point in time.

Buyers have the option to select how the title report is obtained. Common options include:

> ▸ retaining the services of a professional title company
> ▸ hiring a real estate attorney (especially in states that require attorney-managed closings)
> ▸ conducting a search through the local county recorder's office or courthouse
> ▸ ordering a report through an online title service

Regardless of the method, the goal is to ensure a comprehensive and accurate assessment of the property's title history.

As part of the lender's **underwriting** and **due diligence**, the title report is carefully reviewed to identify any potential risks or legal complications. Significant title issues—such as undisclosed liens or unresolved ownership disputes—can affect loan approval or necessitate modifications to the loan terms. Any problems identified in the title report must be fully resolved before the transaction may proceed to closing. If marketable title cannot be established or cured, the sale may be delayed or cancelled

**Title insurance.** Based on the findings of the title search, the title company will issue a **title insurance commitment**. This document outlines the terms under which the company will issue a **title insurance policy** at closing. The commitment includes essential information such as the current owner of the property, a list of **title exceptions** (items not covered by the policy), any requirements that must be satisfied prior to issuing the policy, and the estimated cost of coverage. This commitment is reviewed by all parties involved—including the buyer, seller, agents, and attorneys—to ensure there are no unresolved or unexpected title concerns. Any listed exceptions or conditions must be addressed and cleared before closing can occur. Typically, the borrower is required to pay for the lender's title insurance policy, while the borrower may also elect to purchase a separate owner's title insurance policy for personal protection.

Both the preliminary title report and the title insurance commitment provide valuable early assurances that the property's title will be free of defects and suitable for transfer at closing. However, the final determination is not made until the transaction nears completion.

**Final title report.** A **final title report** is issued after all title-related issues have been resolved and the loan is ready to close. At that point, the title insurance policy becomes a binding agreement that provides ongoing protection against covered title defects. The lender is typically named as the insured party, although the buyer may also be protected if an owner's policy is purchased. Title insurance coverage remains in effect for as long as the insured party retains an interest in the property and serves to protect against future claims or title disputes that were not identified during the original title search.

The timing of title reporting is critical. The title report and title insurance commitment must be obtained and reviewed prior to closing, and the title search process typically requires up to two weeks to complete. However, in cases involving complex ownership histories or rural properties, additional time may be required. The use of thorough, independent title examinations and proper insurance coverage provides both lenders and borrowers with confidence that the property being financed has a clear and insurable title.

In some jurisdictions, the final title report, sometimes referred to as the **title policy jacket** or **title policy package**, is issued after closing and serves as documentation that the title company has fulfilled its obligations under the title insurance commitment. It confirms that the requirements listed in the commitment—such as releasing old liens, correcting ownership issues, or recording necessary documents—have been satisfied and that the title company is now ready to issue the final title insurance policy.

This report includes a summary of the final recorded documents, such as:

▸ the deed transferring ownership from seller to buyer
▸ the mortgage or deed of trust securing the lender's interest
▸ any releases of previously recorded liens
▸ affidavits or supporting documents used to cure defects

It acts as a final verification that:

▸ The chain of title is clear.
▸ The title is insurable.
▸ All conditions in the title commitment's Schedule B, Part I (Requirements) have been met.
▸ No new title defects or encumbrances have appeared since the original title search.

**Lender's policy and owner's policy.** Title insurance protects against financial loss due to defects in the title that were not discovered during the title search. There are two distinct types of title insurance policies, each serving a different party: the lender and the owner.

A **lender's title insurance policy**, also known as a loan policy, is required by most lenders as a condition of mortgage financing. It protects only the lender's interest in the property, not the borrower's, and it covers the amount of the loan, not the full property value. This policy remains in effect only for the life of the loan, so it terminates when the loan is paid in full or refinanced. A lender's policy ensures that the lender has a valid, enforceable lien on the property in first position. If a covered title defect arises—such as a previously undisclosed lien or an ownership dispute—the policy helps protect the lender from loss but does not reimburse the borrower for their equity or investment.

An **owner's title insurance policy** is a separate, optional policy that the buyer may choose to purchase (or negotiate for the seller to provide) to protect the buyer's ownership interest in the property. This policy covers the full purchase price of the property and remains in effect for as long as the buyer (or their heirs) holds title to the property—even after the mortgage is paid off. It provides protection against title claims that could affect the buyer's ability to sell, refinance, or transfer the property in the future and provides legal defense and financial compensation (up to the policy limit) if a covered claim arises.

**Insurance: hazard, homeowners, flood, mortgage**

As a condition of most mortgage loans, lenders require borrowers to maintain various types of **insurance coverage** to protect the lender's financial interest in the property. These insurance requirements serve to mitigate the risk of loss due to damage, destruction, or other unforeseen events that could compromise the property's value or the borrower's ability to repay the loan. In the event of significant property damage, insurance proceeds may be used to repair or rebuild the home, thereby safeguarding both the homeowner and the lender. Required insurance premiums are often collected through **escrow accounts**, and borrowers must provide proof of coverage before the loan can be finalized and the property transaction completed. Documentation typically includes a copy of the insurance policy and evidence of payment for the first year's premium. If the required insurance is not obtained or is cancelled, the lender may impose **force-placed insurance**, which the borrower must pay for. This type of insurance is generally more expensive and may offer less favorable coverage terms.

**Property insurance: hazard and homeowners coverage. Property insurance** is a critical component of the mortgage lending process. Lenders require adequate insurance coverage to protect their financial interest in the property securing the loan. If the property is damaged or destroyed, insurance proceeds help ensure that repairs can be made or the outstanding loan balance can be recovered. Without this protection, a borrower's inability to repair or replace the home could leave the lender with collateral of diminished or no value.

**Hazard insurance**. The most fundamental type of property insurance is **hazard insurance**, which protects the physical structure of the home against specific perils, such as fire, lightning, hail, windstorms, explosions, theft, and vandalism. This coverage generally applies to the dwelling itself—meaning the permanent structure and any attached components, such as garages or decks. Hazard insurance is typically required by the lender as a condition of loan approval and must remain in effect for the life of the loan. The coverage amount must usually be equal to at least the lesser of the loan balance or the cost to rebuild the home, excluding the value of the land.

**Homeowners insurance**. In most cases, hazard insurance is included as part of a more comprehensive **homeowners insurance policy**. This broader policy provides protection not only for the structure but also for personal belongings inside the home, such as furniture, electronics, and clothing. It also includes liability coverage, which protects the homeowner in the event someone is injured on the property and pursues legal action. Additionally, homeowners insurance typically includes coverage for additional living expenses (ALE) if the home becomes uninhabitable due to a covered loss. ALE coverage reimburses costs such as hotel stays, meals, and other temporary housing expenses while the home is being repaired.

Standard homeowners insurance policies are usually issued as **HO-3 policies**, also known as "special form" policies. These policies provide "open peril" coverage for the dwelling—meaning all risks are covered unless specifically excluded—and "named peril" coverage for personal property, meaning coverage only applies to the perils listed in the policy.

Mortgage lenders often require borrowers to submit proof of insurance prior to closing, which may include:

- a copy of the insurance policy declaration page
- an invoice or receipt showing payment of the first year's premium
- the lender listed as a mortgagee on the policy to receive claim payment notifications

If required insurance coverage lapses, is cancelled, or is not obtained, the lender may impose **force-placed insurance** (also known as **lender-placed insurance**). This type of policy is purchased by the lender on the borrower's behalf and typically offers limited coverage at a higher premium. The borrower remains financially responsible for the cost of this coverage, which is often added to the loan's escrow account.

In some regions, especially those prone to certain natural disasters (e.g., hurricanes, wildfires, or earthquakes), <u>additional specialized insurance may be required or recommended</u>. While these are not part of standard hazard or homeowners policies, they may be essential for full protection. Examples include:

- hurricane or windstorm riders
- earthquake insurance
- wildfire coverage or separate deductibles for fire-prone zones

Understanding the scope, limitations, and lender requirements for property insurance ensures that both the borrower and the lender are adequately protected throughout the life of the loan.

**Flood insurance.** In certain areas designated as being at risk of flooding, flood insurance is a mandatory requirement for mortgage approval. Standard homeowners insurance policies do not provide coverage for flood damage, which presents a significant risk to both the homeowner and the lender. Whether flood insurance is required depends on the property's location, elevation, and flood zone designation as determined by federal mapping data.

**FEMA designations and Special Flood Hazard Areas (SFHAs).** The Federal Emergency Management Agency (FEMA) is responsible for maintaining and updating the **Flood Insurance Rate Maps (FIRMs)** that identify areas at varying levels of flood risk. Properties located within **Special Flood Hazard Areas (SFHAs)** are considered high-risk. These zones include designations such as Zones A and V and indicate a 1% or greater annual chance of flooding (commonly referred to as a "100-year flood zone").

If a property is located in an SFHA and the mortgage loan is made through, insured by, or sold to a federally regulated or federally backed lender or investor (including FHA, VA, USDA, Fannie Mae, and Freddie Mac), then flood insurance is federally mandated. Lenders are required to ensure that adequate flood coverage is in place before closing and that the coverage remains active for the duration of the loan.

For properties outside of SFHAs (e.g., Zones B, C, or X), flood insurance is not required under federal law but may still be recommended. In some cases, lenders may impose their own flood insurance requirements as part of loan underwriting.

**Flood zone determination and compliance.** Lenders must obtain a **Standard Flood Hazard Determination Form (SFHDF)** to verify the flood zone status of the subject property. If the determination indicates that the property is in an SFHA, the lender must notify the borrower using a **Notice of Special Flood Hazards and Availability of Federal Disaster Relief Assistance**. The borrower must acknowledge receipt of this notice prior to closing.

Flood insurance must be in place at or before loan consummation. If it lapses or is found to be insufficient, the lender may force-place coverage and pass the premium cost on to the borrower.

**National Flood Insurance Program (NFIP).** Flood insurance coverage is often obtained through the **National Flood Insurance Program (NFIP)**, which is administered by FEMA and available in participating communities. The NFIP offers standardized policies for both building and contents coverage. Current limits include:

> ▸ residential structure coverage is available up to $250,000
> ▸ personal contents coverage is available up to $100,000

These policies have standardized exclusions and deductibles and are backed by the federal government. Participation in the NFIP is contingent upon local governments adopting and enforcing FEMA-approved floodplain management regulations.

**Private flood insurance.** Borrowers may choose to obtain flood coverage through a private flood insurance provider rather than the NFIP. Under the Biggert-Waters Flood Insurance Reform Act and subsequent guidance, private policies must meet specific criteria to be accepted by federally regulated lenders. These criteria include:

> ▸ coverage at least equivalent to an NFIP policy
> ▸ issuance by an insurance company licensed and approved in the state where the property is located
> ▸ legal sufficiency under federal and state law

Lenders must accept private flood insurance that meets these criteria. Some lenders may require legal or underwriting review to verify adequacy before accepting private coverage in lieu of an NFIP policy.

**Life-of-loan flood zone monitoring and map changes.** Lenders are required to perform life-of-loan flood zone monitoring to ensure continued compliance with zoning regulations. If FEMA updates or remaps a flood zone, and a property is newly included in an SFHA, the lender must notify the borrower and ensure flood insurance is obtained within 45 days. Failure to maintain required coverage may result in force-placed insurance.

**Disclosures and borrower education.** Federal regulations require that borrowers purchasing property in SFHAs be informed not only of the insurance requirement but also of the availability of federal disaster relief. However, this relief is not guaranteed and may only apply in presidentially declared disaster areas. Borrowers are encouraged to understand the limits of federal aid and the broader benefits of maintaining adequate flood insurance, even when it is not strictly required.

**Mortgage insurance.** When a borrower obtains a conventional loan with a loan-to-value (LTV) ratio exceeding 80%, the lender typically requires **private mortgage insurance (PMI)** to reduce its risk in the event of borrower default. PMI protects the lender—not the borrower—and is required until the borrower achieves at least 20% equity in the home. PMI may be structured as a **single-premium plan**, in which the borrower pays the full premium at closing. This option can reduce monthly mortgage payments but may not be refundable if the borrower refinances or sells the property before reaching the equity threshold. More commonly, borrowers pay PMI through monthly premiums included in their regular mortgage payments.

**PMI premiums**. PMI premiums are calculated using a mortgage insurance (MI) factor, a percentage based on the loan amount, credit score, loan type, and associated risk factors. The annual premium is determined by multiplying the loan amount by the MI factor. This annual cost is then divided by 12 to calculate the monthly premium. For example, on a $365,000 loan with an MI factor of 1.56% (0.0156), the single premium would be $365,000 × 0.0156 = $5,694. If paid monthly, the cost would be $5,694 ÷ 12 = $474.50 per month.

**FHA mortgage insurance**. Borrowers who use Federal Housing Administration (FHA) loans are subject to a separate form of mortgage insurance known as **Mortgage Insurance Premiums (MIP)**. These premiums are required as part of the FHA program to encourage homeownership by reducing the financial risk to lenders. MIP is paid over the life of the loan and includes both an upfront premium and an annual premium. The upfront premium may be financed into the loan amount, while the annual premium is typically paid in monthly installments. Unlike conventional PMI, FHA mortgage insurance generally cannot be cancelled unless certain criteria are met, such as refinancing into a conventional loan after accumulating sufficient equity.

In all cases, required insurance policies must be maintained according to lender guidelines and applicable federal regulations. Failure to maintain adequate insurance coverage may result in loan default or the imposition of force-placed policies at the borrower's expense. Proper insurance is not only a loan requirement but a critical safeguard for both the borrower's investment and the lender's security interest.

---

## CLOSING

**Settlement agent**
**Closing fees**
**Explanation of documents**
**Funding synopsis**

---

**Settlement agent**

At the heart of the real estate closing process is the **settlement agent**, also referred to as the **closing agent** or **escrow agent**. This professional is responsible for facilitating and overseeing the final steps in a real estate transaction, acting on behalf of the lender to ensure that all legal and financial elements of the transaction are executed accurately and efficiently. The identity of the settlement agent varies by state and may include a **title company, escrow company, real estate attorney**, or, in some cases, a **real estate broker**, depending on local customs and legal requirements.

**Holding funds**. The settlement agent provides substantial value to the transaction by serving as a neutral third party, ensuring fair treatment of all parties and confirming that the terms of the agreement are met. Their expertise in real estate laws and regulations ensures the transaction complies with all applicable legal standards. A core part of their role is to hold funds and documents in escrow, providing a secure and trustworthy means of conducting financial transactions. Settlement agents also assist in resolving discrepancies or outstanding issues that arise during closing, working to keep the transaction on track.

**Key tasks**. The settlement agent's key tasks include coordinating and conducting the closing process, ensuring that all necessary documents are prepared, reviewed, and signed by the buyer, seller, lender, and any other relevant parties. In many transactions, the settlement agent also acts as escrow agent, maintaining custody of critical documents and funds in a secure, neutral account until all contractual conditions are met. They may review and approve any power of attorney (POA) documents if a borrower is unable to attend closing in person. In some cases, they may also conduct or oversee the title search to confirm that the property is free of liens or encumbrances. Additional responsibilities include preparing legal documents such as the settlement statement and deed, scheduling signing appointments, overseeing the closing meeting, recording documents with the appropriate government office, and distributing final copies to the relevant parties.

**Closing fees**

**Educating the borrower**. Throughout the mortgage process, the mortgage loan originator (MLO) is responsible for educating borrowers about the full range of fees associated with obtaining a mortgage loan and completing a real estate transaction. These fees may appear at various stages in the process, from application through closing, and must be disclosed clearly and accurately to help borrowers make informed financial decisions.

**Origination fees.** Origination fees are charges imposed by the lender or mortgage broker for processing, underwriting, and originating the loan. These fees cover administrative tasks such as evaluating the borrower's creditworthiness, verifying documentation, and preparing the loan for funding. Origination fees are typically expressed as a percentage of the loan amount—for example, 1% on a $300,000 loan would equal a $3,000 origination fee.

**Fee disclosure.** Origination fees must be clearly disclosed to borrowers and are prominently displayed on both the Loan Estimate (LE) and the Closing Disclosure (CD). The Loan Estimate provides borrowers with an early breakdown of the costs associated with the loan, including the origination fee. It must be provided to borrowers within three business days of submitting a completed application. The Closing Disclosure, which borrowers must receive at least three business days prior to closing, reflects the final and binding version of those costs. Displaying origination fees on both documents ensures transparency and allows the borrower to confirm that fees have not changed significantly during the application and underwriting process, except where permitted under tolerance rules.

Because origination fees are not standardized across the lending industry, borrowers are strongly encouraged to shop around and compare fee structures among different lenders. Some lenders may charge higher origination fees while offering lower interest rates, whereas others may advertise "no-origination-fee" loans that offset the cost elsewhere, such as through a higher rate. Understanding how the origination fee fits into the total cost of borrowing is essential for informed decision-making. The mortgage loan originator (MLO) plays an important role in helping the borrower evaluate and compare these fees in the broader context of the loan's affordability and terms.

Federal regulations also require MLOs to clearly disclose both the percentage and the total dollar amount of the origination fee. For example, if a lender charges a 1% origination fee on a $250,000 loan, the LE and CD must show both the 1% rate and the corresponding $2,500 cost. This dual presentation ensures clarity and helps borrowers assess how the fee relates to their total loan amount. The MLO must be prepared to explain these disclosures and respond to borrower questions about how the fee is calculated and what services it covers.

**Discount points.** Discount points are optional, upfront fees that a borrower may choose to pay in exchange for a lower interest rate. Each discount point usually equals 1% of the loan amount and reduces the interest rate by a predetermined amount (commonly 0.25%, though this varies by lender and market conditions). This is referred to as "buying down" the rate.

When a borrower elects to pay discount points, the upfront cost of the loan increases, resulting in higher closing costs. However, this payment can yield long-term savings by reducing the mortgage loan's interest rate. A lower interest rate typically translates to reduced monthly payments and less interest paid over the life of the loan, making discount points an appealing option for borrowers who plan to remain in the home for an extended period. While the initial outlay may be significant, the potential long-term financial benefit can be substantial under the right circumstances.

The effectiveness of discount points depends largely on the borrower's intended time horizon for holding the loan. If the borrower plans to sell the home or refinance in a few years, they may not remain in the mortgage long enough to recoup the upfront cost of the discount points. In contrast, borrowers who anticipate living in the home for many years may benefit from the accumulated monthly savings. Therefore, determining whether to pay discount points is not a one-size-fits-all decision—it must be evaluated in light of the borrower's ownership plans and financial objectives.

The mortgage loan originator (MLO) is responsible for guiding the borrower through this decision-making process. This includes helping the borrower understand how much each discount point reduces the interest rate, estimating monthly savings, and calculating the break-even point—the point at which the borrower's interest savings equal the cost of the points paid. MLOs must ensure that the borrower's choice to pay discount points is well-informed and aligned with their broader financial goals, housing plans, and loan strategy.

**Closing costs.** Closing costs encompass a wide range of fees incurred during the finalization of the mortgage and the transfer of property ownership. Although the buyer pays more closing costs than the seller does, the seller generally pays some too.

**Buyer closing costs.** Buyers incur a wide range of closing costs when purchasing a property, especially when financing is involved. These costs typically include both lender-related fees and transaction-related charges, some of which must be paid in advance and others at the time of closing. The total amount can vary significantly based on loan type, lender practices, state and local regulations, and negotiated contract terms.

Common buyer closing costs include:

> ▸ **loan origination and underwriting fees**: Charged by the lender for processing the loan application, evaluating creditworthiness, and preparing the mortgage documents. This often includes a flat origination fee or a percentage of the loan amount.

> ▸ **credit report fee**: A fee to obtain the borrower's credit report from one or more national credit bureaus, used during underwriting.

> ▸ **appraisal fee:** Paid to a licensed appraiser to determine the fair market value of the property. Required by most lenders to confirm the property justifies the loan amount.

- **flood zone determination fee**: A small fee to assess whether the property is located in a FEMA-designated flood zone.

- **prepaid interest:** Covers the interest due between the closing date and the end of the month. This ensures the borrower's first full mortgage payment aligns with the next calendar month.

- **initial escrow deposits:** Lenders often require buyers to deposit several months' worth of property taxes, homeowners insurance, and mortgage insurance (if applicable) into an escrow account to ensure future payments are covered.

- **title insurance** (lender's policy): Typically required by the lender to protect its interest in the property. In some states, the buyer also purchases an owner's title policy, unless negotiated otherwise.

- **title-related fees**: Include title search, settlement/escrow agent fees, document preparation, and recording fees for the deed and mortgage.

- **survey or inspection fees**: Buyers may pay for a property survey (required in some states) or home inspection fees, including specialized inspections (e.g., termite, radon, or structural), depending on the property.

- **attorney fees** (if applicable): In attorney states or where legal review is customary, buyers may retain an attorney to review documents or conduct the closing.

- **mortgage insurance premiums**: If the loan exceeds 80% loan-to-value (LTV), private mortgage insurance (PMI) may be required. Some loans, such as FHA loans, also require upfront mortgage insurance premiums (UFMIP).

- **transfer taxes or government fees**: In some jurisdictions, buyers may pay part or all of the transfer tax, intangible tax, or mortgage recording tax.

- **discount points** (if elected): Optional upfront payments that reduce the loan's interest rate, discussed earlier.

- **homeowners association (HOA) fees**: Buyers may pay initiation fees, application fees, or advance dues if the property is located within an HOA-governed community.

- **homeowners insurance premium**: The first year's premium is typically paid in full at closing, particularly if insurance is being escrowed by the lender.

- **earnest money deposit** (credited): While not technically a closing cost, the earnest money deposit is often applied toward the buyer's closing costs or down payment at settlement.

- **brokerage compensation**: Real estate licensees and their clients negotiate payment as part of their agreement. The licensees are paid according to those agreements, typically at closing.

**Seller closing costs.** While much of the attention in real estate transactions is focused on the buyer's closing costs, sellers also incur costs when transferring ownership of a property. These expenses are typically subtracted from the seller's gross proceeds at closing and vary depending on state laws, local customs, the terms of the purchase agreement, and the nature of the transaction.

Common seller closing costs include:

- **brokerage compensation**: Sellers negotiate pay as part of their agreement with the listing broker for their services in selling the property. Sellers may also pay some or all of the buyer's broker's compensation, either by choice or by negotiation.

- **title insurance** (owner's policy): In many states, the seller pays for the owner's title insurance policy to protect the buyer's interest. This is a one-time premium paid at closing.

- **transfer taxes** / documentary stamp taxes: Some states or municipalities impose transfer taxes or recording fees that must be paid when a property changes hands. These may be based on a flat fee or a percentage of the sales price.

- **outstanding liens or mortgages**: Any mortgage loan balances, home equity loans, or other liens must be paid off at closing. The settlement agent ensures these are satisfied and releases recorded liens.

- **property taxes (prorated)**: The seller is responsible for paying their portion of the property taxes up to and including the closing date, depending on the custom in each state. If property taxes are prepaid, the buyer may reimburse the seller for the unused portion. If taxes are unpaid, the seller's share is deducted from their proceeds.

- **unpaid HOA dues or special assessments** (if applicable): If the property is located in a community with a homeowners association (HOA), the seller may owe prorated dues, transfer fees, or special assessments. these may be negotiable between the buyer and seller.

- **attorney fees (in attorney states):** In states where attorney involvement is required or customary, the seller may retain legal counsel to prepare the deed, review documents, or represent their interests at closing.

> ▸ **repairs or credits agreed upon during negotiations**: If the seller agreed to complete repairs or offer a credit in lieu of repairs, those costs may be reflected on the closing disclosure.

> ▸ **recording fees and document preparation**: In some areas, the seller pays for the preparation and recording of the deed and other documents required to convey the property.

**Prorations and adjustments.** At closing, certain costs related to the property are prorated between the buyer and the seller to ensure each party pays only for the portion of the billing period during which they own the property. Prorations are commonly based on a calendar year or monthly cycle, and the closing date determines how the costs are divided.

These prorated amounts appear on the Closing Disclosure or settlement statement as credits or debits to each party and can affect how much the buyer must bring to closing or how much the seller will receive. Prorated expenses can be either accrued or prepaid.

**Accrued expenses** are costs that have been incurred by the seller but not yet paid as of the closing date. Since these are the seller's responsibility, they are typically credited to the buyer at closing. The buyer will eventually pay the full amount when the bill comes due but will have already been reimbursed for the seller's portion.

Examples of accrued expenses include:

> ▸ Unpaid property taxes for the current year (when billed annually in arrears)
> ▸ Unpaid HOA dues or assessments
> ▸ Utility charges (in some cases, depending on how and when billing occurs)

*Example:*

If the seller has owned the property for 5 months of a 12-month property tax year but the tax bill has not yet been issued, the seller must credit the buyer for 5 months' worth of taxes at closing. The buyer will pay the full tax bill when it arrives but will have already been reimbursed for the seller's share.

**Prepaid expenses** are amounts the seller has already paid in advance for a period that extends beyond the closing date. Since the buyer will benefit from this advance payment, the buyer typically reimburses the seller at closing.

Examples of prepaid expenses include:

> ▸ prepaid property taxes
> ▸ HOA dues paid through the end of the month or year

‣ fuel or oil left in a tank (common in rural properties)

*Example:*

If the seller paid HOA dues through the end of the quarter but is closing mid-month, the buyer will reimburse the seller for the unused portion of the dues.

**Prepaid items and escrow reserves.** In addition to closing costs, borrowers are often required to prepay certain recurring costs into an escrow account, which the lender uses to make future payments on the borrower's behalf. These include:

‣ homeowners insurance premiums (often the first year paid at closing)
‣ property taxes
‣ mortgage insurance premiums (if applicable)
‣ prepaid interest for the partial month between closing and the first full mortgage payment

These prepaid amounts are sometimes confused with closing costs but serve a different function: They ensure the borrower has sufficient reserves to cover upcoming obligations.

**Prepayment penalties.** A **prepayment penalty** is a charge imposed by some lenders if the borrower pays off the mortgage loan early, typically within the first few years. This could occur due to refinancing, selling the property, or making substantial principal reductions. Prepayment penalties are designed to compensate the lender for lost interest income. The MLO is responsible for disclosing whether a loan includes a prepayment penalty and explaining the specific conditions and costs associated with it.

Prepayment penalties are typically structured as a percentage of the remaining loan balance at the time the borrower pays off the loan early. For example, a lender might impose a 2% penalty if the borrower repays the mortgage within the first year of the loan term. This means that a borrower who pays off a $250,000 loan during that period could owe an additional $5,000 in prepayment charges. The intent behind this fee is to compensate the lender for the loss of anticipated interest income, particularly in the early years of the loan when interest makes up a greater portion of the monthly payments.

Some prepayment penalties are designed to decline over time or apply only during a designated "hard prepayment period." A declining structure might begin at 2% in year one, reduce to 1% in year two, and expire altogether in year three. Alternatively, a lender may impose a penalty only if the borrower pays off the loan within the first two or three years of the term, after which the borrower is free to prepay without penalty. These structures are usually outlined clearly in the loan note or prepayment rider, and borrowers should be made aware of any such restrictions during the application and disclosure process.

It is important to note that not all loan programs permit prepayment penalties. Under current federal regulations, prepayment penalties are prohibited on certain types of loans, particularly Qualified Mortgages (QMs)—a category of loans that meet strict underwriting and consumer protection standards set by the Consumer Financial Protection Bureau (CFPB). The prohibition is designed to protect consumers from predatory lending practices and ensure borrowers retain flexibility in managing their home loans. For this reason, many lenders offer loans without prepayment penalties or limit their use to non-QM loans or specialized lending products.

**Explanation of documents**

The closing process involves the execution of several important legal documents, each of which plays a specific role in finalizing the mortgage transaction and transferring ownership of the property. Understanding the purpose and content of these documents is essential for both mortgage professionals and borrowers.

**Promissory note.** The **promissory note** is <u>a legally binding contract in which the borrower agrees to repay the mortgage loan under clearly defined terms</u>. It specifies the principal loan amount, interest rate, monthly payment, repayment schedule, and due dates for each installment. The note also details any applicable late payment penalties, prepayment terms, and the circumstances under which the loan may be considered in default. In the event of default, the promissory note outlines the lender's remedies, including the right to accelerate the loan and pursue foreclosure. <u>Although the note itself is not recorded in public records, it is the borrower's formal acknowledgment of the debt owed</u>.

**Mortgage (security instrument).** The mortgage is a security instrument that pledges the property as collateral for the loan. It creates a voluntary lien on the real estate and provides the lender with a legal claim to the property should the borrower fail to meet the terms of the promissory note. The mortgage document includes a legal description of the property, the names of the parties, and the loan terms. It is recorded in the public records of the county where the property is located, serving as notice to other parties of the lender's secured interest.

In states that use traditional mortgages (often referred to as lien theory states), the borrower holds both legal and equitable title, while the lender holds a lien that must be removed through a satisfaction or release of mortgage once the loan is paid in full.

The mortgage may contain several key clauses.

▸ **acceleration clause**

The **acceleration clause** gives the lender the right to <u>demand full repayment of the outstanding loan balance immediately</u> upon the borrower's breach of the mortgage terms—most commonly, failure to make scheduled payments or failure to maintain required insurance or taxes. This clause does not obligate the lender to accelerate the loan automatically; rather, it gives the lender the option to do so. Once the clause is invoked, the borrower is no longer entitled to repay the loan in installments, and the full remaining balance becomes due. This is often a prerequisite to initiating foreclosure proceedings.

▸ **alienation clause (due-on-sale clause)**

The **alienation clause**, also referred to as a due-on-sale clause, prohibits the borrower from transferring ownership of the property without the lender's written consent. If the borrower sells, gifts, or otherwise conveys the property to another party without permission, the lender may invoke the clause and require immediate repayment of the loan. This clause protects the lender from having to work with a new, possibly unqualified borrower and helps preserve the original loan's terms. It also prevents assumptions of the mortgage unless the lender explicitly allows it.

▸ **defeasance clause**

The **defeasance clause** ensures that the lender's interest in the property is terminated once the loan is paid in full. Upon full repayment of the mortgage debt, the lender must take action to release the lien by recording a satisfaction of mortgage or, in states using a deed of trust, a deed of reconveyance. This clause is critical in restoring clear and marketable title to the borrower and extinguishing the lender's claim on the property.

▸ **escrow clause**

The **escrow clause** requires the borrower to make monthly escrow payments in addition to principal and interest. These payments fund an escrow account held by the lender or servicer, used to pay property taxes, homeowners insurance, mortgage insurance, and sometimes HOA dues. The lender uses this clause to ensure these critical obligations are paid on time, which protects its collateral interest in the property. The borrower receives an annual escrow analysis outlining how the funds are managed.

▸ **maintenance and occupancy clause**

This clause requires the borrower to maintain the property in good condition and to occupy it as a primary residence if that was the original stated intent. Failure to keep the property in habitable condition, or converting it to an investment or vacation home without lender consent, may constitute a default. This provision ensures that the value of the collateral is not diminished through neglect or misuse.

▸ **hazard insurance clause**

The **hazard insurance clause** requires the borrower to maintain adequate insurance coverage to protect the property against damage or destruction. If the borrower fails to maintain the required coverage, the lender has the right to obtain force-placed insurance and charge the borrower for the premiums—often at higher rates. This clause protects the lender's interest in the collateral.

▸ **subordination clause**

A **subordination clause** establishes the priority of liens. In most cases, the mortgage being signed is intended to be the first lien on the property. If a borrower has other loans or liens—such as a home equity line of credit (HELOC)—this clause clarifies that those secondary liens are subordinate to the mortgage lender's claim. In the event of foreclosure, the senior lien holder (the mortgage lender) is paid first.

▸ **power of sale clause (in deeds of trust)**

This clause appears in deeds of trust rather than traditional mortgages and gives the trustee the right to sell the property through a non-judicial foreclosure process if the borrower defaults. The lender does not need to go through the courts, making the process faster and less expensive. This clause must be authorized by state law and is one reason non-judicial foreclosure is allowed in certain jurisdictions.

**Deed of trust.** In some states, particularly those following a title theory model, a **deed of trust** is used in place of a traditional mortgage. While it serves a similar purpose—securing the loan with the property—it involves **three parties**: the borrower (trustor), the lender (beneficiary), and a neutral third party (trustee). The trustee—often a title company or attorney—holds **legal title** to the property on behalf of the lender until the debt is repaid.

The borrower retains **equitable title** and the right to occupy and use the property. If the borrower defaults, the deed of trust often contains a **power of sale clause**, which authorizes the trustee to sell the property through a **non-judicial foreclosure process**, bypassing the court system and allowing for a faster resolution. Like a mortgage, the deed of trust is recorded in public records, and upon full repayment of the loan, a **deed of reconveyance** is issued to clear the lien and return full legal title to the borrower.

## Check Your Understanding

What is the primary difference between a promissory note and a deed of trust?

A. One secures the loan; the other establishes repayment terms.
B. One is recorded publicly; the other is not.
C. One applies only to FHA loans.
D. Both documents serve the same purpose.

If you selected Option A, you are correct! A promissory note outlines loan repayment terms; a deed of trust secures the loan with the property.

**Tax documents.** During the closing process, buyers are often required to sign several tax-related documents that support income verification and reporting obligations tied to the mortgage loan. These documents help ensure the borrower's financial information is accurate and verifiable. They also support the lender's compliance with IRS reporting requirements and protect against identity fraud.

▸ **Form 4506-C: Request for Transcript of Tax Return**

This **form** authorizes the lender to obtain a copy of the borrower's tax return transcript directly from the IRS. It's used to verify income reported on the loan application and helps prevent fraud. Lenders use Form 4506-C to access records through the IRS's Income Verification Express Service (IVES), which speeds up processing.

▸ **Form W-9: Request for Taxpayer Identification Number and Certification**

This form is used to collect the buyer's Social Security number or other taxpayer identification number. It is often required by the lender or servicer for federal tax reporting purposes, including the reporting of mortgage interest paid. The W-9 also includes a certification that the information provided is accurate.

**Compliance and privacy disclosures.** Several documents in the closing package are designed to meet federal legal requirements and protect both the lender and borrower. These disclosures ensure that the borrower's rights are respected and that the lender complies with laws related to identity verification, data privacy, and fair lending.

These disclosures help ensure transparency, protect borrower rights, and confirm that the lender is following federal laws related to fair lending, identity verification, and consumer privacy.

**USA PATRIOT Act disclosure.** This form informs the borrower that the lender is required by federal law to verify their identity. The disclosure explains that the borrower's identification documents (such as a driver's license or passport) will be collected and reviewed as part of the lender's obligation to prevent fraud and comply with anti-terrorism regulations.

**Privacy Notice.** This notice outlines how the lender collects, uses, shares, and protects the borrower's personal information. It also explains the borrower's rights regarding their data and whether they can limit certain types of sharing. Privacy notices are typically required under federal laws like the Gramm-Leach-Bliley Act.

**Equal Credit Opportunity Act (ECOA) Notice.** This notice advises the borrower of their rights under the ECOA, which prohibits discrimination in any aspect of a credit transaction. It confirms that the lender does not discriminate based on race, color, religion, national origin, sex, marital status, age, receipt of public assistance, or because a person has exercised rights under consumer protection laws.

**Additional closing documents.** In addition to the promissory note and the security instrument (mortgage or deed of trust), borrowers typically sign several other important documents at closing, including:

> ▸ **initial escrow disclosure statement**
>
> This explains how the lender will manage escrow accounts for property taxes and insurance, including the expected monthly deposits and disbursement schedule.

> ▸ **borrower's affidavits and certifications**
>
> These may include affirmations that the borrower intends to occupy the property as a primary residence (if applicable), acknowledgments of disclosure receipt, and declarations of accuracy regarding financial and personal information. The Name/Signature Affidavit confirms that the borrower is known by and signs under any name variations used in legal documents.

> ▸ **ALTA Settlement Statement (or HUD-1 in rare cases)**
>
> This is a line-by-line breakdown of the buyer's and seller's transaction costs that helps confirm that funds were distributed accurately. While primarily used by title companies for internal records, it is often shared with the parties for additional clarity alongside the Closing Disclosure.

> ▸ **payoff statement (for seller's mortgage)**

This shows the exact amount needed to pay off the seller's existing loan(s) at closing. It ensures the mortgage is fully paid so the buyer receives clear title.

> ▸ **deed (warranty deed, grant deed, or special warranty deed)**

This is the instrument by which the seller transfers ownership of the property to the buyer. While the seller typically executes the deed, it is a critical closing document for the buyer and must be recorded to evidence title transfer.

**Funding synopsis**

The **funding phase** of the transaction involves executing all financial components of the sale. During closing, the buyer and seller finalize the transfer of ownership, and all payments and financial adjustments are completed.

Some state laws require that all funds brought to the closing table by the borrower and lender qualify as "good funds"—meaning they must be immediately collectible at the time of closing. If the funds are not considered "payable on demand," they cannot be used to complete the transaction. This ensures that all parties have access to cleared, reliable funds when the closing is finalized.

Funds are typically transferred via wire or certified checks and are managed by the settlement agent, who ensures that all disbursements align with the terms of the contract. Other funding arrangements also exist.

**Table funding.** In table funding, the loan is made in the name of the lender who is technically providing the funds at closing. However, that lender sells the loan almost immediately—often on the same day—to another lender or investor (such as one in the secondary market). This allows the original lender to free up their money and reuse it for more loans. For example, a lender might lend $100,000 to one borrower, sell that loan, and then use the proceeds to fund another $100,000 loan. This method keeps their capital in constant circulation.

**Funding by a direct investor (private investors).** Sometimes, a borrower doesn't meet the typical "conforming" loan standards required by traditional lenders (such as banks or mortgage companies). In these cases, a mortgage broker may turn to a direct investor—often a private individual or group of investors who are not affiliated with an institution. These direct investors provide the loan funds themselves, often based on more flexible criteria. This is a common path for funding non-conforming or hard-to-place loans.

**Assignment of mortgages.** After a loan is originated, it can be assigned (sold) from one lender to another. The loan may be sold with or without recourse. If it's sold with recourse, the original lender may have to buy it back if the borrower defaults. The promissory note (the document promising repayment) is endorsed to the new lender. When a loan is sold, both the old and new loan servicers (the companies handling payments and customer service) are required to notify the borrower in writing. This way, the borrower knows who to contact and where to send payments.

## FINANCIAL CALCULATIONS USED IN MORTGAGE LENDING

**Decimals and percentages**
**Interest**
**PITI payments**
**Mortgage insurance**
**Debt-to-income ratios**
**LTV ratio**
**Buydowns**
**Closing costs**
**ARM fully indexed rate**
**VA loan funding fees**

**Decimals and percentages**

It is important to know how to convert percentages to decimals and vice versa. Both are involved in several loan-related calculations.

To convert a percentage to a decimal:

1. Remove the percent sign (%).
2. Divide by 100 OR simply move the decimal point two places to the left.

*Examples*:

Convert 25% to a decimal.

$$25 \div 100 = 0.25$$

Convert 7.5% to a decimal.

$$7.5 \div 100 = 0.075$$

To convert a decimal to a percentage, multiply the decimal by 100 OR simply move the decimal point two places to the right.

*Examples*:

Convert 0.45 to a percentage.

$$0.45 \times 100 = 45\%$$

Convert 0.065 to a percentage.

$$0.065 \times 100 = 6.5\%$$

## Interest

**Interest** is the cost of borrowing money, typically expressed as a percentage of the loan amount. It is the fee that lenders charge borrowers for the use of funds, calculated over time and often paid in periodic installments.

In mortgage financing, interest is considered and calculated in a few different ways.

**Period interest.** Period interest, also known as periodic interest, refers to the interest that accumulates over a defined time period, often on a regular schedule such as monthly or annually. This interest represents the cost of borrowing. i.e., a fee that the borrower pays to the lender in exchange for the lender lending the borrower the money for the purchase.

Period interest is calculated based on the outstanding loan balance, the applicable interest rate, and the loan's terms for the given period. While lenders generally quote interest rates using the annual percentage rate (APR), the interest on most mortgages compounds on a monthly basis, or 12 times per year.

The formula for period interest is:

*Monthly Interest Payment = (Annual Interest Rate in Decimal Form ÷ Number of Compounding Periods) x Principal Balance*

*Example*:

A borrower has an outstanding loan balance of $100,000 and a 4% annual interest rate. Calculate the monthly interest amount.

*Monthly Interest Amount = (0.04 ÷ 12) × 100,000 = 0.00333 × 100,000 = 333.33*

*Monthly Interest = $333.33*

So, the monthly interest amount of $333.33 will be added to the borrower's monthly mortgage payment.

**Per diem interest.** Per diem interest, also known as daily interest, is interest that accumulates each day rather than on a monthly or other periodic basis. This daily interest is commonly applied when determining the amount of prepaid interest due at closing or for calculating partial interest for short periods within a loan term. For per diem calculations, <u>lenders may use either a 365-day or a 360-day year</u>, depending on their specific calculation method.

The formula for per diem interest is:

*Daily Interest = (Loan Amount × Monthly Interest Rate in Decimal Form) ÷ 365*

**Example**:

A borrower has an outstanding loan balance of $250,000 and a 6% annual interest rate. Calculate the per diem interest using the 365-day per year approach.

*Daily Interest = (250,000 × 0.06) ÷ 365 = $41.10*

**Prepaid interest.** Borrowers typically pay mortgage interest in arrears, meaning each monthly payment covers the interest from the previous month. Further, the first monthly mortgage payment is usually due on the first day of the second month following closing.

Mortgage interest, however, begins to accrue on the day after closing through the end of that same month. Because of this, the borrower is responsible for paying for this interest accrual at closing—BEFORE the interest actually accrues. This payment is commonly referred to as **prepaid interest** or interest on closing.

The formula for prepaid interest is:

*(Loan Amount × Monthly Interest Rate in Decimal Form) ÷ 365 × Number of Days*

**Example**:

A borrower is closing on a home loan of $375,000 with an interest rate of 5% on March 15. The first regular mortgage payment will be due May 1, which will include mortgage interest for the month of April because mortgage interest is paid in arrears. At closing, the borrower will need to prepay the mortgage interest for March 16 through March 31.

Using the 365-day year, calculate the interest that accrues for March 16 through the end of the month to determine the amount of prepaid interest the borrower will owe at closing.

*Prepaid Interest Owed at Closing = (375,000 x 0.05) ÷ 365) × 16 days = $821.92*

Borrowers pay **per diem interest (interest per day)** at closing to cover the <u>daily interest</u> for the time between the closing date and the start of their first scheduled mortgage payment.

For per diem calculations, <u>lenders may use either a 365-day or a 360-day year</u>, depending on their specific calculation method.

Remember to round up the cents for dollar amounts: 625.38695 is $625.39

The formula for per diem interest is:

*Per Diem Interest = (Loan Amount × Interest Rate in Decimal Form) ÷ 365*

The resulting per diem interest amount is then used to calculate the prepaid interest that will be due at closing.

The formula for prepaid interest is:

*Prepaid Interest = (Loan Amount × Interest Rate in Decimal Form) ÷ 365) × Number of Days*

1.  Calculate Per Diem Interest

    Loan Amount: $192,300
    Interest Rate: 6.5%
    Method: 365-day

2.  Calculate Total Prepaid Interest

    Loan Amount: $88,000
    Interest Rate: 5.75%
    Calculate for: 12 days
    Method: 365-day

**Interest paid over life of the loan.** Borrowers are often interested in the total amount of interest they will pay over the life of the loan. The numbers used in the calculation are the P&I portion of the mortgage payment, the total number of payments, and the original loan amount (i.e., the principal). The formula is:

*Total Interest Paid = (P&I Monthly Payment × Number of Payments) – Original Loan Amount*

1.  Calculate Total Interest Paid

    Loan Amount: $260,000
    Monthly P&I Payment: $1,375
    Loan Term: 30 years

**Monthly principal and interest payments.** A borrower's monthly payment begins with a principal loan amount (P) payment to pay down the loan balance plus a monthly interest (I) payment. Use this formula for a fixed rate loan:

*Monthly Payment = (Principal + Total Interest Paid) ÷ Loan Term in Months*

1.  Calculate Monthly P&I Payment

    Principal Loan Amount: $289,000

    Total Interest Paid Over Loan Term: $178,200

    Loan Term: 30 years

**Interest-only payment.** Some loan products include an interest-only feature in which a borrower pays only the interest on the loan each month for a set initial period (often 5 to 10 years). After the interest-only period ends, the loan typically converts to a fully amortizing loan, where the borrower must start making higher monthly payments that cover both principal and interest—usually over the remaining loan term.

The formula for an interest-only monthly payment is:

*Monthly Interest = (Principal Loan Amount × Interest Rate) ÷ 12)*

1.  Calculate Interest-Only Payment

    Loan Amount: $325,000

    Interest Rate 5%

**Down payment.** A down payment is the initial lump sum a borrower pays upfront when purchasing a property, usually represented as a percentage of the total purchase price.

The formula to calculate the down payment percentage is:

*Down Payment ÷ Purchase Price = Down Payment Percentage*

Any earnest money accompanying the offer will be credited toward the buyer's costs, usually reducing the amount of down payment and/or closing costs they still owe subtracted from the total amount the buyer must bring to closing.

Here's the formula to use to calculate the remaining down payment due at closing:

*Down Payment Due at Closing = (Purchase Price × Down Payment %) − Earnest Money Paid*

1. Calculate Down Payment Percentage

    Loan Amount: $360,000

    Down Payment: $11,000

2. Calculate Down Payment Due at Closing

    Purchase Price: $280,000

    Down Payment: 5%

3. Earnest Money Paid: $4,000 Calculate Down Payment Percentage

    Loan Amount: $360,000

    Down Payment: $11,000

4. Calculate Down Payment Due at Closing

    Purchase Price: $280,000

    Down Payment: 5%

    Earnest Money Paid: $4,000

**PITI payments**

**PITI** refers to the four components of a typical monthly mortgage payment: principal, interest, taxes, and insurance. Together, these elements make up the total payment a borrower owes each month, per the following formula:

*Total Monthly Mortgage Payment = Monthly Principal + Monthly Interest + Monthly Taxes + Monthly Insurance*

Lenders often collect an **escrow** amount as part of the monthly payment to ensure that expenses like property taxes and homeowners insurance are paid on time and in full. To cover unexpected increases in these expenses, lenders are allowed, under RESPA, to maintain an **escrow cushion** of up to one-sixth (1/6) of the estimated total annual disbursements from the escrow account.

*Monthly Property Tax Escrow Payment = Annual Property Tax Bill ÷ 12*

*Monthly Homeowners Insurance Escrow Payment = Annual Insurance Premium ÷ 12*

*Example scenario*:

A borrower's monthly principal payment is $700, and their monthly interest payment is $500. In addition to principal and interest, the lender collects funds monthly for the escrow account to pay property taxes and homeowners insurance. For this year, the property taxes are $3,600 annually, and the homeowners insurance annual premium is $1,200.

Calculate the borrower's monthly PITI payment.

$$Monthly\ PITI = \$700 + \$500 + (\$3,600 \div 12) + (\$1,200 \div 12) =$$
$$\$700 + \$500 + \$300 + \$100 =$$
$$\$1,600$$

Borrowers often have to fund their escrow account at closing.

*Example scenario:*

A borrower learns that the annual property tax bill for the house they're buying is $15,000, paid in two installments in June and September each year. The closing is in January, so the first mortgage payment will be due March 1.

First, determine how many payments the borrower will pay into escrow before each property tax installment is due. Then calculate any shortage and also add in the permissible cushion to find the amount the borrower will have to pay at closing.

Consider these details:

1. Six months of taxes are due June 1. By then, the borrower will have paid monthly taxes into the escrow account for March, April, and May.

2. Six months of taxes are also due September 1. By then, the borrower will have paid monthly taxes into the escrow account for June, July, and August.

3. The borrower's mortgage payments (which include escrow amounts for taxes) will cover six months of tax payments. That leaves six months unaccounted for, as well as the permissible two months of cushion, for a total of eight months to be paid at closing.

4. The monthly property tax bill: $15,000 \div 12 = $1,250

Because there is a shortage of six months of tax payments, as well as two months' need for cushion, at closing the borrower will pay to fund the escrow account:

$$\$1,250 \times 8 = \$10,000$$

**Mortgage insurance**  Mortgage insurance may be included in the borrower's monthly payment. This insurance could take the form of either Private Mortgage Insurance (PMI) or Mortgage Insurance Premium (MIP), each with distinct requirements and payment options. PMI is typically required for conventional loans when the borrower's down payment is less than 20% of the property's purchase price. Conversely, MIP is mandatory for FHA loans regardless of the down payment amount.

**PMI.** PMI is typically required for conventional loans when the borrower's down payment is less than 20% of the property's purchase price. Annual premium rates generally range from 0.22% to 2.25%. The formula for PMI derivation is:

*Principal Loan Amount × Annual Premium Rate Percentage = Annual PMI*

The formula for monthly PMI, which is the amount that will be added to the borrower's PITI payment, is:

*Annual PMI ÷ 12 = Monthly PMI*

1. Calculate the Annual PMI Amount and the Monthly PMI Amount

Loan Amount: $295,000

Annual PMI Rate: 0.85%

*Examples:*

A borrower has a $350,000 principal loan amount and an annual private mortgage insurance premium rate of 0.75% paid monthly. Calculate the annual PMI amount.

*Principal Loan Amount × Annual Premium Rate Percentage = Annual PMI*

$350,000 × 0.0075 = $2,625 annual PMI

Now calculate the monthly PMI, which will be added to the borrower's PITI payment.

*Annual PMI ÷ 12 = Monthly PMI*

$2,625 ÷ 12 = $218.75

**MIP.** For FHA loans, borrowers are required to pay a Mortgage Insurance Premium (MIP) both upfront at closing and as an annual payment. The **upfront MIP (UFMIP)** is 1.75% of the loan amount, which the borrower can pay in cash at closing or choose to roll into the loan principal.

The formula for calculating UFMIP is:

*Principal Loan Amount × 1.75% = UFMIP*

The **annual MIP** ranges between 0.15% and 0.75% of the loan amount and is paid in monthly installments as part of the mortgage payment. The exact annual rate depends on several factors, including the base loan amount, the loan-to-value

(LTV) ratio, and the mortgage term. Together, these MIP payments help secure the FHA loan by reducing risk to the lender.

The formula for calculating annual MIP is:

*Principal Loan Amount × 0.75% = Annual MIP*

*Examples:*

Calculate the UFMIP, a 0.75% annual MIP, and the monthly MIP payment for a $250,000 FHA loan.

First, calculate the UFMIP:

UFMIP = $250,000 × 0.0175 = $4,375

Then calculate the annual MIP:

Annual MIP: $250,000 × 0.0075 = $1,875

Now, calculate the monthly MIP payment that will be added to the PITI by dividing the annual MIP by 12 and then rounding to 2 decimal places:

$1,875 ÷ 12 = $156.25

## Check Your Understanding

Elizabeth is putting $11,000 down on a home she's purchasing for $360,000. What is her down payment percentage?

A. 2%

B. 3%

C. 5%

D. 6.5%

Option B is correct! To find the down payment percentage, divide the down payment amount by the purchase price: $11,000 ÷ $360,000.

**Debt-to-income ratios**

The **debt-to-income (DTI) ratio** is a critical measure used by lenders to evaluate a borrower's ability to manage monthly debt payments relative to their gross monthly income (income before taxes and other payroll deductions). There are two primary types of DTI ratios: the housing (front-end) ratio and the total (back-end) ratio.

The **housing ratio**, or front-end ratio, focuses specifically on the borrower's housing expenses. It is calculated by dividing all proposed housing expenses—

such as principal, interest, property taxes, hazard and flood insurance, and homeowner association dues—by the borrower's gross monthly income.

The formula for the housing ratio is:

*Housing DTI = All Proposed Housing Expenses ÷ Gross Income*

The **total DTI ratio**, or back-end ratio, takes a broader view by including all of the borrower's monthly debts. This includes proposed housing expenses (PITI), consumer debts like car loans and credit card payments, negative rental income, and court-ordered payments such as alimony or child support.

The formula for the total ratio is:

*Total DTI = All Borrower Debt ÷ Gross Income*

Standard guidelines for DTI ratios typically set acceptable maximums for housing ratios between 33% and 36% of the borrower's income and for total ratios between 36% and 43%. However, automated underwriting systems for conforming conventional loans may allow higher DTIs, up to 50%, by compensating with strong credit scores or substantial assets. For manually underwritten loans, Fannie Mae generally caps the DTI at 36% but may increase it to 45% if the borrower meets certain credit score and reserve requirements.

NOTE: Fannie Mae and Freddie Mac allow the exclusion of installment loans' monthly payments when 10 or fewer payments remain.

By analyzing both housing and total DTI ratios, lenders can determine whether a borrower's debt obligations are manageable and assess the risk associated with extending credit.

### Housing DTI Example:

A borrower's monthly housing expenses are: $1,800 principal and interest payment, $130 in real estate taxes, $25 for homeowners insurance, and $36 HOA fee. The borrower's monthly gross income is $6,840. Calculate the housing ratio.

1. Add up all proposed housing expenses.

$$\$1,800 + \$130 + \$25 + \$36 = \$1,991$$

2. Divide housing expenses total by gross income.

$$\$1,991 \div \$6,840 = 0.29108 = 29\%$$

### Total DTI Example:

A borrower's monthly expenses are: $1,991 total proposed housing expenses, $290 total credit card payments, a $560 car payment, and $75 for car insurance. Calculate the borrower's total DTI ratio.

1. Add up all monthly expenses.

$$\$1{,}991 + \$290 + \$560 + \$75 = \$2{,}916$$

2. Divide total expenses by gross income.

$$\$2{,}916 \div \$6{,}840 = 0.4263 = 43\%$$

**Housing ratios and loan qualification.** Standard guidelines for DTI ratios typically set acceptable maximums for housing ratios between **33% and 36%** of the borrower's income and for total ratios between **36% and 43%.** Automated underwriting systems for conforming conventional loans may allow higher DTIs. For manually underwritten loans, Fannie Mae generally caps the DTI at 36% but may increase it to 45% if the borrower meets certain credit score and reserve requirements.

## Check Your Understanding

A borrower earns $6,000 a month and has a PITI of $1,680. What is their housing ratio?

    A. 26%

    B. 28%

    C. 30%

    D. 32%

If you selected Option B, you are correct! $1,680 ÷ $6,000 = 0.28 or 28%. This is a common acceptable limit for housing ratio under many loan programs.

1. Calculate the Housing Ratio

Principal & Interest (monthly): $1,425.00

Taxes & Insurance (annual): $2,400

HOA Fee (annual): $360

Borrower's Annual Income: $98,000

2. Calculate the Total DTI

Purchase: $310,000 home with a 5% down payment

Principal & Interest (monthly): $1,735.00

Annual Taxes: $3,600

Annual Hazard Insurance: $900

Car Payment: $289/month (8 months remaining)

Credit Card Payment: $45/month

Student Loan Payment: $120/month

Streaming Subscriptions: $35/month

Borrower's Annual Income: $123,000

3.  Calculate the Housing Ratio for Loan Qualification Purposes

Spouse A earns $850.00 bi-weekly

Spouse B earns $1,250.00 monthly

Housing Payment: $895.00/month

## Check Your Understanding

1.  A $200,000 loan with a PMI rate of 0.5% results in what monthly PMI? Round to the nearest dollar.

    A.  $52
    B.  $83
    C.  $102
    D.  $133

If you selected "b," you are correct! Annual PMI = $200,000 × 0.005 = $1,000 → Monthly PMI = $1,000 ÷ 12 = $83.33

2.  Calculate the UFMIP Amount

FHA Loan Amount: $265,000

3.  Calculate the New Loan Amount for UFMIP Rolled into Loan

FHA Loan Amount: $312,000

4.  Calculate the Annual MIP and Monthly MIP

FHA Loan Amount: $278,000

Annual MIP Rate: 0.75%

**Loan-to-Value Ratio**   The **loan-to-value ratio (LTV)** represents the relationship between the mortgage loan amount and the appraised value or purchase price of the property being financed. A higher LTV indicates a smaller borrower equity stake and is considered riskier for the lender. LTV is expressed as a percentage.

The LTV is calculated by dividing the principal loan amount by either the property's purchase price <u>or</u> its appraised value, whichever is lower. The formula for calculating LTV is:

$$LTV = Principal\ Loan\ Amount \div Purchase\ Price\ OR\ Appraised\ Value$$

1. Calculate LTV

Loan Amount: $400,000

Purchase Price: $500,000

Appraised Value: $490,000

2. Calculate LTV

Loan Amount: $375,000

Purchase Price: $500,000

Appraised Value: $505,000

The **combined loan-to-value ratio (CLTV)** expands on the standard LTV by considering the total amount of all outstanding loans secured by the property. This includes the primary mortgage as well as any secondary loans or liens.

Here is the formula:

*CLTV = Total of All Mortgage Balances ÷ Appraised Value OR Purchase Price*

3. Calculate CLTV

Purchase Price: $300,000

First Loan Amount: $250,000

Second Loan (Piggyback Loan): $40,000

Appraised Value: $295,000

The **Home Equity Combined Loan-to-Value Ratio (HCLTV)** is used to assess the risk of a borrower who has, or may take out, multiple loans secured by the same property. Unlike the standard CLTV, which considers only the total balance of existing loans, the HCLTV also includes any available credit from a home equity line of credit (HELOC). This measure helps lenders evaluate the potential exposure if the borrower fully utilizes the available HELOC credit.

The formula is:

$$HCLTV = (Total\ of\ All\ Mortgage\ Balances + HELOC\ Available\ Credit) \div$$
$$Appraised\ Value\ OR\ Purchase\ Price$$

4. Calculate HCLTV

Appraised Value: $700,000

First Mortgage Balance: $500,000

HELOC Available Credit: $100,000

**Buydowns**

A **buydown** is a financing option that allows a borrower to pay a lower interest rate and reduced mortgage payments by paying discount points upfront. A **discount point** is a fee equal to 1% of the total loan amount, paid at closing to reduce the interest rate. Buydowns can be structured as either temporary or permanent.

A **temporary buydown** reduces the loan's interest rate for a specified period, typically three years or fewer. Two forms exist: level payment buydowns and graduate payments buydowns. For level payment buydowns, the payment reduction amount stays the same over the buydown period. With graduated payment buydowns, the mortgage has lower monthly payments that gradually increase over a specific period before leveling off to a fixed amount for the remainder of the loan term.

For example, a 3-2-1 buydown lowers the interest rate by 3 percentage points in the first year, 2 percentage points in the second year, and 1 percentage point in the third year before reverting to the original rate for the remainder of the loan term.

A **permanent buydown**, also known as a fixed-rate buydown, allows the borrower to secure a lower interest rate for the entire life of the loan. This option can result in significant savings over the loan term, making it attractive for borrowers who plan to stay in their home long-term. Both types of buydowns require an upfront cost but offer flexibility depending on the borrower's financial goals.

Buydown calculations are always based on the loan amount. The formula is:

$$\textit{Loan Amount} \times \textit{Discount Points} = \textit{Buydown Cost}$$

*Example:*

A property has a sale price of $349,000 and the loan amount is $255,000. The borrower wants a buydown of 2 discount points. What is the buydown cost for the borrower at closing?

$$\$255,000 \times 0.02 = \$5,100$$

Remember that 1 discount point is 1% of the loan amount. In this case, the borrower's buydown is 2 discount points, so 2% of $255,000.

1. Calculate Buydown Cost

   Sale Price: $349,000

   Loan Amount: $255,000

   Discount Points: 2 points (2%)

**Check Your Understanding**

A borrower is applying for a loan of $375,000 to purchase a home with a purchase price of $500,000 and an appraised value of $520,000. What is the loan-to-value (LTV) ratio?

A. 70%
B. 75%
C. 80%
D. 85%

Option B is correct. LTV is calculated by dividing the loan amount by the lower of the purchase price or appraised value.

**Closing costs: prepaid Items, prorated Items**

**Prepaid items. Prepaid items** are costs that borrowers pay up front at closing to ensure certain expenses are covered in advance.

These items are typically related to the property and mortgage and may include a portion of property taxes, homeowners insurance premiums, mortgage interest from the day of closing until the end of the month, private mortgage insurance (PMI) premiums, and escrow account funding to cover future payments for property taxes and insurance. These payments ensure that the borrower is financially prepared to meet ongoing property-related obligations after closing.

Here is a scenario involving prepaid homeowners insurance:

A borrower's annual homeowners insurance premium is $1,200. The lender requires the first 12 months of homeowners insurance to be prepaid at closing, plus a 2-month escrow cushion. What is the total the borrower will owe at closing for homeowners insurance?

1. Calculate the <u>monthly</u> insurance premium.

   *Annual Insurance Premium ÷ 12 = Monthly Insurance Premium*

   $1,200 ÷ 12 = $100

2. Calculate the total due at closing (annual premium plus 2-month cushion).

   $1,200 + $200 = $1,400

At closing, the buyer will pay $1,400 to cover the first year of homeowners insurance and fund the 2-month escrow cushion. This way, the lender can make insurance payments on time and maintain a reserve for future premiums or any shortfall.

**Prorated items.** Prorated items are ongoing costs that are divided proportionately between the buyer and seller based on the length of time each party owns the property during the billing period.

Common prorated expenses include property taxes, homeowner association (HOA) dues, rent (if the property is a rental), and utility bills. This adjustment ensures that each party only pays for their fair share of the expense during their respective period of ownership.

Consider this scenario about prorated property taxes:

The annual property tax for a home is $6,000, which is paid in 2 installments. The seller has already paid the January 1-June 30 installment of $3,000. Closing is set for April 10. That means the buyer will need to reimburse the seller for the taxes the seller already paid for April 10-June 30.

Calculate how much the buyer will owe the seller at closing.

1. Calculate the daily property tax amount.

$$Annual\ Property\ Tax\ Amount \div 365 = Daily\ Tax\ Amount$$

$$\$6,000 \div 365 = \$16.44\ per\ day$$

2. Determine the number of days the buyer needs to reimburse.

April 10 through June 30 is <u>82 days</u> (21 days in April + 31 days in May + 30 days in June). Remember to count the day of closing in most states.

3. Calculate the prorated property taxes the buyer owes the seller.

$$Daily\ Tax\ Amount\ x\ Number\ of\ Days\ Owed = Prorated\ Property\ Taxes$$

$$\$16.44 \times 82 = \$1,347.08$$

In this scenario, the buyer will reimburse the seller $1,347.08 for the property taxes covering April 10 through June 30 at closing. This amount ensures the seller is compensated for taxes paid in advance for a period when the buyer will own the property. Going forward, the buyer will be responsible for the next tax payment due on July 1.

1. Calculate Prepaid Homeowners Insurance

Annual Homeowners Insurance Premium: $1,200

Lender Requirement: Prepay 12 months of coverage and an escrow cushion of 2 additional months

**Prorated calculations (Property Tax).** Calculate how much the buyer will owe the seller at closing.

Calculate the daily property tax amount.

$$Annual\ Property\ Tax\ Amount \div 365 = Daily\ Tax\ Amount$$

Determine the number of days the buyer needs to reimburse.

Calculate the prorated property taxes the buyer owes the seller.

$$Daily\ Tax\ Amount \times Number\ of\ Days\ Owed = Prorated\ Property\ Taxes$$

2. Calculate Prorated Property Taxes

Annual Property Taxes: $6,000 (paid in two $3,000 installments)

Seller has paid: January 1 – June 30 installment ($3,000)

Closing Date: April 10

Buyer owes seller for: April 10 – June 30

**ARM fully indexed rate**

Adjustable-rate mortgages (ARMs) adjust their interest rates at specified times throughout the loan term, typically after an initial fixed-rate period.

Features include rate **adjustments, margins, and caps**:

**Adjustments.** Adjustments are tied to a specific index. The **index rate** is a benchmark interest rate that fluctuates with the market and serves as the foundation for calculating the new ARM interest rate. Once the initial fixed-rate period ends, the rate adjusts on the **adjustment date**, when the new interest rate takes effect.

**Margins.** The adjustment is determined by adding the **margin**, a fixed number of percentage points set in the loan agreement, to the current index rate, which results in the **fully indexed rate**, the new variable interest rate that applies after the adjustment. Unlike the index rate, the margin remains constant over the life of the loan.

**Caps.** The fully indexed rate is subject to the loan's **periodic cap** (limiting how much the rate can increase per adjustment period) and **lifetime cap** (is the <u>maximum amount the interest rate is allowed to increase over the entire life of the loan,</u> regardless of how market rates change).

**Fully indexed rate.** The formula to calculate the fully indexed rate is:

$$\textit{Fully Indexed Rate = Margin + Current Index Rate}$$

Once you have calculated the fully indexed rate, you apply a cap if applicable:

▸ **apply the periodic cap**

Compare the fully indexed rate to the borrower's current rate. The rate cannot increase more than the periodic cap allows during a single adjustment period.

▸ **check the lifetime cap**

Make sure the new rate does not exceed the maximum rate allowed over the life of the loan. This is based on the original starting interest rate plus the lifetime cap.

1. Calculate the New Interest Rate After the Initial Rate Period Ends

Starting Interest Rate: 5.25%

Margin: 2.00%

Current Index Rate: 1.75%

Periodic Cap: 2%

Lifetime Cap: 6%

**VA loan funding fees**

Borrowers of VA loans pay a one-time, non-refundable funding fee that is typically financed into the loan.

The funding fee is based on the loan amount and the veteran's use history (first-time or subsequent use):

▸ first-time VA loan users with no down payment or less than 5% down: 2.15%
▸ subsequent VA loan users with no down payment or less than 5% down: 3.3%
▸ 5% down payment: 1.5%
▸ 10% or more down payment: 1.25%
▸ interest rate reduction refinances: 0.50%

- cash-out refinance loans with any down payment amount:
    - first-time VA loan use: 2.15%
    - subsequent VA loan use: 3.3%

1. Calculate the Loan Funding Fee

Purchase Price: $300,000

Down Payment: $0

Loan Type: VA, first-time use

VA Funding Fee Rate: 2.15% (0.0215)

Borrower chooses to finance the funding fee

2. Calculate the Loan Funding Fee

Purchase Price: $350,000

Down Payment: $0

Loan Type: VA, second-time use

VA Funding Fee Rate: 3.3% (0.033)

Borrower pays the funding fee in cash at closing

# FINANCIAL CALCULATIONS ANSWER KEY

**Per diem interest**

1. Loan Amount: $192,300
Interest Rate: 6.5%
Method: 365-day
Per Diem Interest = $(0.065 \div 365) \times 192,300 = \$34.25$

2. Loan Amount: $88,000
Interest Rate: 5.75%
Calculate for: 12 days
Method: 365-day
*Solution:*
Per diem interest = $(0.0575 \div 365) \times 88,000 = \$13.87$
Total interest for 12 days = $\$13.87 \times 12 = \$166.44$

**PITI**

1. Monthly Principal: $1,120.00
Monthly Interest: $980.00
Monthly Property Taxes: $275.00
Monthly Homeowners Insurance: $85.00
*Solution*:
PITI = $\$1,120 + \$980 + \$275 + \$85 = \$2,460.00$

2. Loan Amount: $289,000
Monthly Principal & Interest (P&I): $1,550.00
Annual Property Taxes: $3,000 \div 12 = \$250.00$/month
Annual Homeowners Insurance: $960 \div 12 = \$80.00$/month
Annual PMI Rate: 0.70%
PMI paid monthly
*Solution*:
Annual PMI = $\$289,000 \times 0.007 = \$2,023.00$
Monthly PMI = $\$2,023.00 \div 12 = \$168.58$
Total Monthly Mortgage Payment (PITI + PMI) = $1,550 (P&I) + $250 (Taxes) + $80 (Insurance) + $168.58 (PMI) = $2,048.58

3. Loan Amount: $260,000

Monthly P&I Payment: $1,375

Loan Term: 30 years ÷ 12 = 360 payments

*Solution:*

Total Interest Paid = ($1,375 × 360) − $260,000 = $495,000 − $260,000 = $235,000


4. Principal Loan Amount: $289,000

Total Interest Paid Over Loan Term: $178,200

Loan Term: 30 years

*Solution:*

Monthly Mortgage Payment (P&I) = ($289,000 + $178,200) ÷ (30 x 12) = $467,200 ÷ 260 = $1,298.89


5. Loan Amount: $325,000

Interest Rate 5%

*Solution*:

Monthly Interest-Only Payment = ($325,000 × .05) ÷ 12 = $1,354.17


6. Loan Amount: $360,000

Down Payment: $11,000

*Solution:*

Down Payment Percentage = $11,000 ÷ $360,000 = 0.0306 = 3%


7. Purchase Price: $280,000

Down Payment: 5%

Earnest Money Paid: $4,000

*Solution:*

Down Payment Due at Closing = ($280,000 × 0.05) − $4,000 = $14,000 − $4,000 = $10,000


**Mortgage insurance**

1. Loan Amount: $295,000

Annual PMI Rate: 0.85%

*Solution*:

Annual PMI = $295,000 × 0.0085 = $2,507.50

Monthly PMI = $2,507.50 ÷ 12 = $208.96

2. FHA Loan Amount: $265,000

*Solution*:

UFMIP = $265,000 × 0.0175 = $4,637.50

3. FHA Loan Amount: $312,000

*Solution:*

UFMIP = $312,000 × 0.0175 = $5,460.00

New Loan Amount = $312,000 + $5,460.00 = $317,460.00

4. FHA Loan Amount: $278,000

*Solution*:

Annual MIP = $278,000 × 0.0075 = $2,085.00

Monthly MIP = $2,085.00 ÷ 12 = $173.75

**Debt-to-income ratios**

1. Principal & Interest (monthly): $1,425.00

Taxes & Insurance (annual): $2,400 ÷ 12 = $200.00/month

HOA Fee (annual): $360 ÷ 12 = $30.00/month

Borrower's Annual Income: $98,000 ÷ 12 = $8,166.67/month

*Solution:*

Total Monthly Housing Expense = $1,425 + $200 + $30 = $1,655.00

Housing Expense Ratio = $1,655.00 ÷ $8,166.67 = 20.3%

2. Purchase: $310,000 home with a 5% down payment

Principal & Interest (monthly): $1,735.00

Annual Taxes: $3,600 ÷ 12 = $300.00/month

Annual Hazard Insurance: $900 ÷ 12 = $75.00/month

Car Payment: $289/month (8 months remaining)

Credit Card Payment: $45/month

Student Loan Payment: $120/month

Streaming Subscriptions: $35/month (not included in calculation)

Borrower's Annual Income: $123,000 ÷ 12 = $10,250.00/month

*Solution:*

Total Monthly Housing Expense = $1,735 + $300 + $75 = $2,110.00

Total Monthly Debts = $2,110 (housing) + $289 + $45 + $120 = $2,564.00

Total Debt Ratio = $2,564 ÷ $10,250.00 = 25.0%

Loan Qualification

3. Spouse A earns $850.00 bi-weekly

Spouse B earns $1,250.00 monthly

Housing Payment: $895.00/month

*Solution*:

Spouse A monthly income = $850 × 26 ÷ 12 = $1,841.67

Spouse B monthly income = $1,250.00

Total Monthly Income = $1,841.67 + $1,250.00 = $3,091.67

Housing Expense Ratio = $895.00 ÷ $3,091.67 = 28.9%

Do they qualify? Yes

## LTV ratio

1.  Loan Amount: $400,000

Purchase Price: $500,000

Appraised Value: $490,000

*Solution*:

LTV = $400,000 ÷ $490,000 = 81.6%

2.  Loan Amount: $375,000

Purchase Price: $500,000

Appraised Value: $505,000

*Solution*:

LTV = $375,000 ÷ $500,000 = 75.0%

3.  Purchase Price: $300,000

First Loan Amount: $250,000

Second Loan (Piggyback Loan): $40,000

Appraised Value: $295,000

*Solution:*

CLTV = $290,000 ÷ $295,000 = 98.3%

4.  Appraised Value: $700,000

First Mortgage Balance: $500,000

HELOC Available Credit: $100,000

*Solution:*

HCLTV = $600,000 ÷ $700,000 = 85.7%

## Buydowns

1.  Sale Price: $349,000

Loan Amount: $255,000

Discount Points: 2 points (2%)

*Solution:*

$255,000 × 0.02 = $5,100

## Closing costs

1. Annual Homeowners Insurance Premium: $1,200

Lender Requirement: Prepay 12 months of coverage and an escrow cushion of 2 additional months

*Solution*:

$1,200 ÷ 12 = $100 monthly premium

$1,200 + $200 = $1,400

2. Annual Property Taxes: $6,000 (paid in two $3,000 installments)

Seller has paid: January 1 – June 30 installment ($3,000)

Closing Date: April 10

Buyer owes seller for: April 10 – June 30

*Solution*:

Daily Tax = $6,000 ÷ 365 = $16.44

Days owed = 82

Buyer Reimbursement to Seller= 82 × $16.44 = $1,348.08

## ARMs
## fully indexed rate

1. Starting Interest Rate: 5.25%

Margin: 2.00%

Current Index Rate: 1.75%

Periodic Cap: 2%

Lifetime Cap: 6%

*Solution*:

Fully Indexed Rate = 2.00% (margin) + 1.75% (index) = 3.75%

Periodic Cap: Fully Indexed Rate (3.75%) is within 2% of the current rate (5.25%)

Lifetime Cap: The Fully Indexed Rate is well below the maximum allowed (5.25% + 6% = 11.25%)

New Interest Rate = 3.75%

Because the fully indexed rate is below the periodic cap limit, the borrower receives the full benefit of the lower rate.

**VA loan funding fees**

1. Purchase Price: $300,000

Down Payment: $0

Loan Type: VA, first-time use

VA Funding Fee Rate: 2.15% (0.0215)

Borrower chooses to finance the funding fee

*Solution*:

Funding Fee = $300,000 × 0.0215 = $6,450

Total Loan Amount (with funding fee added) = $300,000 + $6,450 = $306,450

Answer: The borrower's total loan amount will be $306,450 after rolling in the VA funding fee.

2. Calculate the Loan Funding Fee

Purchase Price: $350,000

Down Payment: $0

Loan Type: VA, second-time use

VA Funding Fee Rate: 3.3% (0.033)

Borrower pays the funding fee in cash at closing

*Solution*:

Funding Fee = $350,000 × 0.033 = $11,550

Since the borrower is not financing the fee, the loan amount remains $350,000

Total due out of pocket at closing for the funding fee = $11,550

# Chapter 3 Mortgage Loan Origination Activities
## Snapshot Review

**APPLICATION
INFORMATION
AND
REQUIREMENTS**

**Loan origination
process**
- Begins with pre-qualification (informal, no documentation required) and moves to pre-approval (formal, with verified documentation).
- Steps include: initial consultation, application, verification, processing, underwriting, approval/denial, closing, and post-closing servicing or sale.

**Role of the MLO**
- MLO collaborates with processors, underwriters, appraisers, title agents, and escrow officers.

**Pre-qualification
Phase**
- MLO evaluates borrower's financial profile: calculates estimated loan amount; prepares non-binding pre-qualification letter

**Initial
consultation**
- A relationship-building opportunity to understand borrower goals, explain the process, and introduce typical loan products and fees.
- Non-binding rate quotes and fee overviews are discussed but not finalized.
- Sets expectations for documentation, timelines, and next steps.
- Interest rates discussed in general terms; borrowers learn the difference between rate and APR.
- MLO may explain discount points and loan pricing.
- Typical fees include origination, processing, underwriting, appraisal, title, escrow, and prepaid items.

**Borrower
application**
- URLA / Form 1003the industry-standard form for collecting borrower and loan information; used at both application and closing stages.
- Includes borrower details, employment and income, assets and liabilities, declarations, and loan product details.
- An application is considered received when six key pieces of information are collected (name, income, SSN, address, value, and loan amount).
- MLO ascertains ability to repay loan.
- Gift funds must be from eligible donors (e.g., relatives, domestic partners) and accompanied by a signed gift letter.
- Restrictions may apply depending on loan type and borrower credit score.
- MLO must follow up on incomplete applications per ECOA.
- If not resolved, must issue a Notice of Incompleteness or Adverse Action Notice with required content.

**Application
verification**
- Verifies employment, income, assets, and availability of funds using VODs, VOEs, pay stubs, W-2s, and tax returns.
- Lenders prefer "seasoned funds" (held at least 60 days).
- Employment status is often re-verified shortly before closing.

| | |
|---|---|
| **Suitability of products and programs** | • MLO must assess borrower's short- and long-term plans, risk tolerance, and financial goals to recommend suitable loan options.<br>• Must explain product differences (e.g., fixed vs. ARM), risks, and benefits. |
| **Accuracy (tolerances)** | • TRID rule establishes accuracy tolerance thresholds<br>• Zero tolerance: lender/MLO fees, transfer taxes.<br>• 10% cumulative tolerance: third-party fees from lender's list.<br>• No/Unlimited tolerance: borrower-selected third-party services outside the list. |
| **MLO disclosure documents** | • Loan Estimate (LE): Delivered within 3 business days of application; revised if key changes occur.<br>• Mortgage Servicing Disclosure: Discloses whether the lender will service the loan or transfer servicing.<br>• Home Loan Toolkit: For purchase transactions only.<br>• List of Providers: Includes third-party service options.<br>• Affiliated Business Disclosure: Must disclose any affiliated financial interest in recommended providers.<br>• ARM Disclosures: CHARM booklet + loan-specific ARM disclosure due within 3 business days of completed ARM application.<br>• Homeownership Counseling Disclosure: Notifies borrower of counseling availability.<br>• Closing Disclosure (CD): Must be received at least 3 business days before closing; major changes trigger a new 3-day waiting period.<br>• 3-7-3 rule summarizes timing requirements for initial disclosures; iInitial disclosures within 3 business days.<br>• Closing cannot occur until at least 7 business days after disclosure delivery.<br>• If redisclosure is needed, allow 3 additional business days. |
| **QUALIFICATION PROCESSING AND UNDERWRITING** | |
| **Borrower analysis** | • Evaluates the borrower's assets, liabilities, income, and creditworthiness.<br>• Assets must be verifiable and often "seasoned" for 60+ days.<br>• Liabilities include mortgages, loans, credit cards, court-ordered payments, and tax liens.<br>• Income must be stable, verifiable, and likely to continue for 3+ years if it has an expiration (e.g., alimony).<br>• Varying income (commissions, bonuses) usually averaged over 2 years.<br>• Acceptable sources: wages, self-employment, rental, retirement, alimony, and certain non-taxable benefits.<br>• Gaps in employment under 6 months may require minimal documentation; over 6 months requires proof of current full-time work.<br>• Credit scores and reports are key to assessing borrower risk.<br>• FICO score components: payment history (35%), utilization (30%), age (15%), mix (10%), inquiries (10%).<br>• Undisclosed debts must be clarified and verified by the MLO. |

- Delinquencies, charge-offs, and bankruptcies must be considered in underwriting.
- Qualifying ratios: housing ratio (front-end): PITI ÷ gross income, typically ≤ 28–31%; DTI ratio (back-end): all monthly debts ÷ gross income, typically ≤ 43%, but may vary; LTV ratio: loan amount ÷ property value; higher LTV = greater risk; >80% usually requires PMI.
- ATR rules require lenders to verify 8 key underwriting factors.
- QM loans must avoid risky features and meet standards for safe harbor or rebuttable presumption.
- Refinance analysis must show a net tangible benefit (e.g., lower rate, shorter term, fixed over ARM).
- Repeated refinancing without borrower benefit (churning) may violate lending laws.

**Automated underwriting systems (AUS)**

- DU (Fannie Mae) and LPA (Freddie Mac) are commonly used AUS tools.
- Evaluate loan data for guideline compliance and issue recommendation (approve, refer, or deny).
- Final decisions may also consider lender overlays or investor requirements.

**Appraisals**

- Determine market value using comps, condition, and valuation methods.
- Three primary approaches: sales comparison, cost, and income.
- Appraisal types: full, exterior-only (drive-by), and desktop.
- Government loans have additional property standards (FHA, VA, USDA).
- Reports must meet USPAP standards and be conducted by certified/licensed appraisers.
- ECOA Valuations Rule: borrower must receive appraisal ≥ 3 business days before closing.
- Appraisals governed by FIRREA and USPAP.
- Prohibits coercion or influence over appraisers; often uses AMCs.
- Reconsideration of value allowed with supporting documentation—no undue pressure permitted.
- Second appraisals or updates may be required for aged or conditional reports.

**Title reports, binders and title insurance**

- Title search reviews ownership history, liens, easements, and defects to confirm marketable title.
- Preliminary title report (title binder) identifies current status and exceptions.
- Final title report confirms marketable title and compliance with closing requirements.
- Title insurance types: lender's policy protects lender up to loan amount (required); owner's policy: optional; protects buyer's full interest for as long as they own the home.

**Insurance: hazard, homeowners, flood, mortgage**

- Required coverage for property damage (fire, wind, theft, etc.).
- HO-3 policies are most common: structure = open peril; contents = named peril.
- Force-placed insurance may be imposed if borrower fails to maintain coverage.
- Flood insurance mandatory in FEMA Special Flood Hazard Areas (Zones A & V).
- Verified through a Standard Flood Hazard Determination Form (SFHDF).

- May be obtained via NFIP or private insurer (must meet federal requirements).
- Lenders must monitor flood zone status for life of loan and ensure continuous coverage.
- PMI required for conventional loans with LTV > 80%; paid monthly or upfront.
- FHA loans require MIP: upfront + annual premiums, typically not cancellable.
- Lender must be listed on insurance policies to ensure payment protections.

## CLOSING

**Settlement agent**
- Neutral third party (title/escrow company, attorney, or broker, depending on state) who coordinates the final transaction steps.
- Oversees document preparation, escrow funds, title clearance, closing appointments, and recording of legal documents.
- Ensures legal compliance and protects interests of all parties.

**Closing fees**
- Origination fees are charged by lender for processing and underwriting the loan (typically 0.5%–1% of loan amount).
- Disclosed on both Loan Estimate (LE) and Closing Disclosure (CD).
- Must be explained clearly by the MLO to help borrower comparison shop.
- Discount points are optional upfront fees to "buy down" the interest rate (1 point = 1% of loan amount).
- May make sense for long-term borrowers; not ideal for those who plan to sell or refinance soon.
- MLO should help borrower calculate break-even point.
- Closing costs: buyer typically pays more than the seller.
- Buyer costs include: loan origination, appraisal, credit report, title insurance, taxes, escrow deposits, prepaid interest, inspection fees, MIPs, discount points, earnest money deposit, homeowners insurance.
- Seller costs include: brokerage commissions, title insurance (in some states), taxes, payoff of liens, and negotiated repairs or credits.
- Certain costs are prorated (e.g., property taxes, HOA dues) depending on the closing date.
- Prepaid items include prepaid interest, first-year insurance premiums, and escrow deposits for taxes and insurance; ensure funds are available for upcoming payments.
- Prepayment penalty charged by some lenders if loan is paid off early within a set period.
- Declining or fixed structures; not permitted on qualified mortgages (QMs).
- MLO must disclose and explain clearly if applicable.

**Explanation of documents**
- Promissory note outlines borrower's loan terms and repayment obligations.
- Mortgage / deed of trust secures the loan with the property; recorded publicly; include clauses such as acceleration, alienation, defeasance, escrow, maintenance, hazard insurance, and subordination.
- Deed of Trust used in title theory states; includes trustee and power of sale clause for non-judicial foreclosure.
- Form 4506-C authorizes lender to access IRS tax transcripts.
- Form W-9 provides taxpayer ID for reporting.
- USA PATRIOT Act Disclosure verifies borrower's identity.
- Privacy Notice explains how personal data is used and shared.
- ECOA Notice confirms borrower rights under anti-discrimination law.

- Initial Escrow Disclosure explains escrow account funding and disbursements.
- Borrower affidavits confirm information accuracy and intent to occupy property.
- ALTA Settlement Statement breaks down costs line by line.
- Payoff Statement shows seller's outstanding mortgage payoff.
- Deed transfers ownership from seller to buyer; recorded after closing.

**Funding Synopsis**

- Final stage where funds are disbursed, documents recorded, and ownership officially transfers.
- Funds must be "good funds" (immediately collectible) and transferred via wire or certified check.
- Table Funding: originating lender funds loan and sells it immediately.
- Direct Investor Funding: used for non-conforming loans; funded by private individuals or groups.
- Assignment of mortgage: after funding, loan may be sold to another lender; borrower receives notice of servicer change.

# Chapter 3 Quiz: Mortgage Loan Origination Activities

1. At which stage does the lender make a credit decision based on a full risk assessment of the borrower and property?

   a. Application
   b. Processing
   c. Underwriting
   d. Post-closing

2. What marks the transition from underwriting to the closing phase of the loan origination process?

   a. The borrower schedules the property inspection.
   b. The loan is approved, and all conditions are satisfied.
   c. The appraiser submits the final report.
   d. The borrower opens a checking account with the lender.

3. Which professional serves as the borrower's main point of contact throughout the mortgage loan origination process?

   a. Underwriter
   b. Loan processor
   c. Mortgage loan originator
   d. Escrow officer

4. Which of the following is typically NOT included in the pre-qualification process?

   a. Review of recent pay stubs and W-2s
   b. Reporting estimated income and debts
   c. Verbal discussion with an MLO
   d. Providing an estimate of how much a borrower may qualify to borrow

5. What does a pre-approval letter represent in the homebuying process?

   a. A non-binding estimate of the loan amount a borrower would qualify for based on Fannie Mae or VA guidelines
   b. A final commitment to lend a specified amount
   c. A loan offer valid for up to 60 days
   d. A conditional commitment to lend up to a specific amount

6. A borrower is charged a fee to cover the lender's risk evaluation and final loan decision. Which type of fee is this?

   a. Underwriting fee
   b. Processing fee
   c. Credit report fee
   d. Closing fee

7. A borrower decides to lower his interest rate by paying three discount points at closing. If the loan amount is $250,000, how much will he pay in discount points?

   a. $2,500
   b. $5,000
   c. $7,500
   d. $10,000

8.  At what two points in the mortgage process is the URLA typically completed?

    a.  At home inspection and loan disbursement
    b.  At application and again at closing to reflect final loan terms
    c.  During pre-qualification and final walk-through
    d.  Before the appraisal and after the title search

9.  Maya's aunt gives her a financial gift to help cover the down payment on her first home. Maya plans to apply for a conventional loan with a 25% down payment. Can she use the gift funds for the entire down payment, and what must she provide to verify the gift?

    a.  Yes, and she must provide a signed gift letter and verify the transfer of funds.
    b.  Yes, but only if the gift is less than $10,000.
    c.  No, gift funds are never allowed for down payments on conventional loans.
    d.  No, only parents are allowed to give gift funds.

10. What does it mean when a lender requires funds to be "seasoned"?

    a.  The funds must come from a tax-exempt account.
    b.  The funds must have been earned through employment.
    c.  The funds must have been in the borrower's account for at least 60 days.
    d.  The funds must have been approved by a title company.

11. How many years of verifiable income history do most lenders require for loan qualification?

    a.  One year
    b.  Two years
    c.  Three years
    d.  Four years

12. Which type of fee falls under TRID's no or unlimited tolerance category?

    a.  Recording fees selected from the lender's provider list
    b.  Charges for services required by the lender
    c.  Origination fees paid directly to the MLO
    d.  Owner's title insurance selected by the borrower outside the lender's provider list

13. Under which of the following conditions may a lender issue a revised Loan Estimate (LE)?

    a.  The borrower requests a lower interest rate.
    b.  The borrower misses a document deadline.
    c.  The cumulative fees exceed TRID tolerance thresholds.
    d.  The borrower changes their home insurance provider.

14. When must the Mortgage Loan Servicing Disclosure be provided to the borrower?

    a.  At closing
    b.  Within three business days of a completed loan application
    c.  Before the first mortgage payment is due
    d.  Only if the borrower requests it in writing

15. In the "3-7-3 Rule" under TILA (15 U.S.C. §1601 et seq.) and the Mortgage Disclosure Improvement Act (MDIA), what does the "7" refer to?

   a. The number of pages in the Loan Estimate
   b. The maximum number of loan options that can be presented
   c. The minimum number of business days that must pass before closing
   d. The number of disclosures required at application

16. Which of the following borrowers is presenting a liquid asset as part of the mortgage application?

   a. Mea has $12,000 in a checking account.
   b. Harold owns an investment property in another state.
   c. Jenna just paid off her car, which is now fully owned.
   d. Lin has antique furniture valued at $5,000.

17. Under what condition can a co-signed loan be excluded from a borrower's liabilities during underwriting?

   a. If the loan is less than $10,000
   b. If the primary borrower has made payments from their own funds for the past year
   c. If the borrower signs an affidavit of intent to refinance
   d. If the co-signed loan was opened more than 5 years ago

18. How do lenders typically evaluate variable income such as bonuses or commissions?

   a. They count only the most recent bonus or commission.
   b. They average it over a two-year period.
   c. They exclude it unless it exceeds 26% of the borrower's salary.
   d. They estimate based on the borrower's projections.

19. Marisol is a freelance writer who works as a sole proprietor. She's applying for a mortgage and plans to use her self-employment income to qualify. Which documentation will she most likely be required to provide?

   a. Her business license and three client testimonials
   b. Two years of W-2s and pay stubs from freelance clients
   c. Her last two years of federal tax returns, including Form 1040 with Schedule C
   d. A notarized affidavit from her accountant stating her income is stable

20. Carlos is applying for a mortgage. His estimated monthly housing expenses, including principal, interest, property taxes, and homeowner's insurance (PITI), total $1,820. He earns a gross monthly income of $6,500. What is Carlos' housing ratio?

   a. 26%
   b. 28%
   c. 30%
   d. 32%

21. Taylor is applying for a mortgage and earns a gross monthly income of $7,000. Her monthly debts include PITI of $1,850, $300 car payment, $150 in credit card payments, and $400 in alimony payments. What is Taylor's debt-to-income (DTI) ratio?

   a. 37%
   b. 39%
   c. 41%
   d. 43%

22. What is the Safe Harbor legal protection associated with Qualified Mortgages?

    a. It applies when the borrower's DTI is 43% or less and the loan meets QM criteria.
    b. It shields lenders from underwriting oversight, allowing for faster loan approval.
    c. It allows lenders to issue QMs without verifying the borrower's income.
    d. It applies only to HELOCs and reverse mortgages for senior citizens.

23. Which borrower is most likely to benefit from paying discount points?

    a. A buyer who plans to refinance in 12 months
    b. A buyer who expects to sell the home within five years
    c. A buyer planning to keep the home for 15 years or more
    d. A buyer seeking the lowest possible upfront costs

24. A seller has owned the home for five months of the year, and property taxes are billed annually in arrears. How is this handled at closing?

    a. The seller credits the buyer for five months' worth of taxes.
    b. The seller pays the entire year's taxes in advance.
    c. The buyer pays no taxes after closing.
    d. The taxes are split evenly between the parties.

25. Which of the following best describes a declining prepayment penalty structure?

    a. The penalty increases as the loan matures.
    b. The penalty remains fixed for the life of the loan.
    c. The penalty applies only if the borrower misses a payment.
    d. The penalty decreases over time, then expires.

26. Which of the following details is NOT typically included in a promissory note?

    a. The loan's interest rate
    b. The property's appraised value
    c. The monthly repayment schedule
    d. Prepayment and late payment terms

27. Alicia has a mortgage with an alienation clause. She decides to transfer her home's title to her son as a gift but does not inform the lender or get written permission. What can the lender legally do in response to this transfer?

    a. Modify the loan to reflect the new owner.
    b. Automatically approve the transfer since it's a family member.
    c. Require immediate repayment of the loan under the due-on-sale clause.
    d. Refinance the loan in Alicia's son's name without documentation.

28. Nathan buys a home in a state that uses a deed of trust rather than a traditional mortgage. His loan agreement includes a power-of-sale clause, and legal title is held by a trustee until he repays the debt. If Nathan defaults on the loan, what is the most likely outcome under this arrangement?

    a. The lender must sue Nathan in court to initiate foreclosure.
    b. The trustee can sell the property through a non-judicial foreclosure process.
    c. The borrower automatically retains full title and cannot be foreclosed on.
    d. The court will appoint a new lender to take ownership of the property.

29. A local mortgage lender funds a $250,000 loan in their name and closes the transaction with the borrower. The same day, they sell that loan to a large national investor in the secondary market and immediately use the proceeds to fund a new loan. What type of funding model is this lender using?

    a. Warehouse funding
    b. Portfolio lending
    c. Flip-over lending
    d. Table funding

30. A borrower takes out a $280,000 conventional loan with a PMI rate of 0.75% annually. What is the borrower's monthly PMI payment?

    a. $140
    b. $175
    c. $210
    d. $260

31. Jason has a 30-year fixed-rate mortgage with a monthly principal and interest (P&I) payment of $1,450 and a loan amount of $300,000. What is the total interest Jason will pay over the life of the loan?

    a. $192,000
    b. $222,000
    c. $240,000
    d. $262,000

32. A borrower takes out a $240,000 loan and will pay $160,000 in total interest over a 30-year loan term. What is the borrower's monthly principal and interest payment?

    a. $980
    b. $1,050
    c. $1,111
    d. $1,200

33. How long are most pre-approval letters valid before the borrower's financial data must be updated?

    a. 15 to 30 days
    b. 30 to 45 days
    c. 60 to 90 days
    d. 120 to 180 days

34. A borrower receives a rate quote during their initial meeting with the MLO. Which of the following statements about that quote is most accurate?

    a. It is based on preliminary information and subject to change.
    b. It is legally binding once provided in writing.
    c. It can only be offered after full application and underwriting.
    d. It requires the borrower to pay discount points.

35. What is the purpose of the Declarations section of the URLA?

    a. To declare borrower citizenship only
    b. To summarize estimated closing costs
    c. To gather information about the borrower's financial background
    d. To collect the borrower's preferred mortgage term

36. Which of the following borrower characteristics would most likely suggest that an adjustable-rate mortgage (ARM) is appropriate?

    a. Plans to relocate or refinance within a few years
    b. Prefers stable, long-term payments
    c. Has a fixed income and low risk tolerance
    d. Is purchasing an investment property to hold for 20+ years

37. When must the AfBA disclosure be provided to the borrower?

    a. Within 10 days of loan closing
    b. At the time of underwriting approval
    c. At or before the time of loan application
    d. At or before the time the affiliated business is recommended

38. How far in advance must lenders send ongoing adjustment notices before subsequent ARM payment changes?

    a. 10 to 30 days
    b. 60 to 120 days
    c. 180 to 210 days
    d. 12 months

# *4* Ethics

## Introduction
## Ethical issues related to federal laws
## Ethical behavior in loan origination

### Learning Objectives

- Define and describe ethics related to the mortgage industry.
- List and describe UDAAPs in the categories of unfair acts or practices, deceptive acts or practices, and abusive acts or practices.
- Identify the general principles behind fairness in lending, including prohibited acts and protected classes under the Equal Credit Opportunity Act (15 U.S.C. §1691 et seq.) and the Fair Housing Act.
- Distinguish between fraudulent misrepresentation, negligent misrepresentation, and puffing.
- Define and identify examples of fraud for housing and fraud for profit.
- Identify red flags for various types of mortgage fraud.
- Identify mortgage-related advertising requirements and prohibitions.
- Describe predatory lending practices.

**INTRODUCTION**

The process of originating mortgage loans is fundamental to the housing finance system. It impacts not only individual borrowers but also the entire economy. Consider the profound impact unethical mortgage lending practices had on the housing and economic crisis of 2007-2008.

Experts generally agree that subprime loans, risky adjustable-rate mortgages, the failure to properly secure mortgage loans, and other predatory lending practices contributed greatly to the crisis. These practices contributed to a massive number of foreclosures when borrowers found they owed more on their homes than they were worth or when increased interest rates on adjustable-rate mortgages resulted in borrowers who could not afford their mortgage payments.

In a field where financial decisions are deeply personal and have a significant impact on individuals' lives, ethical practices are critical to maintaining the integrity of the mortgage lending profession and safeguarding lenders, borrowers, and the overall economy.

At its core, mortgage loan origination involves creating and structuring loans that allow borrowers to obtain affordable home financing. However, the importance of ethical practices in the industry cannot be overstated. Decisions that loan officers, brokers, and other stakeholders make have broad consequences for borrowers and the financial institutions they represent.

This chapter explores the ethical responsibilities of mortgage loan originators and examines the challenges these professionals face as they navigate the complex mortgage lending landscape. We will examine key ethical issues, such as the duty to provide accurate, transparent information to consumers, the impact of predatory lending, and the role of self-regulation within the industry.

As you review this content, you will see references to many of the laws introduced in the first chapter of this book. We present these here again because of their relationship to ethics in the mortgage industry. Also, as you proceed, remember that when we mention a mortgage loan originator, we refer to mortgage bankers, lenders, and brokers.

## ETHICAL ISSUES RELATED TO FEDERAL LAWS

**Mortgage industry ethical benchmarks**
**UDAAP guidelines**
**Ethics and RESPA**
**Ethics and the Civil Rights Act**
**Ethics and the Fair Housing Act**
**Ethics and other financing laws**
**Prohibited acts**
**Mortgage fraud**
**Advertising ethics**
**Predatory lending**
**Recent mortgage ethics cases**

**Mortgage industry ethical benchmarks**
In a general sense, ethics are a set of moral principles or values that govern an individual or a group of individuals engaged in similar practices. Like many industries, the mortgage industry and its participants have at times been scrutinized for failing to comply with ethical lending practices, resulting in numerous federal and state laws governing lending.

Ethics in the mortgage industry is a critical topic, especially given the industry's history of contributing to financial crises and impacting consumers. The following table provides an overview of key ethical factors in the mortgage industry:

## Key Ethical Benchmarks in the Mortgage Industry

| Factor | Prohibition Benchmark | Best Practice |
|---|---|---|
| Truthful marketing and advertising | **Misleading advertising** used to attract borrowers | Be transparent about loan terms, fees, and qualifications; provide clear, honest communication. |
| Fair lending practices | **Discriminatory lending**, such as denying loans or charging higher interest rates based on membership in a protected class | Comply with laws such as the Equal Credit Opportunity Act and the Fair Housing Act; provide unbiased credit evaluations. |
| Predatory lending | **Taking advantage** of vulnerable borrowers (elderly, low-income) by offering loans with excessive fees or terms that borrowers cannot realistically afford | Offer loans suitable for a specific borrower's situation; clearly explain terms and risks. |
| Loan origination and documentation integrity | **Falsifying** income, inflating appraisals, or manipulating credit applications to obtain loan approval | Ensure that all information used to evaluate and process a loan is accurate and verified. Loan officers must act with integrity, even when under pressure to close deals. |
| Duty to borrowers | **Conflicts of interest**, such as pushing higher-commission products that may not be right for the consumer | Mortgage professionals should act in the best interests of their clients, offering advice and products that suit the borrower's needs. |
| Transparency in loan servicing | **Ambiguous loan servicing** practices, poor communication during loan modifications, or wrongful foreclosures | Provide clear, timely communication about payment changes, foreclosure risks, and assistance options. |
| Regulatory compliance | **Failure to stay up to date** on or comply with relevant laws and regulations | Mortgage professionals should become familiar with related federal and state legislation and stay current on changes in the regulatory environment. |

**NAMB Code of Ethics**

Federal mortgage legislation does not explicitly define ethical conduct. Federal and state laws focus on actions that lenders are required to perform or are prohibited from performing.

Various professional organizations provide their own ethical guidelines for the mortgage industry. For example, the **National Association of Mortgage Brokers (NAMB)** opens its brief code of ethics by stating,

> *"The members of the National Association of Mortgage Brokers, believing that the interests of the public and private sector are best served through the voluntary observance of ethical standards of practice, hereby subscribe to the following Code of Ethics."*

**NAMB ethics code overview**. The NAMB Code of Ethics, which you can find at https://secure.namb.org/np/viewDocument?orgId=namb&id=402889258fc82944 018fd16609fc0068, outlines the following standards, stating that NAMB members shall:

1. conduct business in a manner reflecting honesty, honor, and integrity.

2. conduct their business activities in a professional manner. Members shall not pressure any provider of services, goods, or facilities to circumvent industry professional standards. Equally, Members shall not respond to any such pressures placed upon them.

3. provide accurate information in all advertisements and solicitations.

4. not disclose unauthorized confidential information.

5. conduct their business in compliance with all applicable laws and regulations.

6. disclose any equity or financial interest they may have in the collateral being offered to secure a loan.

In addition to this Code of Ethics, NAMB provides an Events Code of Conduct outlining the behavior expected of members at conferences, meetings, and events. This code applies not only to NAMB members but also to sponsors, hosts, and other attendees. To view or download a PDF file of this Code of Conduct, visit https://secure.namb.org/np/viewDocument?orgId=namb&id=402889728f2e4b65 018f2f6689220006.

Finally, NAMB invites members to earn a **Lending Integrity Seal of Approval**. The approval process includes additional continuing education, a criminal background check, and a pledge to comply with the Code of Ethics, best business practices, and an outlined grievance review process. For more information, visit https://www.lendingintegrity.org/.

Similarly, other groups, such as the National Association of Mortgage Underwriters and several regional and state mortgage associations, offer ethical codes for their members.

Of course, these ethical codes cannot guarantee that individuals or firms in the mortgage lending industry will comply with ethical standards. Thus, the myriad laws promulgated by federal and state governments come into play.

**UDAAP guidelines**     Federal and state laws expressly prohibit certain actions. The Dodd-Frank (12 U.S.C. §5301 et seq.) Act introduced the concept of unethical actions as being "unfair, deceptive, or abusive acts or practices" (UDAAP).

Per Dodd-Frank, it is illegal for lenders or other firms that offer financial services **to engage in unfair, deceptive, or abusive acts or practices.** The Consumer Financial Protection Bureau and the Federal Trade Commission are the main agencies tasked with enforcing regulations that protect consumers from predatory lenders and unethical lending practices. The CFPB is authorized to regulate UDAPPs and, together with the FTC, enforce compliance. The CFPB applies specific "tests" to various situations to determine if a particular action meets the criteria for unfair, deceptive, or abusive practices.

Many other federal laws prohibit financial product and service providers from making false or misleading claims about their products and services or pressuring or deceiving consumers into making unwanted purchases.

**UDAAP is the ethics enforcement doctrine**. CFPB and FTC regulators use UDAAP standards to evaluate mortgage-related entities for practices such as using misleading advertising, hampering consumers' understanding of a transaction, or concealing information that results in a consumer obtaining an unsuitable or unaffordable mortgage loan.

### Check Your Understanding

The general premise of UDAAP is to

    A. force compliance with multiple statutes and regulations that govern the mortgage lending industry
    B. prevent unfair, deceptive, and abusive acts and practices in the mortgage lending industry
    C. strengthen the relationship between mortgage lenders and governing agencies
    D. prevent discriminatory behaviors in the foreclosure process

If you selected "B," you are correct! UDAAP refers to unfair, deceptive, and abusive acts or practices in the mortgage industry. Those acts and practices include discrimination and a multitude of other practices that result in or could result in harm to consumers.

**UDAAP-prohibited practices.** The Dodd-Frank Act charges the CFPB with detecting and assessing risks to consumers and markets for financial products and services, and defines unfair, deceptive, and abusive acts or practices.

What tests does the CFPB use to determine if an act or practice is unfair? A practice may be categorized as unfair for any of the following reasons.

▸ **Substantial injury**.

First, regulators determine if the act causes or is likely to cause substantial injury to consumers. In this context, substantial injury typically involves financial harm, such as costs or fees a consumer pays because of an unfair practice.

An act or practice that causes a small amount of harm to a large number of people may constitute *substantial injury*. It is important to note that actual injury is not required; a significant risk of concrete harm may be sufficient to result in a charge of substantial injury.

▸ **Unfair if injury is unavoidable**.

Second, an act or practice is unfair if consumers cannot reasonably avoid the injury. This includes, for example, an act or practice that interferes with a consumer's ability to make an informed decision (such as failing to provide timely disclosures or misrepresenting financing terms). This failure may result in consumers committing to loan products that do not fit their needs or that they cannot afford. According to the CFPB, a key consideration in determining whether a practice is unfair is whether it hinders a consumer's decision-making process. Actions consumers are expected to take to avoid injury must be reasonable.

▸ **Benefits must outweigh injury**.

Third, an act or practice is unfair if the offsetting benefits do not outweigh the injury. For instance, if an act or practice results in lower consumer prices or wider availability of products and services, it may be considered balanced and, therefore, not unfair.

An FTC enforcement action may better illustrate the three criteria.

## Case Study – Unfair Acts or Practices

The FTC brought an enforcement action against a mortgage lender that was believed to have established a practice of failing to release liens after borrowers paid off their mortgage loans. To determine if this practice was unfair, the FTC applied the three questions:

1) Did the act or practice cause substantial injury?
2) Could the consumer have reasonably avoided the issue?
3) Did certain benefits outweigh the harm caused by the act?

In this case, the FTC found that the mortgage company's behavior met the three criteria for unfair acts and practices by repeatedly failing to release liens after consumers paid off their mortgages.

- ▶ First, the agency found that the practice economically injured consumers.

- ▶ Second, consumers had no way of knowing the mortgage servicer would not release the lien, so they could not avoid the injury.

- ▶ Finally, there were no proven benefits that outweighed the injuries sustained. (https://files.consumerfinance.gov/f/documents/cfpb_unfair-deceptive-abusive-acts-practices-udaaps_procedures_2023-09.pdf)

## Check Your Understanding

A local lender overcharged hundreds of loan applicants by $5 each because it unintentionally overstated the fee paid to a third-party provider to run credit reports. Which of these statements about this overcharge is most accurate?

A. This overcharge is unfair by UDAAP standards because it had a small impact on a large number of consumers.
B. This overcharge is not unfair by UDAAP standards because it had an insubstantial impact on each consumer.
C. This overcharge is not unfair by UDAPP standards because it was unintentional.

If you selected "A," you are correct! An act with a small impact on a single consumer is not likely to be considered unfair; however, a small act that impacts a large number of consumers could be unfair under UDAAP standards.

**Testing ads for deception**. The CFPB tests whether a representation, omission, act, or practice is deceptive by identifying if 1) it is likely to mislead a consumer,

2) the consumer's interpretation of it is reasonable in the given situation, and 3) it is material.

First, an act or practice <u>may be considered deceptive if it has or is likely to deceive consumers</u>. The FTC has a "four Ps" test that helps identify whether a representation, omission, act, or practice is misleading or likely to mislead:

> ▸ Is the information **prominent** enough to gain a consumer's attention?
> ▸ Is the information provided in a **clear, concise format** that parallels other information in the package without distracting the consumer's attention?
> ▸ Is the **information located** where consumers are naturally expected to hear or see it?
> ▸ Is the information **close to the claim** that it qualifies (verbally or in print)?

**Is the ad reasonable?** Second, it is important to note that <u>investigators analyze deception under the microscope of "reasonableness."</u> Is the consumer's interpretation of the omission, act, or practice reasonable in the context of the situation? For example, if an advertisement targets elderly borrowers, is it considered deceptive to that audience?

**Did the ad affect the buying decision?** Third, a representation, omission, act, or practice is material if it has or is likely to impact a consumer's choice about a product or service. Governing agencies automatically consider certain categories of information material:

> ▸ Information related to cost, benefits, or restrictions on use or availability is material.
> ▸ Specific claims about a financial product or service are material.
> ▸ Implied claims are material if an institution intended to make the claim, even if the intent was not to deceive consumers.
> ▸ Purposely making false claims is material.
> ▸ Omissions are material when the lender knew or should have known consumers needed the omitted information to make an informed decision.

Examples of deceptive acts or practices include **failing to provide adequate disclosures, misrepresenting loan terms, or otherwise providing misleading or untruthful information**.

The following case involves a mortgage company that engaged in deceptive acts or practices.

## Case Study – New Day Financial, LLC

In 2024, the CFPB ordered New Day Financial, LLC, a non-bank direct mortgage lender, to pay a $2.25 million civil penalty and stop misrepresenting loan costs to consumers.

The details? New Day provides cash-out refinance loans. Some states where New Day offered these loans required the firm to provide consumers with a "net benefit" analysis detailing the benefits of refinancing.

The CFPB determined New Day "engaged in deceptive acts and practices" when the firm issued net benefit worksheets. In those worksheets, New Day compared payments before and after the refinance. However, it used PITI calculations for the "before" payments but included only principal and interest in the "after" payments to make the payments after the refinance appear lower. In reality, many consumers faced higher payments after the refinance. (https://www.consumerfinance.gov/about-us/newsroom/cfpb-orders-newday-usa-to-pay-2-25-million-for-illegally-luring-veterans-and-military-families-into-cash-out-refinance-loans/)

**UDAAP and Dodd-Frank's "abusiveness".** The Dodd-Frank Act deems an act or practice **abusive** if it **materially hinders a consumer's ability to understand** a transaction **or takes unreasonable advantage** of a consumer's:

- lack of understanding about the product or the mortgage market
- inability to protect his or her own interests in selecting a financial product or service
- reasonable reliance on the mortgage loan originator or institution acting in the consumer's best interests

Note that there is likely some crossover between the three types of acts. For example, abusive acts may also be unfair or deceptive. However, the legal standards for each category are separate and distinct.

Another critical point to remember is that unfair, deceptive, or abusive acts or practices likely violate other federal and state laws. For example, failure to properly disclose loan costs violates UDAAP standards as well as Truth in Lending requirements.

Finally, it is important to understand that a particular action may comply with other federal or state mortgage laws but still violate UDAAP provisions. For instance, an advertisement may properly disclose loan terms based on TILA (15 U.S.C. §1601 et seq.) requirements but contain other false or misleading information that violates UDAAP standards.

**Ethics and RESPA (12 U.S.C. §2601 et seq.)**

**Loan terms transparency.** As you know, RESPA requires transparency of loan terms (i.e., proper disclosures) and prohibits third-party actions, such as kickbacks and illegal compensation, that increase the cost to consumers seeking mortgage loans.

**Must render specific service to charge a fee**. In addition, RESPA prohibits service providers from charging fees for anything other than services actually provided. While providers cannot charge a fee for preparing transaction-related documents, including the LE and the CD, certain other fees and charges are permitted.

> ▶ bona fide salaries or compensation for services rendered
> ▶ ordinary promotional and educational activities that are not tied to referrals and do not cover expenses that the recipient would otherwise bear when referring settlement services or business.
> ▶ payments from listing brokers to cooperating brokers or bona fide referral payments between real estate licensees
> ▶ attorney fees for services rendered
> ▶ title company fees for services rendered (title insurance and closing fees)
> ▶ loan origination fees

In short, third-party service providers, such as attorneys, lenders, or real estate licensees, who will receive compensation for standard services performed can receive additional compensation for extra services only if those services are actual, necessary, and distinct from standard services.

**Cannot require use of a given provider**. As addressed previously in this text, an additional RESPA protection relates to required use. Lenders cannot require borrowers to use a specific provider for settlement services. However, providers can offer legitimate discounts for consumers, either on single or bundled services. Consumers must be allowed to choose whether or not to use such services, and the discount on these services cannot be covered by higher prices on other settlement services.

Cannot discriminate. In addition to RESPA, other federal laws impact mortgage industry ethics. These laws include the Civil Rights Act of 1966, the Fair Housing Act, the Americans with Disabilities Act, the Home Mortgage Disclosure Act (12 U.S.C. §2801 et seq.), and the Community Reinvestment Act all address discrimination.

**Ethics and the Civil Rights Act of 1866**

The **Civil Rights Act of 1866** provides all United States citizens with "the same rights to inherit, purchase, lease, sell, hold, or convey real and personal property." Victims of discrimination based on this law can sue in federal district court. Possible penalties include injunctions, compensatory damages, and punitive damages. These penalties may be in addition to or instead of remedies provided under other federal laws for the specific violation. No exemptions to this law exist.

## Ethics and the Fair Housing Act

The Fair Housing Act (Title VIII of the Civil Rights Act of 1968) prohibits discrimination in the sale or lease of residential property. This definition includes vacant land that buyers or owners intend to use for residential housing. The FHA lists seven specific protected classes:

- race
- color
- religion
- national origin
- sex
- disability
- familial status

**Fair housing exemptions**. Unlike the Civil Rights Act, the Fair Housing Act exempts some residential transactions:

- owners who occupy one unit of a one- to four-unit multi-family property or those who rent out a room in their primary residence
- private owners who sell or rent a single-family home without a real estate broker's assistance, as long as the individual doesn't own more than three such homes at a time
- religious organizations and private clubs that offer housing to members as long as they do not discriminate in membership
- housing communities for the elderly that meet the Act's requirements

Be aware that some state and local laws may eliminate or restrict these exemptions. In addition, remember that it is illegal under any circumstances to discriminate on the basis of race.

### Check Your Understanding

Select the item below that best represents a fair housing violation.

- A. A couple applies to rent a one-bedroom apartment. The couple has three children under the age of six. The landlord denies the application based on occupancy standards.
- B. An elderly man rents the basement of his home to help make his mortgage payments. He refused the application of a young woman to rent the basement.
- C. The manager for a 75-unit apartment complex places all families with children in one of two buildings in the back of the complex so they don't disturb other tenants.
- D. A landlord denies an application from a 20-year-old renter because he doesn't want "kids" renting his apartment.

If you selected item "C," you are correct! This manager's actions discriminate against families with children, which violates the prohibition against familial status discrimination. Note that the FHA does not prohibit discrimination based on age.

**Ethics and other financing laws**

Several other federal laws highlighted previously serve to enforce ethical behavior in the mortgage industry. These laws include the following.

The **Equal Credit Opportunity Act (ECOA)**. This Act addresses discrimination against borrowers and transparency in loan terms.

The **Home Mortgage Disclosure Act** (HMDA). The HMDA focuses on discrimination by requiring lenders to report application, loan, and demographic data collected. Note that the HMDA is a reporting-only regulation. It does not require or prohibit other lender actions or implement any type of quota system for loan funding in specific geographical areas. What is the potential impact of HMDA violations? In 2023, the Bureau ordered Freedom Mortgage Corporation to pay a $3.95 million civil penalty for inaccurate reporting under the HMDA. (https://www.consumerfinance.gov/enforcement/actions/freedom-mortgage-corporation-hmda-2023/)

The **Community Reinvestment Act (CRA)**. The CRA encourages financial institutions to meet the credit needs of consumers in the communities they serve, regardless of the socioeconomic status of those consumers in those areas. While the focus is not only on mortgage loans, CRA provisions include these loans. Governed by the Federal Deposit Insurance Corporation, the Federal Reserve Board, and the Office of the Comptroller of the Currency, the CRA requires financial institutions to provide records that are scrutinized to determine the institution's activity in the prescribed communities. Regulators review records submitted to ensure that lenders promote fair access to credit and do not engage in activities such as redlining.

**Prohibited acts**

As you can see from reviewing federal legislation in mortgage lending, existing laws overlap in some instances and diverge in others. We have already discussed many of these federal laws, but, we are presenting some of them again in the context of specific prohibitions, including RESPA, the Gramm-Leach-Bliley (15 U.S.C. §6801 et seq.) Act, and the Fair Housing Act.

**RESPA-prohibitions.** In review, RESPA prohibits the following practices:

- compromising a client's interest to benefit a referral source
- giving or receiving a thing of value in exchange for referral fees or kickbacks from settlement service providers
- requiring consumers to use a specific settlement service provider
- steering consumers to specific settlement service providers to benefit the steering party
- charging fees for something other than actual services provided

**Gramm-Leach-Bliley prohibitions.** To review, GLB specifically prohibits lenders from sharing account numbers or other access numbers for use in marketing. The third component of the Act, *pretexting protection,* prohibits anyone from **pretexting**, which is defined as *using false* pretenses *to obtain customer information from financial institutions.* Generally, pretexting occurs when a scammer uses a fake scenario or impersonation to gain an individual's trust and access secure data.

More specifically, pretexting often involves a scammer who develops a compelling, though false, story in an attempt to gain someone's trust. Once trust is established, the scammer uses it to convince the victim to send money, share sensitive information, or download malware (usually through clicking a link or opening a document).

The mortgage loan and real estate industries have seen numerous scams of this type, many of which have led to serious financial injuries to victims. Consider the multiple victims of wire fraud, where borrowers receive last-minute instructions from their "closing agent" to redirect wired funds to a different account than originally agreed on. Sadly, the "closing agent" is a scammer, and once the borrower wires the funds, they are nearly impossible to retrieve.

GLB standards require that mortgage professionals use appropriate staff training and other techniques to recognize and avoid social engineering and phishing scams.

**Fair Housing Act prohibitions.** The Fair Housing Act prohibits discrimination in housing-related transactions, including mortgage lending, based on the protected classes noted previously. The FHA explicitly prohibits redlining, steering, and blockbusting.

> ▸ **redlining**
>
> The illegal practice of redlining occurs when lenders refuse to write loans based on geographic area or neighborhood characteristics, or write loans with less favorable terms based solely on these factors. Lenders are, however, allowed to deny loans or offer higher-priced loans in neighborhoods where property values are declining. Such decisions must be based only on objective criteria about the property's condition, value, or area.

> ▸ **steering**
>
> Steering, as it relates specifically to mortgage lending, is guiding borrowers to certain loan products to benefit the lender, often to the borrower's detriment. Note that the term "steering" is also used to describe the practice of guiding buyers to or away from certain neighborhoods based on protected class status.

▸ **blockbusting**

While specifically targeted to real estate agents, but relevant to mortgage lenders as well, **blockbusting** is the practice of convincing owners to list their homes at below-market prices. Agents lead homeowners to believe that because members of a minority class have moved into or are moving into a neighborhood, property values will drop.

While these three practices are less common than before legislation was enacted to prevent them, evidence suggests that lending discrimination still exists.

In addition, the Fair Housing Act specifically prohibits the following acts if the act is based on protected class status. While these prohibitions relate primarily to real estate licensees, there are implications for mortgage lenders as well.

▸ refusing to rent or sell residential property after receiving a bona fide offer
▸ refusing to negotiate for housing or making housing unavailable
▸ denying a dwelling
▸ setting different terms, conditions, or privileges for the sale or rental of a dwelling
▸ providing different housing services or facilities
▸ falsely denying that housing is unavailable for inspection, sale, or rental
▸ denying access to or membership in a facility or service related to the sale or rental of housing (aimed at membership in professional organizations such as mortgage loan originator groups or MLSs)

**Supreme Court prohibition.** A U.S. Supreme Court ruling in 2015 made it illegal for lenders to discriminate against married same-sex loan applicants or borrowers.

**Additional prohibitions.** The following actions are discriminatory and thus prohibited if taken based on an applicant's or borrower's protected class status:

▸ refusing to make a mortgage loan to qualified applicants
▸ refusing to provide information regarding loans
▸ imposing different terms or conditions on loans (higher interest rates, points, origination fees, or other fees)
▸ imposing different terms or conditions for equally qualified buyers depending on the geographic location of the property to be purchased
▸ discriminating in property appraisals
▸ refusing to purchase a loan

**Equal Credit Opportunity Act (ECOA) prohibitions.** Generally, fairness in lending refers to freedom from discrimination in the mortgage industry. Both the Equal Credit Opportunity Act (ECOA) and the Fair Housing Act (FHA) protect consumers from discrimination in real estate and mortgage transactions.

Similar to the Fair Housing Act, the ECOA prohibits discrimination in lending based on certain characteristics. The protected classes under the ECOA are similar to those noted by the Fair Housing Act, but some differences exist. The ECOA names the following protected classes:

- race
- color
- national origin
- religion
- sex
- marital status
- the receipt of public assistance (source of income)
- age

Age is a prohibited factor unless the applicant is not of legal age and, therefore, cannot enter into a contract. Age can be considered if it relates to the ability to repay.

This legislation also protects applicants who, in good faith, exercise any of their rights under the Consumer Credit Protection Act. In short, the ECOA requires that lenders treat all consumers applying for credit or seeking information equally.

Of course, "equal access and treatment" does not mean that all applicants receive identical loan terms; however, applicants in similar financial situations should receive similar loan terms regardless of protected class status. Remember, federal and state laws require lenders to evaluate all loan applications based only on an applicant's financial qualifications.

**Americans with Disabilities Act (ADA) prohibitions.** The ADA requires providers to make reasonable accommodations to serve borrowers with disabilities. The act also prohibits discrimination in the form of denying credit, offering unfavorable terms, or treating unequally based on disability.

Lenders must be cautious to examine policies and procedures to ensure they do not engage in indirect discrimination or disparate impact, which, as addressed previously, occurs when a policy or action that seems neutral has a disproportionate impact on individuals with disabilities and is, therefore, discriminatory.

## Check Your Understanding

Two consumers submit loan applications to a lender. The first applicant's credit score is 841, debt-to-income ratio is 25%, housing expense ratio is 18%, and the borrower's down payment is 30%. The second applicant's credit score is 712, the debt-to-income ratio is 35%, the housing expense ratio is 26%, and the borrower's down payment is 20%. Because these two borrowers fall within the lender's lending limits, both should receive identical loan terms.

    A.  True
    B.  False

If you selected "B," you are correct! Even though both borrowers fall within the lender's minimum requirements, the second applicant does not have as strong a financial foundation as the first, and the lender is within its rights to offer different loan terms and products to the two applicants.

**Mortgage fraud**

Mortgage fraud occurs when an individual or entity deceives another for personal gain or to cause harm. More specifically, mortgage fraud is any *intentional, deceptive, or fraudulent act related to obtaining a mortgage loan*. The fraudulent act may occur at any stage in the mortgage loan process, including during the application phase, document gathering and processing, loan approval (underwriting), or closing. It may involve only the loan process or the real estate transaction itself. In addition, it may involve only a single party or multiple parties to the transaction, including the buyer, seller, lender, and appraiser.

Defrauding parties could include:

- a borrower who inflates income or assets to appear more financially sound for loan qualification
- a real estate professional who facilitates an undisclosed second mortgage from the seller (aka a **silent second**)
- a lender who provides a borrower with loan documents containing different terms than those agreed upon
- an MLO who steals identities to create fraudulent loan applications
- an appraiser who falsifies an appraisal report so a borrower obtains approval for a larger loan

**Misrepresentation versus puffing.** When discussing fraud, it is essential to understand related terminology as well as the relationship between **misrepresentation** and fraud. It is also important to understand the term "puffing" as it relates to misrepresentation.

**Intentional misrepresentation.** Intentional misrepresentation, also known as **fraudulent misrepresentation** or **actual fraud**, occurs when one party purposely provides false information or conceals **material facts** to deceive another party. You learned previously that in the mortgage industry, a material fact is information that, if known, would likely result in a reasonable consumer making a different decision about a loan product or lender. For example, information about loan terms (the APR, interest rate, and **prepayment penalties**), the nature of the loan (fixed or adjustable rate), origination fees, and prepayment penalties is material. The importance of this type of information to the consumer is made clear by various lender disclosure requirements.

Intentional misrepresentation is a serious legal offense. It can lead to civil liability, financial penalties, and criminal charges.

**Unintentional misrepresentation; negligence.** Also known as **constructive fraud** or **negligent misrepresentation,** unintentional misrepresentation occurs when individuals breach their duty of care by committing errors or omissions or fail to fulfill their responsibilities. While not purposeful, this type of fraud can still raise liability concerns, especially if the courts determine the party should have known better.

Understanding the distinction between misrepresentation and a practice known as **puffing** or **puffery** is also crucial. Puffing involves making a statement that exaggerates the benefits of a product or service. For example, a mortgage loan broker placed an advertisement that stated, in part, "Contact Ed Burns for all your mortgage needs. He is the best, and you won't regret it!" While puffing may not be a best business practice, it is not illegal. The courts typically view puffing as "non-actionable" and acceptable because it doesn't provide false concrete statements, and a "reasonable person" would recognize the practice as a marketing technique.

The website Legal Clarity (https://legalclarity.org/what-is-puffing-in-law-and-how-does-it-differ-from-misrepresentation/) notes that the "*distinction between puffing and misrepresentation often depends on the specificity and verifiability of claims.*" When lawsuits occur, courts evaluate whether statements could *reasonably* be interpreted as facts. Interestingly, cases related to puffing and misrepresentation date back to the 1700s and perhaps even further.

## Check Your Understanding

A mortgage lender placed an advertisement stating that she was the most efficient, consumer-friendly MLO in the area. This statement is an example of which of the following?

    A. Fraudulent misrepresentation
    B. Intentional misrepresentation
    C. Puffing
    D. Negligence

If you selected "C," you are correct! This statement is an example of puffing, as it simply exaggerates the benefits this MLO can provide.

**Categories of mortgage fraud.** As previously noted, mortgage fraud may be committed by an individual, such as a buyer, or multiple parties to the transaction. There are as many types of mortgage fraud as there are unscrupulous people who think them up. While federal, state, and local laws assist in reducing fraud, vigilant professionals in the field must also do their part.

We can categorize mortgage fraud as either fraud for housing or fraud for profit.

> ▸ **Fraud for housing** (aka **fraud for property**)
>
> This occurs when a borrower purposely provides false statements about income, debts, employment, assets, property value, intent to occupy, or the borrower's financial situation to qualify for a loan or to purchase a property.

> ▸ **Fraud for profit**
>
> This occurs when industry insiders, such as bank officers, appraisers, mortgage brokers, attorneys, loan originators, and title officials, use their knowledge, authority, and contacts to commit or facilitate fraud. Note that fraud for profit may also involve the buyer and/or seller.

Fraud schemes of both types are varied and can occur in every area of real estate lending. A few examples follow.

**Deed or home title theft.** This practice is one of the newest and fastest-growing types of mortgage fraud. Fraudsters steal a property by forging signatures on a deed or creating a fake sale wherein title is transferred without the true owner's knowledge. Scammers use these false documents to take out a mortgage on the property.

The lender is unaware that the individual does not own the property and takes appropriate steps to secure the loan. The scammer disappears with the new loan funds, the lender attempts to foreclose, and the true owner of the property is left trying to clean up the mess and save the home from foreclosure.

In a similar con, scammers file false documents with the secretary of state claiming a change in ownership of an LLC or corporation, then "sell" the property. Agencies are actively implementing systems to help consumers avoid this scam, but awareness is critical.

Red flags for this type of fraud include parties to the transaction insisting on remote notarization or on working only with their own vendors, likely also remote, for title insurance and other services. Refusing to meet with the real estate agent or lender in person is another potential red flag.

**Using a straw buyer.** This is a scheme that may involve an individual who lacks good credit or is otherwise prohibited from buying a property. Multiple variations of this tactic exist.

In one, the actual buyer engages and pays for the services of a **straw buyer.** The straw buyer applies for and obtains a loan to purchase the desired property. The actual buyer promises to make all mortgage payments and meet other purchase terms. Individuals use straw buyers because they cannot qualify for a loan, they qualify for a loan with less favorable terms than another buyer with better credit might receive, or they are legally prohibited from buying a property. Schemes such as this typically fall in the fraud-for-housing category.

Straw buying may also involve an unscrupulous lender who creates a fictitious person who subsequently applies for and obtains a loan. The lender creates and funds an **air loan** on a non-existent property to illegally collect the loan proceeds. This particular scheme is quite complex as it requires the fraudster to create a "back story" that will meet underwriting scrutiny. Schemes such as this typically fall in the fraud-for-profit category.

Red flags for this scheme include an unexplained large deposit or down payment. Also, a mismatch between a buyer's financial means and the price or even the concept of buying a new property may indicate the need for closer inspection.

**Asset and liability fraud.** This is another fraud-for-housing scheme, involves individuals, usually buyers, who manipulate financial information related to assets and liabilities to deceive lenders into approving loans under false pretenses. Examples include failing to report unrecorded debts or other required payments, overstating the value of real estate holdings, bank accounts, and investment portfolios, or even working with friends or family members who deposit funds into the borrower's account or place the borrower's name on accounts belonging to others to make it appear that they have more cash on hand than they do.

**Income and employment fraud.** This is yet another form of fraud-for-housing, occurs when individuals misrepresent their income or employment history to enhance their creditworthiness. For example, borrowers may inflate reported income to meet lender loan approval requirements. They may provide false or misleading information about their employment history and status or fabricate employment positions and income sources.

Again, several circumstances may indicate this type of mortgage fraud:

- ▸ suspicious gaps or inconsistencies in a borrower's employment history, including extended periods of unemployment or frequent job changes
- ▸ a borrower's unwillingness or inability to provide supporting documentation for stated income sources
- ▸ discrepancies between a borrower's reported income and employment history, industry norms, or standard wage levels for the stated occupation

- a borrower claiming rapid or unrealistic income growth over a short period without corresponding evidence
- incomplete or inconsistent employment verification documentation
- a borrower providing vague or unverifiable details about employers
- a borrower reluctance to disclose employer information

Lenders and underwriters can help detect fraud of this type by carefully asking detailed questions and following up on discrepancies or missing information. They should <u>thoroughly verify income and employment documentation with third parties, such as financial institutions and employers</u>.

**Warning signs of income and employment fraud.** Lenders and underwriters should be aware of the following red flags that may indicate asset and liability fraud:

- discrepancies between the information provided on the loan application and supporting documentation
- significant fluctuations in asset balances or debt levels with no reasonable explanation
- failure to adequately verify the authenticity of assets or liabilities claimed by the borrower
- a history of frequent loan applications or unexplained multiple credit inquiries within a short period
- failure to disclose all assets, liabilities, or financial obligations during the application process
- large deposits or the transfer of funds from undisclosed sources, especially if noted as gifts or loans

Mortgage professionals can help detect this type of fraud by carefully scrutinizing documents for irregularities or inconsistencies that may indicate falsified information. <u>Lenders should verify the authenticity of assets and liabilities directly with financial institutions, creditors, or other relevant sources, and pay close attention to unusual or suspicious financial transactions</u>.

## Check Your Understanding

A lender's best defense against income and employment fraud is to

   A. require the applicant to certify statements made regarding income and employment
   B. verify the applicant's income and employment during the initial application process
   C. verify the applicant's income and employment during the initial application process and loan underwriting
   D. require the applicant's employer to certify, in writing, the applicant's income, employment, and continued employment outlook

If you selected "C," you are correct! Most lenders conduct a preliminary review of income and employment, followed by a second check shortly before approving loan funding.

**Occupancy fraud.** The practice known as occupancy fraud may be either a fraud-for-housing or a fraud-for-profit scheme. It involves providing false or misleading information about the buyer's intended occupancy status of a property in the mortgage loan application. This scheme is typically used to help borrowers qualify for favorable loan terms reserved for owner-occupied properties or to assist borrowers who lack sufficient income in obtaining certain loan types.

Examples of occupancy fraud include claiming a property will be a primary residence when, in fact, it will be used as a second home or investment property or misrepresenting a property as a primary residence when it is actually vacant or intended for speculative purposes. Borrowers implementing this scheme generally do so to circumvent certain loan restrictions or even purchase through certain more restrictive government programs.

**Buy and bail fraud.** In a slightly different iteration of occupancy fraud, known as **buy-and-bail fraud**, borrowers create a lease arrangement with someone to make it appear that they are or will be receiving rental income for their current property. The borrower then uses that nonexistent "rental income" to help them qualify for a new, perhaps more affordable mortgage. The borrower moves into the newly purchased home and walks away from the mortgage on the previous home, on which the payments may have become unaffordable, often allowing it to go into foreclosure.

Lenders may see the following red flags:

> ▸ The buyers do not own a primary residence but claim the loan is for investment purposes (a form of reverse occupancy fraud in which the borrower uses potential rental income to help qualify for a loan).
> ▸ The borrowers are moving from a single-family home to a multi-unit home in the same geographic area.
> ▸ The borrowers are purchasing a property in an area with a high concentration of vacation homes or investment properties, but claiming the property will be their primary residence.
> ▸ The borrowers are moving from larger homes to smaller ones, keeping the larger ones as investment properties.

Lenders can help prevent this type of fraud by requiring borrowers to certify their intended occupancy status in the loan application. Lenders may also conduct post-closing occupancy verifications to ensure compliance. Such verifications may include physical inspections, utility bill reviews, or confirmation of occupancy from an affiliated HOA.

**Appraisal fraud.** Fraud in valuing properties may occur when an appraiser colludes with a lender, real estate agent, or mortgage broker to <u>intentionally inflate or deflate the property's value</u>. Because subsequent appraisals of other similar properties may rely on this appraisal as a comparable sale, inflated or deflated appraisals can lead to unfounded changes in property values in a specific geographic area.

Appraisal fraud has largely been curbed because the mortgage crisis of 2007-2008-spawned requirements for how appraisers operate and, perhaps more specifically, how lenders select appraisers.

Before the 2007 meltdown, lenders could select and work with a specific appraiser or group of appraisers. For most lenders, a solid working relationship with a select appraiser helped ensure the timely completion of work on behalf of the lender; however, some lenders selected appraisers who were complicit in the lender's fraudulent activities.

Appraisers now must comply with the **Uniform Standards of Professional Appraisal Practice** (USPAP) and hold a specific certification level to appraise various property types. USPAP requires that appraisers act independently, impartially, and objectively in valuing all properties they are engaged to appraise. In addition, most loan programs in the current mortgage lending environment prohibit lenders, mortgage loan originators, and buyers from selecting the appraiser to perform the appraisal. Most lenders establish or locate one or more appraisal management companies (ACM). As an added layer of protection, lenders typically create an impartial committee of external members to select which AMC(s) to work with. The appraisal management company employs appraisers and manages the appraisal process, so there are fewer opportunities and more layers to work through to perpetrate fraud.

Red flags for mortgage fraud include using limited, incomplete, or unverified comparables and drastic property value increases without verification of upgrades.

**General red flags.** In addition to the red flags presented with each type of fraud scheme, there are more general red flags that mortgage professionals should be aware of (from https://singlefamily.fanniemae.com/mortgage-fraud-prevention).

- loan file discrepancies, such as mismatched Social Security numbers or addresses
- verification documents addressed to a specific party's attention
- obviously edited information verifications and other loan documents
- verification completions on the same day requested or on the weekend
- loan's purpose is cash-out refinance on a recent purchase
- the buyer is not the loan applicant
- no or very little credit history
- recently issued Social Security number
- applicant's salary does not support bank account balances

**Fraud enforcement.** Under the **Fraud Enforcement and Recovery Act (FERA)**, it is a felony to falsify loan documents. Individual loan programs, such as FHA, VA, and first-time homebuyer programs, may have additional enforcement options.

Lending institutions and individual lenders can subscribe to organizations that provide access to a database of fraud and suspected fraud cases reported by the organization's members, as well as governing agencies. One such agency is **MARI,** the **Mortgage Asset Research Institute**.

**Bank Secrecy Act.** As noted previously, the **Bank Secrecy Act** requires financial institutions to file suspicious activity reports (SARs) whenever they detect a potentially suspicious or unusual activity that may indicate money laundering, fraud, or other illegal financial transactions. Each mortgage firm should have a policy identifying how and when to file a SAR. Mortgage loan originators are protected from legal liability for filing SARs in good faith, even if the reported activity does not result in criminal charges or prosecution.

The FBI is the primary agency that investigates mortgage fraud. Conviction on fraud charges carries significant penalties as outlined in federal law, including fines, imprisonment, or both.

Mortgage professionals can help detect fraud by carefully scrutinizing documents for irregularities or inconsistencies that may indicate falsified information. Lenders should verify the authenticity of assets and liabilities directly with financial institutions, creditors, or other relevant sources, and pay close attention to unusual or suspicious financial transactions.

## Check Your Understanding

A lender's best defense against income and employment fraud is to

- A. require the applicant to certify statements made regarding income and employment
- B. verify the applicant's income and employment during the initial application process
- C. verify the applicant's income and employment during the initial application process and loan underwriting
- D. require the applicant's employer to certify, in writing, the applicant's income, employment, and continued employment outlook

If you selected "C," you are correct! Most lenders conduct a preliminary review of income and employment, followed by a second check shortly before approving loan funding.

Advertising ethics

Regulatory agencies overseeing MLO activity. Mortgage industry advertising raises multiple ethical issues, especially given the complex nature of mortgage products and the vulnerability of potential borrowers. As you know, multiple federal agencies and regulations govern mortgage industry advertising, including the CFPB, FTC, HUD, and FCC. TILA's Regulation Z (12 CFR §1026), the Federal Trade Commission Act (FTCA), and the Map rule (Regulation N) place rigorous requirements on mortgage advertising.

As in any industry, individuals who work in the mortgage industry have the luxury of understanding the intricacies of the industry. Mortgage professionals who deal with these complex products daily sometimes forget or fail to understand that the average consumer lacks knowledge of the mortgage process. While many laws to protect consumers exist, consumers typically rely on mortgage professionals to be honest and fair. Thus, mortgage professionals must ensure that advertising does not mislead or deceive consumers.

**Due diligence in observing TILA, Fair housing requirements.** In general, advertising regulations prohibit lenders from any of the following:

- misrepresenting material facts or making false promises that could influence an applicant's decision regarding a mortgage loan
- making misleading statements (untrue claims) or failing to provide relevant information
- concealing a material fact related to the transaction, including loan terms or conditions, and undisclosed third-party payments to the MLO

Advertisers must ensure they comply with the underlying principles of advertising law, including the following guidelines:

- Advertisements must be truthful and not deceptive or misleading.
- Advertisements must be fair.
- Advertisers must be able to support advertising claims.

**Advertising defined.** What exactly is classified as advertising? Advertising in today's mortgage industry includes print, broadcast, and electronic media. It is important to recognize that advertising regulations govern all forms of advertising, and advertisers must comply with advertising regulations no matter the medium used.

For instance, you likely have heard mortgage advertisements on the radio where the narrator very rapidly addresses various terms. This is an attempt on the advertiser's part to include all required information and disclosures in the short time allotted to the advertisement.

In a similar vein, advertising on the Internet can pose challenges due to limited space on the device and the user's ability to navigate around the site. Advertisers must be aware of the proper use and placement of required information, particularly disclosures, as well as the limitations posed by using frames or pop-up windows on a site.

**Required advertising disclosures.** Advertising disclosures must be *clear and conspicuous* in both online and print environments.

> ▸ Disclosures should appear as close as possible to the triggering claim, preferably on the same page.
> ▸ Site design should include visual cues encouraging consumers to scroll to the disclosure location.
> ▸ Sites that use hyperlinks to access disclosures should use standard web design protocols to make the links obvious, including labeling, formatting, placement, scrolling
> ▸ Hyperlinks should lead consumers directly to the disclosure on the click-through page.

Advertisers should routinely test the effectiveness of the hyperlink by observing click-through rates and carefully evaluate and address technological limitations of providing disclosures, including using frames or pop-ups.

Lenders should ask the following questions when placing advertisements to ensure they meet the "clear and conspicuous" test:

> ▸ Can the required information be placed in the advertisement instead of being accessed through a link?
> ▸ Are the required disclosures difficult for a consumer to see or easy to miss?
> ▸ Is the advertisement lengthy, thereby requiring repeated disclosures?
> ▸ Do sounds or other factors distract from the provided disclosures?
> ▸ Are disclosures made using appropriate graphic design rules for font size, color, type, and location?
> ▸ Are verbal disclosures made using adequate volume and cadence?
> ▸ Do video-based disclosures appear for an adequate duration?
> ▸ Will the intended audience understand the disclosure wording?

The FTC notes that if advertisers are unable to meet the requirements as outlined, they should not place the advertisement.

For additional guidance, consult the FTC's "Dot Com Disclosures" report, available here: https://www.ftc.gov/sites/default/files/attachments/press-releases/ftc-staff-issues-guidelines-internet-advertising/0005dotcomstaffreport.pdf.

**Mortgage Acts and Practices (Regulation N) (MAP).** The Truth in Lending Act(TILA) and Regulation Z define advertising as a *commercial message in any medium that directly or indirectly promotes a credit transaction*. Thus, as previously discussed, using certain terms in mortgage advertising also requires lenders to disclose related terms..

The FTC established **Regulation N, the Mortgage Acts and Practices (MAP) Advertising Rule,** to prevent deceptive advertising practices in mortgage advertising. The CFPB subsequently adopted and currently enforces the rule.

Essentially, MAP prohibits mortgage advertisers from using misleading language or omitting key details that could lead consumers to make bad decisions. Regulation N further pinpoints specific areas that are common pitfall areas of misleading advertising:

- interest rates and APR
- fee and down payment requirements
- loan qualification and eligibility
- prepayment penalties
- bait-and-switch tactics

To illustrate, the following practices are considered misleading and predatory:

- highlighting a low introductory rate without clearly noting that it will increase significantly after a short time
- failing to disclose the annual percentage rate when required
- advertising rates that are much lower than most consumers may qualify for
- misrepresenting the down payment required to qualify for a loan
- omitting the full cost of a loan, including fees, prepayment penalties, or other charges that increase the cost of the loan
- suggesting that "anyone" can qualify for a mortgage, no matter what their financial situation is
- promising "easy approval" without disclosing that qualifying for these mortgages may require higher-than-typical costs, rates, or stringent terms
- failing to disclose prepayment penalties
- offering low introductory rates or terms and then unnecessarily switching consumers to a different, more costly loan product

Individual states are charged with enforcing MAP. Neither lenders nor borrowers can waive MAP provisions. Regulations require that advertisers retain copies of advertisements placed for at least 24 months from the last date they were disseminated.

You read previously about TILA and FHA advertising requirements. In addition to those prohibitions and requirements, professionals should be knowledgeable about *discriminatory phrases and words* as well as certain words that may be considered offensive, though they are not illegal.

**"Equal Housing Lender" poster**. In today's mortgage lending industry, the FHA requires lenders to display the "Equal Housing Lender" logo in print-based advertisements. Similarly, in verbal advertisements, lenders must make a statement indicating that the lender is an "Equal Housing Lender." Lenders that fund residential mortgage loans must conspicuously display the "Equal Housing Lender" or "Equal Housing Opportunity" poster available from HUD.

**Complaints**. Fair housing violations can damage a firm's reputation and be costly and time-consuming. Individuals who believe they have been victims of housing discrimination may file a complaint with HUD within one year of the alleged incident. HUD may investigate or defer the investigation to a state or local agency approved to perform such investigations.

Courts may grant injunctions against lenders as well as impose fines that include compensatory damages, punitive damages, and payment of attorney's fees. Severe cases or those that appear to be patterns of abuse may result in the U.S. Attorney General bringing a civil lawsuit.

## Check Your Understanding

Bright Future Mortgage Lending presented a radio advertisement touting its "low introductory rate" on 30-year mortgage loans. To comply with federal regulations, what else must this advertisement state?

      A. The application deadline
      B. The fact that the rate will increase
      C. The lender's contact information
      D. The implementing regulation for any governing statutes

If you selected "B," you are correct! For this advertisement not to be misleading, consumers must be aware that the interest rate will significantly increase.

**Vulnerable populations in advertising.** Unscrupulous lenders sometimes target **vulnerable populations**—those who are financially vulnerable or lack financial literacy. These lenders may tailor advertisements to low-income, elderly, or first-time homebuyers. They may also target borrowers who are facing pre-foreclosure or foreclosure. Ethical issues arise when advertisers exploit these borrowers.

For example, lenders may offer subprime loans to people with poor credit, promising easy access to home buying but at terms that are not financially sustainable. They sometimes target senior citizens with reverse mortgage products that may be financially detrimental over time. Sadly, unethical practices such as these have caused many borrowers to default on loans or be otherwise harmed because of the lender's failure to properly disclose all relevant information and ensure that borrowers understand the consequences of signing for the loan.

Advertisements focusing on "quick cash, easy refinancing, or low monthly payments" tend to target individuals already in difficult financial situations.

Lenders may employ other tactics in conjunction with these advertisements, such as high pressure to act quickly, resulting in consumers acquiring loans that may not be in their best interests.

**Avoid confusing terminology.** Like most industries, the mortgage lending industry uses complex jargon that can confuse consumers. Ethical lending professionals should ensure that their advertisements and conversations clearly explain key terms so consumers understand the impact of the loan products they are considering. Lenders should provide and discuss easy-to-understand tools such as the Loan Estimate to help consumers evaluate and compare loan offers from different lenders.

**Bait advertising.** The Code of Federal Regulations Part 238 (16 CFR §238) addresses bait advertising. While it speaks to the sale of merchandise, it is also relevant to mortgage loan products and related advertising.

**Bait advertising defined.** Code advertising defines bait advertising as *"an alluring but insincere offer to sell a product or service which the advertiser in truth does not intend or want to sell. Its purpose is to switch consumers from buying the advertised merchandise in order to sell something else, usually at a higher price or on a basis more advantageous to the advertiser. The primary aim of a bait advertisement is to obtain leads as to persons interested in buying merchandise of the advertised type."* (https://www.ecfr.gov/current/title-16/chapter-I/subchapter-B/part-238).

Note that this regulation defines advertising as ANY form of public notice, however disseminated or used. Thus, a presentation to a group of consumers could be classified as advertising for the purposes of this legislation.

This regulation also prohibits advertisers from making any statement in an initial advertisement that creates a false impression of the product being offered. Such statements may not misrepresent the product in a way that, when the facts are revealed to the borrower, the borrower may be switched from the advertised product to another. In an important sidenote, even if the lender later makes the facts known to the borrower, the lender has violated the law by making the initial misleading offer in an attempt to rope the borrower in.

An example of **bait advertising** in the mortgage industry is the practice of advertising an advantageous interest rate or other loan term that, upon investigation, becomes "unavailable" or requires that borrowers meet other conditions. When borrowers respond to these advertisements, lenders attempt to steer them to other loan products that are more beneficial to the loan originator and potentially less beneficial to the borrower.

This statute distinguishes between two types of bait advertising: discouraging the purchase of advertised products and switching after the sale. The statute identifies factors regulators use to determine whether an offer is bona fide, noting that any of the following may indicate a fraudulent advertisement:

- refusing to provide or discuss the product offered under the terms of the offer
- disparaging, by acts or words, the advertised product or its guarantee, credit terms, or availability
- failing to make an advertised product available at all advertised outlets
- refusing to take orders (applications) for the advertised product within a reasonable time period
- showing, demonstrating, or advertising a product that is unusable or impractical for the purposes noted in the advertisement
- discouraging or penalizing salespeople (loan originators) for offering the advertised product

## Check Your Understanding

Which one of the following is NOT an example of bait advertising?

A.  A lender advertises a low-interest ARM in an advertisement that meets all requirements. A couple meets with the lender to discuss applying for the loan. The lender cautions them that because they barely qualify for the loan at the existing interest rate, an increase in the rate might put them in danger of being unable to make their loan payments.

B.  A lender advertises a low long-term interest rate with no down payment in an advertisement that meets all requirements. When consumers ask to apply for this mortgage loan, the lender directs them to another loan product, indicating that the maximum number of applicants has already applied for the advertised loan.

C.  A lender advertises a low long-term interest rate with no down payment in an advertisement that meets all requirements. When consumers ask to apply for this loan, the lender notes that applications for this particular product are accepted only at the lender's main branch in the next city.

If you selected "A," you are correct! In this example, the lender is performing due diligence to inform potential borrowers of the dangers of an ARM.

**Switch After Sale (Bait and Switch).** The tactic referred to as "**switch after sale**" occurs when lenders advertise a particular loan's terms and then discourage or prohibit applicants from applying for the loan. Instead, they guide borrowers to a different loan product.

Legislation prohibits lenders from "unselling" an advertised product with the intention of substituting another product. Regulators consider the following acts or practices, among others, when determining if an advertiser engaged in switch marketing after a sale:

> The advertiser accepted a deposit for the product as advertised and then switched the buyer to a higher-priced product.
> The advertiser failed to deliver the advertised product within a reasonable amount of time.
> The advertiser disparaged the product by act or words or by disparaging the guarantee, credit terms, availability of service, repairs, or in any other respect, in connection with the product.
> The advertiser delivered a defective, unusable, or impractical product.

As with all "red flags," the practices noted above do not guarantee that a lender has taken fraudulent or illegal actions. Changed borrower circumstances or new loan products may make offers such as those outlined both legal and beneficial for the consumer. Typically, regulators will look for a pattern of such actions to determine whether to investigate.

**Regulation enforcement by FTC and CFPB.** You have learned that the FTC and the CFPB are the primary agencies responsible for preventing deceptive and unfair acts or practices, including misleading or deceptive advertising. Both individual advertisers and advertising agencies are subject to advertising regulations.

The FTC requires lenders to have a reasonable basis, or objective evidence, to support all advertising claims. If an advertisement does not make a specific claim, the FTC looks at other factors to determine if it is reasonable. In determining whether to bring a case against an advertiser, the FTC considers multiple factors:

> Does the agency have jurisdiction over the specific industry?
> What is the scope of the advertising? The FTC focuses on national advertising and refers local matters to relevant local jurisdictions.
> What is the extent of the deception? Is it a pattern?
> What is the amount of injury to consumers' health and safety, or, in the case of mortgage lending, wallets, that has occurred or could occur as a result of the deceptive advertising?

If advertisers target a specific group of individuals, especially vulnerable consumers such as elderly or low-income borrowers, an FTC investigation will primarily consider the harm it may cause to that particular group.

For example, consider advertisements that use buzzwords such as "low down payments," "low monthly payments," "low fixed mortgage rates," or "low interest rates." While these advertisements may be legitimate, they may also be an attempt to target individuals who are already facing financial hardship and coerce them into accepting a loan they cannot afford, or one with egregious terms.

Another example is advertising for reverse mortgages. While well-known actors often tout the benefits of a reverse mortgage, these advertisements may not reveal all the pertinent details that allow consumers to make informed decisions.

The FTC offers advice to consumers who are shopping for a mortgage, including a discussion of mortgage basics and tips on recognizing deceptive mortgage loan advertisements and offers. Visit https://consumer.ftc.gov/credit-loans-and-debt/loans-and-mortgages for more information.

**Best practices for Regulation N compliance**. Mortgage lenders should consider the following best practices to ensure compliance with Regulation N and other mortgage advertising legislation:

- ▸ Establish clear advertising guidelines. Create detailed policies that define acceptable advertising standards, ensuring that advertisements are not misleading.
- ▸ Provide ongoing training. Consistently educate employees on the requirements of relevant legislation and the critical role compliance plays in advertising and the firm's reputation.
- ▸ Perform routine compliance reviews. Develop and follow an audit schedule to review advertising content and identify any concerns.
- ▸ Implement compliance monitoring solutions. Use technology to track and archive advertising content, regardless of the medium.
- ▸ Keep comprehensive records. The MAP rule requires advertisers to retain complete documentation of all advertising content and supporting materials for at least 24 months.

**Penalties for advertising violations.** If a case gets to the penalty phase, the FTC or the courts can issue cease and desist orders, impose civil penalties and other monetary remedies, require consumer redress, and call for corrective advertising, disclosures, or other informational remedies. The FTC's website notes that some advertisers found guilty of violations have been required to "take out new advertisements to correct previous misinformation, notify purchasers about deceptive advertisements, include specific disclosures in future advertisements, or provide other information to consumers."

**Predatory lending**

**Characteristics of predatory lending.** Predatory lending is defined as unethical or abusive lending practices that exploit vulnerable borrowers, often resulting in financial harm or disadvantage. This type of lending bears the following characteristics:

- ▸ targets individuals who may have severe financial issues, limited financial knowledge, poor credit history, or low income
- ▸ uses deceptive tactics to entice borrowers into loans with unfavorable terms and conditions
- ▸ uses deceptive advertising, false promises, and bait-and-switch tactics to lure borrowers into loans they do not understand and cannot afford

▸ misrepresents loan terms or conceals fees to exploit a borrower's lack of financial knowledge

**Forms of predatory lending.** Predatory lending often results in borrowers being unable to repay their loans. This can also trigger foreclosures and the associated poor credit scores and histories. Examples of predatory lending include the following:

▸ **loan flipping--** the practice of encouraging borrowers to refinance (or "flip") their loans repeatedly, charging exorbitant fees each time and extending the repayment period, ultimately increasing the cost of the loan, often by a substantial amount

▸ **asset-based lending--** the practice of offering loans based on equity in the borrower's home or other assets instead of on the consumer's ability to repay the debt, putting the borrower's property at risk of foreclosure

▸ **imposing excessive fees**, penalties, and charges on borrowers, often without their knowledge or understanding, thereby increasing the overall cost of the loan

▸ **imposing a high prepayment penalty** or a prepayment penalty over the life of the loan to trap borrowers in unfavorable loans, inhibiting their ability to refinance the loan or pay off debts

▸ **refinancing a high-cost loan** with another high-cost loan in less than one year with no benefit to the borrower

**Additional predatory lending red flags**. In addition to the above examples, many other factors can signal potential predatory lending:

▸ offering balloon payments
▸ lacking transparency/failure to provide disclosures
▸ negative amortization loans
▸ requiring autopay for mortgage payments
▸ instantly approving or offering no credit check
▸ offering subprime mortgages
▸ encouraging borrowers to lie about their finances
▸ lending more money than the borrower can afford to repay
▸ pressuring borrowers to accept a specific loan product
▸ encouraging cash-out refinances to borrowers who can't afford them
▸ telling borrowers they will not be able to get a loan anywhere else
▸ asking borrowers to sign blank or incomplete forms
▸ providing false information about the need for or purpose of mortgage insurance

Not all of these are definite indicators of predatory lending, though many are. In the following paragraphs, we will review some practices that may or may not be considered predatory, depending on the circumstances.

**Subprime mortgages**. A **subprime mortgage** is a home loan that lenders offer to borrowers with low credit scores or income and negative credit histories.

These loans are made under the assumption that lower credit scores equate to higher risk and usually come at a higher interest rate than prime mortgages. Processing fees are often higher, too. These loans do not qualify for sale to the secondary market, so they may not be subject to all the protective requirements of federally backed loans. However, not all subprime loans are predatory. They become predatory when lenders aggressively promote them to borrowers who cannot afford them or do not understand that they qualify for a loan with better terms.

**Balloon payments.** Loans with balloon payments are generally for a short term, such as five years, with a final large (balloon) payment. Similar to subprime loans, balloon payments are not always a sign of predatory lending. However, lenders must be sure to fully disclose all loan features and educate consumers about the impact of a mortgage with a balloon payment. These mortgages are enticing to borrowers because the payments appear lower than traditional mortgage loans. However, borrowers may be unable to make the balloon payment or refinance out of it, making foreclosure a real possibility.

**Negative amortization.** Negative amortization occurs when a loan calls for payments that are less than the interest charged on the loan, resulting in a continual increase in the principal balance. Adjustable-rate mortgages may feature negative amortization because of the fluctuation in interest rates. Again, because the initial payments are low, these loans can be enticing to borrowers.

While loans with negative amortization are not always predatory, lenders must be certain to make all required disclosures and educate borrowers about the impact of these loans and a potential "payment recast" clause. With a recast in play, lenders can add the deferred interest back to the loan balance and increase the monthly payments, potentially making it difficult for borrowers to afford the higher payments.

TILA regulates negative amortization loans through the CFPB. Regulations require clear, comprehensive disclosures and a complete breakdown of loan terms, including the possibility of negative amortization, payment recast examples, and the maximum potential increase in monthly payments. TILA also imposes strict advertising guidelines on negative amortization loans.

**Prepayment penalties.** You may recall that the Loan Estimate and Closing Disclosure require lenders to identify the potential for a prepayment penalty on the loan. Most lenders today do not charge a prepayment penalty, and not all prepayment penalties are predatory. When does this penalty become predatory? When the fee is extremely high or extends over a large part or the entire life of the loan, it is likely to be considered predatory.

**Excessive fees.** While less-qualified borrowers sometimes pay higher fees to obtain a mortgage loan because of the increased risk to the lenders, predatory lenders may charge (and attempt to hide) exorbitant fees such as excessive late fees, unnecessary inspection fees, mortgage insurance premiums for unnecessary policies, and fees charged unlawfully when a buyer enters a loss mitigation program. Typically, fees in excess of 4-5% of the loan amount are considered high and may indicate predatory lending.

**Foreclosure relief.** While not strictly a predatory lending practice, foreclosure relief scams are closely related to some predatory lending practices. Numerous variations of these scams exist.

These scams target desperate homeowners who are fearful of losing their homes. The scammers may encourage homeowners to turn all foreclosure-related communications over to them, saying they will negotiate the foreclosure with the lender for a fee. The scammer takes the fee and disappears. In an escalated iteration of this scam, the scammer may convince homeowners to make the mortgage payments directly to them instead of the bank while the "negotiations are taking place," but of course, they are not transferring these payments to the lender, putting the homeowner at even greater risk.

Other schemes result in the homeowner turning title to the property over to the scammer, who promises to use various techniques to save the property, including renting the property back to the owner. One scheme offers a new loan to borrowers so they can bring their mortgage current. Buried in the loan documents is verbiage that turns title to the property over to the scammer.

Several federal agencies provide foreclosure protections, as do many states.

## Check Your Understanding

A borrower obtains a mortgage loan from the First State Bank and Trust Company. After closing on the loan, the lender sells the mortgage loan to another service provider without providing the proper notifications to the borrower. This sale is an example of illegal loan flipping.

    A. True
    B. False

If you selected "B," you are correct! While it is illegal for the lender to sell a mortgage loan without proper notification to the borrower, this is not an example of loan flipping.

**Steering.** As noted previously, steering in the mortgage industry is the act of directing or guiding borrowers to certain loan products or lenders based on factors other than the borrower's best interests. Unscrupulous lenders engage in steering to enable them to collect financial incentives or commissions for promoting certain loan products over others. When conversing with borrowers, these lenders focus on loans that are more lucrative for the lender or MLO, such as high-cost or other subprime loans, and attempt to limit a borrower's ability to shop around for the best terms.

**Steering regulation**. <u>Current regulations do not require proof that a borrower was harmed to establish that steering occurred</u>. Thus, MLOs must be cautious when recommending loan products to borrowers, ensuring they fully disclose all loan terms and conditions and discuss with borrowers the best loan product available based on the borrower's needs. If necessary, MLOs should document these discussions with borrowers as proof that the borrower received all pertinent information.

Various laws and regulations prohibit mortgage steering, including the Home Mortgage Disclosure Act, the Real Estate Settlement Procedures Act, and the Truth in Lending Act.

**Consequences of unethical behavior.** Unethical behavior can lead to damaged reputations and legal repercussions. Lenders found guilty of unethical behavior may face fines, loss of licensure, civil actions, and even criminal actions. Professional organizations can also take disciplinary action.

**Recent mortgage ethics cases**

In recent years, federal and state authorities have aggressively pursued mortgage lenders and brokers for ethical violations.

If you thought redlining was a thing of the past, consider this: Many recent fair-lending actions have targeted discriminatory redlining. The U.S. Department of Justice announced more than ten cases against banks and mortgage firms accused of avoiding Black and Hispanic neighborhoods. Some examples of redlining cases dated from 2023-2024 follow.

| Lender | Results |
|---|---|
| City National Bank, Los Angeles, CA (2023) | $31 million settlement |
| Patriot Bank, Memphis, TN (2024) | $1.9 million settlement |
| Trident Mortgage, PA (first non-bank redlining settlement) (2023) | Provide $22 million in subsidies to support new mortgages in majority-minority neighborhoods |
| Citadel Federal Credit Union, Philadelphia, PA (first credit union case) (2024) | $6.5 million settlement |

In addition to the DOJ crackdown on redlining, cases related to fraud and misrepresentation have also surfaced. For example, a Georgia mortgage broker, Kimberly Johnson, entered a guilty plea in early 2025 for fabricating income and asset documents on loans totaling $161 million to qualify unqualified borrowers. Many of these were FHA-insured loans. Ms. Johnson falsified pay stubs, bank statements, and W-2s to induce lenders to fund loans. She has been ordered to pay restitution. https://www.justice.gov/usao-ndga/pr/hampton-woman-pleads-guilty-161-million-mortgage-fraud-scheme

In yet another case, highlighted in National Mortgage News (https://www.nationalmortgagenews.com/list/2024-mortgage-wars-lawsuits-over-fraud-poaching-and-ot) and on the U.S. Department of Justice website, Christopher J. Gallo, a New Jersey loan originator, and Mahmet Ali Elmas, his aide, face a hefty prison sentence after being indicted by the Department of Justice for mortgage fraud. The two operated out of a privately owned licensed residential mortgage lending business.

They are accused of falsifying loan origination documents sent to mortgage lenders about how borrowers planned to use the purchased property. Their goal was to lock in lower interest rates by claiming the borrowers would occupy the properties as a primary residence. The pair is also accused of falsifying various property records to facilitate loan approval. The specific charges levied include conspiracy to commit bank fraud, bank fraud, and false statements to a financial institution.

These cases and many others illustrate that even with myriad statutory protections in place to prevent mortgage fraud and ethics violations, unscrupulous lenders and other "professionals" are still willing to take advantage of consumers or other individuals and institutions.

---

## ETHICAL BEHAVIOR IN LOAN ORIGINATION

**Financial responsibility**
**MLO & cybersecurity**
**Truth in marketing and advertising**
**Consumer education**
**General business ethics**

---

As demonstrated leading up to the economic and housing crisis of the early 2000s, unscrupulous lending practices can have a disastrous impact on individual consumers as well as the overall economy. While external factors are largely out of the control of individual lenders and the entities they work with, those same lenders and entities must uphold the highest industry standards to protect themselves, their customers and clients, and the mortgage industry.

This section addresses certain requirements of mortgage lenders, including how to handle consumer complaints, compliance and self-reporting, and the lender's fiduciary relationship with clients. Increasingly complex and ever-changing **cybersecurity concerns** are critical components of mortgage industry functions, as is the lender's responsibility to educate consumers regarding mortgage loan processes and impacts.

**Financial**
responsibility

MLO integrity and responsibility. The federal SAFE Act (12 U.S.C. §5101 et seq.), which will be covered in more detail in the next chapter, requires mortgage loan originators to maintain a certain level of personal financial integrity and responsibility. For example, MLOs must maintain a clean financial record with no recent bankruptcies due to financial mismanagement and no patterns of poor money handling. Essentially, for MLOs to advise others and manage mortgage funds, they must demonstrate that they successfully manage their own funds.

Loan applicants bear some responsibility, too, and are expected to have achieved an acceptable level of financial responsibility to be approved for a loan. Lenders and loan underwriters determine whether or not an applicant has achieved this goal. These parties will review the applicant's employment and credit history, income, debt-to-income ratio, and savings to determine if the applicant can manage the financial obligations of the mortgage loan and any other expenses or indebtedness. The lender needs to see evidence that the borrower can make payments on time and solidly qualify for the desired loan amount.

As illustrated throughout this text, mortgage lenders are accountable for ensuring compliance with legislation regarding permitted fees and compensation, fee changes and closing costs, referral fees, and fee splitting.

**Handling consumer complaints.** As in any industry, the mortgage industry and those who work in it are subject to occasional consumer complaints. MLOs must always act professionally, even if consumer complaints seem unjustified or unfair. It is important to acknowledge the consumer's feelings, communicate steps the MLO will take to address the issue, and follow the lending company's policies and procedures for managing complaints.

**Complaint response deadlines.** Federal law requires that lenders log all consumer complaints, including details of the complaint facts, the date received, and the final disposition of the complaint. Lenders must make this complaint log available to state or CFPB examiners upon request.

The CFPB requires lenders to respond to formal complaints within 15 days of receipt. If the lender needs additional time to address the complaint, it must notify the complainant within that 15-day timeframe and provide a final response within 60 days.

Note that fair lending standards apply to complaint management; thus, the complaint management process should be uniform for all consumers.

**Check Your Understanding**

Which one of the following statements regarding the complaint process in the mortgage industry is true?

    A. Lenders must provide an annual report to the CFPB outlining any consumer complaints received regarding the firm's loan products or processes.
    B. Lenders must notify the CFPB each time a consumer lodges a complaint about the firm's loan products or processes.
    C. Lenders must maintain a log of complaints and resolutions and make it available to the CFPB on request.
    D. Lenders must engage the services of a third party.

If you selected "C," you are correct! Lenders must maintain a log of consumer complaints and make it available to regulators on request.

**Company compliance, self-reporting.** All mortgage lending entities must comply with federal and state mortgage laws. Lenders are expected to monitor compliance management systems continuously to ensure the timely identification of concerns. Lending companies are expected to self-report all detected compliance violations to the applicable regulatory entities. These reports must identify the violation that occurred, the steps taken to correct it, and any procedures enacted to prevent recurrence.

Adequate and accurate self-reporting may lessen penalties for violations; concealing violations will result in harsh penalties once discovered.

## MLO and cybersecurity

**Cybersecurity.** Cybersecurity issues pose a significant risk to the mortgage industry. Security breaches that compromise consumers' sensitive information, financial transactions, and the integrity of the lending process are all too common. Because of the sensitive nature of information that consumers share with lenders, it is especially critical that lenders take proper care to protect that information from hackers and other fraudsters.

**Redirecting transaction funds.** Specific cybersecurity threats include scams where cybercriminals intercept or divert funds during the closing process. Unsuspecting borrowers receive a notice that provides them with "new" wiring instructions. These borrowers wire the funds, which are often never recovered.

**Ransomware.** Ransomware is a scam that involves malicious software that encrypts files or systems, resulting in users being locked out of their systems until they pay the ransom.

**Phishing schemes.** Ransomware attacks and other cybersecurity issues are often the result of phishing schemes, where deceptive emails, messages, or websites trick users into divulging sensitive information or clicking on malicious links. These links then allow hackers access to the user's computer, allowing them to steal information used for other cyber-attacks, identity theft, and more.

**Cybersecurity programs.** The Gramm-Leach-Bliley Act requires financial institutions to develop written cybersecurity programs outlining how they intend to protect the security, confidentiality, and integrity of their consumers' information. In developing these programs, lenders must focus on certain factors:

- identify and assess potential risks to the security of consumer information in their possession, including unauthorized access, data breaches, or cyberattacks
- implement safeguards to address the risks identified; such safeguards may include access controls, encryption, firewalls, password requirements, and more
- regularly monitor, evaluate, test, and update information security programs to adapt to changing threats and ensure their effectiveness in safeguarding consumer information
- train all employees on program details and methods to be used to properly protect client data

Individuals within the firm should also implement precautions to protect sensitive information:

- comply with the firm's cybersecurity program
- use antivirus software and spam filters
- implement multi-factor authentication (MFA) for accessing sensitive systems and accounts
- use encryption technologies for email communications, file storage, and data transmission to ensure confidentiality
- connect only to secure, password-protected Wi-Fi networks

**Truth in marketing and advertising**

**Regulation N and MAP.** Regulation N, the implementing regulation for Mortgage Acts and Practices in Advertising (MAPs), specifically prohibits deceptive or misleading advertising of mortgage loan products.

**Compliance with MAP.** In order to comply, lenders must provide accurate, understandable, and comprehensive information in all advertising about mortgage products and terms, including rates, fees, payments, taxes, insurance, and other components. Advertisements must use simple, clear and accessible language, and the content included must present credit terms and other critical facts clearly and conspicuously for potential borrowers.

**The purpose of MAP.** The purpose of MAP is to ensure accuracy and transparency regarding the mortgage loan process and foster integrity and fairness in mortgage advertising. The ultimate goal is to provide advertising that permits consumers to gain a sense of the risks and rewards related to the advertised product. Based on the advertisement's content, they should be able to assess if the product aligns with their risk tolerances.

**MAP prohibitions**. The MAPs rule expressly prohibits misrepresenting any of the following:

- the interest charged, including the monthly interest owed, the loan amount, or the total amount due, and whether the difference between the interest owed and the interest paid is added to the total amount due
- the annual percentage rate, simple annual rate, periodic rate, or any other rate
- the fees or costs associated with the mortgage, including any misrepresentations about the absence of fees
- the existence, cost, payment terms, or other terms associated with additional products or features sold alongside the mortgage, such as credit or credit disability insurance
- the terms, amounts, payments, or other requirements relating to taxes or insurance, including any misrepresentations about whether the payment includes property taxes and insurance
- the existence and terms of any prepayment penalty
- the terms "fixed" or "variable" related to the loan's interest rate
- a comparison of a temporary rate or payment to any actual or hypothetical rate or payment
- the type of mortgage product and whether it is fully amortizing
- the loan amount, available cash, or credit, including false claims about cash or credit the consumer will receive
- payment requirements, including claims that no payments are needed in a reverse mortgage or other loan
- default risks, such as when a consumer could default due to unpaid taxes, insurance, or maintenance
- a mortgagee's ability to resolve debt issues, including false claims about debt reduction, elimination, restructuring, or forgiveness
- the association of a mortgage product or provider with any person or program, including falsely claiming the provider is affiliated with a government entity or organization OR suggesting the product is a government benefit or is endorsed, sponsored, or affiliated with a government or other program, including misleading use of symbols, logos, or formats
- the source of messages or correspondence, such as falsely claiming it is from the consumer's current lender or servicer
- a consumer's right to remain in his or her home, including misleading claims about how long or under what conditions a reverse mortgage holder can stay
- a consumer's likelihood of obtaining a mortgage product or term, including false claims of preapproval or guarantees
- the chances of refinancing or modifying a mortgage, including false claims of preapproval or guarantees

> ▸ the availability, nature, or credibility of counseling or expert advice regarding mortgage products, including the qualifications of those providing the services

## Check Your Understanding

Regulation N, or MAPS, addresses which component of the mortgage lending process?

> A. Lender disclosures such as the LE and CD
> B. MLO qualifications
> C. Underwriting
> D. Advertising

If you selected "D," you are correct. MAPS (Mortgage Acts and Practices – Advertising) outlines requirements and prohibitions related to advertising mortgage loan products.

**Consumer education**

As a mortgage loan originator's priority is to ensure they meet borrowers' needs while also complying with pertinent state and federal regulations. In addition, they should consider their role as a consumer educator.

*Consumer Affairs* noted in January 2024 that first-time buyers made up 32% of all homebuyers during 2023. The National Association of REALTORS® notes that this number remained largely unchanged over the previous ten years. What does that mean to MLOs?

**Promote client rights in loan acquisition process.** Purchasing a home is likely the single most expensive purchase most individuals will ever make, and the home-buying process, including the mortgage loan process, can be daunting. Ethical MLOs consider it their legal obligation to ensure that consumers understand the mortgage loan process and their rights in that process.

As an example, consider lenders' statutory obligation to provide a Loan Estimate within three days of receiving a loan application. Lenders that comply with this directive have met their legal obligation. But have they met their ethical obligation? Perhaps not. Taking time to thoroughly explain the LE, including the information it contains, the borrower's rights and obligations, and the impact of the loan terms, demonstrates the lender's commitment to ethical lending practices.

**Consumer education considerations.** These considerations include personalized, professional service in helping borrowers understand their financial situation and the options available for mortgage financing. Lenders should help borrowers develop a clear understanding of the mortgage loan process as it unfolds, including tactful but honest discussions about necessary changes in the down payment amount, interest rates, fees, or other loan terms, and the use of a power of attorney if needed. If relevant, lenders must make borrowers aware of the implications of having a non-occupant co-borrower who will be responsible for the loan if the borrower fails to make payments but will not have an ownership stake in the home.

**General business ethics**

What are *general business ethics*? These moral principles and standards guide the behavior and conduct of individuals and businesses. For the mortgage industry, it refers to upholding the highest standards of integrity and service, which benefits lenders, loan originators, other professionals, clients, consumers, and the entire industry.

The values that ethical individuals and organizations display include honesty, integrity, fairness, respect, and responsibility in all aspects of business operations. Such attributes should be present in interactions with customers, employees, suppliers, competitors, and the community. Ethical decisions balance business and finances with stakeholders' needs and rights.

As mentioned previously, many companies and most professional organizations have a code of ethics that serves as a formal set of guidelines and principles that outline the expected standards of behavior and conduct for everyone in the organization. This code of ethics should do the following:

- set clear standards and expectations regarding ethical behavior for employees
- serve as a reference point for employees who face ethical challenges
- promote accountability by holding individuals responsible for their actions and behaviors
- help mitigate legal, financial, and reputational risks associated with unethical behavior.

**Stay current with new ethics-related legislation.** Businesses should periodically review and update their codes of ethics to ensure they remain in line with the latest legal requirements and incorporate new standards and benchmarks as appropriate. The review should identify and address new ethical challenges as they emerge and confirm that the code aligns with the company's values, culture, and strategic objectives. Periodic review reduces the risk of legal battles and reputational harm and fosters a culture of accountability in upholding ethical standards.

**Stay in your lane.** Behaving ethically also encompasses knowing when to offer advice and when to refrain from unsolicited or unnecessary advice. Any advice to borrowers should remain relevant to the transaction, and MLOs *should not provide advice outside their area of expertise*.

MLOs are responsible for their actions as well as the actions of their workplace and even their clients, to a certain extent. Anyone who suspects fraud must report it. They must exhibit professionalism, honesty, integrity, and transparency in all interactions with other professionals and consumers. MLOs and mortgage firms must comply with multiple regulations, including the SAFE Act and the Gramm-Leach-Bliley Act, to protect the firm, the firm's investors, the MLO, and clients.

Remember, most unethical acts are also illegal:

- encouraging appraisers to provide inaccurate property valuations
- funding mortgage loans on considerations other than a borrower's ability to repay
- presenting misleading marketing or advertising materials
- discriminating in the lending process
- mishandling (purposely or inadvertently) a borrower's funds
- failing to protect a borrower's confidential information

**ETHICAL ISSUES
RELATED
TO FEDERAL
LAWS**

**Mortgage industry
ethical
benchmarks**

- truthful marketing and advertising, fair lending practices, no predatory lending, loan origination and documentation integrity, duty to borrowers, transparency in loan servicing, and regulatory compliance.
- Federal and state laws do not specifically address or define ethical conduct.
- **The National Association of Mortgage Brokers** (NAMB) and other professional organizations have established codes of ethics for mortgage industry professionals.

**UDAAP
guidelines**

- **Dodd-Frank** defines and prohibits UDAPP (unfair, deceptive, or abusive acts and practices). CFPB and FTC regulators use UDAAP standards to investigate lenders for illegal practices.

**Ethics and
RESPA**

- **RESPA** focuses on loan term transparency and illegal kickbacks and compensation.

**Ethics and the
Civil Rights Act**

- **The Civil Rights Act of 1866** was the first U.S. law to prohibit discrimination in the inheritance, purchase, lease, sale, or conveyance of real or personal property.

**Ethics and the
Fair Housing Act**

- **The Fair Housing Act** prohibits housing discrimination based on race, color, religion, national origin, sex, disability, and familial status, with some exemptions for owner-occupants, private owners, housing for the elderly, and religious organizations or private clubs.

**Ethics and other
financing laws**

- **HMDA, ECOA, and CRA** all work to prohibit unethical or discriminatory treatment of loan applicants and borrowers.

**Prohibited acts**

- **RESPA, the Gramm-Leach-Bliley, and the Fair Housing Act** also include specific prohibitions aimed at unethical and discriminatory treatment.
- **Federal legislation specifically prohibits redlining** (refusing to write loans or insurance on properties in specific geographic areas), steering (guiding borrowers to more expensive loan products for the lender's benefit), and blockbusting (frightening owners into listing below market price.
- **ECOA** prohibits unethical and discriminatory treatment in lending based on race, color, national origin, religion, sex, marital status, income source, and age.

| | |
|---|---|
| **Mortgage fraud** | • Defined as any intentional, deceptive, or fraudulent act related to obtaining a mortgage loan. |
| | • Fraud may be perpetrated by borrowers, lenders, or others related to the mortgage lending and purchasing process. |
| | • Intentional misrepresentation occurs when one party purposely provides false information or conceals material facts with the intent to deceive. |
| | • Unintentional misrepresentation occurs when individuals breach their duty of care by committing errors or omissions or fail to fulfill their responsibilities. |
| | • Puffing involves making a statement that obviously exaggerates a product or service. It is not considered fraud. |
| | • Mortgage fraud may be categorized as fraud for housing or fraud for property. |
| | • Multiple fraud schemes exist, including deed or home title theft, straw buyers, air loans, asset and liability fraud, income and employment fraud, occupancy fraud, and appraisal fraud. |
| | • The Fraud Enforcement and Recovery Act (FERA) makes it a felony to falsify loan documents. FHA, VA, and other lending programs have additional enforcement options. |
| **Advertising ethics** | • Many agencies prohibit fraudulent mortgage lending advertising no matter the advertising medium used. |
| | • Federal agencies are especially concerned with fraudulent advertising such as confusing terminology, bait advertising, and switch after sale aimed at vulnerable populations. |
| | • Disclosures must be clear and conspicuous. |
| **Predatory lending** | • Predatory lending and steering activities include loan flipping, asset-based lending, excessive fees, penalties or charges, and excessive or lengthy prepayment penalties. |
| | • Subprime lending, negative amortization loans, loans with balloon payments, and other activities may also be considered predatory lending, depending on the circumstances. |
| **Recent mortgage ethics cases** | • examples include Redlining, fabricating documents, misrepresentation |

## ETHICAL BEHAVIOR IN LOAN ORIGINATION

| | |
|---|---|
| **Financial responsibility** | • The SAFE Act requires MLOs to maintain a certain level of personal financial accountability, including no bankruptcies or patterns of poor money handling. |
| | • Loan applicants and borrowers also bear some responsibility to demonstrate an acceptable level of responsibility to receive loan approval. |
| | • Lenders are responsible for effectively handling consumer complaints and must log all complaints, the date received, and how they resolved the complaint. The CFPB may audit this complaint log at any time. |

|  |  |
|---|---|
|  | • Mortgage lenders must comply with all federal and state mortgage laws and monitor their firms to identify areas of concern. They must self-report any detected compliance violations. |
|  | • MLOs have a fiduciary relationship with clients and must act accordingly, including disclosing discovered information material to the transaction. |
|  | • MLOs must protect their company or investors and comply with established policies and procedures. |
| **MLO and cybersecurity** | • MLOs must be mindful of cybersecurity issues and take appropriate steps to ensure client confidentiality. Gramm-Leach-Bliley mandates various steps MLOs must take to prevent cybersecurity concerns. |
| **Truth in marketing and advertising** | • MAP governs ethical advertising methods, such as accuracy and transparency regarding loan products and processes. |
|  | • Compliance with MAP and Regulation N enables consumers to make informed decisions. |
| **Consumer education** | • MLOs are expected to meet borrowers' needs and educate them so they understand the mortgage loan process and its impact on their finances. |
| **General business ethics** | • Honesty, integrity, fairness, respect, and responsibility in all aspects of business operations. |

# Chapter 4 Quiz: Ethics

1.  Which federal agencies are primarily responsible for enforcing UDAAP regulations?

    a.  CFPB and FHA
    b.  FTC and FDIC
    c.  CFPB and FTC
    d.  NAMB and FNMA

2.  A closing attorney prepares documents for a mortgage transaction and charges an extra fee for "document preparation." No additional or distinct services are performed. According to RESPA (12 U.S.C. §2601 et seq.), this fee is

    a.  permitted, as long as the attorney is licensed
    b.  prohibited, because it is for a standard service already compensated
    c.  allowed if disclosed in advance on the Loan Estimate
    d.  acceptable if the borrower does not object

3.  A lender includes critical cost disclosures in a small, hard-to-read font at the bottom of a web page. According to the FTC's "four Ps" test, this placement would likely be considered

    a.  appropriate, since the information is technically present
    b.  abusive, because it limits consumer choice
    c.  unfair, because it increases loan processing time
    d.  deceptive, because it is not prominent or well-located

4.  Which of the following statements best describes the purpose of the Home Mortgage Disclosure Act (HMDA (12 U.S.C. §2801 et seq.))?

    a.  It requires lenders to allocate a percentage of loans to underserved communities.
    b.  It prohibits redlining and mandates lending in low-income areas.
    c.  It requires lenders to report application and demographic data to monitor fair lending practices.
    d.  It enforces penalties against loan officers who discriminate against applicants.

5.  Under the Equal Credit Opportunity (15 U.S.C. §1691 et seq.) Act, when may a lender legally consider an applicant's age during the mortgage approval process?

    a.  When the applicant is over 70, and the lender believes retirement may affect repayment
    b.  When the applicant is under 25 and applying for their first loan
    c.  When the applicant is a senior citizen, and the lender wants to offer better terms
    d.  When the applicant is not of legal age to enter a binding contract or when age affects the ability to repay

6.  Which of the following best distinguishes intentional misrepresentation from unintentional misrepresentation?

    a.  Intentional misrepresentation involves errors made in good faith.
    b.  Unintentional misrepresentation includes deliberate concealment of loan terms.
    c.  Intentional misrepresentation is purposeful deception, while unintentional misrepresentation results from negligence or failure to meet professional duties.
    d.  Unintentional misrepresentation cannot lead to any legal consequences.

7. A lender approves a mortgage loan for Darren, who appears to be the legal owner of a residential property. Darren provides a deed, title documents, and even a remote notarization verifying the sale. A few weeks later, the true homeowners discover a foreclosure notice on their property and learn that a mortgage was taken out in their name—without their knowledge or consent. The real owners never met Darren, never sold the home, and had no idea title had been transferred. What type of mortgage fraud scheme does this scenario most likely represent?

   a. Straw buyer scheme
   b. Deed or home title theft
   c. Asset and liability fraud
   d. Fraud-for-housing misrepresentation

8. A mortgage lender detects potentially suspicious activity during the underwriting process and files a suspicious activity report (SAR). Later, it was determined that no fraud occurred. What is the legal consequence for the lender?

   a. The lender may be penalized for filing a false report.
   b. The lender is protected from liability under the Bank Secrecy Act.
   c. The borrower may sue for damages related to the SAR.
   d. The lender must notify the borrower that a SAR was filed.

9. A lender launches an online ad campaign promoting "low monthly payments" with a hyperlink labeled "More info" that directs users to a disclosure page via a pop-up window. What's the primary compliance concern in this situation?

   a. The use of pop-up windows could prevent effective disclosure delivery.
   b. The ad may violate fair lending laws by failing to target all audiences equally.
   c. The ad lacks a toll-free number for consumer questions.
   d. The hyperlink should have directed users to the loan application instead.

10. Which of the following practices would most likely violate the MAP Rule (Regulation N)?

    a. Disclosing an adjustable interest rate and including a link to the full APR
    b. Advertising a low rate without mentioning that it increases after six months
    c. Promoting a mortgage with a required 20% down payment
    d. Including a prepayment penalty disclosure in the fine print of a loan agreement

11. Which of the following scenarios is the best example of a "switch after sale" tactic prohibited under mortgage advertising rules?

    a. A borrower applies for a loan with a low interest rate but is denied due to poor credit and offered a different loan with higher terms.
    b. A borrower requests an advertised loan, but the lender requires additional documentation before proceeding with the application.
    c. A borrower sees an ad for a fixed-rate mortgage but ultimately chooses an adjustable-rate loan after reviewing the pros and cons with their loan officer.
    d. A borrower applies for a loan advertised with no closing costs, pays a deposit, and is later told that the loan is unavailable and must choose one with closing costs.

12. Ryan refinanced his mortgage 10 months ago. His lender contacts him, saying interest rates have dropped and encourages him to refinance again. Ryan agrees. After this refinance, Ryan's total loan balance and overall repayment costs are significantly higher—even though he's only received a minimal short-term benefit. Which type of predatory lending practice does this scenario best illustrate?

    a. Asset-based lending
    b. Excessive prepayment penalties
    c. Loan flipping
    d. Charging excessive fees

13. What is negative amortization?

    a. A decrease in loan balance due to extra principal payments
    b. A loan feature where the interest rate is fixed but monthly payments fluctuate
    c. When loan payments are less than the interest charged, causing the loan balance to increase
    d. A penalty for paying off the loan before the end of the term

14. Which of the following statements about consumer complaints and regulatory requirements is correct?

    a. MLOs should file complaints without investigation even if they believe the complaints are unjustified, unless instructed otherwise by management.
    b. Federal law requires lenders to respond to consumer complaints within 30 days of receipt.
    c. Complaint logs must be kept confidential and may not be shared with examiners unless subpoenaed.
    d. Lenders must log all complaints and respond within 15 days, with a final response due within 60 days if more time is needed.

15. Which of the following best supports a key expectation for a compliance management system within a mortgage company's operations?

    a. The system must balance loan processing time with required regulatory checks, prioritizing a desired number of loan approvals per month.
    b. The system must perform quarterly audits for monitoring compliance.
    c. The system must support continuous monitoring and timely identification of concerns.
    d. The system must operate independently from regulatory oversight, only involving regulators when fraud or other serious violations are suspected.

16. Jared, an MLO, meets with several consumers at a homebuyer event. One attendee, Nina, expresses general interest in learning more about mortgage loans but doesn't provide any personal information. Another attendee, Tyler, fills out a loan application and submits income documentation later that day. According to industry expectations and fiduciary standards, which individual(s) would now be considered Jared's client?

    a. Neither Nina nor Tyler, because fiduciary duty applies only after underwriting begins
    b. Both Nina and Tyler, because they both showed interest in a mortgage loan
    c. Only Tyler, because he has taken concrete steps to begin the application process
    d. Only Nina, because she expressed interest before Tyler did

17. A mortgage company's system suddenly becomes inaccessible. Staff personnel are locked out of email, loan files, and closing software. A message appears demanding payment in cryptocurrency to restore access. The IT department later confirms that a staff member clicked a link in what appeared to be an internal HR email. What type of cybersecurity threat does this situation most likely represent?

    a. Social engineering
    b. Ransomware attack
    c. Phishing-based identity theft
    d. Wire transfer fraud

18. A mailer features a U.S. flag and a bald eagle, using official-looking fonts and a subject line reading, "You've been selected for a federally backed refinance of your amortized loan!" The mailer directs borrowers to call a third-party mortgage broker unaffiliated with any federal agency. What type of MAP violation does this scenario illustrate?

    a. Misrepresentation of debt resolution options
    b. Misrepresentation of loan payment requirements
    c. Misrepresentation of loan amortization status
    d. Misrepresentation of affiliation with a government program

19. Paulette is a first-time homebuyer who expresses anxiety and confusion after receiving her Loan Estimate. Her MLO, Devon, reassures her that everything looks fine but doesn't walk her through the document or offer any additional guidance. What ethical misstep has Devon made?

    a. Violating RESPA's consumer support requirements
    b. Overestimating the borrower's financial literacy
    c. Failing to provide the Loan Estimate Explanation pamphlet
    d. Meeting legal standards but falling short on consumer education

20. A mortgage loan originator receives a commission bonus offer for selling a certain high-cost loan product. Although the product isn't the best fit for the borrower, the MLO knows it will increase their earnings. Instead, the MLO recommends a more affordable loan better suited to the borrower's long-term goals. What ethical principle is the MLO demonstrating?

    a. Integrity and putting the client's needs first
    b. Transparency in advertising
    c. Loyalty to the lender's financial goals
    d. Obedience to marketing strategy

21. Which of the following is an ethical obligation of an MLO under professional codes of conduct?

    a. Avoiding reporting client behavior to protect the fiduciary relationship and reputation of MLOs.
    b. Promoting higher-interest products to increase revenue and ensure the financial stability of the lending industry.
    c. Reporting suspected fraud and exhibiting integrity in all interactions.
    d. Complying with borrower requests even when they conflict with the law, to demonstrate undivided loyalty to the client.

22. Which of the following best describes a "substantial injury" under the CFPB's definition of an unfair act or practice?

    a. Financial harm or a significant risk of concrete harm to the consumer
    b. A small, unavoidable fee disclosed in the loan terms
    c. Physical harm that results from a consumer misunderstanding
    d. Harm caused by a competitor's lower rates

23. What makes a misrepresentation or omission "material" under the CFPB's deception standard?

    a. It was made during loan servicing rather than during origination.
    b. It influences or is likely to influence a consumer's choice or behavior.
    c. It occurs only when a consumer files a formal complaint.
    d. It results in the loss of money, personal property, or other material possessions.

24. Mrs. Ellis, who owns and lives in one unit of a four-unit building, decides to rent out the other three units without the help of a broker. She sets rental terms but does not advertise publicly. Which statement best describes her legal obligations under the Fair Housing Act?

    a. She is fully exempt from the FHA and may discriminate on any basis.
    b. She is exempt from the Act unless she rents to someone of a different religion.
    c. She is partially exempt from the Act but still may not discriminate based on race.
    d. She must comply fully with the Fair Housing Act because the building has more than one unit.

25. What is the primary purpose of the Community Reinvestment Act (CRA)?

    a. To regulate interest rates on residential mortgages
    b. To require equitable home prices in low-income neighborhoods
    c. To ensure financial institutions meet the credit needs of all communities they serve
    d. To prohibit the use of automated underwriting systems in mortgage lending

# 5

# Uniform State Content

**SAFE Act and CSBS/AARMR Model State Law**
**State mortgage regulatory agencies**
**License law and regulation**
**Compliance**

## Learning Objectives

- Describe the purpose and role of the SAFE Act and its relation to MLO licensing and registration.
- Identify the purpose of the NMLS in relation to MLO licensing and registration.
- Define MLO-related terminology.
- Identify who needs to hold a state-issued MLO license and who needs to register through the NMLS.
- Identify licensing laws and regulations that govern mortgage loan originators.
- Describe compliance-related activities and prohibitions.

---

## SAFE ACT, CSBS, AND AARMR MODEL STATE LAW

**The SAFE Act and HERA**
**The NMLS**

---

## The SAFE Act and HERA

**The Secure and Fair Enforcement for Mortgage Licensing Act (SAFE Act).**
**The Housing and Economic Recovery Act**, is codified as Public Law 110-289 and comprises several **sub-statutes**. One of these sub-statutes is the **SAFE Act**, or **Secure and Fair Enforcement for Mortgage Licensing Act**, which is codified as 12 USC Ch. 51, Title V. The SAFE Act governs individual mortgage loan originators, entity mortgage loan originators, states, and federal agencies. The CFPB currently administers this Act. The SAFE Act impacts only residential mortgage loans.

The SAFE Act gave states two years to pass legislation requiring the licensure of mortgage loan originators according to national standards and the participation of state agencies on the Nationwide Multistate Licensing System (NMLS). Mortgage loan originators who work for an insured depository or its owned or controlled subsidiary that is regulated by a federal banking agency, or for an institution regulated by the Farm Credit Administration, are registered. All other mortgage loan originators are licensed by the states.

SAFE Act administrators are NOT responsible for licensing MLOs. Instead, the act governs state-level MLO licensing in all 50 states, the District of Columbia, and the U.S. territories of Puerto Rico, Guam, the U.S. Virgin Islands, American Samoa, and the Northern Mariana Islands.

The SAFE Act protects consumers by ensuring that MLOs meet minimum professional standards. It reduces fraud and abuse in the mortgage industry and improves accountability and tracking of MLOs through a nationwide database. It promotes uniformity in mortgage licensing across states and increases transparency in the mortgage lending process.

## Check Your Understanding

Carlotta works for a commercial lending entity. She writes business loans primarily for small businesses in her community. Which of these statements about Carlotta is most likely true?

> A. She is NMLS-registered.
> B. She holds a state MLO license.
> C. She is both registered and licensed.
> D. She does not need to be registered or licensed.

If you selected "D," you are correct. The SAFE Act applies only to residential mortgage loan originators.

**The NMLS**

In an attempt to combat fraud in the mortgage industry and standardize state regulations, the SAFE Act places licensing and registration requirements on individuals who serve as mortgage loan originators.

The Nationwide Multistate Licensing System (NMLS). At its inception, the act required each state to develop minimum MLO licensing and registration standards. It mandated that the Conference of State Bank Supervisors (CSBS) and the American Association of Residential Mortgage Regulators (AARMR) create and maintain a nationwide mortgage licensing system and registry for residential mortgage loan originators. To that end, these organizations partnered with states and the financial services industry to develop what is known today as the Nationwide Multistate Licensing System (NMLS), originally the Nationwide Multistate Licensing System Registry (NMLS-R). At the same time, they created a governing agency called the State Regulatory Registry, which is not a governmental organization but a wholly owned subsidiary of the CSBS.

In addition, the CSBS and AARMR developed a **model state law** to help states enact MLO licensing legislation that complies with the SAFE Act.

**NMLS functions.** The NMLS has several functions:

- standardize application forms and requirements for state-licensed loan originators
- maintain a central database with comprehensive licensing and supervision information
- consolidate and optimize the flow of data between regulatory bodies
- strengthen accountability and tracking mechanisms for loan originators
- make the licensing process smoother and less burdensome
- reinforce consumer protections and anti-fraud efforts
- grant consumers free access to information about loan originators (license history, disciplinary actions)
- create a system that requires MLOs to prioritize consumers' best interests
- encourage responsible practices in the subprime mortgage market
- expedite and facilitate the handling of consumer complaints

Licensees and registrants pay a fee to maintain access to the NMLS. Consumers may access the system free of charge to research various MLOs.

## Check Your Understanding

What is the NMLS?

 A. A professional organization designed for networking among mortgage loan originators
 B. A federal organization that governs MLO licensing and registration
 C. A nationwide database of and for mortgage loan originators
 D. A state-level agency in each state charged with providing MLO licensing exams

If you selected "C," you are correct. The NMLS, created by mandate from the SAFE Act, is an online platform that assists states in managing licensing and registration processes for mortgage loan originators.

## STATE MORTGAGE REGULATING AGENCIES

**Registered v. licensed loan originator**
**Regulatory agency responsibilities**
**State law and regulation definitions**

---

**Registered v.
licensed loan
originator**

**Registered originator.** The SAFE Act defines two categories of loan originators. A **registered loan originator** is typically employed by a covered financial institution. A covered institution is a federally regulated depository, such as a bank or a credit union. These individuals must obtain and maintain their NMLS registration annually. **They do not typically have to hold a state license.** Regulation G implements the registration requirement for MLOs and focuses on facilitating the information flow to and between regulators and increasing MLO accountability and tracking.

**Licensed originator.** A **state-licensed loan originator** is an individual, such as a mortgage broker, who originates mortgage loans but is **not employed by a covered financial institution.** These individuals obtain a valid loan originator license from a state, register with the NMLSR and maintain their licenses annually.

In addition to individual MLO licensing, loan origination companies typically must also be licensed. Sole proprietors must hold two licenses: one for the business owner and one for the business itself.

### Check Your Understanding

1. Martina originates mortgage loans for her employer, First Federal Bank and Loan, in Winston-Salem, North Carolina. Martina most likely _____.

   A. holds a North Carolina MLO license
   B. has an NMLS unique identifier and a North Carolina MLO license
   C. has an NMLS unique identifier but not a state MLO license
   D. is neither licensed nor registered since she is not an independent contractor

If you selected "C," you are correct. Since Martina works for a federally regulated bank, she most likely does not have an MLO license but instead is simply registered with the NMLS.

2. All mortgage loan originators must hold a state license and be registered with the NMLS.

    A. True
    B. False

If you selected "B," you are correct! All mortgage loan originators must be registered, but not all must be licensed by an individual state.

**Regulatory agency responsibilities**

The SAFE Act delegates MLO licensing tasks to an agency in each state. Each state assigns a name to its regulatory agency. For example, the State Board of Financial Institutions/Consumer Finance Division governs MLO licensing in South Carolina. In California, the governing body is the Department of Financial Protection and Innovation, and in Iowa, the Division of Banking Finance Bureau performs the required duties. Each state manages its own licensing process that complies with SAFE Act standards and issues licenses through the NMLS.

**Regulatory loan originator responsibilities.** Under SAFE Act mandates, each state regulatory agency must possess broad authority to oversee, interpret, and enforce the SAFE Act, as well as take an active role in developing and communicating related rules and regulations to loan originators within the state.

Each state's regulatory program must meet the following criteria:

- provide adequate supervision of MLOs, enforce the law, conduct investigations, and take disciplinary action against MLOs who violate federal or state mortgage laws
- ensure NMLS registration of all state-licensed MLOs
- report relevant violations and enforcement actions to the NMLS
- establish a process for challenging inaccurate information in the NMLS
- require licensed MLOs to provide periodic reports about loans closed
- implement a mechanism for assessing and collecting civil financial penalties against individuals operating without a license or registration
- establish the authority to conduct license examinations
- implement a mechanism for accessing MLO and mortgage entity records to facilitate initial licensing and license maintenance
- establish requirements for amending, transferring, surrendering, or making other license status changes
- establish requirements for financial protections, such as a minimum net worth, a surety bond, or a recovery fund

In addition, state regulatory authorities must set minimum requirements for state-chartered MLO licensing programs; develop criteria for licensing eligibility, education, training, continuing education, and testing; and grant the CFPB permission to review and approve the state's licensing programs.

## Check Your Understanding

1. Which of the following is NOT a required component of a state's regulatory authority?

    A. Providing supervision and enforcement actions against MLOs
    B. Requiring MLOs to report personal income annually
    C. Ensuring NMLS registration of state-licensed MLOs
    D. Establishing the authority to conduct license examinations

If you selected "B," you are correct! The SAFE Act does not require that MLOs report their personal income annually.

2. According to the SAFE Act, want entity is responsible for ensuring that MLOs are properly licensed?

    A. The state regulatory authority
    B. The NMLS
    C. The CFPB
    D. The attorney general

If you selected "A," you are correct! Each state has a regulatory authority that governs MLO licensing in that state.

**Mortgage Call Reports.** You likely recall that mortgage loan companies must be licensed. Part of that licensure process is to complete and submit periodic reports called **Mortgage Call Reports (MCR)**.

The Mortgage Call Report comprises two components. First is the **Residential Mortgage Loan Activity (RMLA)** report. Lending institutions collect and report data related to submitted applications, closed loans, individual MLOs, lines of credit, and servicing, categorized by state (for firms that operate in more than one state). The RMLA is due quarterly within 45 days of the end of each calendar quarter.

The second component is the **Financial Condition (FC)** report. This report includes company-level financial information. It does not have to be completed for each state in which the firm operates. Instead, it is a consolidated report of the firm's activities across all locations. Mortgage servicers and lenders must submit the FC quarterly at the same time as the RMLA. Mortgage brokers must submit the FC annually within 90 days of the calendar year's end.

Companies approved as Fannie Mae or Freddie Mac sellers/servicers or **Ginnie Mae (GNMA)** issuers must submit an **expanded MCR (EMCR)**. The EMCR includes a financial condition component and one or more residential mortgage loan activity components, depending on where the company is licensed and required to file. Lenders must submit the EMCR quarterly within 45 days of the end of each calendar quarter.

For more information regarding the MCR and EMCR, consult the NMLS Mortgage Call Report User Guide at https://mortgage.nationwidelicensingsystem.org/licensees/resources/LicenseeResources/mcrUserGuide.pdf.

## Check Your Understanding

1. What criterion determines if a company must submit an expanded MCR?

   A. The company's annual income from mortgage loan origination activities
   B. The number of MLOs working for a given company in all states in which the firm operates
   C. The company's approval to sell or service Fannie Mae or Freddie Mac loans
   D. The number of states in which the company offers mortgage loan origination services

If you selected "C," you are correct! Companies approved as Fannie Mae or Freddie Mac sellers/servicers or Ginnie Mae issuers must submit an EMCR.

2. Which of the following does a lender submit as a consolidated report of information for all states where the lender operates?

   A. RMLA
   B. FC
   C. MCR
   D. EMCR

If you selected "B," you are correct! Mortgage origination firms operating in more than one state must submit a Residential Mortgage Loan Activity report for each state but must submit only a single Financial Condition document.

**Federal agency mandates.** In addition to the mandate placed on the CSBS and AARMR to develop the NMLS/R, the SAFE Act initially required the Department of Housing and Urban Development (HUD) to verify that each state's MLO licensing standards met the federally mandated minimums and that the state was participating in the NMLS. If a state was out of compliance, HUD was required to implement a similar system for all state-licensed mortgage loan originators in a given state.

These governing and enforcement actions have been handed off to the CFPB, which is currently the regulating body for the SAFE Act and the NMLS.

The act requires federal banking agencies, the Federal Financial Institutions Examination Council, and the Farm Credit Administration to develop and maintain a system for registering employees who originate mortgage loans with the NMLS.

## Check Your Understanding

Under the SAFE Act, which of these responsibilities is relegated to the federal level instead of the state level?

    A. Establish standards for NMLS licensing and registration
    B. Ensure NMLS licensure and/or registration for all residential MLOs
    C. Verify that the state system complies with the SAFE Act mandates
    D. Submit Mortgage Call Reports to the appropriate agency

If you selected "C," you are correct. The act initially charged HUD with verifying the compliance of each state system. The CFPB is now responsible for this verification.

**Enforcement.** State regulatory authorities are permitted to engage attorneys, accountants, or other specialists to assist in examining, auditing, and investigating MLOs.

If the state regulatory authority discovers violations and provides proper notice and an opportunity for a hearing to the alleged violators, the authority can (and must) impose fines on individuals and entities subject to the SAFE Act.

Each violation or failure to comply with orders or directives from the state regulatory agency is considered a separate and distinct violation and can be penalized as such. The fine for an individual violation is inflation-adjusted each year and, as of January 2025, is more than $35,000 per violation. (https://www.federalregister.gov/documents/2025/01/08/2025-00167/civil-penalty-inflation-adjustments)

State and federal regulating authorities are not empowered to impose prison sentences on violators.

**State law and regulation definitions**

To ensure understanding of the content in this chapter, we will review some definitions here.

**Administrative and clerical tasks** are tasks for which no MLO license or registration is required. For example, individuals who collect, receive, or distribute information common to the mortgage loan process or communicate with consumers to obtain common information are performing clerical tasks.

The **American Association of Residential Mortgage Regulators (AARR)** is a national organization representing state residential mortgage regulators responsible for directing and controlling mortgage lending, brokering, or servicing activities.

An **application** is the official document consumers submit to a lender to express their interest in obtaining a mortgage loan. Lenders use application information to consider the consumer's request. Those who take or receive consumer applications are considered to be loan originators.

The **Conference of State Bank Supervisors (CSBS)** is a nationwide organization representing state regulators who oversee all types of banks, including those involved in mortgage lending. This organization plays a significant role in the creation and ongoing oversight of the NMLS and model licensing laws.

An **immediate family member** is a spouse, child, sibling, parent, grandparent, or grandchild. In this context, an individual originating a loan with or on behalf of an immediate family member is not required to hold an MLO license.

An **independent contractor** in the mortgage industry is self-employed and finds clients, sets fees, and self-manages taxes. This individual is responsible for obtaining and maintaining an individual MLO license in each state in which they operate.

A **loan originator** is an individual or entity that initiates the process of securing a loan for a borrower in exchange for compensation (such as origination fees). This individual can offer a range of loan types, including mortgages, personal loans, car loans, and business loans.

A **loan processor/underwriter** is an individual who performs support and clerical tasks under the loan originator's supervision. Some states require that loan processors obtain MLO licensing. In addition, certain certifications are available from the National Association of Mortgage Underwriters, Fannie Mae, Freddie Mac, and the VA.

A **non-traditional mortgage product** is a mortgage product that is NOT a 30-year, fixed-rate loan. ARM, balloon, interest-only, and non-QM loans are all considered non-traditional mortgage products.

A **registered loan originator** is registered with the NMLS and traditionally employed by a covered depository institution, a subsidiary of a depository institution, or an institution administered by the Farm Credit Administration. These individuals usually do NOT need a state-issued MLO license.

A **residential mortgage loan** is a specific loan type designed to finance the purchase or refinance of a property intended for use as a residence (including primary, secondary, or investment property purchases).

A **state-licensed loan originator** has obtained a state-issued MLO license through the required education and testing process. State-licensed MLOs must also register with the NMLS. They typically work for mortgage companies, mortgage brokers, and mortgage lenders not affiliated with depository institutions.

The **State Regulatory Registry** operates the NMLS and is a wholly owned subsidiary of the Conference of State Bank Supervisors.

A **unique identifier** is issued to every registered MLO that maintains an account on the NMLS platform. This number permits regulators, industry professionals, and consumers to track the activity and history of any MLO, regardless of the MLO's location.

## LICENSE LAW AND REGULATION

**Persons required to be licensed**
**Engaging in the business of an MLO**
**Licensee qualifications**
**Temporary authority to operate**
**Grounds for denying a license**
**License maintenance**
**NMLS requirements**

### Persons required to be licensed

This section will cover state licensing by addressing who must be licensed, who is exempt from licensing, licensee qualifications, license denials, and license maintenance.

As noted earlier in this text, <u>individuals who take residential mortgage loan applications and offer or negotiate the terms of a residential mortgage loan for compensation must be licensed or registered</u>. You may recall that Dodd-Frank characterizes a mortgage loan originator as someone who performs the following activities:

- takes residential mortgage loan applications
- offers or negotiates residential mortgage loan terms (or individuals who represent or advertise that they perform such services)
- offers or negotiates a loan for compensation or gain

We'll explore these three criteria in more detail in the next few pages.

**Taking a mortgage application.** What does it mean to *take* a mortgage application? The SAFE Act defines the term "*taking a mortgage application*" as "*Receipt by an individual, for the purpose of facilitating a decision whether to* *extend an offer of loan terms to a borrower or prospective borrower, of an application as defined in Section 1008.23 (a request in any form for an offer, or a response to a solicitation of an offer, of residential mortgage loan terms, and the information about the borrower or prospective borrower that is customary or necessary in a decision whether to make such an offer."*

Specific actions that constitute the taking of a loan application include

> - receiving information a consumer provides when requesting a loan, with the information to be used to determine if the consumer qualifies for a loan, even if the employee
>
>   - receives the information indirectly for the purpose of making an offer or negotiating a loan (this prevents individuals from avoiding licensing requirements by having someone else physically receive the application and then passing it on)
>   - is not responsible for verifying information
>   - inputs information into an online application or other automated system for the consumer
>   - is not involved in loan approval or qualification

Certain activities do NOT constitute *taking an application:*

> - accepting an application package and routing it to the appropriate department or individual for processing without reviewing it or making any related decisions
> - contacting a consumer to request additional documentation to verify application information
> - answering general questions about the application or application process, fees, or deadlines without engaging in fact-finding or eligibility assessments
> - describing offered loan products or services without discussing specific terms or rates that might apply to a particular individual
> - recommending a lender or specific loan terms to a borrower under an agreement with someone other than the borrower
> - providing a revised loan offer on a pending application in response to a borrower's request for a different rate or different fees than those proposed
> - responding to consumers who have received prequalified offers and collecting only basic identifying information to be forwarded to the MLO
> - receiving information related to modifying the terms of an existing loan for consumers who are participating in the firm's loss mitigation process

## Check Your Understanding

An individual who _____ has taken a loan application, based on criteria in the SAFE Act.

    A. opens an envelope that contains a consumer's mortgage application
    B. contacts a loan applicant to obtain a phone number for the applicant's employer
    C. has the authority to determine if a consumer qualifies for a loan
    D. is authorized to describe offered loan products, but not discuss specific terms or rates

If you selected "C," you are correct! An individual with the authority to determine whether an applicant is qualified for a mortgage loan has taken an application.

**Offering or negotiating loan terms.** A second criterion for determining if an individual should be licensed is whether the individual **offers or negotiates loan terms** related to the definition in Section 1008.103(c)(2). Offering or negotiating loan terms includes the following actions when performed for compensation:

- presenting a loan offer to a consumer for acceptance, whether verbally or in writing, including providing TILA disclosures, even if

  - additional information from the borrower is needed
  - the offer is conditional
  - other individuals have to complete the loan process
  - only the rate approved by the relevant financial institution's loan approval process for a specific loan product is provided without authority to negotiate the rate

- providing a revised loan offer (verbally or in writing) in response to a consumer's request for a lower interest rate or points on a pending application
- communicating with a borrower or prospective borrower, directly or indirectly, with the intent of coming to an agreement about residential mortgage loan terms
- recommending, referring, or steering a borrower or prospective borrower to a specific lender or set of residential mortgage loan terms based on a duty to or incentive from someone other than the borrower or prospective borrower

The following actions do not constitute offering or negotiating loan terms:

- sharing general information or definitions about different loan types, interest rates, and repayment options without recommending specific products or lenders

- responding to consumer inquiries about publicly available loan rates for specific loan products, without determining if the consumer qualifies for those rates
- gathering consumer information to later provide details about loan products they might be eligible for, without extending a specific loan offer for acceptance
- coordinating aspects of the loan closing process or related steps, as long as communication is limited to confirming terms that have already been offered or negotiated
- providing information that does not pertain to loan terms
- making underwriting decisions
- explaining the necessary steps or eligibility criteria a consumer must meet to obtain a loan offer
- relaying messages from a mortgage loan originator to a consumer indicating that the lender has sent a written offer and required the disclosures

### Check Your Understanding

Select the action that is an example of offering or negotiating loan terms.

A. In answer to a caller's questions regarding VA loans, a loan assistant in the firm responds by saying that the firm does offer VA loans, emphasizes that the VA does not require a down payment, and that the most common VA repayment terms are 15 and 30 years.

B. After reviewing a loan application and documentation, an underwriter determined that the applicants are qualified for the loan they applied for.

C. After the firm's initial review, an applicant is offered a 30-year mortgage at 6.25% interest with a 15% down payment.

D. A loan assistant notifies a consumer that the loan officer has mailed an offer and the required disclosures.

If you selected "C," you are correct! An offer with information specific to a potential borrower is classified as offering or negotiating loan terms.

**Offering or negotiating a loan for compensation or gain.** The third criterion for determining if any individual should be licensed is whether an individual is deemed to be offering or negotiating a loan for any compensation or gain (based on Section 1008.103[c][2][ii] if the activities are conducted as part of their job responsibilities, regardless of whether additional compensation is received.

**Underwriter licensing.** In general, the SAFE Act does not require loan processors and underwriters to hold a state-issued MLO license. However, certain circumstances may require these individuals to be licensed:

- underwriters or loan processors who also perform origination activities
- independent contractors who perform clerical or support duties in the loan origination field
- independent contractors who collect, receive, distribute, or analyze information related to making a credit decision
- independent contractors who communicate with consumers to obtain information necessary for making a credit decision

Underwriters and loan processors who serve as managers are typically licensed due to their supervisory role and must register through NMLS as required by the licensing platform.

States do not have to license loan processors or underwriters who perform only clerical or support duties under the direct supervision of a licensed MLO or a duly registered MLO. However, a licensed MLO must supervise unlicensed processors, and the SAFE Act requires an actual **nexus** (an active connection through which the MLO provides training and supervision for the underwriter).

Loan processors or underwriters are required to obtain and maintain a state loan originator license if they fall into any of the following categories:

- any individual who acts as a loan originator, as defined in §1008.103
- any individual who performs clerical or support duties and is classified as an independent contractor, as defined in §1008.23
- any independent contract who collects, receives, distributes, or analyzes information related to making a credit decision, as defined in §1008.23
- any independent contractor who communicates with consumers to gather information necessary for making a credit decision, as defined in §1008.23

States do not have to require compliance with SAFE Act licensing standards from individuals who, for example:

- perform only clerical or support duties, meaning they do not offer or negotiate loan terms or counsel borrowers and do so under the supervision of either a licensed or exempt MLO
- are employed by a mortgage lender or mortgage brokerage firm, perform only clerical or support duties, and work under the supervision and direction of a licensed employee of the same company, in accordance with §1008.103(a)
- work for a loan processing or underwriting company that contracts with mortgage lenders or brokers, performs only clerical or support duties, and operates under the supervision of a licensed loan originator employed by the same company
- do not perform loan originator activities and are not involved in collecting, analyzing, or handling loan-related information, nor communicate with consumers to gather such information

## Check Your Understanding

Which of the following situations best illustrates an actual nexus between a licensed or registered mortgage loan originator and an unlicensed assistant?

  A. An assistant completed the mortgage firm's required orientation process.
  B. The firm's underwriter reviews loan documentation under the direct supervision of the MLO.
  C. The firm's human resource records indicate that the unlicensed assistant reports directly to the MLO.
  D. An internship contract between the local university and the firm indicates that the MLO will oversee the intern's work.

If you selected "B," you are correct! To demonstrate an actual nexus between the licensed and unlicensed individuals, a licensed MLO must directly supervise the unlicensed individual.

## Engaging in the business of an MLO

**License-required activities.** Individuals who perform the functions of a mortgage loan originator or present themselves as doing so with a certain level of regularity or repetition are considered to be "engaging in the business of an MLO," meaning they must be licensed by the state (for non-depository employees) or registered (for depository employees). An individual, unless specifically exempted, shall not engage in the business of a mortgage loan originator without first obtaining and maintaining annually a license under applicable state law. Each licensed mortgage loan originator must register with and maintain a valid unique identifier issued by the NMLS. Additionally, MLOs facilitate loans; they do not provide financing.

Another factor that determines if an individual is engaging in the business of an MLO is whether or not the individual regularly or periodically (habitually) acts as an MLO or provides mortgage financing.

**Activities exempted from licensing.** The following scenarios illustrate situations in which an individual is generally not considered to be "engaged in the business of a loan originator" as long as the practice is not regular or habitual:

  ▸ individuals who arrange financing for the sale of their own primary residence or another property they own
  ▸ parents who provide financing to their child(ren)
  ▸ government employees who originate loans solely as part of their official responsibilities, provided all requirements under §1008.103(e)(6) are met
  ▸ employees of a bona fide nonprofit as recognized by the relevant state authority who originate loans as part of their job duties, assuming all criteria under §1008.103(e)(7) are met
  ▸ individuals who do not habitually or repeatedly act as a loan originator

**Additional exemptions**. Other factors may exempt individuals from MLO licensing and registration requirements:

> ▸ the individual is a licensed real estate professional who is not compensated by a lender
> ▸ the loans are business loans, not residential mortgage loans (state licensure may be required)
> ▸ the individual is arranging timeshare credits
> ▸ the individual is an attorney originating loans as part of an attorney-client relationship
> ▸ the individual is working as a registered loan originator (remember, licensed MLOs must be registered, but not all registered MLOs must be licensed)

## Check Your Understanding

A seller acts as an MLO in selling a property she owns. Which of the following factors would require her to hold an MLO license?

> A. She is a licensed real estate professional.
> B. The property is not her primary residence.
> C. The property is her primary residence.
> D. She regularly finances her own sales.

If you selected "D," you are correct. She is exempt unless she regularly performs the actions of an MLO.

**Licensee qualifications**

To obtain and maintain an MLO license, individuals must perform the following tasks:

> ▸ obtain a criminal background check
> ▸ submit to a credit check
> ▸ complete prelicensure education and testing
> ▸ complete all required annual continuing education
> ▸ establish at least one source of financial protection
>
>> • defined minimum net worth
>> • purchase of a surety bond
>> • participate in an established recovery fund

**Education and exam requirements.** The education and exam requirements for license applicants include successful completion of a 20-hour prelicensure course. The course must incorporate three hours on federal laws and regulations, three hours on ethics, and two hours on nontraditional mortgage products.

Candidates must achieve a score of 75% or higher to pass. The following table illustrates the impact of failed exams:

| Initial exam | 30-day waiting period |
|---|---|
| Second exam | 30-day waiting period |
| Third exam | 180-day waiting period |

This cycle starts over after the 180-day waiting period and follows the same pattern for subsequent exams, if necessary.

## Check Your Understanding

Which of these tasks is NOT required to obtain a state MLO license, based on provisions in the SAFE Act?

    A. Complete 30 hours of prelicensure education.
    B. Obtain a criminal background check.
    C. Submit to a credit check.
    D. Establish a source of financial protection.

If you selected "A," you are correct! License applicants must complete 20 hours of prelicensure education.

**The MLO exam.** The national SAFE exam with Uniform State Content consists of 120 questions. Of those questions, 115 are scored, and five are not. The questions are distributed among five major content areas, listed here in order based on the number of questions in each category:

- mortgage loan origination activities (27%)
- federal mortgage-related laws (24%)
- general mortgage knowledge (20%)
- ethics (18%)
- uniform state content (11%)

Applicants are not required to complete prelicensure coursework before taking the exam but must complete the coursework before applying for a license. Before taking the MLO test, candidates must

- have or create an NMLS account
- create and pay for a test enrollment window in the NMLS
- accept the Candidate Test Security and Confidentiality Agreement (Candidate Agreement)
- schedule a test appointment with Prometric, the test provider.

The test enrollment window is open for 180 days after a candidate pays for the exam.

For additional information regarding the exam, you can visit this link on the NMLS portal: https://nmlsportal.csbs.org/csm?id=kb_article_view&sys_kb_id=a5f7955b1b30d6904d74c957624bcba9.

**Obtain unique identifier.** During the application process, applicants must obtain a unique identifier through the NMLS Registry.

- Each MLO is assigned a unique registry number through the NMLS.
- This number assists regulators in distinguishing between individuals and tracking MLO conduct.
- MLOs must include this unique identifier on all applications, business cards, and advertisements.
- This identifier may be used in place of a Social Security number for SAFE Act purposes.

## Temporary authority to operate

The CFPB does not mandate license portability between states. It does provide a mechanism by which states can issue a license to individuals licensed in another state, provided the applicant meets all requirements posed by the new state. States are NOT permitted to issue licenses to registered loan originators who do not have a state license. Loan officers who are registered but not licensed must complete the full license process in at least one state before being eligible for a state license under this process.

In 2018, the CFPB added a third category of mortgage originators (beyond licensed and registered MLOs), authorizing a loan administrator with **temporary authority**. These LOs may originate loans for a limited time while applying for a state loan originator license.

These temporary authority provisions streamline the transition for federally registered MLOs seeking a state license and state-licensed individuals seeking licensure in another state.

Temporary authority authorizes eligible MLOs to originate loans before obtaining full state licensure under the following conditions:

- The applicant must have submitted all required state license application documents via the NMLS.
- No disqualifying issues may exist, such as denial of licensure in another state, license revocation in another state, conviction for certain financial crimes, or other disciplinary actions.
- The applicant must have previously completed all pre-licensure requirements and passed the MLO licensing exam.

If the applicant meets these conditions, state regulating authorities can grant temporary authority within 48 hours of applying for a new state license. However, the approval period may extend up to nine days if more information is needed based on background check results.

Temporary authority can last up to 120 days after submitting the license application. The MLO can originate loans while the license application is being processed. Temporary authority ends when any of the following occurs:

> ▸ the applicant's permanent license is approved
> ▸ the MLO withdraws the temporary authority application
> ▸ the licensing authority denies the applicant's application
> ▸ the 120-day period expires, and the applicant's application in the NMLS is incomplete

**Grounds for license denial**

Agencies can deny licensure to applicants based on multiple factors:

> ▸ financial concerns
>   - outstanding judgments, other than medical-related expenses
>   - tax or other government liens
>   - foreclosure(s) within the past three years
>   - a pattern of delinquent account(s) during the past three years
>
> ▸ legal issues
>   - convicted or pled guilty to a felony in the past seven years, unless pardoned
>   - convicted or pled guilty to a felony for any of the following (unless pardoned)
>     - fraud
>     - dishonesty
>     - breach of trust
>     - money laundering
>
> ▸ license revocation in another state

## Check Your Understanding

An MLO from one state decides to begin working in another state. Which one of the best illustrates the MLO's options to begin operating in the new state?

    A.  The MLO must take the state licensing exam in the new state.
    B.  The MLO's license from the previous state ports over to the new state.
    C.  The MLO may obtain temporary permission to operate in the new state.
    D.  The MLO does not need a license for the new state.

If you selected "C," you are correct! CFPB and SAFE Act provisions permit licensed MLOs to request temporary permission to operate in the new state pending receipt of a permanent license.

**License maintenance**

**Renewal.** Licensed MLOs must renew their licenses annually. The renewal period is from November 1 through December 31. Licenses not renewed by December 31 expire, and licensees may not perform MLO tasks with an expired license.

Some states have identified a late renewal period from January 1 through February 28. Licenses not renewed by the late renewal deadline terminate.

**Continuing education.** To renew a license, licensees must continue to meet all initial qualifications related to financial accountability and criminal stipulations. In addition, all renewal candidates must have completed at least the minimum required continuing education coursework, which is eight hours annually of NMLS-approved courses. Specific requirements may vary by state, but courses typically include the following:

- three hours of federal law and regulations
- two hours of ethics, which must include fraud, consumer protection, and fair lending issues
- two hours of non-traditional mortgage lending
- one hour of elective education

Continuing education credits apply in the same year in which a course is taken. No credits carry forward or may be applied to a previous year's requirements. State laws may mandate additional courses or requirements for renewal. Licensees may not take the same course two years in a row for credit.

Individuals who teach approved continuing education courses can receive two hours of continuing education credit for every hour taught.

**Extended absence renewals.** MLOs who leave the industry and wish to return must comply with the following requirements:

| Licenses expired for... | Requirements |
|---|---|
| Less than 3 years | Take the Late CE course, which serves as the last year of licensure's CE requirement, and apply for a new license. |
| 3 – 5 years | Retake all prelicensing education (which is valid for 3 years) and submit a new license application. |
| More than 5 years | Complete all prelicensure education, retake and pass the NMLS SAFE exam, and submit a new license application. |

**NMLS requirements**

The SAFE Act imposes certain requirements on licensees, state-level regulating authorities, and education providers.

  ▸ Individuals who hold a state MLO license must register with the NMLS.
  ▸ State-level regulating authorities must report MLO license violations and enforcement actions to the NMLS.
  ▸ All mortgage loan originators must include their unique NMLS identifier on all advertising, transaction documents, solicitation materials (including emails, social media posts, and mailings), websites/online profiles, business cards, and stationery.
  ▸ MLO courses and education providers must be NMLS-approved.
  ▸ State-licensed companies and companies employing state-licensed MLOs must submit the quarterly Mortgage Call Reports noted previously.
  ▸ Registered and licensed MLOs must provide the NMLS with current employment and address information; individual NMLS profiles must be current to renew a license.

## COMPLIANCE

**Prohibited conduct and practices**
**Required conduct**
**Advertising**

**Prohibited conduct and practices**

The overall purpose of the SAFE Act is to protect the general public by ensuring that mortgage loan originators are well-qualified and behave professionally. Thus, in addition to testing and continuing education requirements, the act prohibits certain conduct and practices and promotes other actions.

The SAFE Act prohibits the following conduct:

- engage in MLO activities without proper registration or licensing
- assist or allow any unlicensed or unregistered individual to perform MLO activities
- employ unlicensed mortgage loan originators
- fail to meet minimum licensing standards
- provide false or misleading information to regulatory authorities
- fail to maintain proper records or comply with reporting requirements
- violate the confidentiality of NMLS information
- engage in any scheme, device, or artifice to defraud or mislead borrowers or lenders or to defraud anyone
- obtain property by fraud or misrepresentation
- ask or require borrowers to compensate the MLO even if the MLO does not obtain a loan for them
- offer specific loan terms unless the terms are actually available at the time of the offer
- fail to make any required disclosures
- fail to comply with any federal or state laws applicable to business governed by the SAFE Act
- make any false or misleading statements regarding terms
- engage in bait-and-switch advertising
- attempt to influence the independent judgment of any official in a mortgage-related transaction, including lenders and appraisers
- collect or attempt to collect any fee or charge prohibited by the SAFE Act
- cause or require a borrower to obtain insurance in excess of what is necessary
- fail to truthfully account for funds belonging to a party to a residential mortgage transaction

**Required conduct**     Whether licensed or registered, mortgage loan originators must demonstrate good character, financial responsibility, and general suitability to serve consumers.

MLOs must include their unique identifier (NMLS) number on all applications, transaction documents, advertisements, and solicitations. Various federal laws and agencies require that MLOs include this number on operating documents.

- TILA requires that the NMLS number appear on all loan documents.
- FHA mandates that Fannie Mae and Freddie Mac require all mortgage loan applications to include the NMLS number.

MLOs must also employ appropriate record-keeping practices, including mechanisms for securing both paper and electronic records.

**Advertising**

As addressed in previous chapters, multiple federal laws impact MLO advertising, including Regulation Z and the Fair Housing Act. The SAFE Act reiterates the need for lender advertising to be honest and accurate. It also requires that MLOs include their NMLS unique identifier in all ads.

## SAFE ACT, CSBS AND AARMR MODEL STATE LAW

**The SAFE Act and HERA**

- The SAFE Act is a sub-statute of HERA and governs MLOs, lending institutions, and state and federal mortgage-related agencies in all 50 states, the District of Columbia, and U.S. territories.
- The CFPB oversees compliance with this act.
- SAFE Act protects consumers by its focus on mortgage lender and lending institution registration and licensing.
- When the act was implemented, states were required to develop minimum MLO licensing and registration standards.

**The NMLS**

- The Conference of State Bank Supervisors (CSBS) and the American Association of Residential Mortgage Regulators (AARMR) were tasked with creating and maintaining a nationwide mortgage licensing and registry system, which is now called the Nationwide Multistate Licensing System (NMLS).
- NMLS standardizes forms and requirements, manages databases, maintains information about MLOs, facilitates handling of consumer complaints

## STATE MORTGAGE REGULATING AGENCIES

**Registered v. licensed loan originator**

- Loan originators are categorized as registered or licensed.
- Licensing is handled at the state level. Registration is handled at the national level through the NMLS.
- Lenders affiliated with a covered financial institution (a federally regulated depository) typically register with the NMLS but are not required to hold a state license.
- Lenders not affiliated with a covered financial institution must obtain a state license by completing appropriate coursework, passing an examination, and registering with the NMLS. These individuals must complete continuing education courses to qualify for license renewal.
- Loan origination companies must be licensed by the state(s) in which they operate.

**Regulatory agency responsibilities**

- Each state is responsible for licensing but must adhere to SAFE Act standards.

- The governing agency in each state oversees compliance with federal and state laws, must adequately supervise MLOs, and be authorized to take necessary disciplinary action for any violations.
- To maintain licensure, mortgage companies must submit periodic reports called Mortgage Call Reports (MCR).
- One component of the MCR is data on submitted applications, closed loans, individual MLO activity, lines of credit, and loan servicing for each state in which the firm operates.
- The second component of the MCR is a Financial Condition (FC) report that includes company-level financial information.
- Fannie Mae- and Freddie Mac-approved firms must submit an expanded MCR with additional data on financial condition and residential mortgage loan activity.
- State governing agencies may engage attorneys and other experts to assist in necessary audits and investigations. Violators may be subject to fines.

## State law and regulation definitions

- Individuals in the mortgage industry who take a mortgage license, offer or negotiate loan terms or loans for compensation or gain must comply with licensing and registration laws.
- Specific criteria determine whether or not an individual has "taken" a mortgage application, offered or negotiated loan terms, or offered or negotiated loan terms for compensation. In general, clerical workers with no decision-making or negotiating authority are not considered to be subject to licensing or registration requirements.
- Underwriters are typically not licensed, though some states may require licensure for those who supervise other underwriters or perform loan origination tasks.
- Individuals who act as mortgage loan originators or present themselves as doing so for compensation are considered to be "engaging in the business of an MLO" and must be duly licensed or registered.
- Some licensing exemptions exist, such as individuals who arrange financing for property they own, parents who provide financing to their children, government or nonprofit employees who perform tasks as part of their job duties, and anyone who does not habitually or repeatedly perform loan origination activities.
- To qualify for licensure, individuals must submit to a background and credit check, complete required education and testing, and establish one source of financial protection, such as a certain threshold of net worth, purchase of a surety bond, or participation in an established recovery fund.

## LICENSE LAW AND REGULATION

## Persons required to be licensed

- for compensation, take residential loan applications; offer and negotiate terms of such loans
- generally do not need license: loan processors and underwriters, unless engaged in loan origination or credit information related to credit decision

**Engaging in the business of an MLO**

- performing licensed activities for compensation
- excluded: handling own property; financing own children; government employee performing official function; employee of certain non-profits; real estate licensee not compensated by a lender; business lender; attorney performing client duties; registered loan originator; arranging timeshare credits

**Licensee qualifications**

- criminal background check; credit check; pre-license education; required continuing education; one source of financial protection
- pass MLO exam

**Temporary authority to operate**

- states may grant temporary authority to originate loans to some loan administrators and out-of-state licensees

**Grounds for denying a license**

- license may be denied to applicant for financial or legal concerns or for license revocation in another state

**License maintenance**

- annual renewal required by December 31
- eight hours of NMLS approved continuing education annually

**NMLS requirements**

- SAFE Act places many requirements and restrictions on those who perform MLO activities, including licensing and registration requirements
- must include NMLS identification on all advertising and transaction-related documents and websites
- must keep contact and employment information current with NMLS

**COMPLIANCE**

**Prohibited conduct and practices**

- must act within all ethical and legal boundaries

**Required conduct**

- must demonstrate good character, financial responsibility, and general suitability to serve consumers
- must include issued NMLS number on all loan documents and advertisements
- must maintain paper and electronic records appropriately

**Advertising**

- must comply with all federal laws impacting advertising, such as Reg Z, Fair Housing Act, SAFE Act

# Chapter 5 Quiz: Uniform State Content

1. Under the SAFE Act (12 U.S.C. §5101 et seq.), what must all licensed and registered mortgage loan originators do?

   a. Submit loan documents and borrower demographic data directly to the CFPB.
   b. Maintain annual membership with the Federal Reserve.
   c. Register with the Nationwide Multistate Licensing System (NMLS).
   d. Complete their own underwriting for each residential loan they approve.

2. Why did CSBS and AARMR develop a model state law (MSL)?

   a. To establish a uniform code for mortgage interest rate setting
   b. To help states enact consistent MLO licensing laws that comply with the SAFE Act
   c. To allow federally chartered banks to avoid licensing requirements
   d. To create a new federal agency for regulating state banks

3. Which of the following individuals is required to obtain a state-issued license under the SAFE Act?

   a. An independent mortgage broker originating loans in multiple states
   b. An MLO working for a federally regulated credit union
   c. A loan officer employed by a national bank
   d. A customer service representative at a federal credit union

4. Which companies are required to submit an Expanded Mortgage Call Report (EMCR)?

   a. Any company that underwrites more than 90 loans per calendar year
   b. Mortgage brokers operating in multiple states
   c. Companies approved as Fannie Mae or Freddie Mac sellers/servicers or Ginnie Mae issuers
   d. Any company that employs both mortgage lenders and mortgage brokers

5. Which of the following individuals would NOT meet the Dodd-Frank (12 U.S.C. §5301 et seq.) definition of a mortgage loan originator?

   a. A licensed mortgage broker offering residential loan terms for a commission
   b. A customer service representative who answers basic loan questions but doesn't negotiate terms
   c. An individual who takes applications and negotiates loan terms for a fee
   d. A person who advertises that they can negotiate residential mortgage loans

6. Evan is applying for an MLO license in his state. He's completed the prelicensure education, passed the exam, and submitted his background and credit checks. However, he does not meet the state's minimum net worth requirement. Which of the following options could Evan pursue to meet the SAFE Act's financial responsibility requirement and obtain his license?

   a. Purchase a surety bond or participate in a recovery fund, depending on what his state allows.
   b. This is Evan's only option for demonstrating financial responsibility, so he must reapply when he has achieved the required net worth.
   c. Apply for a waiver through the NMLS, providing documented evidence of his financial stability.
   d. Submit evidence of employment at a federally regulated institution or notarized affidavits from a witness attesting to his financial condition.

7. Which of the following financial issues could result in a denial of an MLO license application?

    a. A single late credit card payment from four years ago
    b. A foreclosure that occurred five years ago
    c. An unresolved government tax lien
    d. An unpaid parking ticket from the previous year

8. Which of the following documents is required by federal law to include an MLO's NMLS unique identifier?

    a. A borrower's credit report
    b. Loan applications
    c. Appraisal summaries
    d. Closing disclosures issued by a title company

9. Which of the following is a prohibited act under the SAFE Act?

    a. Making required disclosures via both email and printed hard copy
    b. Charging a borrower for multiple third-party services rendered by licensed vendors
    c. Employing an unlicensed mortgage loan originator who has a real estate broker's license
    d. Referring borrowers to a title company for convenience

10. By what date must a licensed MLO renew their license to avoid expiration?

    a. October 31
    b. December 15
    c. December 31
    d. January 31

11. Which of the following is part of the annual continuing education requirement for MLO license renewal?

    a. Four hours of federal law and regulations
    b. Two hours of ethics, including fraud, consumer protection, and fair lending law
    c. Three hours of elective education
    d. One hour of social media and digital marketing compliance

12. How long can "temporary authority" status last for a mortgage loan originator?

    a. Up to 120 days after submitting a complete license application
    b. Up to 90 days after completing pre-licensing education and passing the licensing exam
    c. Until the company hires a new licensed mortgage loan originator
    d. Until the CFPB confirms the NMLS registration

13. Which of the following individuals is NOT required to be licensed as a mortgage loan originator?

    a. Kiera finances the sale of her own home.
    b. Bryan works for a mortgage brokerage and regularly takes residential loan applications for compensation.
    c. Trina helps multiple friends each year apply for residential mortgage loans in exchange for a referral fee.
    d. Luis is a real estate agent who is paid by a lender for recommending specific mortgage products to clients.

14. Angela works for a lender and helps applicants by entering their financial information into an online system. She doesn't verify the data, approve loans, or speak to underwriters. Which of the following statements best applies to Angela's role?

   a. Angela does not need to be licensed because she isn't involved in loan approval.
   b. Angela is taking a mortgage application and must be licensed or registered.
   c. Angela may complete this work only if she passes a federal background check.
   d. Angela is exempt from being licensed or registered as an MLO because she works under a licensed MLO.

15. Which of the following underwriter actions would require the individual to be licensed as a mortgage loan originator under the SAFE Act?

   a. Reviewing income and asset documentation to assess risk
   b. Sending automated underwriting results to the MLO
   c. Offering loan terms or negotiating conditions with the borrower
   d. Submitting the file for final approval

# Answer Key for Quizzes

## Chapter 1: Federal Mortgage-Related Laws

1.  **(a) The Dodd-Frank Act created the Consumer Financial Protection Bureau in response to the housing and financial crisis of 2007-2008.**
    Due to mortgage-related actions by lenders, appraisers, etc., that led to the housing and financial crisis, the Dodd-Frank Act created the Consumer Financial Protection Bureau to alleviate concerns about fraud and predatory lending practices.

2.  **(b) HUD**
    The U.S. Department of Housing and Urban Development (HUD) enforces the Fair Housing Act.

3.  **(d) Fostering homeownership and affordable housing**
    HUD's primary focus is on fostering homeownership and housing affordability, though the agency is also involved in enforcing fair housing laws, solutions to homelessness, and rental assistance.

4.  **(c) Purchase mortgage loans from independent lenders**
    The FHFA primarily supervises and regulates Fannie Mae, Freddie Mac, and the Federal Home Loan Banks. It does not directly engage in buying lenders' loans.

5.  **(d) OCC**
    The Office of the Comptroller of the Currency (OCC) is an independent bureau of the U.S. Treasury Department. In its role of chartering, regulating, and supervising national banks and savings and loan associations, the OCC monitors mortgage market trends to identify risks.

6.  **(a) Each person has an individual checking account, and they have a joint checking account, all at the same bank.**
    The FDIC insures bank accounts based on the account category and ownership. Each of the three accounts in this scenario has a different owner, so each would be insured for the maximum amount.

7.  **(d) Seller's financial condition statement**
    RESPA governs service providers in the lending environment. It does not place disclosure requirements on individual buyers or sellers.

8.  **(b) The applicant has not supplied an address for the property to be purchased.**
    Borrowers who request loan preapproval from a lender typically do so at the beginning of their housing search and thus do not have a specific property address. An address is one of the six pieces of information that trigger an LE.

9.  **(c) Portfolio lenders**
    Many mortgage lenders retain and service some or all of the mortgage loans they write in their own "portfolio" and are therefore referred to as portfolio lenders.

10. **(a) mortgage broker**
    Mortgage brokers serve as intermediaries between borrowers and lending institutions. They do not fund or service mortgage loans.

11. **(c) An investor is paying cash for a property to fix up and resell**
    RESPA governs most residential mortgage loans. Because it primarily focuses on mortgage provider disclosures and requirements, it does not govern purchases made with cash.

12. **(b) Movers**
    Parties who provide services to a buyer outside the purchase transaction and after the transaction closes are not considered third-party service providers and are not subject to RESPA provisions.

13. **(c) The borrower's estimated annual property tax bill is $1,875, insurance is $1,295, and a three-year flood insurance policy is $2,160. The lender calculates the borrower's monthly escrow payment to be $444.17.**
    Lenders may collect only 1/12 of the estimated annual expenditures from the escrow account. In this scenario, that equates to $264.17 for taxes and insurance plus 1/36 of the monthly premium for a three-year flood insurance policy.

14. **(b) A lender offers a substantial discount to buyers who choose to use its preferred title company.**
    Lenders may offer discounts to borrowers who use their preferred service providers as long as the appropriate disclosures are made and, if offering the discount because of bundled services, the lender does not increase charges elsewhere in the transaction to make up for the discount.

15. **(a) The seller is paying for the title insurance and all related services.**
    Sellers can require buyers to use a specific title insurance company if the seller agrees to pay for the title insurance and all related services. If the borrower is to pay for title insurance, the borrower gets to select the firm.
16. **(d) The borrower conveyed title to the property into the borrower's trust.**
    The due-on-sale clause in security documents is generally triggered when a borrower transfers title to the property without paying off the loan. In some cases, transfer of title from an individual's name to an entity name, such as a trust or LLC, may trigger the clause.
17. **(b) Both laws prohibit discrimination based on race, religion, nationality, and sex.**
    Protected classes under the Fair Housing Act are race, religion, color, national origin, sex, disability, and familial status. Under the ECOA (15 U.S.C. §1691 et seq.) & Regulation B (12 CFR §1002), age and source of income are also protected, but disability is not.
18. **(c) A lender established a policy not to offer loans for single-family residences for less than $150,000.**
    Disparate impact occurs when a seemingly innocuous policy adversely impacts a particular group of borrowers more than other groups.
19. **(a) Insufficient income**
    Federal laws are clear regarding the factors lenders can use to deny a mortgage loan. Insufficient income is such a factor.
20. **(b) Margaret is applying for a mortgage loan based on only her income. The property will be titled in her name, though her spouse will reside with her.**
    Lenders may not inquire about marital status to approve or deny a loan if the borrower is basing the loan on only their income.
21. **(c) What is your immigration status?**
    Lenders can question immigration status, but only as it pertains to loan repayment.
22. **(a) Loan approval**
    Lenders must provide a Notice of Action Taken when any ADVERSE action is taken on a loan application or when a loan application is incomplete, but the lender believes the borrower intends to pursue the loan.
23. **(b) Lenders may not discriminate based on any legal source of income.**
    Lenders are required to consider any legal, stable source of income reported by the borrower when determining loan eligibility.
24. **(a) require lenders to make appropriate disclosures to consumers regarding the cost of a loan**
    The primary purpose of TRID is to ensure that consumers are well informed regarding the cost of any loan they consummate. Thus, TRID requires that lenders provide proper disclosures to loan applicants.
25. **(a) must be provided to borrowers within three days after submission of an application**
    Federal legislation places strict timing requirements on the issuance of the LE and CD. The LE must be issued within three days after application submission.
26. **(c) Lenders must issue a new LE if the borrower's work hours, and thus wages, were reduced.**
    Certain changes in either the borrower's status or the lender's terms trigger the requirement for a new LE. A reduction in the borrower's income is likely to require a new LE.
27. **(a) The lender origination charge increased by $250.**
    Certain tolerance limits are in place regarding changes in costs to the buyer from the LE to the CD, and certain charges, no matter the amount, are not permitted. Any increase in fees to the lender is included in this zero-tolerance category.
28. **(b) The lender must provide a new CD, and a new three-day waiting period is required.**
    A change in loan type triggers the need for a new LE because costs to the borrower will change.
29. **(c) prevent discriminatory lending by requiring lenders to gather and report certain lending information**
    The HMDA (12 U.S.C. §2801 et seq.) focuses primarily on lender reporting to ensure that lenders are not discriminating.
30. **(d) FCRA**
    The Fair Credit Reporting Act (FCRA (15 U.S.C. §1681 et seq.)) addresses consumer privacy, record accuracy, and identity theft.
31. **(c) failing to provide a telephone number via Caller ID**
    Federal do-not-call laws require telemarketers to provide a telephone number via Caller ID.
32. **(a) When an account holder makes sudden, unexplained deposits**
    Any unusual or suspicious activity in an account may trigger a bank to submit a SAR.
33. **(d) Gramm-Leach-Bliley Act**
    The Gramm-Leach-Bliley Act requires lenders to protect consumers' personal financial information and provide consumers with information about how the lender shares the information.

34. **(d) regarding the loan terms of any of the lender's loan products**
While multiple laws regulate mortgage advertising, MAP prohibits misleading marketing or advertising related to the terms of a lender's loan products.

35. **(c) allows electronic documents to take the place of printed documents**
The E-SIGN Act allows electronic signatures on many documents and allows electronic documents to take the place of printed documents.

36. **(a) borrowers can request PMI termination when the mortgage balance reaches 80% of the home's original value based on payments made or appreciation**
The HPA permits borrowers to request removal of PMI when the mortgage balance reaches 80% of the home's original value.

# Chapter 2: General Mortgage Knowledge

1. **(b) A restriction or claim that may affect a property's value or transfer**
An encumbrance is a legal claim, right, or restriction on a property that can affect its value or how it's transferred—such as a mortgage lien.

2. **(c) A jumbo loan that doesn't meet Fannie Mae standards**
Non-conforming loans don't meet Fannie Mae or Freddie Mac standards; jumbo loans are one example because they exceed conforming loan limits.

3. **(a) Primary mortgage market**
Jason is working directly with a lender to secure a new loan, which takes place in the primary mortgage market.

4. **(c) It ensures investors receive timely payments of principal and interest, even if the borrower defaults.**
Both Fannie Mae and Freddie Mac guarantee that investors receive timely principal and interest payments on mortgage-backed securities, even if the borrower defaults.

5. **(b) Agency MBS**
Agency MBS are considered relatively safe because they contain conforming loans and are issued by government-sponsored entities like Fannie Mae, Freddie Mac, or Ginnie Mae.

6. **(a) The borrower's total DTI ratio must be 43% or less.**
To qualify as a QM, a loan must meet a 43% debt-to-income cap to ensure the borrower can realistically repay the loan.

7. **(c) Balloon-payment QM**
Balloon-payment qualified mortgages (QMs) are a special category for small creditors operating in rural or underserved areas. These QMs allow for balloon payments, which are typically prohibited under other QM categories.

8. **(b) It qualifies as a conventional, non-conforming loan due to the loan amount.**
Loans that exceed the conforming loan limit—even if conventional—are classified as non-conforming.

9. **(d) The borrower has a high LTV ratio and a low credit score.**
LLPAs are based on risk-related factors like credit score, LTV ratio, loan purpose, property type, and loan features—and apply only to conventional loans, not government-backed ones.

10. **(a) UFMIP has a higher rate, typically 1.75% of the loan amount.**
The UFMIP is a one-time fee typically set at 1.75% of the loan amount, while the annual MIP is a smaller, recurring fee (generally between 0.45% and 1.05%) paid monthly.

11. **(d) Loan origination fee**
The VA limits the loan origination fee to no more than 1% of the loan amount, helping to keep borrower costs reasonable.

12. **(c) A primary residence for the borrower**
USDA Guaranteed Loans apply only to owner-occupied, single-family homes.

13. **(d) They carry higher risk for the lender.**
Lenders charge higher interest rates on subprime loans to offset the increased risk of lending to borrowers with weaker credit profiles.

14. **(c) $1,200**
Monthly interest = $(0.06 \div 12) \times 250{,}000 = 0.005 \times 250{,}000 = \$1{,}250$.

15. **(d) $1,800**
Monthly PITI = $850 + $450 + ($4,200 ÷ 12) + ($1,800 ÷ 12), or $850 + $450 + $350 + $150 = $1,800.

16. **(c) 6%**
    For primary residences with a 10% to 25% down payment, the IPC cap is 6%.
17. **(b) They may experience payment shock when the teaser rate ends and adjustments begin.**
    Borrowers with ARMs can face payment shock—sudden increases in monthly payments—once the teaser rate ends and the rate adjusts based on the index and margin.
18. **(b) The percentage of the home's value covered by the first mortgage**
    The "80" in an 80-10-10 structure represents the portion of the home's value financed by the primary mortgage, which helps avoid PMI by keeping the first loan at or below 80% LTV.
19. **(c) It remains the same because only interest is being paid.**
    During the interest-only period, the borrower pays only interest—no principal—so the loan balance stays the same.
20. **(a) Someone who expects to sell or refinance before the balloon payment is due**
    Balloon mortgages are best suited for borrowers who expect to refinance, sell, or otherwise pay off the loan before the large balloon payment comes due at the end of the term.
21. **(b) The loan becomes due, and the home will typically be sold to repay the loan.**
    When a borrower with a reverse mortgage permanently leaves the home, it triggers repayment of the loan. The home is usually sold, and the sale proceeds are used to repay the loan balance.
22. **(a) He will no longer be able to access any of the unused credit.**
    Once the draw period ends, the borrower can no longer access the line of credit. They must begin repaying both principal and interest on the amount borrowed—$20,000 in Marcus's case.
23. **(c) To prepare for unexpected expenses or cost overruns during construction**
    Contingency funds help cover unforeseen expenses during construction, ensuring the project can move forward even if costs exceed the original budget.
24. **(d) By providing regional funding access that may not be available through national lenders**
    The FHLB's regional structure helps ensure that even small, local lenders have access to funding for housing and development—supporting economic growth at the community level.
25. **(b) 25%**
    Housing DTI = ($1,450 + $250 + $50 +$45) ÷ $7,250 = $1,795 ÷ $7,250 = 0.2476 or 25%
26. **(c) Borrowers must occupy the home within 60 days and live there for at least one year.**
    FHA borrowers must occupy the home within 60 days of closing and live there for at least 12 months to meet FHA residency rules.
27. **(b) To confirm the property provides a safe and sanitary living environment**
    VA MPRs are designed to ensure homes are safe, structurally sound, and sanitary—protecting both the borrower and the VA from costly property issues.
28. **(d) Higher interest rates and limited access to the secondary mortgage market**
    Alt-A loans carry higher interest rates and are not typically bought or sold in the secondary mortgage market due to their increased risk.

# Chapter 3: Mortgage Loan Origination Activities

1. **(c) Underwriting**
   During the underwriting phase, the underwriter evaluates borrower risk and ensures compliance with lending guidelines before issuing a credit decision.
2. **(b) The loan is approved, and all conditions are satisfied.**
   Once the loan is approved and all underwriting conditions are met, the file moves to closing, where documents are signed and the mortgage is finalized.
3. **(c) Mortgage loan originator**
   The mortgage loan originator (MLO) guides the borrower through the loan process, evaluates financial readiness, and collects documentation from inquiry to closing.
4. **(a) Review of recent pay stubs and W-2s**
   Unlike pre-approval, pre-qualification does not involve document verification like pay stubs, tax returns, or a credit report—it's meant to be a quick, informal assessment.
5. **(d) A conditional commitment to lend up to a specific amount**
   A pre-approval letter is a conditional commitment from the lender based on verified financial information, signaling the borrower's strong position to make an offer.

6. **(a) Underwriting fee**
   The lender charges an underwriting fee to cover the cost of evaluating loan risk and making the final approval decision.
7. **(c) $7,500**
   One discount point equals 1% of the loan amount. Three points = 3% of $250,000 = $7,500.
8. **(b) At application and again at closing to reflect final loan terms**
   The URLA is generally completed at the start of the application process and again at closing to confirm the loan's final terms and conditions.
9. **(a) Yes, and she must provide a signed gift letter and verify the transfer of funds.**
   On conventional loans with 20% or more down, the borrower can use gift funds for the entire transaction, provided they submit a signed gift letter and the lender verifies the transfer.
10. **(c) The funds must have been in the borrower's account for at least 60 days.**
    Seasoned funds have been held in the borrower's account for at least 60 days, helping demonstrate that they were not recently acquired from an ineligible or undisclosed source.
11. **(b) Two years**
    Most lenders require a minimum of two years of verifiable income to assess consistency and stability in the borrower's employment history.
12. **(d) Owner's title insurance selected by the borrower outside the lender's provider list**
    Optional services—such as owner's title insurance—chosen by the borrower from outside the lender's provider list fall under the no tolerance category and can vary without restriction.
13. **(c) The cumulative fees exceed TRID tolerance thresholds.**
    A revised LE may be issued if cumulative fee changes exceed tolerance limits or if other material changes affect the loan terms—triggering the need for updated disclosures.
14. **(b) Within three business days of a completed loan application**
    The Mortgage Loan Servicing Disclosure must be delivered within three business days of receiving a completed loan application, as required under RESPA (12 U.S.C. §2601 et seq.).
15. **(c) The minimum number of business days that must pass before closing**
    The "7" refers to the requirement that the loan may not close until at least seven business days have passed after the initial disclosures are delivered to the borrower.
16. **(a) Mea has $12,000 in a checking account.**
    Liquid assets include funds that can be quickly and easily converted into cash, such as money held in checking or savings accounts.
17. **(b) If the primary borrower has made payments from their own funds for the past year**
    A contingent liability, such as a co-signed loan, can be excluded if it's documented that the primary borrower—not the applicant—has made all payments from their own funds for the past 12 months.
18. **(b) They average it over a two-year period.**
    Lenders use a two-year average for variable income like commissions or bonuses to account for fluctuations and assess income stability.
19. **(c) Her last two years of federal tax returns, including Form 1040 with Schedule C**
    Sole proprietors must typically submit two years of federal tax returns, including Form 1040 with Schedule C, to verify income for mortgage qualification.
20. **(b) 28%**
    Housing Ratio = PITI on Primary Residence ÷ Gross Monthly Income, or $1,820 ÷ $6,500 = 28%.
21. **(b) 39%**
    DTI Ratio = Total Recurring Monthly Debt ÷ Gross Monthly Income, or ($1,850 + $300 + $150 + $400) ÷ $7,000 = $2,700 ÷ $7,000 = 39%
22. **(a) It applies when the borrower's DTI is 43% or less and the loan meets QM criteria.**
    Safe Harbor protection applies when the loan meets QM standards—including a DTI ratio of 43% or less—providing lenders strong legal protection against ability-to-repay (ATR)-related claims.
23. **(c) A buyer planning to keep the home for 15 years or more**
    Borrowers who plan to remain in the home long term are more likely to benefit from paying discount points, since the upfront cost can be offset by long-term interest savings.
24. **(a) The seller credits the buyer for five months' worth of taxes.**
    When taxes are billed in arrears, the seller credits the buyer for their share (five months, in this case), and the buyer pays the full bill when it arrives.

25. **(d) The penalty decreases over time, then expires.**
A declining prepayment penalty starts high (e.g., 2% in year one), decreases in subsequent years (e.g., 1% in year two), and eventually disappears—often after three years.

26. **(b) The property's appraised value**
While the promissory note includes loan terms, interest rate, and repayment obligations, it does not include the appraised value of the property.

27. **(c) Require immediate repayment of the loan under the due-on-sale clause.**
An alienation clause gives the lender the right to demand full repayment if the borrower transfers ownership without the lender's written consent, regardless of the reason for the transfer.

28. **(b) The trustee can sell the property through a non-judicial foreclosure process.**
In a deed of trust with a power-of-sale clause, the trustee may conduct a non-judicial foreclosure, allowing the lender to recover the property without going through the court system.

29. **(d) Table funding**
In table funding, the originating lender closes the loan in their name but sells it immediately to an investor—freeing up capital to fund additional loans.

30. **(b) $175**
Principal Loan Amount ×Annual Premium Rate Percentage = Annual PMI, or $280,000 × 0.0075 = $2,100; Monthly PMI = $2,100 ÷ 12 = $175.

31. **(b) $222,000**
Total Interest Paid = (P&I Monthly Payment × Number of Payments) – Original Loan Amount, or ($1,450 × 360) – $300,000 = $222,000

32. **(c) $1,111**
Monthly Payment = (Principal + Total Interest Paid) ÷ Loan Term in Months, or ($240,000 + $160,000) ÷ 360 = $1,111.11

33. **(c) 60 to 90 days**
Most pre-approval letters are valid for 60 to 90 days before the borrower's information must be reviewed and updated to remain valid.

34. **(a) It is based on preliminary information and subject to change.**
Early rate quotes are non-binding and based on preliminary data—they can change once full documentation is reviewed during underwriting.

35. **(c) To gather information about the borrower's financial background**
The Declarations section asks about the borrower's financial history, including bankruptcies, foreclosures, judgments, and property occupancy plans.

36. **(a) Plans to relocate or refinance within a few years**
Borrowers who plan to move or refinance soon may benefit from the lower initial rates of an ARM, as they're less exposed to future rate adjustments.

37. **(c) At or before the time of loan application**
To comply with RESPA regulations, the AfBA must be provided at or before loan application, so the borrower has full transparency before choosing a service provider.

38. **(b) 60 to 120 days**
For each subsequent adjustment, ARM notices must be sent 60 to 120 days before the new payment takes effect.

# Chapter 4: Ethics

1. **(c) CFPB and FTC**
The Consumer Financial Protection Bureau (CFPB) and the Federal Trade Commission (FTC) are the main agencies that enforce protections against unfair, deceptive, or abusive acts or practices (UDAAP) in the mortgage industry.

2. **(b) prohibited, because it is for a standard service already compensated**
RESPA prohibits charging additional fees for services that are already compensated or required—like standard document preparation—unless the extra service is actual, necessary, and distinct from those already performed.

3. **(d) deceptive, because it is not prominent or well-located**
The FTC's "four Ps" test helps determine whether information is likely to mislead. For disclosures to be effective, they must be prominent, clear, and placed where consumers are likely to see or hear them—none of which is true in this scenario.

4. **(c) It requires lenders to report application and demographic data to monitor fair lending practices.**
The HMDA is a reporting-only rule that provides transparency into lending patterns by requiring institutions to report key loan and demographic data. It does not mandate lending quotas or prohibit specific behaviors but helps regulators detect discrimination through data.

5. **(d) When the applicant is not of legal age to enter a binding contract or when age affects the ability to repay**
The ECOA generally prohibits age-based discrimination. However, a lender may consider age if the applicant is not legally able to enter a contract or if age is relevant to assessing the applicant's ability to repay the loan.

6. **(c) Intentional misrepresentation is purposeful deception, while unintentional misrepresentation results from negligence or failure to meet professional duties.**
Intentional misrepresentation (fraudulent misrepresentation) is done knowingly to deceive, while unintentional misrepresentation (constructive or negligent fraud) results from a breach of duty or care, not deliberate dishonesty.

7. **(b) Deed or home title theft**
This scenario describes deed or home title theft, where a fraudster forges ownership documents to transfer title, secures a mortgage loan, and vanishes with the proceeds—leaving the true homeowner and the lender in legal and financial chaos. Red flags include remote notarizations, exclusive vendor use, and refusal to meet in person.

8. **(b) The lender is protected from liability under the Bank Secrecy Act.**
The Bank Secrecy Act provides legal protection to those who file SARs in good faith, even if no fraud is ultimately proven. This encourages proactive reporting without fear of retaliation or legal consequence.

9. **(a) The use of pop-up windows could prevent effective disclosure delivery.**
Advertisers should routinely test the effectiveness of the hyperlink by observing click-through rates and carefully evaluate and address technological limitations of providing disclosures, including using frames or pop-ups. Ineffective delivery of disclosures can lead to regulatory violations and consumer confusion.

10. **(b) Advertising a low rate without mentioning that it increases after six months**
Highlighting a low introductory rate without disclosing that it will increase is a direct violation of Regulation N, which prohibits misleading advertising practices in mortgage marketing.

11. **(d) A borrower applies for a loan advertised with no closing costs, pays a deposit, and is later told that the loan is unavailable and must choose one with closing costs.**
This scenario reflects a classic switch after sale tactic: the borrower acts on an advertised loan, provides a deposit, and is then discouraged or blocked from proceeding with that product—being pushed toward a costlier alternative instead. This practice may be deemed deceptive if it forms a pattern.

12. **(c) Loan flipping**
Loan flipping involves repeatedly encouraging borrowers to refinance their loans—often with no real benefit to the borrower—while collecting high fees and extending the loan term. This practice increases the long-term cost of borrowing and is a classic predatory tactic.

13. **(c) When loan payments are less than the interest charged, causing the loan balance to increase**
Negative amortization occurs when monthly payments don't cover the full interest due, causing unpaid interest to be added to the loan balance. Over time, this increases the total amount owed.

14. **(d) Lenders must log all complaints and respond within 15 days, with a final response due within 60 days if more time is needed.**
Lenders must log all consumer complaints and make those logs available to investigators or state examiners. A formal response is required within 15 days, and if more time is needed, a final resolution must be provided within 60 days.

15. **(c) The system must support continuous monitoring and timely identification of concerns.**
A strong compliance management system involves ongoing monitoring to detect and correct violations promptly. Regulators expect proactive, not passive, oversight of internal operations.

16. **(c) Only Tyler, because he has taken concrete steps to begin the application process**
An MLO is presumed to have a fiduciary relationship once a consumer decides to move forward with the loan process. In this scenario, Tyler is considered a client because he submitted a loan application and documentation—triggering the MLO's fiduciary duty to act in his best interest.

17. **(b) Ransomware attack**
This is a ransomware attack, where malicious software encrypts files or systems and demands payment for release. These attacks are often triggered by phishing emails that fool employees into clicking malicious links.

18. **(d) Misrepresentation of affiliation with a government program**
MAPs prohibit any false claims of government affiliation or endorsement, including using symbols or language that imply the lender is tied to a government entity or program.

19. **(d) Meeting legal standards but falling short on consumer education**
While Devon complied with disclosure timing, he failed to meet his ethical obligation to help Paulette—especially as a first-time buyer—understand the information critical to her financial decision.

20. **(a) Integrity and putting the client's needs first**
Acting with integrity means placing the borrower's best interests above personal gain—a key component of ethical behavior in the mortgage industry.

21. **(c) Reporting suspected fraud and exhibiting integrity in all interactions.**
MLOs must act with integrity, honesty, and professionalism and are ethically and legally required to report suspected fraud to protect clients, the firm, and the industry.

22. **(a) Financial harm or a significant risk of concrete harm to the consumer**
Substantial injury generally refers to financial harm, but actual injury is not required—a significant risk of harm may also meet this standard.

23. **(b) It influences or is likely to influence a consumer's choice or behavior.**
A representation or omission is material if it would reasonably affect a consumer's decision-making, such as whether to take out a loan, accept a rate, or believe a product feature.

24. **(c) She is partially exempt from the Act but still may not discriminate based on race.**
Owner-occupied one- to four-unit properties qualify for limited FHA exemptions, but discrimination based on race is never permitted.

25. **(c) To ensure financial institutions meet the credit needs of all communities they serve**
The CRA is designed to encourage lenders to serve all segments of their communities, including low- and moderate-income areas, helping to ensure fair and equal access to credit.

# Chapter 5: Uniform State Content

1. **(c) Register with the Nationwide Multistate Licensing System (NMLS).**
The SAFE Act requires all licensed and registered MLOs to be listed in the NMLS, which tracks licensing, maintains records, and promotes accountability nationwide.

2. **(b) To help states enact consistent MLO licensing laws that comply with the SAFE Act**
The model state law (MSL) was developed to help states ensure their licensing frameworks aligned with the SAFE Act, promoting uniformity and consistency in regulatory standards.

3. **(a) An independent mortgage broker originating loans in multiple states**
State-licensed loan originators—such as mortgage brokers not employed by covered institutions—must obtain and maintain a state-issued license in each state where they originate loans and register with the NMLS.

4. **(c) Companies approved as Fannie Mae or Freddie Mac sellers/servicers or Ginnie Mae issuers**
Companies approved as sellers and/or servicers for Fannie Mae or Freddie Mac or issuers for Ginnie Mae must submit the Expanded Mortgage Call Report, which includes both loan activity and financial condition components.

5. **(b) A customer service representative who answers basic loan questions but doesn't negotiate terms**
Under Dodd-Frank, someone must be actively taking applications or negotiating terms for compensation or gain (or represent themselves as doing so) to be considered a mortgage loan originator.

6. **(a) Purchase a surety bond or participate in a recovery fund, depending on what his state allows.**
If an applicant cannot meet the minimum net worth requirement, they may still satisfy the financial protection standard by purchasing a surety bond or participating in a state recovery fund, depending on what their state allows.

7. **(c) An unresolved government tax lien**
Outstanding tax or government liens and other significant unresolved financial obligations can disqualify an applicant under the SAFE Act's financial responsibility standards.

8. **(b) Loan applications**
The NMLS unique identifier must appear on applications, loan documents, advertisements, and solicitations, as required by TILA, FHA, and GSE guidelines.

9. **(c) Employing an unlicensed mortgage loan originator who has a real estate broker's license**
Under the SAFE Act, it is prohibited to employ or allow any unlicensed or unregistered individual to perform mortgage loan origination activities—regardless of whether they hold another type of license, such as a real estate broker's license.

10. **(c) December 31**
    Licensed MLOs must renew annually between November 1 and December 31. Licenses expire after December 31 if not renewed, and the MLO may not legally perform MLO activities.
11. **(b) Two hours of ethics, including fraud, consumer protection, and fair lending law**
    The SAFE Act requires eight hours of NMLS-approved CE annually, including two hours of ethics focused on fraud, consumer protection, and fair lending topics.
12. **(a) Up to 120 days after submitting a complete license application**
    "Temporary authority" may remain active for up to 120 days, allowing the MLO to originate loans while awaiting full state licensure—as long as the application remains complete and in process.
13. **(a) Kiera finances the sale of her own home.**
    Individuals who finance the sale of their own property—such as a primary residence—are generally not considered MLOs under the SAFE Act, provided the activity is not habitual or done for others.
14. **(b) Angela is taking a mortgage application and must be licensed or registered.**
    Even if Angela isn't approving loans, she is receiving and inputting borrower data for the purpose of a loan decision, which qualifies as taking an application under the SAFE Act and requires licensure or registration.
15. **(c) Offering loan terms or negotiating conditions with the borrower**
    Once an underwriter or processor begins engaging in origination activities—like offering or negotiating loan terms—they must meet the licensing and registration requirements under the SAFE Act.

# Index

*If you liked Essentials of Mortgage Loan Origination, check out the other real estate licensing titles of Performance Programs Company!*

**Cramming for your NMLS licensing exam? You need Mortgage Loan Originator License Exam Prep!**

**Where can you buy Mortgage Loan Originator License Exam Prep?**
Mortgage Loan Originator License Exam Prep (MOLEP) is available as a printed book or e-book through nearly all online retailers.

**Looking for a real estate principles textbook? Get what all the students love -- Principles of Real Estate Practice!**

Principles of Real Estate Practice is invaluable reference material for real estate professionals. Its 495-pages contain the essentials of real estate law, principles, and practices taught in real estate schools and colleges across the country. For many states, there are now state-specific versions of Principles of Real Estate Practice.

**Where can you buy Principles of Real Estate Practice?**
Principles Real Estate Practice is available as a printed book or e-book through nearly all online retailers.

**Struggling with real estate math?  The solution to that equation is Real Estate Math Express!**

Real Estate Math Express is a concise, easy-to-study test preparation guide to help real estate students improve their real estate math scores to pass the state licensing test. The primary feature of Real Estate Math Express is that it contains all necessary formulas and practice questions in 100+ pages.

**Where can you buy Real Estate Math Express?**
Real Estate Math Express is available as a printed book or e-book through nearly all online retailers.

**Publisher Contact**
Ryan Mettling
Performance Programs Company
6810 190th St E, Bradenton, FL 34211
ryan@performanceprogramscompany.com
www.performanceprogramscompany.com

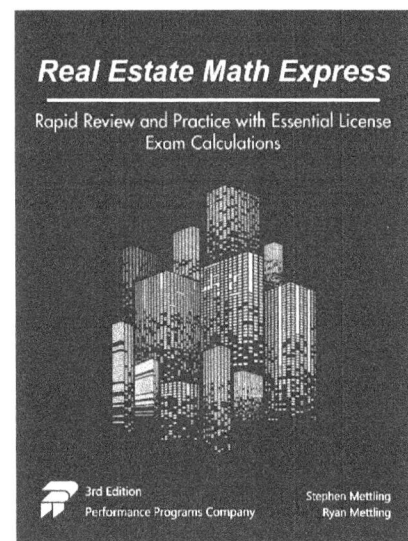

www.ingramcontent.com/pod-product-compliance
Lightning Source LLC
Chambersburg PA
CBHW080932220326
41598CB00034B/5764